ILLU

Beyond their mansion gates, the power-elite left no sin unexplored . . . and Katharine Darktower walked amongst them, as if in a dream, searching for love, redemption . . . and

ILLUSIONS

Once again, the audacious, uncompromising Barney Leason weaves a shocking, sensuous tale of money, power and greed as he lays bare the lives and lusts of the 'privileged people' who can have anything money can buy – and still want a little bit more . . .

ILLUSIONS

a novel by

Barney Leason – author of the three international bestsellers, RODEO DRIVE, SCANDALS and PASSIONS

ILLUSIONS

Barney Leason

ARROW BOOKS

Arrow Books Limited
62-65 Chandos Place, London WC2N 4NW

An imprint of Century Hutchinson Limited

London Melbourne Sydney Auckland
Johannesburg and agencies throughout
the world

First published in Great Britain 1983
Reprinted 1984 and 1987

Printed and bound in Great Britain by
Anchor Brendon Limited, Tiptree, Essex

ISBN 0 09 932650 7

In memory of
Gaye Tardy

One

She sat silently, motionlessly, beside him in the car, her eyes fixed on the icy surface of Plymouth Avenue, which led into the center of Port London, then beyond, toward New York. The tires made crisp, crunching noises and he drove slowly for, despite the sand strewn earlier that morning, it was slippery, here and there treacherous.

Katharine was warm, though he hadn't yet turned on the heat inside the Mercedes, and the sun, if there was still a sun in the sky, had not broken through the haze of the morning. She had dressed carefully for the trip back to the city and now she was conscious of the wool tweed of the pantsuit, the snugness of the brilliant red cashmere turtleneck against her breasts and arms.

She folded her hands in her lap, switching her eyes for a second down to brown medium-heeled loafers, the kind one had bought at Gucci before everyone began shopping at Gucci.

Her feet were small, although she was not under average height. Erik had always said they were aristocratic feet and he should know, shouldn't he? Aristocratic, too, he assured her, was the shape of her face; her blonde hair, cut short in back, was sculpted to her head. Yes, Erik said, her features might have been carved by a Greek master.

They glided under the bare trees, through the magic mile of those magnificent mansions, the incredible summer homes built in Port London, and most of them along Plymouth Avenue, by the incredibly rich before the turn of the century. Palaces even then, costing millions in imported marble, domestic stone, wood of a hundred varie-

1

ties from every forest of the globe . . . crystal and gold and pearl inlays. Legions of cheap Irish labor had rigged them up in record time; no one wanted to wait to enjoy their little summer place, once they had discovered Port London.

To her right, Katharine realized drowsily, was the ten-ton wrought-iron gate leading into the acres of grounds around the Palazzo Merano, constructed just before 1900, reminding the residents of an especially ornate northern Italian lake-district showplace. Gardens and walks led down to the ocean and a bridle path called Peach Run which, a half-mile farther north, separated the more modest property called, simply, Maples, from Long Island Sound.

Maples was the summer home of Erik and Katharine Moss but they used it as well from time to time in the winter, on such a February weekend as this. Maples was far smaller than places like Palazzo Merano, or Ocean House, a brooding gray granite pile, or Gullwings, a Victorian wooden edifice with three floors of gables and porches so expensive to insure that only the wealthiest of the wealthy could afford it, just for a month in the summer.

Indeed, by now most of the truly gigantic homes had been deeded to the very active Port London Heritage Assembly, a body dedicated to tradition for its own sake and as a means of heading off property developers seem-ingly just as determined to bring the curse of the condomin-ium to Port London.

"Chateau Biarritz," she said, almost in a whisper, as they slid past three hundred yards of white picket fence, behind which solemnly squatted the stone and timbered "chateau," turreted and buttressed against the invader.

"What?"

"Chateau Biarritz," Katharine repeated, just as softly.

"Yes," Erik grunted, not even glancing at her. "Dolly and I were talking about it yesterday. Next summer, the assembly gets to put Biarritz on the house tour. Georgina Scully died last month and Horace won't be far behind."

"Georgina," Katharine muttered. "I remember her."

"Of course you do," Erik said sharply. "Horace will never see Biarritz again . . . the family says go ahead. We get it anyway when he dies."

Katharine felt a tear collect in the corner of one eye. "Pretty soon the assembly will own everything in Port London."

Annoyance showed on his somber face. "There's no single family that can afford to run these places any more. It's not such a tragic thing, you know, darling," he said reprovingly. "We take the houses off their hands . . . and so they escape the deathbed guilt of knowing that as soon as they're cold, house, property and all will go straight into some developer's pocket."

"How kind of you," Katharine murmured. "You and Dolly. . . . How is Mrs. Percy?"

"Fine," Erik said shortly.

They were approaching Dolly's house which lay, like theirs, on a more twentieth-century-sized piece of property, between Chateau Biarritz and Regatta Place, the latter designed by a stockbroking sailing buff and complete with a "cottage" on the back stretch of lawn resembling a Chinese junk.

"Here's Villa Dolly," Katharine said dryly. This was her name for her best friend's home. Dolly, following the death of Harrison Percy, had taken to living in Port London almost the year around.

"Correct," Erik commented humorlessly, "and there's Fiat Dolly parked in front. She must be home. Shall we stop? She was sorry not to see her friend Kitty."

"I was too tired to go out," Katharine complained. "You know that."

"Yes," Erik replied, "I do know that. You were extremely tired, Kathy—and you must rest."

Dolly's home, built late, not until the middle twenties, was reminiscent of the transplanted southern antebellum architecture so popular in the horse racing capital of Saratoga Springs in the nineteenth century. It was white, porticoed with stately columns and wide windows. Like Dolly, it was airy, frivolous; in the snow, it seemed to float over the ground. Like Dolly, yes, Katharine thought fondly. But not so fondly, either.

"Shall we stop?" he repeated.

"No," Katharine said.

"You don't wish to see your best friend in all the world?" he asked ironically.

"No. Not today. Sometimes . . . you know, Dolly is hard to take."

"Perhaps," Erik agreed, "but together, we are the most aggressive team on the Heritage Assembly. When we are finished restoring the Smithers House, it will be the center-piece of the Port London colonial collection."

"I'm sure," she said. "It's been a derelict so long."

"It is a very worthwhile project," Erik said firmly, as though she were trying to get him to drop it.

"I know. It's what you like doing better than anything else."

"Better than what?"

Wearily, Katharine said, "A ruin better than the living. Old wood better than a living tree. Bones better than flesh."

"*Verdamnt!*" Erik blurted the German curse. "Why do you say such things?"

"Because they're true." She tried to smile at him.

"They are *not* true. It is a morbid thing for you to say, Kathy. Sometimes . . ." He paused sorrowfully. "Some-times you disturb me very much."

She shook her head listlessly. "No, don't. *Weltschmertz*—your word. 'World weariness,' *your* translation."

"Yes, world weariness," Erik snapped, "but not my *weltschmertz*. Yours! I love life. It is you who insist on riding your steed—its name is *sadness*. . . ."

"Sadness? Not *madness?*"

"Madness?" Erik's right eyebrow lofted. "Does it strike you so? Is that your diagnosis?"

"Don't worry," she said softly. "I know what you're thinking."

"You do not," he said firmly. "There is no way you could know."

"I know! I *do* know," Katharine insisted, feeling the deep wound of hopelessness across her heart. "You think I'm a lost soul, wandering in and out of a cloud. *Do* you think I'm suicidal? You've said so. You've told people, haven't you? I know you have. You've told Dolly. You're afraid of me. Yes, that's true." She glared at him now. His face was set rigidly. "You think I'm a bad mother to Margaret."

"Stop!" he exclaimed. "I won't hear this. Don't go on."

"I'm more than you bargained for, isn't that so?" she demanded cruelly, more cruelly to herself than to him. "The gay divorcee, remember? Katharine Darktower Ratoff, ex-wife of an international fag."

Miserably, he growled, "I am going to stop. Turn. Go back to the house. I cannot drive to New York like this."

"No. . . ." Katharine nodded slowly. "Well, you can always get a divorce, you know."

"Damnation," he snarled. "I am your husband."

"You're not responsible for me." She reached to pat his right arm. "You're much too honorable," she taunted. "Why do you drive yourself crazy? *My darling*, is it the money?"

He stiffened under her hand, looked at her, smiling disdainfully. "You know that I have never needed your money."

"So they say," she pressed, hurting, and wanting to hurt. "I know—you'd already made a pile of your own before ever we met. Yes, you were James Merriwether's right-hand man in Europe, long before you ever saw Kathy Darktower."

"That is true, as it happens," he said icily. He drew a deep breath. "We are in the center of Port London now, if you haven't noticed. Do you want to stop at the Lobster Claw for coffee before we go on?"

Katharine laughed hoarsely. "What you mean is—do you need a drink? Can you hold until New York, *my darling?* Do you need to go into the john to take some pills? *Say* it!"

"Do you want to stop at the Claw for coffee?" he repeated stoically.

"Shit, no! Drive to New York."

He turned off Plymouth Avenue to the left, toward the ocean and then after several blocks right again into Henley

Street, a wider thoroughfare that would take them out of Port London.

More heavily traveled, Henley Street was slick but not slippery. Across Erik's shoulder, Katharine gazed toward the harbor on the other side of the Lobster Claw. Tops of ships' masts tipped back and forth in the light wind and beyond that was the gray glinting of the sea, a few whitecaps, under the green-gray sky. Erik picked up speed as they passed the border of Old Town. His beloved Smithers House was a few blocks to the right off the main road, in the colonial-era enclave of Port London, to be distinguished, as it was in the guide books, from the "Gay Nineties" ostentation of the Plymouth Avenue mansions.

About one thing, at least, she agreed with Erik—she wouldn't have wasted an hour of her volunteered time on the likes of Chateau Biarritz but would have given months to the Smithers House, if she'd been properly asked. But that was beside the point—the Heritage Assembly existed and the Smithers place would be restored, thanks to the garish architectural rubbish along Plymouth Avenue— summer tourists were far more interested in the marble and gold and glitter of Chateau Biarritz than they ever could be by the stark and simple clapboard Smithers House.

Katharine hummed to herself, drifting away, descending toward the numbness of her own interior, appreciating the warmth, the comfort of the leather bucket seats. No more talking now, as they departed the city limits of Port London and swished along glistening Sound Road, to the left again the gray and troubled sea. She would enjoy the trip in silence, as if a journey back to the womb. In a moment, she would be asking herself why they couldn't drive along like this forever.

But they were only going as far as Park Avenue, New York City. Warily, she studied Erik again. He drove deliberately, his big hands gripping the steering wheel as they might have a neck he was wringing. His face was set in despair, or ill humor, or both, the lips drawn down in a pout. But it could not be a pout because Erik was not a spoiled person. Katharine *was*, so they said. Aristocratic of foot size, classical of features, and fashionably spoiled. Elegantly neurotic, Erik would say.

He was angry with her now, frustrated by her logic. But there was nothing new in that. After all, they'd had their usual weekend, the likes of which usually left him in a dither. While he'd been out with Dolly Percy, up to God knows what, Katharine had rested, talked a little while to Mrs. Rogers, the woman who ran Maples, then "rested" some more with a couple of vodkas, lunch, a brandy. . . . She needed so much rest. Everyone said so, including her doctor Hank Hodges. She was *so* tired, but she didn't look so very tired. Everyone said Katharine Darktower Ratoff Moss was as beautiful as ever, even more so, though, as most people knew, she would be turning forty in a couple of years. Katharine was such a placid, classically beautiful blonde, people said, but primarily so placid, often seeming to be walking through a dream of her own making. Nothing, but nothing, disturbed her, worried her, aggravated her.

And that's our Kathy, she told herself sardonically.

Erik's eyes were hooded, heavy eyelids half-closed over the blazing blue Germanic eyes that scorned distance and obstacle. It was not the car that was so especially powerful. It was the man who drove it, pushing it, forcing it forward over the macadam, a winding black mark in the land, stretching ahead, merging at hillsides and then disappearing into the horizon. A dusting of beige-colored sand covered the black nerve, a ganglion which moaned under the heavy wheels of the Mercedes.

Erik might have bent the steering wheel with those hands, wrists broad with light golden hair lying over the veins, the skin. The hair on his head must once have been golden too; it was graying a little in his forty-fifth year but thick and wavy where he brushed it away from a high bony forehead. The hair was long at the back and around his ears, big ears, convoluted, like shells, which he liked to tug by the lobes when he was interested or anxious.

Katharine knew without looking any closer that the eyes were opaque, even in their open and honest-to-goodness blueness, guarded, giving nothing away. Even when he smiled—everybody said that when he flashed a real uninhibited smile the world could come apart—the eyes did not change but remained, as always, distant, reserved, secretive, yes . . . and cold.

Katharine shivered. Could she love him? Maybe, maybe not. She had once but that was a while ago now, ten years. He was not much older than she, but he seemed a million years old, a very old soul. She didn't know him, but he knew her, every square inch of her. In a way, he was her father, Richard Darktower, also a man she had never known.

Erik felt her eyes and noticed it. Then she shivered again. He turned his head and the white teeth broke the tan of his face. He was smiling at her with the lower half of his face.

"Do you want your coat?" Her long mink lay behind the seats.

"No. I'm all right."

Warmly, as if nothing had been said before, he flattered her, told her she looked wonderful this morning, that the rest had, indeed, done her good. Then, quickly veering away from the subject of *her*, he continued to speak, about himself. His voice was heavy, blurred by a trace of accent, but deep, resonant.

"It went well yesterday," Erik stated carefully. "I feel they accept me now in Port London. It has taken some time, has it not?" He chuckled comfortably. "But, given time, all things come to he who waits and now at the assembly they are quite concussed by Dolly and myself—we are determined to return the Smithers House to its colonial grandeur. It is such a lovely house," he chattered, taking his eyes off the road for a second to assure her it was so. "It is such a *solid* house, brick covered by clapboard, the walls are thick, not like your flimsy twentieth-century houses. The wood is so beautiful, old, patinaed with history. Walking through this house, one can feel the presence of Captain Joshua Smithers. I should say *I* can feel it; perhaps other people would not. But I am intuitive, my senses are more acute than those of most *Americans*. *I* can *feel* the energy field of Captain Joshua Smithers. You see, my sweetheart," Erik went on in staccato beat, "people do not ever completely die. They die, their bodies rot to dust in time but not at once—and their energy never dies. This is the reason why powerful men leave monuments. They live on within their monuments.''

He glanced briefly at her again to see if she was listening.

Katharine nodded dully. ''I've heard all this before, you know. You're preoccupied with death and rotting.'' She returned his look with a frown. ''You talk like Death is a neighbor of Captain Joshua Smithers.''

Erik chuckled mirthlessly. ''Our colleagues at the Hermitage Assembly take it for granted that you are also involved in our restoration project. Never mind! It is not required, sweetheart. It is enough that I honor the history of this country. Is that so amazing? No. One must honor history, for we are all history in the making.''

''Potentially dead bodies,'' she interjected.

''Precisely. Also dead events, wars, et cetera, all history.'' He laughed abruptly, almost scornfully. ''They seem amazed I speak English so well. Should I bother to explain that my mother was English and that I went to school in England?'' He shrugged. ''Why bother? I accept their compliments, their pleasure that such a poor refugee as myself has given to their language the respect of learning it so well. Ha! It is all part and parcel of my *winning ways*. After these years, they finally admire me, respect me and they are always eager to hear my opinion.''

''Your opinion *and* Dolly's opinion.''

''Yes,'' he agreed, ''at the moment we two are quite the most influential members of the assembly.'' He switched his eyes toward her again. ''She was sorry not to see you.''

''So you said,'' she muttered. Katharine paused to think, allowing a grumbling stomach cramp to pass. She had eaten breakfast; she couldn't be hungry again. No, it was all the damned pills and God knows why she took so many.

''Dolly will be down in New York in a week or so,'' Erik said. ''She said she'll be calling you about lunch.''

''If I'm feeling up to it.''

''Sweetheart,'' he said intently, ''it is simply a matter of making up your mind to feel up to it. Tell yourself—I *am* up to it. Dolly wants to see you.''

"All right, all right!'' She was thinking seriously of a drink, picturing the glass, the ice, the steaming vodka, the lemon twist. She swore to herself, thrusting the image away. "You don't have to talk me into lunching with Dolly, you know.'' She could not, however, at this moment force her own feelings about Dolly past the lukewarm point. Dolly had everything Katharine didn't have. Dolly did not give a damn about anything. She was bright, energetic, reckless, and her only purpose in life was to live it as well as she could. "I've *always* loved Dolly,'' she said emphatically. "When we were young we were so alike people called us the Dolly Sisters—not the Kathy Sisters, you notice. She was always the leader. I was her blonde shadow.'' Then, rashly, before he was ready for it, she demanded, "Could you fall in love with Dolly?''

His right fist thumped the steering wheel. "A stupid question,'' he said harshly.

"I mean it,'' Katharine said fiercely. She turned to look him full in the face, fearing the emptiness of her life. "I won't live long, you know. I feel that. When I'm gone, *could* you fall in love with Dolly?''

His face seemed pallid under his deep tan. "My sweetheart, please don't say such awful things.''

"Goddamn it! Answer the question! Could you?''

"No. Never. She is not a serious woman.''

"She has plenty of money!''

His look agonized, bitingly he said, "Money? What do I care about money?'' He let his scorn rise. "Besides, *sweetheart*, if you were to die, as you morbidly suggest, I wouldn't need her money. I'd have yours, wouldn't I?''

The stomach twisted again, knotted, burned, hurting her. "Maybe not as much as you think.''

She was ready to drop the subject, to let her body relax. Furiously, he stepped on the gas and the car shot forward. "This is a stupid conversation and I refuse to engage in stupid conversation.''

Katharine quavered. "You'll have to promise you'll take care of Margaret.''

"Verdamnt!" His anger was real. "I tell you, stop talking like this, at once!"

"Will you?"

"Of course." His voice was deadened. "If you ask, if you must torture me, yes, of course."

"Margaret, yes," she whispered. "And you'll look after Conrad."

He cursed indistinctly. "Your dear *little* lost brother? The prince? Why? He can take care of himself, my darling. If he needs help, let him go to his father . . . or," he stuttered, "to Ratoff, your most wonderful first husband. They got on far better than I have, ever, with the little prince."

"Steve?" Katherine smiled hopelessly. "We hardly know where he is."

Bitterly, he corrected her. "Once and for all, it is not Steve. His name is *Stefan.* He is not an American accountant. He is a Bulgarian, some sort of Slav."

"I know, I know," she said quickly. "What do you care what I call him?"

"It is best to be correct," Erik snapped.

"What does it matter? A name . . . yours. . . ." Musingly, Katharine stroked him the wrong way. "Erik *Mossberg.*"

"Damnation. Is it necessary to taunt me? Erik Moss—I have always considered that a sufficiency."

But she continued, almost recklessly. "You Europeans— always so much activity in the haystacks. Nobody has got their real names anymore."

Grimly, Erik scoffed, "Hallucinating again? Tell me about your great Republic where indiscriminate sex has become the great leveler."

Despite her weariness, Katharine muttered, "You chopped your name because you were afraid somebody might think you were a Jew."

"My God!" Visibly shaken, his hands trembled on the steering wheel. "You can say such things so easily to me? Have you no respect for my feelings?"

"Some." Katharine studied the long face. Erik would have classified, she supposed, as a handsome man. The thick gray hair; he made the most of that, constantly running his hands through it. But his face was possibly too long, jaw too pronounced, the nose almost too straight for comfort. But he had good teeth, strong teeth and the eyes, deep-set and dead blue, were most impressive. "I do respect *your* feelings," she murmured.

Katharine clenched her hands in her lap. Her fingers were vital enough. Weariness settled on her like fog. Weariness, was it simple weariness? Or boredom? Lately, she had begun to think, defensively, that perhaps it was merely that Erik bored her to distraction.

"No more of this," he said curtly. "Forget it, please. I am American now. I adopted your country. *Erik Mossberg* with an umlaut is a thing of the past."

He tried to smile at her but his lips wouldn't move. He had been so cocky about his conquest of the Hermitage Assembly and the Port London hierarchy. And, so easily, she had reduced him to ashes. She made her point a second time. "I know . . . when I'm gone . . . you'll do the right thing."

"I always do the right thing."

"Yes, you are an honorable man," she said quietly, surprised at the sarcasm in her voice. "You've always said so."

"And so I am." He turned momentarily, his expression troubled. The eyes were the same, steady, penetrating, giving nothing back. "Sweetheart, why do you go on about death?"

She shook her head. "I think because you taught me to dwell on it."

"Oh, no!"

"Oh, yes. You're always talking about it. Just now, about the spirit of Captain Joshua Smithers wandering his house, the supremacy of the spirit."

His lips tightened. "But sweetheart, I do believe in the supremacy of the spirit. A Christian must—"

"But you're not a Christian," Katharine interrupted. "You're a pagan, Erik, I've always thought so."

They did not speak again until Erik was cruising across town toward Park Avenue. Home at last, she thought, holding her roiling stomach steady with her forearms.

God, she *was* tired. She had to rest. But there was another thing. She hated to disturb the uneasy peace, especially as he began to hum to himself, the louder as they neared Park Avenue, thinking he was home, free and clear.

"Did you sleep with Dolly yesterday?"

He reacted coolly enough, as if he had been prepared for the question earlier.

"I beg your pardon?"

"I said did you sleep with Dolly yesterday?"

"No, I did not."

"I see."

"What do you see?" he asked coldly. "You see *nothing*. I was with Dolly yesterday, as you know, at the assembly meeting and luncheon. I then drove her home and she asked me in. She wanted me to examine a piece of furniture, an antique highboy she proposes to install in the Smithers House when the restoration is complete. I then," he related rigidly, "returned home and found you were . . . resting. I did not disturb you."

Katharine shook her head listlessly. "I know you do—it doesn't matter what you say. Maybe not with her. . . . They say since Harrison Percy died, Dolly has had at least a dozen lovers. She wouldn't need you, if that's so. . . . But I know—since my illness—you've gone with other women."

Evenly, bitterly, concentrating on the light Sunday traffic on Park, he said, "From where do you date these fantasies of yours, my sweetheart? I think perhaps from the time your mother left your father—this made you feel inadequate, no? Then your first husband, the Slav Mongrel Ratoff," he added sardonically. "This union was not the most splendid. Ratoff was sent away with a large bundle of Darktower money. And then . . . me, Erik Moss, harmless and defenseless European. The second of Katharine's fortune-hunters, *n'est ce pas?*" His voice was cutting. "And so to our fantasies, our delusions of inferiority, not of grandeur." His voice rose. "Where do you get these ideas? Who puts them in your head?" he demanded. The closer they got to home, she knew, the more he was reminded of Helen Ryan, their nursemaid since Margaret's birth eight years before. "I know—from that Irish *bitch!*" he panted, as if reading her mind. "She is telling lies about me again. I tell you, Helen Ryan must go! She is destructive and has been since the beginning. She is poison in our lives."

"I'm not going to fire her," she said calmly. "She doesn't say anything about you."

"She hates me," he exclaimed. "She is a snooping Irish-Catholic bitch." He was right about Helen, to a degree. Helen had disliked him and been, for some reason, suspicious of Erik since the moment she'd been hired to take care of baby Margaret. Helen had come to them out of a strict religious upbringing; her mother for years had worked as housekeeper for a parish priest in Brooklyn. Helen was fulsomely religious; Erik, in one blessed flight of humor, said Helen perspired holy water.

Soothingly, though she didn't care, Katharine said, "She doesn't hate you. . . . You frighten her. All she wants is a little encouragement. I think she's utterly *fascinated* by you."

He made a rude sound. "She is disgusting! So pious, bah! Humble and self-righteous at the same time. So self-critical, so goddamned patient. *Merde!* If we wished, we could whip her into bruises and torn flesh and she would be convinced she deserved it. She would welcome it and turn the other cheek and then pray for us. I forbid her to pray for me!"

"For God's sake, darling, she's just a poor little thing."

"Little?" he cried. "She eats us out of house and home."

"I mean . . . mentally. She's loyal anyway."

His lips drew down. "As opposed to? I suppose *me!* I am not loyal?"

Very quietly, holding herself in control, knowing they would be home within a few more minutes, Katharine droned, "Don't forget, I do know about Dolly. Dolly is a barracuda, darling, everybody says so."

The remark put him back on the original track, and for the moment, Helen was forgotten. "Everybody says so. . . ." He mimicked her ferociously. "What do I care what everybody says? What bearing does that have on me? I refuse to fuel their ridiculous malice. How *dare* you suggest anything between Dolly and me?''

"I dare," she said indifferently. "Why shouldn't I dare?" She took her right hand from her belly and passed it across her damp forehead. "God, I have a headache, the most terrible headache."

"Of course," he said stonily, "you need a drink. Yes, when you're upstairs, have your Irish dear one bring you a *very* large vodka martini."

Erik braked the car violently in front of the gray, canopied entrance to Park Tower. He jumped out of the car and was pulling their two overnight bags out of the trunk before the blue-uniformed doorman managed to get himself outside.

"Afternoon, Mr. Moss."

"Hello, Peter." Erik's pronunciation of the name was gutteral. "Help Mrs. Moss out, will you, then bring up the bags."

"Sure thing, Mr. Moss. Oh, by the way, Miss Ryan has gone for a walk. She told me to tell you, in case you got here before she's back."

"Splendid," Erik snarled.

Two

The entrance to their duplex was on the sixteenth floor, opening straight out of the private elevator into a high-ceilinged living room whose tall windows looked out to Park Avenue and west toward Central Park. A study, wood-paneled and cozy, lay off the living room, its smaller, leaded windows also facing west. The dining room, airy, bright, furnished with gleaming woods, was at the rear of the apartment, close to a kitchen which, by New York standards, was gigantic. Upstairs, there was a master bedroom suite in the front, spare bedrooms, and Helen's quarters. An interior staircase, steep and winding, connected living room with the second floor and just recently they had had installed a small elevator in the space of what had been a butler's pantry and rising to a former linen closet.

"Shall you walk or ride?" he asked.

"Ride."

"Very well. Since Bitch is not here, I'll make you the drink. Double or triple?"

"Quadruple," she murmured sardonically.

"It will be done," he said, steadfast. "I am making your drink, so in the meantime there is no reason for you to take any pills."

She flinched. "Not even a tiny little tranquilizer? You used to say they were so good for me . . . a handful of aspirin?"

"Please don't endeavor to be amusing," Erik said stiffly.

"I do know what I'm doing," she barked. "Just bring the drink."

"Very well."

He opened the elevator door and formally assisted her into the padded and cushioned interior. It was, she thought, like a mini-booby hatch. Once, between Stefan and Erik, when everything had suddenly become too much for her, she had overnighted in such a place.

She sat down. "Farewell."

"Farewell, sweetheart," he muttered.

As he closed the door, she said, teasingly, "You wouldn't let me be trapped in here, would you? They'd never find me, you know."

Erik exhaled scornfully. "Yes, no doubt. The perfect murder—perhaps the very thing for an Independence Day weekend."

Katharine hit the *UP* button and, haltingly, the luxurious little box began to move. It stopped at its appointed place and quickly she pushed the door open and stepped into the hallway outside the master suite.

Katharine dropped her pocketbook on the bedside chair and flexed her shoulders, yawning and stretching. Actually she did not feel too bad and at least she was home, back in the cocoon. For some reason, after the bitter exchange in the car, she was in a more spritely mood; was there really any *real* cause to be depressed at all? It was something she did not understand very well.

She took off the jacket of the pantsuit, then sat on the side of the bed to remove the loafers. Up again to drag off the heavy slacks and then she stood, unencumbered, in bra and panties, in front of her mirrored closets. She was slim—fragile, Erik said. But no, fragile was the wrong word. She had grown to be more full-bodied than she had been, her breasts possibly too big for her slim waist and hips. The breasts undoubtedly were not as taut as childless Dolly's and maybe the cleavage not as dramatic but, on the other hand, her tits did not droop to her waist and, for a woman who had borne a child, they were quite respectably firm . . . luscious, Erik said, if you could believe Erik. She wondered what he told Dolly about hers.

Whatever, she admitted there was no solid reason why she could not be as healthy as a horse. Briefly, she strutted before the mirror, back and forth on the lush carpet where, sometimes, she suddenly remembered, on a bad night the pink polo danced for her. She grimaced, gasped in unexpected panic, remembering also how at night, infrequently though, the pink polo pony, whose head was Picasso's, gored her on the carpet, as if he'd been a unicorn and his horn a penis, a long, pink thing splitting her from end to end.

Katharine shivered and wished Erik would get up here with her drink. Carelessly, she slid out of her underthings and dropped them on the floor. She was on her way into the bathroom when the door opened and Erik stood there, holding the frosty glass, frowning. Just behind him was Helen Ryan, of all people, still in her cloth coat, a plaid scarf around her neck.

Katharine smiled at them, not bothering to cover her nakedness. Helen's face reddened, not so much because she was seeing Miss Katharine stark naked but because Erik was there too.

"Back from your walk, Helen?"

"Oh . . . I'm sorry . . . I. . . ."

"Get out," Erik grunted.

"I would have brought you the drink," Helen stammered, beginning her retreat down the hallway.

"I said, get out!" Erik stepped quickly inside and slammed the door. "You see . . . that bitch. She bursts right in."

"Where angels fear to tread," Katharine said blithely. She reached for the glass and put it to her lips, tasting the vodka gratefully. "Thank you."

He shrugged. "It is nothing." He sat down on the bed, shifted the pillows behind his head and threw his legs up, stretching out. Then, indolently, an expression on his face that was somehow insulting, he reached into the pocket of his shirt and pulled out a package of Rothman's. He lit a cigarette and drew in smoke. "You are beautiful," he drawled. His hard blue eyes roved her body from face to bosom to belly, studying her, she thought, analyzing, as if she were a piece of beef, deciding whether she was prime enough to the eating. He held her with those eyes and, for the moment, she forgot about her vodka. "You are beautiful," he repeated, "but you are so inaccessible. I cannot reach your interior. What is it about you?"

"Nothing," she said vaguely. "You're more inaccessible than I am, far more mysterious than I'll ever be. Maybe I'm just cold . . . and dead."

"No, not dead," he said quickly. "If you were dead, I could understand it." He gestured toward the other half of the bed. "You lay there, hardly breathing, talking to yourself. Do you dream, is that it?"

"I hardly ever dream," she said. "No, I do dream. I dream about a pink polo pony."

"Oh?" He was amused. "How interesting. From where comes this . . . pink polo pony?"

"I don't know, Dr. Freud," she said thinly. "I know my father used to play when he was younger. I remember going to polo matches."

"Not Stefan Ratoff? He did not play polo?"

"Steve?" She giggled softly. "Not Steve. He hated horses and he never had the money to play polo and by the time I was around to give him the money, he was past it."

Erik nodded. "Yes, by the time Stefan arrived, all there was left to do was drink. You learned that from him."

"A little, I suppose," she admitted.

"Pity," Erik grunted, "somebody in the Soviet Army didn't do the world a favor in 1944 and remove Stefan Ratoff from the face of it."

He said it so nastily, she had to have a sip of the vodka. "I expect Steve will take care of that himself."

"Well," he announced, "we can say for sure you did not learn bad things from me. From me, you have learned only steadiness and devotion."

Katharine shifted her bare feet on the carpet, away from the warm patches she'd made into coolness. "Oh, yes. . . ."

"When is your mother bringing the girl home?"

"After tea." Margaret had been taken for the weekend by her doting grandmother, Margo Himmelmann, the ex-Mrs. Darktower. "We have a few hours," she said.

"For what?"

"For whatever you want," she said meekly.

"All right," he said soberly. "I will allow you to make love to me."

"Oh, thank you, thank you," she cried. "You are too kind!"

"Are you on your way to the bath?" He ignored her sarcasm.

"I want a hot shower."

"I will be here," Erik said. He puffed smoke, folded his hands on his chest, the cigarette jutting from between his fingers.

"Laying doggo," she observed.

"Dead men tell no tales."

Shaking her head, Katharine went into the bathroom and closed the door. Now, finally, she could drink boldly from the vodka. Doing so, she turned on the shower with her other hand, and when it was adjusted properly, put the glass down on her makeup table and stepped into the stall. She gasped at the warmth of it. A sybarite, yes, Katharine stood in the rising steam, scalding herself for five minutes, rivulets of hot water running down her body into her crotch, sopping, matted, tender, and drowsiness came back at her powerfully. Recalling herself, she turned off the water and stepped out, reaching for an oversized towel to dry off. Finishing her drink, she slipped into the golden nightgown and silently opened the door.

Erik was there, as she had left him, except that he had undressed and lay naked on the covers, his limbs straight and eyes closed. He hardly seemed to be breathing. His hands were crossed, without the cigarette, at the wrists over his broad and nearly hairless chest. His masculinity scented the room and she almost reeled from it. Of course, Erik knew she was there, staring at him, but he did not move a muscle. Dead men tell no tales. . . .

Katharine lifted the skirt of her golden gown and trailed it along his leg to his hairy groin. The great muscled penis stirred to the touch of the silk and, marveling, she watched it grow stiffer and larger until it was distended, jutting in angry erection. Breathing carefully, pacing herself, Katharine placed one knee on the side of the bed and lifted the other over him, moving the billowing bottom of her gown until it covered nearly all of him like a tent.

Beneath her, she could feel the ramming head of it pulsing against her. She let it rest on her, trying not to disturb him, and slowly, so very slowly, she swayed over him and maneuvered her body to take it within her, first just the ram, and then, eyes tightly closed, she lowered herself on it, impaling herself as if on a stake. The thrill, it *was* like a jagged wooden stake penetrating her innards. She could not help moaning; but still he did not move, not a muscle. She circled him, using her hips, holding him as snugly as she could, then finally pushing down brutally, trying perhaps to wake him from the dead. In a second, a part of him reacted and a hot jet burst into her, a molten force that she pulled at, trying to retain it, hoping for relief and then, desperately, knowing from the dull throbbing in her belly that she would not have it.

She slowed her motion, stopping finally and, giving up, drew away from him. Wetness ran down her legs onto him and she huddled on the bed, distant from him, gathering the gown, her sacrificial gown, between her knees.

His voice encroached on her solitariness. "I seem to have dreamt a very satisfactory dream, my darling."

"For you. . . ."

"Not about you? Why should that be so?"

Katharine sighed bitterly, then dully said, "I don't understand what you're doing to me . . . or why. I think you must hate me. Why do you always have to pretend you're asleep or unconscious?"

"But I am unconscious . . . far away . . . on a mountain top. You like that, I believe. It gives you a sense of power, as if you were defiling a sleeping prince."

"Yes, or a cold dead body. A corpse."

"My darling! You cannot say such things!"

Katharine began to cry silently, biting her knuckles so he could not notice. Perhaps it would be easier for her to die. But why should she die for him? He was so unfathomable, unfeeling. No, not for him. Tears ran down her cheeks to her pillow.

"Some day," she whispered to herself, "it'll all end. Everything."

"What do you say, my darling?"

"Nothing," she answered.

Three

It was not unusual for Richard Darktower to appear unexpectedly for a visit with his granddaughter, little Margaret. Without ever saying so directly, he had the genius to make it clear with only a word, or gesture, that he had seignorial privilege here—after all, he paid for the apartment, didn't he, and if it went co-op in the future he'd buy it, wouldn't he?

Sunday afternoon, late, was always a good time to find the child home with mother and father.

Darktower, following divorce from Margo, now Mrs. Herman Himmelmann, had lapsed into semi-retirement, not undeserved since at the time he had been fifty-five and now was verging on sixty-five. He was of the species they called hale and hearty, a white-haired, no-nonsense man. He spent most of his time now in Long Island, well within commuting distance of the city. Nonetheless he came in progressively less often, booking himself a room at the Princeton Club on Forty-Third Street when prompted.

Today, however, Darktower's sudden, very nearly unannounced arrival was inconvenient. Before Erik was able to advise him on the phone that even then Margo Himmelmann, formerly Darktower, with Margaret and the young and dismal Conrad, was en route from the Himmelmann place on Fifth Avenue, Richard Darktower had merely said he was on his way and then hung up.

Grimly, Erik reminded himself that this was not, of course, the first time Margo and Richard had seen each other since their divorce. Collisions and confrontations were frequent at holiday times; more than that, Herman Himmelmann was often present at these gatherings, not an outrageous coincidence either, since Darktower and Himmelmann had been acquainted, although not bosom buddies, for many years on Wall Street. Seemingly, Darktower bore Himmelmann no resentment for having become his successor in the plumpish arms of vampish Margo but privately, Richard Darktower never ceased expressing puzzlement about how his former wife had fallen under the spell of a man like Himmelmann who, even if he was not now, Darktower said, had at some point been a card-carrying Jew.

Erik showered and was ready to go downstairs as Katharine returned bearing another powerful-looking vodka-on-ice. Glumly, she announced she was going to go to bed and watch TV and didn't want to see anybody except Margaret who was to say goodnight before she went to sleep.

Erik was able to tell her there had been a phone call while she was busy downstairs. Her father was coming to visit and her mother and the rest would also be here in a few minutes. Didn't she want to say hello?

"Not if they're here together, good God! If it was Daddy by himself. . . ."

"So, therefore, it is up to me to entertain your family and keep the peace."

Indifferently, she murmured, "They don't fight in public." Katharine had already placed her glass on the night table and slid her long legs under the sheet. She reached for the TV remote control, pressed *ON*, and began switching stations, completely ignoring him.

He didn't try to argue with her, merely went downstairs where, curtly, he told Helen Ryan to get ice in a bucket and place it on the drinks wagon, which anchored the spot where living room entered study. He followed her angry back with his eyes as she made for the kitchen. In different circumstances, he realized, Helen could have been an attractive little piece. Not exactly *little*. Eight years of rich food at the Moss's had filled out the scrawny little *nun-manque*, who had arrived like a gift from heaven, or somewhere, a few days before Kathy and Margaret came home from the hospital. Helen was about twenty-five now, he supposed, well-rounded in the physical, if not intellectual, sense. Her smooth Irish skin was pink and still baby fresh, dimpled; she possessed clear, snapping eyes and a generous portion of jet black hair. No, there could be no doubt that Helen Ryan was Irish and as Catholic as it was possible to be without breaking out in stigmata. Her stalwart haunches moved boldly beneath her tight black skirt and the line of her brassiere, harnessing untamed mammaries, unexplored, yes, uncharted mammaries was visible at the rear of a plain white blouse. She was still wearing flat walking shoes which made her calves bulge.

Erik turned on the lights in the library-study and prepared himself a Scotch and soda, without ice, then walked to the Park Avenue windows. He might catch sight of Margo Himmelmann and her procession coming from the west. He didn't give a damn about any of them, did he, any of the wastrel Darktowers? Except for *Margaret, his daughter*.

It was very nearly dark and the streets, on this blustery, late Sunday afternoon in February were deserted. It looked so cold outside, even colder than it actually was, a time for hibernation; he should appropriate a beast like Helen Ryan and crawl into a cave with her and remain there, rutting, until the first light of spring.

Or Dolly, he mused delightedly, remembering her heat, depth, so resonantly deep-chested, boldly breasted, richly loined Dolly Percy, the electricity of her sweaty ivory-toned skin. Nubile Dolly, yes, nubile the perfect word for her, shouting up mental paintings of dusky maidens with passion unquenchable. He grew dizzy just thinking about her. He was guilty, he confessed to himself, Kathy had had it right. He had slept with Dolly Percy the afternoon before and, as usual, she had been exciting, wonderful.

He turned from the window. It was dismal now, gloomy, this witching hour of a Sunday afternoon. Erik turned on lamps at each end of the sofa in front of the window, then the table lamps by the fireplace and finally the wall sconces. He hated gloom and darkness. That was better. He was warmed again by the thought of Dolly, the bliss of her bed, and thus ready for bitchy Helen Ryan when she ploughed back from the kitchen bearing ice. She put the bucket, with a gesture disdainful and at the same time defiant, down on the drinks wagon. Erik smiled at her distantly, wondering whether she would have thawed, or frozen even stiffer, if he'd whipped his baton out of his pants and pointed it at her virginity.

"Anything else, Mr. Moss?" Her dark eyes were fearless.

Slowly, Erik nodded. "Yes," he murmured, smiling crookedly. Helen started in surprise; what would he say? Would it be something very rude? She was plainly convinced he was a very rude man. No. "Try not to hate me quite so bitterly, Helen. This hostility must have an end."

"Hostility?" She flushed slightly. "I'm afraid I don't understand, Mr. Moss."

"Oh, yes, you do." He lifted his head so that he might stare down at her along the bridge of his nose, his eyes half closed. "I would pray you not to tell Mrs. Moss bad stories about me. She is very susceptible, as you know."

She blushed bright red at the cheekbones. "I don't know what you mean."

"Yes, Helen, you do. And it is inappropriate. I am prepared to be . . . your friend. But you too must be prepared."

Helen put her hands nervously together, cracking her knuckles. "I . . . uh . . . I do *respect* you as Mrs. Moss's husband, Mr. Moss. And *I* pray for the whole family."

"Oh?" he echoed her distantly, thinking this was exactly what he despised, her praying for him, "Thank you so much." He was prepared to go on when the doorbell chimed. *"Pray,"* he muttered, "answer the door."

Again, amused, he watched her retreat. He thought he had the better of her. Helen walked more self-consciously now, obviously realizing he could be thinking thoughts about her which were new and unexpected and, in a way, threatening.

Erik heard Richard Darktower's voice in the foyer, saying hello to Helen. In a moment, rubbing his hands together against the afternoon cold, Darktower entered the living room. Erik pointed to his glass, questioningly.

"Please," Darktower said smartly, "a Scotch and soda, Erik, if you would."

Erik poured a twenty-year-old Chivas Regal over ice, then squirted soda. "Are you down for the night, Richard?"

"Yes. Dinner. An old crony." Darktower didn't ever elaborate. "Where's my granddaughter?"

"They'll *all* be here in a few minutes, sir. Margaret spent the weekend with her grandmother. Mrs. Himmelmann is bringing her home. Conrad is with them too."

"Oh, hell," Darktower said disgustedly. "Why didn't you tell me? I'd have come later. Margo's not bringing the Jewboy with her, is she?" Darktower glowered at Erik over his glass. "What's Conrad want?"

"I was about to warn you," Erik said, "but you'd already hung up." Even retirement hadn't relaxed Darktower's abrupt business habits. "Poof! You were gone."

Darktower shrugged irritably. "Can't waste time on the goddamn telephone, Erik. Worst time-waster the good Lord ever gifted us. Well . . . so be it." He turned from Erik and strolled toward the windows. He grunted distastefully. "Jammed in, you are. I couldn't live in New York again. The city smells. Full of niggers and Puerto Ricans. Dangerous. Before it's done, we'll probably have to find a final solution, like you Krauts did."

Jesus Christ! Erik felt a claw of misery rake his heart. Again, there it was again. Did it always have to come up like this? Mention of it, so callously, made him feel sick. Why did Darktower do this? He was well aware of how Erik felt.

Slowly, he said, "Even as a joke, Richard, such talk is not funny."

Darktower spun around. "What? Funny? It's not meant to be funny. Just what do *you* think is going to happen to the world the way it's going? You think it's going to come out sunny-side-up? Don't be a fool. What happened in Germany was only the beginning of the horror."

Erik stared at him, feeling his eyes water. "It is terrible."

"I'm not saying it's not terrible, for Christ's sake," Darktower cried in exasperation. "I'm trying to be realistic."

"Terrible to think there is no hope," Erik murmured. "You forget, as you speak, you are touching something very sensitive in me."

"I'm sorry," Darktower said harshly. "I always forget I'm dealing with such a sensitive soul. I forget how sensitive you Germans are."

"All Germans are not murderers, I remind you, sir," Erik said faintly.

"Oh . . . Well . . . never mind," Darktower grunted. "Where's Kate?" His voice was cautious, as if he knew what the answer would be.

"Resting."

Darktower nodded disconsolately, turning his head to look at everything in the room except Erik. But then, brusquely, he snapped, "I've been thinking there's something very wrong. I don't know what it is—I don't know that I want to know what it is. Are you two all right? Why is she so goddamned depressed all the time?" His eyes became fierce. "I'm thinking it's not good for her, this marriage. Maybe we should end it. There's something very wrong," he repeated.

Carefully, Erik lifted his Scotch and finished it. Before speaking, letting Darktower see that he was unflustered, he chose ice and poured Chivas and squirted soda.

"The marriage is good," he said firmly. "So far as I am concerned, very good. I do my best. I do not understand what ails Kathy any more than you do, or any better. I do try my best. It is," he added sorrowfully, "not easy for me, as you can imagine. I worry about her continuously."

"Do you? Do you then?" Darktower retorted. "Tell me why you left your job. I thought I'd set you up very well. I did *my* best to see to that."

Readily, Erik explained, "I left because of Kathy. It was her request, not my idea. And now. . . ." He drew a long breath. "I *am* with her all the time—and she rests."

Darktower bared his teeth. "I don't know why I have to concern myself with these things. I live in the country, I'm finished with business, the world of commerce. Now, I'm

forced to worry about her . . . about you.'' His voice rose
from its low, insistent pitch. "And now about that bastard
Steve Ratoff. . . . Why?''

"Ratoff?'' Erik asked quickly.

"Yes, I heard from him," Darktower growled. "He's
coming to this country and the goddamn fairy wants
money." His face froze with disgust. "I'm at a loss to
know why Kate had to marry two Germans."

Erik stepped back, slammed his heels together and bowed
ironically. "I appreciate your lumping me with Ratoff . . .
It is not my fault if you have heard from Stefan Ratoff.
Stefan Ratoff is *not* a German!''

The glass moved impatiently in Darktower's right hand.
"It makes no difference. Don't try to bullshit me, Erik. I
know all about men like Ratoff and you. I'm not saying
you married Kate for her money, but I know he did. I also
think it's fairly certain that if Kate hadn't any money you
wouldn't have married her, even if you'd been head over
heels in love with her.''

Erik inclined his head again. Bitterly, he said, "After so
many years—thank you for your confidence. Believe it or
not, I repeat . . . I do love your daughter.''

Darktower glared openly at him. "All right," he grunted.
"There's nothing I can do about it—but don't ever make a
false move. That's a serious warning." He held out his
glass. "I'll have another, please.''

Damnation, Erik thought as he took the glass, Darktower
was like the polite assassin, ruthlessly waiting to strike—no
hard feelings, old boy. Men like Darktower had no illu-
sions about anything and when it became a matter of
money, power or position, no one, not family or friends—
and particularly not business associates—was unexpendable.
Once, in the old days, in Milan, Erik had heard the theory
propounded that when business negotiation failed, when
deep crisis threatened or blackmail loomed, his old employer James Merriwether sometimes, albeit rarely, had
recourse to lethal resolution. Erik despised such rumors,
considering it impossible that a man of Merriwether's
international stature could stoop so low. Now, having
watched Darktower for these ten years, he realized it was

neither a matter of stooping nor elevating one's self. It was merely something that was done, like closing a bank account.

"You're clever," Darktower said pleasantly, taking the fresh drink. "Tell me what I'm supposed to do about Steve Ratoff."

If he had been a more optimistic man, Erik might have taken the question as an invitation to alliance. But he knew better than that. "Send him packing," he said coldly. "By what right does he ask for money? He had his settlement, did he not?"

"Yes. He's run through it, obviously. Just tell me, how do I tell this Kraut pansy to get lost?"

"Refuse to see him," Erik cried, "He will not, I assure you, be admitted here."

Darktower tensely asked, "And what about Conrad?"

Erik shrugged. "What Conrad does is his own business. He's over twenty-one years old. He has his allowance and he earns some money lecturing at Columbia. If he wishes to see Ratoff, no one can stop him."

"Yes, true." Darktower became vastly discouraged. This was the sore point, an open wound still. Richard Darktower would never be convinced that somehow Stefan Ratoff had not tried, those dozen years ago, to ruin Conrad Darktower. "School," Darktower muttered. "Lecturing. . . ."

"I believe Conrad is very good at what he does. He is only an instructor now. But he will have his doctorate, perhaps a bright future in the scholastic world."

"Scholastic world!" Darktower might have yelled Humbug! "I'm surprised to hear you say a good word for him," the older man mentioned. "You've *never* gotten along with him."

Erik shrugged calmly. "He has always resented me, as you know, sir. I have tried my best with him. But . . . you understand the whole business as well as I."

"Ratoff," Darktower grunted ferociously, "the son-of-a-bitch. The boy is too goddamned pretty."

Erik smiled hollowly. "He takes after you."

"Yes?" Darktower made a face. "Naturally—I suppose that's what dear Margo says. I have no doubt she's blaming me for everything—heredity will pay the tab."

Thoughtfully, he inspected his glass. "Too bad I didn't know in time—I'd have had the bastard Ratoff barred from the country on moral turpitude. I'll be at my farm—if the son-of-a-bitch comes near me, I'll put the dog on him."

"He won't."

"He better not," Darktower grated. "But never mind him—what the hell are you going to do about Kate?"

"I have considered taking her away in the spring."

"Where to?" Darktower asked suspiciously.

"To Europe. A few weeks in London, Italy, Switzerland. . . ."

"Is she well enough to travel that far?"

"I hoped travel would stimulate her. Here, she merely sits."

"Drinks! Let's be frank about it," Darktower muttered.

"No," Erik said hastily, "I am pleased to tell you, she doesn't drink that much. Her tolerance to alcohol is low." Why bother to deny it? He could see Darktower didn't believe him.

"Yes . . . all right," Darktower said. "If you go, what about Margaret?"

"She remains here, with Helen Ryan, a completely trustworthy woman. After school is finished, she could come to visit you, I trust."

Darktower fidgeted with his drink petulantly, dissatisfied, and was about to say something else when the doorbell rang.

"That will be them," Erik said.

Margaret came in first, bouncing. She was eight years old and her hair so blonde as to be almost silver-white. In this characteristic, she took after both mother and grandmother and the latter relationship became apparent when Margo Himmelmann followed her into the living room. Margo, at close to age sixty, was a stately being. Her hair was more silver than blonde now but her face was clear, eyes bright and she had by no means lost her shape.

Erik's daughter put her arms gravely around his neck and kissed him on both cheeks as he had taught her to do but Richard Darktower pulled her away at once.

"Come to me, child." Margaret had learned already,

Erik told himself acidly—she twined her hands at the back of Darktower's head when he knelt before her and, giggling breathlessly, kissed him wetly on the face and lips. Darktower huffed and puffed deliriously, rummaged in his pocket and pulled out a small velvet jewelry box. He opened it and showed her what was inside.

"Grandfather!" Margaret's eyes popped appropriately. "It's a chain with a locket! And it's gold!"

"Damn right it's gold," Darktower barked. "Would I give Margaret anything else?"

Margo Himmelmann watched her former husband with what seemed to be strained tolerance. "Well, Richard," she remarked, "you never gave *Margo* gold. And once," she said, turning to tall, thin, adamantly frowning Conrad behind her, "he even gave me a fake diamond."

Darktower didn't look at her. "Good thing too," he muttered. He was concentrating on catching the tiny clasp of the gold chain around his granddaughter's neck. "Damned if I know why I should've built a dowry for Mrs. Himmelmann."

Margo chuckled good-naturedly. "Beastly man. Your father was always a beastly man, Conrad."

Darktower was right about his son. Conrad was definitely too beautiful. His face was blond, unblemished; his lips were puckish—pouty when he was in a bad mood. Erik yearned to order him to get his slick blond hair cut to manly length.

"Hello, Conrad," he said.

"Hello, Erik." Conrad's voice was cold, neutral and his look merely absorbed Erik. He did not change expression. "Hello, Dad."

Alertly, Darktower raised his head. "Well, it's been a while, hasn't it? To what do I owe this honor, Conny? You haven't been out to see me in a year."

Conrad wasn't impressed with the rebuff. Coolly, he said, "You owe the honor to an accident. I didn't know you'd be here."

Darktower's face reddened. "And if you had? You're telling me you wouldn't have come?"

"Oh, Dick!" Margo Himmelmann cut in. "Can't you two at least try to be civil?"

Darktower returned his attention to Margaret. "Civil is as civil does," he muttered nonsensically.

Conrad didn't blink. "No—I probably would have come," he said.

"How wonderful," Darktower muttered.

Margo cast her eyes toward Heaven and at Erik. "Where's Katharine? Did you have a nice weekend?"

Erik stepped forward and kissed her cheek. Margo smiled; she liked being kissed. "Kathy is upstairs. . . ."

"Resting," Darktower interjected.

"So? She's tired," Margo exclaimed. Then she wanted to know what they'd done and Erik told her they'd spent two full days dashing madly about, between the Heritage Assembly and the old Smithers House, in aid of their restoration project. He stretched reality a bit but why not make Margo happy?

Hearing the Smithers business mentioned, Conrad felt bound, for some reason, to interrupt. "Par for Port London, isn't it? Pay more attention to the dead then the living."

Margo snapped, "Don't be a silly ass, Conrad. I don't understand you. This course of yours—you're turning into some sort of revolutionary."

Darktower murmured smugly, "I'm not surprised, after he's spent an afternoon with Madame Frivolous."

Margo stared at him hatefully, then laughed vivaciously and flopped down in one of the fireplace armchairs. "My feet hurt." She kicked off her shoes and crossed her legs, these fine and dandy in a Chanel skirt. The suit top was buttoned as far as a string of pearls, which glimmered on her firm chest. "Anyway, what's wrong with preserving history?" she asked idly.

Conrad, give him credit, did not retreat. "The future is more important than the past." He glanced boldly at Erik. "Or isn't it?"

"Without our history," Erik said, "we can have no future."

Conrad's eyes flickered. Erik knew what he wanted to say: Bullshit!

Darktower chuckled complacently. "For once, I happen to agree with Conrad. History is all very well but it doesn't move stock market issues. We'll talk about it, Conny," he added, overly hearty. "I think you and I are on the same wavelength."

"*Maybe* . . . on some things."

Conrad took everything so bloody solemnly. Not that Erik was a comedian—he was not. But he was a positive clown compared to Conrad.

"Columbia!" Darktower summed it up peevishly. "Haven't you had enough of it by now?"

Conrad shook his head. "Not yet," he stonewalled.

"Goddamn it! Join the firm! You're headed for a job with the firm and don't forget it! You're going to do *very well.*"

"I'm not sure I want that," Conrad said quietly.

Darktower stared at him incredulously. How could anyone *not* want what he'd ordained for them? "What *do* you want then?"

"I don't know . . . I just don't know."

Darktower groaned desperately. "My God! Mrs. Himmelmann is right—you've gone mad!"

Margo laughed again, gaily. "Don't *you* be silly, Richard. He's just a young squirt."

Quietly, though he did not have the slightest interest in what Conrad finally chose for a career, or non-career, Erik said, "I'm sure Conrad will do the right thing, whatever that is."

Conrad's eyes flashed sardonically. "I'm so pleased you have confidence in me."

Erik looked back at him icily. Well, he thought, they could all see that once again he had tried.

"Don't be a bore, Conrad," Margo sighed. "Children, so full of themselves. Boring."

"Margo," Erik asked, "would you like some tea . . . or a drink?"

"A little sherry," she said, her voice faint. She grimaced at Darktower, "You look well, dear."

"I am well. I live in good air and I am well."

"Still all by yourself?" she teased, but she was curious.

"Just me and the squirrels, Mrs. Himmelmann."

Margaret sat quietly with her grandfather, tucked into the sanctuary of his armpit on the sofa near the tall windows. She was oblivious of the cutting banter, or so it seemed. Actually, Erik knew, she absorbed *everything* and she was deeply sensitive to all, as he was; this was a trait he and she had from the ancient Mongol tribes who had left their mystic stamp on the Baltic north. He would have liked to remember a father whose eyes slanted Orientally. But he could not remember such a Prussian-born father; Erik's eyes were deep-set, heavily hooded but they were not Oriental. They were simply Germanic, an Aryan blue.

"How *is* Mr. Himmelmann these days?" Darktower inquired. "Still strong-arming everybody on Wall Street?"

"No," Margo said sharply, "as you know he never did, Richard."

Wryly, Conrad spoke up from his place on the far side of Margo. "Mr. Himmelmann agrees with you about higher education."

Darktower's eyebrows jumped. "Which proves that whatever else Mr. Himmelmann is, he is not a fool."

"And whatever else *is* he, Richard?" Margo demanded

Erik hoped Darktower was not going to call Himmelmann a Jewboy, not now. He crossed the room, pointing at Darktower's empty glass.

"No more, Erik. I'll be having a few tonight. I've got to be going soon."

"I want to see Katharine," Margo Himmelmann announced.

"Well . . ." Erik hesitated. "She said she was going to sleep. She said she didn't want you to bother about her."

"Bother?" Margo yelped. "I'm her mother!"

Margaret supplied further advice, very seriously too, like Conrad. "When she's resting, Mommie doesn't like anybody to disturb her."

"Indeed!" Margo exclaimed. "I never minded being disturbed when I was resting."

Erik gave up. "Go then. Wake her up. She'll be happy that you did."

Moodily, Darktower said, "If she wants to see me, she can goddamn well come downstairs."

"Richard, stop being a beast!"

"Mrs. Himmelmann," Darktower said angrily, "I would appreciate it if you would cease and desist calling me a beast."

"I'm only making a little joke, Margaret," Margo Himmelmann said sourly. "Mr. Darktower isn't really a beast."

Darktower snorted. "Hope not! Else how did you survive with me for thirty-odd years?"

"Thirty-odd years! Erik, please, another sherry!"

"Of course." *Why didn't they all go home?* Erik glumly passed Conrad a second drink to give his mother and made himself a new Scotch and soda. God, if they'd only go, he'd turn Margaret over to Helen Ryan and try to get through the Sunday *New York Times*.

But, damnation, there was still more family ground to cover. Defiantly, Conrad took a new position between mother and father in the center of the living room and said, "I had a letter from Stefan Ratoff. He's coming to New York."

Darktower looked pained, but resigned. "From whence is he coming?"

"The letter was from Geneva. Steve said he'll be traveling with an old friend of his, a man named Marco Fortuna."

"Wonderful," Richard Darktower hissed. "They'll fly cheap. They wouldn't need an airplane, would they?"

Erik almost laughed aloud and Margo twitched in her chair. "Richard! Now *that* is a horrible and unfriendly thing to say."

"As well as filthy," Conrad muttered angrily. His blond face turned rosy. "It's all very well if you don't want to see him, but I think it's unkind of you to say things like that. Steve has always been a friend to me, in case you didn't know. . . ."

"I know . . . I know," Darktower glowered. "I'm sorry—I wouldn't want to be . . . unkind . . . about a *dear* friend of yours, Conny."

"Now, Richard . . ." Margo's voice rose.

"I know what you're trying to say," Conrad said in a low voice. "And you're not being very clever about it. You know," he said frankly, eyeing his father hotly, "the time might come when *you'll* grow up—you're always telling me to grow up. The same goes for you."

Margo thumped her glass on the table next to her armchair and jumped up. "Botheration! I'm going upstairs. Come along, Margaret."

Richard Darktower didn't speak. He was breathing in short, irritated bursts. Erik knew he had plenty more to say but he was holding himself back. Conrad stood looking at him, waiting. But he waited in vain.

Darktower pushed himself up and off the couch. "I'm going to go now," he said softly.

"I'll get your coat," Erik left them, going into the hallway by the front door of the apartment.

He heard Darktower speak.

"Conrad . . . all right. I'll say nothing more to you. I won't take offense, though I could. You're right about one thing—I won't see Ratoff. If you want to see him, go ahead. It's nothing to me. I've told you this before—I'm not going to worry about you, not anymore. . . . Perhaps you're right to think kindly of people. That's fine. I *don't* think kindly of many people and for that I'm sorry. But that's the way I am. . . ."

When Erik returned with his topcoat, Darktower slipped into it and took his hat from Erik's hands.

"I'm sorry," Conrad said humbly.

"Forget it," Darktower said strongly. "So long."

Four

The expression of his mother's generosity, also of her guilt feelings, according to some of his friends, was Conrad Darktower's comfortable apartment on the third floor of a Village walk-up, a few blocks from the place where Fifth Avenue dead-ended in Washington Square.

He paid off the cab at Tenth Street to walk the rest of the way. A good many members of his new intellectual set viewed with class disgust the use of a taxi when public transportation was available. Paying cab fares, they charged, was more than ostentation—it isolated one from the masses, from the *people*. And Conrad wouldn't want to be branded a class-enemy.

He found them amusing and he half-believed all the trivia and drivel they talked. Conrad lectured now two or three times a week in Nineteenth Century American Literature and for this he was paid a pittance. But it did serve to make him a member of the working class. And so he had met Roberto who went by that single name. Roberto had been in Conrad's class and then, only a few years younger than Conrad, he became his friend—something of a friend. Roberto, Conrad judged, was what the Russians would have called a firebrand: he loved to talk. And Conrad didn't object to listening. Roberto was somehow different from most of the people he knew. He came from Boston for starters and there was Irish in his language. Sometimes he acted as though he was from outer space. But certainly, somehow, he had become a self-appointed spokesman for a world of which Conrad had no knowledge.

Conrad jammed his hands into his raincoat pockets and bent his head to the wind that ripped off Washington Square. The streets down here were crowded, despite the weather. People hustled past him, buried in windbreakers, down vests, flannel shirts, ski caps and hiking boots. There had been some sort of political rally in the park.

Thinking about the useless and frustrating four hours he'd spent in upper Manhattan, Conrad picked up his feet. He had behaved like a pig, and he knew it, like a spoiled child. There was no reason he should have been surprised at his father's reaction when he'd mentioned Ratoff and no excusable motive for bearing such a grudge against Erik Moss. It was not Moss's fault that his sister had married him. It was not Moss's sin that he was so unlike Ratoff, that he was such a droning bore compared to the light-hearted Stefan Ratoff.

But, leaving reason aside, Conrad did not like Moss. He did not think he would have liked him in any circumstances.

Conrad burned with embarrassment when he thought about his father, Richard Darktower. Tough as nails the old man was and Conrad knew what his father suspected . . . and feared. That somehow Stefan Ratoff had debauched him. Christ! He wouldn't believe otherwise, no matter what they told him. Darktower hated Ratoff as he would have hated the Devil himself.

And of his mother, Mrs. Himmelmann, the less said the better. She loved him but she was the original dilettante, never mind about Ratoff.

He pushed the wind around the corner of Fifth, dodged overturned garbage cans and split plastic refuse bags at which rats rummaged in the night, side-stepped dog shit and decaying fruit and finally trotted the last few steps to the door of his apartment house.

Lilly would be waiting—yes, Lilly, Mr. Darktower— the only person in the world he had ever let get close enough to understand him. She had come with Roberto, off the streets, to love him, and he was content with her.

Conrad let himself in and rushed up the three flights to the top floor. Not wanting to frighten her, he knocked, then yelled, "Lilly, it's me." Then he unlocked the door.

She was sitting in a wicker armchair, dim light from the street over her shoulder, staring at her easel. Coolly, she turned her face to him. She was thin and small, like a waif, but she was so alive. A mass of kinky red hair stood out from her head. Between her paint-stained fingers, she held a cigarette. Her blue sweatshirt was marked with slashes of dried color and smudges of cigarette ash. Dirty blue corduroy jeans covered her crossed legs. One sandal plopped up and down as she swung her foot.

"Hello, lovey," she said softly.

"What have you been doing?"

"Sitting here—looking at this thing. No." She jumped up quickly. "It's not done. You can't see." She threw an old sheet over the easel.

"I won't. Are you hungry?"

"Starved."

"Lilly, you forget all about yourself."

"That's it," she said. "I suppose *you've* been gorging yourself all day at your mother's."

"No." He shook his head glumly. "It's a pain. We walked over to my sister's. My *father* was there—Jesus! And Erik, looking anxious, and stuttering. Kate? *Resting*, as usual."

Lilly clicked her tongue on her small white teeth. "What a way to go. Why don't they do something about it?"

"Yes, why not?" He nodded grimly. "Because— wouldn't do for them to admit she's unhappy, would it?"

"All that money," she said disgustedly. "I *know* about money. And Erik?"

Conrad shrugged. "What can he do? He's not going to rock the boat. One false word and Erik is out on his ass, just like Steve Ratoff. The old man would have him shipped off to Africa or someplace."

Dropping her cigarette in a choked ashtray, Lilly put her sticky hands on either side of his face. "You're here now, lovey. Don't feel bad. You did your thing. None of it is your fault."

"I know." But still he felt miserable. "Let's have a glass of wine, then go eat."

Swaying in her tight jeans, Lilly went into the kitchen,

the size of a double closet and came back carrying a diminished jug of California red and two smudgy glasses.

"Here, I'll wash those," Conrad said.

"No. Why? It's just our own lips marks." Lilly put the glasses down on a littered coffee table, then pulled the cork out of the bottle and poured. "Cheers." The redness slicked her lips. "Roberto was here about two," she reported, "on his way to that rally."

Conrad nodded loosely. "I might've known. As soon as I go out, Roberto shows up."

Lilly grinned. "He wanted to see *you*, not me."

"What about?"

She made a face. "What else? The revolution. Raising money. How they're going to kill everybody and with what's left create the perfect society."

"You're not interested, are you?" he asked. "Me neither, not hardly at all. Killing—they'll probably start with me."

She laughed, her voice tickling him. "Not if you give them a lot of money."

"Does Roberto make you tired? He does me."

"He's your friend, not mine."

"He was *your* friend before he was mine," he pointed out.

"Lovey, I don't mind if you're a capitalist. My father's one too, you know. I like it better here than living in Roberto's tenement. I like money. I can get more work done here, where it's warm, and work is important. I'm not a masochist. As far as I'm concerned, Roberto can take his revolution and shove it."

Conrad told her what Richard Darktower had said a few hours before, about the family business. "He thinks I'm a fool to stick around school."

"You wouldn't have to struggle like everybody else."

"You're struggling," he pointed out.

"That's different. Artists are supposed to. Listen to me. I want you to be a success. Who knows—you may have to support me."

"I would. If that's what I have to do, I'll do it."

"You'd be working with Kate's husband, wouldn't you?"

Conrad shook his head. "No more. Erik quit." He frowned. "Why should he work? Kate's rich. . . ."

"Doesn't he treat her well? Why do you always have such a hard-on for him?"

He shrugged, not understanding either. "I don't know—I must be jealous—or something."

She muttered wisely. "You're in love with your sister and you hate Erik because he screws her."

"Yeah . . . sure." Conrad's nerves sang. "Jesus!"

"Don't like the truth?"

"Truth? Lilly. . . ."

Lilly worked her arms around him, huddling close. "Listen, kid, I'm older than you—maybe not in years. Dump your complexes. Don't I do you well? They don't call me super-bang for nothing, you know." She yanked on his hair. "Well, are we going out, or not? Do I change, or what?"

Conrad smiled. If only everything else could be as uncomplicated as Lilly was, as life *should* be. He tucked his free hand under her sweatshirt, caressing the line of her back, her ribs, one tiny breast.

She squirmed against him. "Not now. I'm hungry."

"So am I." Conrad slid her sweatshirt up above her breasts, baring the pert little things and lowering his head to the nipples, pink and pointed. "Did you miss me today?"

Silently, Lilly nodded, fondling the back of his head, curling his hair with her fingers. She shifted her body to give him space to unbutton the top of her corduroys and tug down the zipper. Lifting her gently, Conrad pulled the pants over her hips and dropped his face to kiss her navel, no more than a twist of dimple in her flat belly. Lilly smelled strong; she'd been working all day and never took a shower in the morning. But that was all right. He liked her scent, pungent, musky. He circled the indentation of the bellybutton with his tongue, stroking the sparse reddish patch at her crotch.

"Lovey. . . ."

"Yes?" he muttered, wanting her not to talk.

"When I was working today," she sighed, "all day,

every time I stopped for a cigarette I thought about you. It's so nice to have you for me, anytime I want.''

"Morning . . . noon . . . and night," he whispered. He began to tremble, wanting his stuff, as Lilly called it.

"Damn," she said, "let's. Now. A quickie before I get dressed and then another one when we get back. Spaghetti makes me unbelievably horny and I want spaghetti. Red wine too."

She unbuttoned his shirt and pulled off his shoes and pants and underwear, then grabbed him in her hands. "You're like a barge pole."

"The better to. . . ." He stared at her, unable to complete the thought. She was so beautiful. Conrad was not completely unexperienced but this was his first real love. It was the continuity which was so comfortable, and comforting. This was all his: the little breasts and nipples, so small, yet so fiery and responsive when he touched them with his mouth, the fuzzy slash of vagina. He knelt over her on the couch and she pulled him forward and down.

She held his stuff cautiously. "I'd give you head," she said, "except you'd come instantly and I want you inside me. Down, Conrad!"

He moved between her legs, spread widely to make room; always, at the outset, she was tiny within. When, at last, he was all in, she twisted her legs over the backs of his thighs.

"You're so huge, I don't know what to do with it all." He turned his head to kiss her lips. Her belly tensed and she started to moan. "Oh!" She stroked his hips as Conrad thrust wildly, then without warning, gasping loudly, spending. He kept bearing down, puffing, snorting, so pleasurable that it hurt and finally Lilly crested, with a reedy scream.

"You're so fast," she protested.

"I can't help it. Sorry. I can keep going now. Don't stop."

"Thank God," she exclaimed softly. "I've caught you near your prime. But we've got to stop. Otherwise, we'll never get anything to eat." She breathed laboriously.

"Lilly—I love you."

She chuckled moistly. "You just love fucking." Rocking under him, tugging him forward, she explained, "Best is when you're young. They say when you get older you lost interest."

"I don't believe that."

"No," she said decidedly, "that's why you've got to get as much as you can before you're twenty-one. After that, it's downhill all the way—*you're* already past it. You were at your best a couple of years ago."

"Lilly, don't talk so much. I feel sad."

"That is what they call post-coital depression—do I have to teach you everything?"

"Yes, because you're older than me and you know more." He fastened his lips to a spot on her neck. "I'm going to put my mark on you. My property. Everybody at the restaurant will know we've just screwed."

"Beast. I'll wear a scarf on my neck."

He remembered the afternoon. "Margo called my father a beast. It made him roar."

"They still talk? I guess," she said thoughtfully, "they never get over some kind of love."

"If you can call *that* love."

Lilly tightened her arms around his back, squeezing air out of him. "Oh, we're so lucky, you know, to be young. A lot of people think being young is miserable, they'd never want to be young again. I don't feel that way about it, do you?"

"I used to—before we came together."

"We should make the most of it," she urged. "Umm . . . umm . . . push. You're getting hard again. If you were fifty you couldn't do that." She jerked at him ecstatically, her red hair flaming against the blue sofa. "Jesus! I'm just so happy! I don't know who thought this up but it's got to be the best thing going—better than anything."

"Better than spaghetti?"

She thought about it. "Yes, I'd have to say so."

Later, when she dressed, it was in a blue wool-knit dress he'd bought for her at Bonwit's uptown, explaining to the ever-critical Roberto that it'd come from the Good-will and cost five bucks.

"You look good in the dress," he said. "You're a shrimp but you're beautiful."

"Lovey," she said brightly, "I'm built like a mouse."

"A red-haired mouse," he said emotionally.

"With a little red-haired mouse-hole."

"Don't talk like that."

"You hate it when I talk dirty." She sat down again and pulled on her soft, high, brown boots.

They descended arm-in-arm to the cold and dark of the street. The restaurant was a ten-block walk, across the Square and on the other side of the university. Wind-blown dust and winter's left-over leaves tossed on the walks among soggy, torn remnants of the afternoon's placards, boosting whatever cause it had been. The victory arch from a forgotten war dominated the park, the benches where, in the summer, old men gathered to play chess and checkers, and young men, black or white, drugged or drunk, baited the passers-by. Now it was empty, and dirty with winter's grime.

The scene darkened her mood. "Christ. Utter desolation. It grinds my very artistic soul, lovey."

"It should stimulate you."

"My mood is quite mournful enough as it is. I need light, and lots of laughing, and lots of love."

"Yes, love," he agreed. "Love, love, love."

She pressed his arm and grinned up at him. "I'm not wearing any panties so you can play with me in the restaurant."

"I wouldn't!"

She giggled. "If you don't promise to, I'll flash Gino. I'll pull up my dress and show it to him."

Sunday night at Gino's place was never crowded and, easily, they got a booth in the dark at the far end of the bar. Conrad ordered a bottle of chianti and, taking charge, Lilly arranged for the spaghetti with meatballs and lots of garlic.

"Nature's own disinfectant," she said brightly. "How do you think your mother would like a dump like this?"

"She'd pass out."

"What about Kate and Erik?"

"He'd probably hate it too. He's such a fucking snob. He'd want to know the history of the place before he ordered . . . Kate," Conrad added darkly. "She'd have a good time with us."

"Well," Lilly said sensibly, "then why the hell don't we ever ask her to come down? I know—you think Kate would be jealous of me, like you're so goddamn awful jealous of Erik."

"No, no." But how was he to know?

"Family," Lilly sniffed. "They never understand anything."

Lilly Royce came from Chicago but she didn't talk about it. She had cut loose at the age of eighteen after one semester at Northwestern and headed for New York. The family of Benjamin Royce was well-to-do, enough to send her a living allowance, but her father made it just that, enough to exist on but not enough to encourage lifelong devotion to art. If they'd known, Lilly chortled, that she'd gotten connected with the great and wealthy Darktower clan, they'd have been a bit more pleased with her. But she'd never dared hint in a letter that she was shacked up, let alone with whom.

"I suppose," she said, "that I'm never going to get to meet your mother."

"You can meet her whenever you want."

"You're not ashamed of me, are you, lovey?"

" 'Course not." Impulsively, he asked the question which seemed most natural in the circumstances. "We could get engaged, couldn't we?"

"I don't meet her until we're engaged? God, you really are a straight arrow, ain't you?"

"I love you."

"*They* might not approve," she said. "Besides, it's so *ordinary* a thing to do."

"I know. It's what . . . our kind of people *do*. Yours too. My father would be as happy as a loon—he thinks I'm queer."

Lilly pinched his arm angrily. "Don't say things like

that. They can go fuck themselves,'' she hissed. "You're not queer! I can testify to that. You're a mad fucker, it's all you ever think about.''

She dropped her hand under the tablecloth and slid it up his thigh to his stuff, bulging in his pants. He felt the juices running on his leg.

"Lilly, please . . . not here. I'm. . . .''

She grinned at him boldly, her small face elfin with mischief, her eyes dancing. Making her point again, she muttered, "We'll hear no more talk about that. Give me your hand.''

He couldn't stop her. She guided his hand under her wool skirt, up her thigh to the warm wetness of her place. He touched her lightly with one finger but, still holding his hand, she pushed the finger inside her, grunting, biting on her tongue between her teeth and just like that he made her come again. She groaned softly, her eyes half-closed but she kept on grinning.

"Nice, very nice.''

Conrad glanced around furtively. Nobody had noticed; of course, if they had they weren't going to say anything. Not to be outdone, he held his fingers to his nose, then licked the tips. The smell was acridly sweet, the taste like that of bitter chocolate.

Lilly whispered, "Tell me it's not fun to be young.''

Five

Richard Darktower's friend Leland Penton lived in a solid, old apartment building on Madison, not far north of the Carlyle Hotel and it was there Darktower headed when he'd finished with his several hours in the bosom of his family.

Bosom of his family, indeed, he told himself maliciously, as he stepped out vigorously from the Moss's place on Park Avenue to keep company with newly bereaved Lee Penton. Penton's wife, Pauline, had died just before Christmas and this was the first chance Darktower had had to extend his sympathies personally. He could have come sooner but the prospect of facing a weeping Penton was not his idea of a good time; so he had pleaded flu, the weather and simply despair over the state of American politics as excuses for not making the trip to New York in December. In fact, he hadn't come into the city at Christmastime at all. No reason he should have, really. Kate and family had driven out a few days after Christmas and he'd distributed his parcels of good cheer, checks, greetings and assorted balderdash. And he'd had the pleasure of enjoying New Year's Eve by himself too. He had made turkey sandwiches from leftover bird, popped on the TV for a while, then polished off a cold bottle of Dom Perignon and after that a good bit of an old Napoleon brandy he'd been saving. After toasting himself to life eternal, he'd stumbled to bed at eleven-thirty.

There was much to be said for being alone, Darktower assured himself, turning right on Madison, and he would have to convince Lee Penton of the same. There was even more to be said for solitude and privacy after an hour or two with his neurotic family. Bosom of the family, hell! If that was a bosom, he grunted to himself, then it had had a double mastectomy. About the only joy attached to it was seeing Margaret, his granddaughter, and perhaps heckling Margo Himmelmann. Conrad always managed to turn his acids loose.

Mrs. Himmelmann! He hummed sourly to himself. Mrs. Himmelmann, the former Margo Darktower, pillar of New York society. Bullshit! Mrs. Himmelmann was, in truth, a demanding wanton and he was still altogether very happy he had got rid of her, although her going from him to the Jewboy seemed often as if she had pissed on his integrity. Herman Himmelmann was never far from Darktower's mind. He wondered how Herman fared with Margo's sex drive, for she was a gorgon, as many-faceted in her desires as hydra-headed Medusa. Herman would have to be a veritable Priam to keep up with her. But enough of the old classical stuff—he remembered his shock soon after their picture-book marriage all those thirty-eight or forty years ago that Margo was Sex Incorporated—he could have sold shares in her.

Margo, at eighteen, had been a virgin, innocent and pure. Once that had been taken care of, she had emerged a ravenous animal, of imaginative insatiability. It was really no exaggeration, he mused, to say that in the beginning she had been next door to a nymphomaniac. He had been able at first to match her, screw for screw, but as the months waned, so did he. After all, he was a working man and he needed rest. But not Margo. He wondered again how, with the longevity of her passion, she managed to keep so well. Never a flicker of remorse, that was one answer—for, even in the heyday of their so-proper marriage, she had cheated on him, often. He knew that for a fact, and at the time he had raised holy hell about it. She had been appropriately contrite for, in those faraway days, divorce was much frowned upon; then she had gone on as before. Surrendering to reality, Darktower had begun spending more time with business and less and less wondering which lover she had discarded and who would be next.

There was, however, a worrying aspect to this. Darktower had often suspected Kate had known—and did that secret knowledge, a form of shame, lay at the center of her trouble? There had to be a good, logical reason for her depressions. Her moods could not be due to unabated adoration of that son of a bitch Stefan Ratoff, Stevie the sweetie. Kate had agreed with her father that divorce was the answer and the sooner the better; one did not stay married to a fairy. He gladly admitted to having forced the issue once the rumors had grown to fact and couldn't be ignored. And, goddamn, yes, he had worried about Conrad, when it was probably too late.

If there was blame to be attached, it was on Margo's shoulders. Darktower did not like to dwell on the sordid past but he remembered the most flagrant episode. Margo had been caught making love to Leonard Libby in the back seat of a Rolls on a hot, sticky summer's day at a horse show near Wainscott, and Darktower was more convinced every year that Kate had been witness to the terrible scene—Margo grunting and rutting and panting and squealing as that son-of-a-bitch Libby rammed it to her. If his, Darktower's, scar had not healed, then what were they to expect of Kate? Margo had a hell of a nerve showing her face at Kate's house after what she'd done, pretending it had never happened; and that, he knew, had been only the most obvious of her escapades.

His stride slowed in discouragement. Kate was not happy. It surely was ironic that she had been such a gloriously *happy* baby, young child, little girl . . . until she began adjusting to life so mechanically. Kate did not become the reckless and hilarious debutante into which Dolly Percy had blossomed. Margo Darktower, silly fool, had panicked when Dolly married Harrison Percy and Kate was still single. Off to Europe they went and there, goddamn it, found Ratoff under a rock in the Alps. For a time, Kate had seemed happy again but then she had declined into the first of her bouts of depression. The family feared suicide and never left her alone. And then came Ratoff's disgrace and quick, another husband. This time Erik Moss, Mossberg, whatever his goddamn name was. They should have mated her to a psychiatrist instead. . . .

Erik Moss was not the man for her. There was something about Erik that frightened Darktower . . . his ominous quiet, deadly reserve, the reticence, the icy grip he kept on his nerves.

"Mister. . . ."

Too late, he remembered what they said in New York. Take a cab, don't walk alone. Darktower turned toward the voice and found himself staring at a gun held firmly in the hand of a man whose face, when he reached it with his eyes, was both mocking and determined.

"Yes?"

"Hand me whatever you've got in your pocket. A couple of twenties will do, fifty, a hundred. Give me everything you've got."

"I—I don't carry much cash," Darktower stuttered, surprised he was not more frightened.

"Dressed like you are, in a homburg and nice wool coat, you've got to have a fifty on you, maybe more."

Darktower edged toward the man, undoing his topcoat. "I'm about to put my hand in my pocket," he warned. "Don't get nervous."

"I'm not nervous," the man sneered. "Get the cash up."

Darktower stared into his eyes. "You're white," he observed.

"So? You think niggers got a monopoly on sticking people up?"

Darktower felt in his pocket for his bankroll, trying to extricate the money from its gold clip. He didn't want to give up the gold.

"Monopoly? I can understand a word like that. I used to work on Wall Street. I never thought of stick-ups in terms of monopolistic practice."

"Look—don't talk shit. Just give me the money. I'm in a hurry."

"I suppose you're out of work," Darktower said sarcastically, "a victim of the recession."

"Right," the man snarled. "Trickle-down hasn't wet my lips yet. I used to be a computer engineer but things being what they are, I had to change professions in order to support myself and my expensive habits."

"If you need a job . . ." Darktower stopped. He wasn't in any position to offer this man a job. "Here." He pulled his hand out of his trousers pocket, the money folded in it. "This is about a hundred, I think. Do you want my watch?"

"I've already got a watch," the man said.

"We could trade."

"Are you crazy, for Christ's sake? You're too cool."

"Yes, I am, aren't I?" Darktower murmured. "Here, let me give you my card. If you feel like it, give me a call."

"Shit," the man said disgustedly, "I'm not interested in that, just the money." He grabbed the bills out of Darktower's hand and stuffed them in the left pocket of his raincoat.

"Just a second," Darktower said angrily. He moved his hand toward his suitcoat pocket.

"Watch it!"

"I'm about to present you with my card."

"Jesus! I ought to present you with the butt of this gun. Look, just take off! Start walkin'. Don't do anything funny."

Darktower found the leather case in which he kept his calling cards. "Here. My card. Phone number."

The man snatched it out of his hand impatiently. "Okay, okay! Why should I call you anyway?"

Darktower shrugged. "One is always looking for men of ability and daring."

The man snorted scornfully. "Take off, weirdo!"

Darktower marched away briskly. He didn't turn around until he'd gone a block, and by then, the man was gone. Darktower chuckled merrily. He'd pulled it off, like he'd always boasted he would. Only one of the twenties he'd handed over was real. The rest of the money was counterfeit cash he'd bought a long time ago from a slimy character who'd worked very briefly for him, before heading off to Dannemora State Prison.

He made the rest of the trip to Lee Penton's with accelerated speed and high spirits. He couldn't wait to tell Lee how he'd handled himself. A story like this was enough to shake Death himself out of black.

"Dick! Man, you're a sight for sore eyes," Penton cried.

"Lee! Let me tell you what just happened to me."

Penton poured him a mammoth Scotch as Darktower related how he'd been held up just down the street but then conned the stick-up man. Penton roared when he heard Dick had had the balls to give the guy his card. "The only trouble is, Dick, what if he comes to see you when he realizes you've stiffed him?"

Darktower frowned. In his euphoria, he'd forgotten about that. "Maybe I'm not as smart as I thought," he admitted. "But no—he was a gentleman. Once he realizes what happened, he'll have a good laugh."

"Unless he's in the mood for a vacation by the sea." Penton guffawed bronchially. A heavyset man, sorrow had not caused Penton to lose any weight or the high-blood-pressure floridness of face that had inspired people to call him Beefy, for Beefeater gin, back in the good old days. "Dick," he repeated, "it's wonderful to see you. I've been a lonely fellow since December."

"I know you have, Lee, and I'm sorry, I really am. It was a great loss. You and Pauline were married a long time—and you were so in love with her." It twisted his gut talking like this, but there were the soppy things one was expected to say.

"Almost fifty years, Dick." Penton's lower lip quivered pendulously.

"If Margo and I had stuck it out, we'd be around forty-eight years together. Long time, Lee," Darktower reflected.

Penton nodded solemnly. "Is Margo still married to Herman? I always thought he was a boring man. Can't understand yet how that happened, Dick. Oh, well, that's life, isn't it? Let's talk of happy things. What's new?"

"I don't have much to report," he said. "I saw Mrs. Himmelmann this afternoon, by the way. Naturally, she had to show up when I stopped in to say hello to my granddaughter."

"Little Margaret," Penton remembered. "How's Katharine?"

Darktower shook his head glumly. "I'm worried about her. I can't figure out what's going on there with her and that husband of hers. He's a funny son-of-a-bitch, Lee."

Penton nodded sympathetically. "Not funny like the other one, I hope."

"Oh, no, Jesus! Please! He's not funny that way—as far as I know." He paused. "Although nothing surprises me anymore. I can't help thinking he's done something to hurt her."

"Something? Of what nature?"

"I don't know—that's the trouble. I just don't know."

Penton frowned furiously. "He's another of those Goddamn Europeans, Dick. Even though they've been our allies in time of war. I've never really trusted those fellows. Except for the Germans—you can do good business with the Germans."

"Moss *is* a goddamn German," Darktower barked. "But maybe not the sort of German you're thinking of. He claims he's a Prussian. His mother was English, he says."

"Well, there you go—the English side is probably the funny side. Look at their foreign service—they're all goddamn Russian spies."

Darktower took another appreciative swallow of mellow Scotch. "Trouble now is the fag one's coming back to this country. I know he's going to make trouble."

"Dick," Penton said solemnly, "I've come to the conclusion in these last couple of months that nobody is going to make trouble for *me*—not ever again. It's not worth it. I refuse to be bothered by any goddamn thing at all. So let's just enjoy ourselves." Penton's beady eyes danced in his fat cheeks. "Harvey is going to serve us some roast beef for dinner, Dick, and we'll have some Bordeaux, then brandy afterward. How's that sound?"

"Great, Lee. Just what the doctor ordered."

The two old friends chatted another twenty minutes until Harvey, a black gentleman who'd been with the Pentons forever, rolled a dining table into the room. When they were seated across from each other, Harvey sliced the roast beef off a well-braised joint. "Now, I serve the wine, Mr. Penton? And leave the bottle right here?"

"Right you are, Harve," Penton said jovially, "and put the brandy and the glasses over there by the fire. And then, it's good night, and thank you, Harvey. I want you to go straight to bed."

"Yes, sir, Mr. Penton, and sleep is what I'm needin'," Harvey muttered. "Good night, you gent'emens."

They'd finished the beef and the bottle of Bordeaux when the doorbell pealed. Penton jumped up so quickly he almost tipped the table with his stomach. "Don't want old Harvey getting that," he muttered.

Darktower leaned back comfortably, thinking to himself that while all might not be right with the world, that part of it, which was within his power to control, he had by the short hairs.

Lee Penton returned, red-faced and smiling cagily, and Darktower saw why. Penton ushered two women into the room and quickly closed the door. Darktower scrambled to his feet. He had not expected their evening to be interrupted, particularly by two such personages as now faced him. Both women were very chubby, one of them even amazingly fat. Both, he noted, were wearing dresses of a shocking pink shade, both were highly powdered and rouged and both had yellow hair at the high-frequency end of bleaching.

"Richard," Penton said proudly, "I'd like you to meet two of my cousins just up to town from their home in New Jersey. On my right, we have Miss Bum and to my left, Miss Tits."

Darktower experienced a slackening of his jaw, that is to say his mouth fell open. He was at a loss, but as calmly as he could, he murmured, "How do you do, Miss. . . ."

"Teats," said the one, with dignity, "not tits."

"And *ass*," said the other, "not bum."

"I beg your pardon," Penton said. He bowed, his eyes glittering.

"Lee. . . ."

"My friend, no buts about it. . . ."

"Not *butts*," said the woman named Miss Ass, "*ass*!"

"And Teats," the other said again, "so's you'll have it straight."

"Well," Darktower muttered.

Miss Ass glanced at the wine bottle, which she saw was empty, then spotted the brandy. "I would much appreciate a *soupcon* of that," she said. "In French, as you may know, that means a little."

"But, of course!" Penton exclaimed. He hurled himself toward the brandy bottle, pulled out the cork, and poured what Darktower thought had to be triple shots. "Ladies, please do drink with us. More glasses, quickly, Dick!"

They drank gravely to each other and then the lady known as Miss Teats said, "Now, pray, where are we to perform?"

"I thought . . . right here," Penton said hesitantly.

Miss Teats looked around, not distastefully, but as though she were measuring square footage. "I expect this will do all right, so long as we move the table out of the way. Come, Gloria."

"Yes, Clara."

"Sit down, Dick," Penton cried enthusiastically, "for you've got a treat coming."

"Lee, I don't understand," Darktower said, his back to the two women. "Isn't this . . .?"

"Dick," Penton whispered urgently, "no point being a widower unless you enjoy yourself a little."

When he sat down in the dining chair again, Darktower realized to his amazement that the two women were undressing.

"Dick, these little sisters are one of the great acts of modern times."

"I'm sure," Darktower said stiffly.

"We have played to bigger audiences than this," Clara declared snootily.

"But none more appreciative," Penton raved.

"We shall see," said Clara.

Darktower told himself that he could not believe this of his friend. He had come merely to comfort Lee Penton, not to engage in depravity with him. Before his eyes, the two ladies disrobed down to very large-sized G-strings, allowing two pair of substantial breasts to roll loose and free round about their chests and down to the shelf where began their bellies. Actually, it had to be said that Miss Ass was by far the bigger of the two. Miss Teats, called Clara, was a large woman, heavy limbed but not so strikingly overweight as her companion. In fact, Darktower decided, she was rather attractive.

Now they were ready, Clara was in a better mood. Both were pros, he realized, and they would give of their best. They joined arms, like proper chorus girls, and hopped around on Penton's oriental carpet, kicking quite surprisingly high, fringes of G-strings swinging wildly, concealing and then revealing two of what Darktower considered must be most extensive snatches in all Christendom. Different hued than the blonde hair on their heads, these recesses were thickly matted with black hair and whatever was true of Clara was doubly true for Gloria. Gloria's thighs rubbed together as she danced and kicked, and the noise transmitted like the mating sounds of giant flies. The first song, performed in falsetto, was an embarrassingly lascivious rendition of *The Good Ship Lollypop*, accompanied by much lip-smacking, and show of tongue, along with exaggerated bumps and grinds.

Darktower had been to the now long-gone Minsky burlesque theatre on Forty-second Street enough times to recognize good stripping. The fact of the matter was that Teats & Ass had started out almost as naked as jaybirds and, thus, there was little left for them to take off. Suddenly, he understood their act was more farce than it was fanciful.

Darktower was still somewhat shocked—wasn't Penton supposed to be in mourning? Seemingly not. Penton watched avidly, his eyes jumping, cheeks puffing and his stomach rolling with glee. He pulled manfully on his brandy.

"By George," he cried, "Dick, look at that, would

you? What do you think? By God, Dick, I do like 'em chubby. Don't you?''

"Oh, yes, Lee."

Naturally, he did not want to insult the ladies but, in truth, he was stricken now by the fearful question of what was going to happen when they'd finished the song-and-dance routine. He found out soon enough. Gloria and Clara breathlessly concluded *Roll Me Over in the Clover*, and grinned wildly at Penton's applause.

"Now then," said Gloria, "we come to the finale."

With that, and in unison, Gloria and Clara fiddled with their G-strings and ripped them away. What had been partially public was now open for the staring. Gloria and Clara whirled around, put their hands on their knees and waggled their bottoms at Lee Penton and Richard Darktower.

"My God, Dick, will you look at that!"

Wantonly, Gloria and Clara glared at them for a moment, then, seemingly having chosen, attacked.

Miss Gloria dropped to her fat knees before Penton and made a sucking noise with her cupid lips. "Let's see what you got, fatty!"

Penton chuffed with delight when Gloria grabbed at his belt, unfastened it, and, without shame, hauled out Penton's pecker. It was as limp, Darktower realized with embarrassment, as his own.

Clara was not quite as brazen as her colleague. "Now, sir," she murmured, somehow shyly, "may I have the distinct pleasure?"

She was so polite, he marveled. What could he do? He was powerless. Gently, she undid his pin-striped suit and laid aside his white shirt tails. And, of a sudden, thrilled, Darktower exulted to himself: what the hell! "I am in your capable hands," he complied, abandoning himself to her.

"A handsome, youthful roger have we here," she whispered studiously.

Darktower felt himself stiffening. He glanced at his friend Penton. Penton by now was fully engrossed, his head against the back of his chair, a ravishing smile on his fat face. Gloria, lost in his rumpled clothing, produced unearthly noises.

The yellow hair on the nape of Clara's neck was curly and moist from her exertion. He felt her lips and the ragged edges of teeth and, by George, if she didn't pull him to a nifty erection, perhaps the first in a week or more. It was not that Richard Darktower didn't think about sex anymore; he just didn't think about it very often. Her lips were soft and undemanding, casually playful. Stretching a little, he felt for her mammaries. They were big, should have weighed a ton, yet they were as light as whipped cream. He touched the nipples with his fingers. She grunted at his pressure; her body swayed between his legs, her lips tightened and her tongue fluttered. She rolled her head to the side and grinned mischievously.

When Darktower did ejaculate, the sensation was jolting—sharp, clear and clean, a distinct relief, not what he had expected in the sordidness of the circumstances. Clara complacently accepted his discharge in her mouth and, staring at him so he could see exactly what she was doing, swallowed it calmly.

She let herself back on her haunches. "Now then, that was very respectable, sir. And to your satisfaction, I trust. Would you pass me my brandy?"

He did, watching her curiously. He was *very* impressed with her, not least because at the moment he felt that what she had done was very *right*, *very* therapeutic. In no way did she make him feel soiled.

"Well," he mumbled, "you are a true professional, aren't you?"

"I like to think so."

It was about then that they both realized all was not right with Leland Penton.

Gloria emitted a shrill cry. "He's turned cold. . . ."

Penton's eyes were closed, the grin across his face still beatific but his head had fallen to the side, awkwardly against the shoulder of his gray flannel jacket.

"My God!"

Darktower scrambled to his feet, holding up his pants with one hand. Gloria slumped backwards, fright all over her face. Gingerly, Darktower moved his friend's head to an upright angle. But when he removed his hand, it tipped again. He put his face next to Penton's nose but there was no murmur of breathing. Likewise, Penton's wrist was inert and, Jesus, when Darktower laid his head next to Penton's chest and listened, there was not a sound of heartbeat.

Lee was dead and if there could be any doubt of it, the latter was dispelled by a heavy, revolting odor, a stench which began to fill the room. Darktower realized what had happened. *In extremis,* his poor friend had voided himself.

Gloria had commenced to whimper, like an animal in the presence of the mysterious. "I could have told him he was too fat for so much excitement." She stared at Penton's slack body.

"Too fat? It's never bothered you, has it?" Darktower said unkindly. "Can you zip him up?"

"Must I touch him?" Gloria wilted.

At that, Darktower's companion somehow brushed Gloria aside. "Here, I'll see to that," she said briskly. "Move away, Gloria."

Darktower had buttoned up his pants. "Now, get dressed, quickly. I'll have to wake up his butler in a minute, call a doctor. You've both got to be out of here."

"Heavens, yes," Gloria moaned. She had turned out, despite her impressive bulk, to be the less brave of the two. "Hurry, Clara, hurry!"

Clara frowned judiciously. "Of course . . . *Quelle scandale.* That wouldn't do, would it, *Mr. Darktower?*"

"You know my name?" He felt his heart muscles constrict: *Blackmail!*

"Of course I do," she said sternly, tucking herself into a large brassiere, then squirming into tight pink panties. As she zipped Gloria's dress, and turned for the same favor, Clara murmured coldly, "Don't worry, Mr. Darktower, we won't make trouble."

"I'm sorry," he apologized. "I didn't mean to give the impression that I thought you would."

Very formally Clara opened her pocketbook and pulled

out a calling card. "This is for you, sir, if I am needed in any connection with this sad event."

Darktower thanked her automatically.

"What are we supposed to say," Gloria demanded. "In case there is trouble? They saw us downstairs."

"Yes," he muttered, "of course they would have. That's a bother. Well, any excuse is better than none. If anybody asks, say you're bond salesmen, and we were up here discussing a new issue. I'll just say poor Lee kicked off not moments after you left. That'll cover it, I should think."

It was flimsy, admittedly, but if it came to that, the authorities would just have to take his word for it. Darktower didn't think they would seriously doubt him. If necessary, he thought wearily, he could always have a word with the mayor.

"Our furs are outside," said Clara.

Cautiously, Darktower opened the door into the foyer and was relieved to see no sign of Harvey. He helped Teats & Ass into voluminous minks. "Good night, ladies. Perhaps we'll be in touch," he whispered to Clara.

She shrugged, obviously still put out he might think her a potential blackmailer. "As you wish."

When they were safely in the elevator and on their way, Darktower went back to the living room. Penton's deathly scent was, by now, almost overpowering. He did not approach the body, still wedged into its chair. The only corrective needed was to get rid of the two lipstick-smeared brandy glasses. He carried them to the butler's pantry, washed and returned them to their proper shelf. Now, he thought, he would give it fifteen minutes, then wake Harvey and begin going through the motions of seeing off his friend Lee Penton. Darktower added brandy to his snifter and sat down gingerly opposite Penton. So humiliating . . . better to fall out of an airplane than go like this, stinking, in front of strangers. Poor Lee. But, on the other hand, it wasn't such a bad way to go. He assumed there hadn't been any pain, more like a pleasurable last few moments. Trying to ignore the smell, he knocked back brandy. Strange how the smile remained fixed on Penton's face. When

62

family viewed him, they would be made to feel sentimental. Such a joyful man he'd always been, Lee Penton, father, uncle, cousin, such a generous and happy man.

As he waited, Darktower was aware he should focus on the memory and good works of his old friend. But he found himself thinking of something else.

By her card, he saw her full name was Clara Riding and that she advertised herself as a clairvoyant. He smiled to himself as his own vision came—of Clara Riding gamboling through his Wainscott meadows in an advanced state of undress.

And dare they say Dick Darktower was finished, a man of the past, yesterday's news? Ha! Not yet, old friend, old dead, Lee.

Six

In the morning, Helen Ryan brought Katharine tea and dry toast at nine. She had a hairdresser's appointment at eleven but today she knew without question she was not going to get herself together at all.

"Where's Mr. Moss?"

"Gone out," Helen said.

"He's early. Did he say where he was going, Helen?" she asked lazily.

"No, Mrs. Moss."

Katharine turned away from the breakfast tray. "I've got the most terrible headache. I think I'll skip everything, Helen."

"You're supposed to meet Mrs. Percy," Helen said. "She's expecting you."

"How do you know that?" Katharine said sharply.

Patiently, Helen said, "She called yesterday afternoon . . . when you were resting. She told me to make sure you made it."

"I *can't* make it, Helen. I don't want to make it. I don't want to see Mrs. Percy."

Helen watched her impassively. "Drink the tea. You'll feel better."

"You think I'm a spoiled fool."

"No, I don't," Helen murmured. Her expression gave nothing away. Her eyes were blank. But it was obvious what she thought.

"Sit down a minute, Helen." Katharine patted the edge of the bed. "Don't think badly of me, please."

Primly, Helen lowered herself, clasping her smooth-skinned hands in her lap. Although her knuckles appeared slightly reddened, it could not have been from doing dishes, since Helen was the favorite of the Moss household. There was a cook for the kitchen and a housemaid who spent five hours in the apartment every day. Helen's post was more exalted—she took care of little Margaret and, Katharine thought morosely, of big Kate.

"You don't need to go to the hairdresser," Helen said. "I can fix your hair. But you've really got to have lunch with Mrs. Percy."

"Have to? I don't *have* to do anything."

Helen flushed. "I'm saying for your own good, you should meet her."

"You talk like my mother," Katharine said. "And you're not. Why, you're not even twenty-five."

"I'm going on twenty-six," Helen declared.

"You were seventeen when you came here. Margaret's eight years old now . . . okay, so you're twenty-five. I'm thirty-eight and I hate going out. I have nothing to say to anybody."

"Not true," Helen said stolidly.

"Helen . . ." Katharine reached for Helen's left hand and held it, in her own, on the comforter.

"Dolly Percy is an old friend of yours," Helen said, undeterred, "and you'll have a lot to say to her."

"No—the older the friends, the less there is to say to each other. You can't keep covering the same old territory all the time." Katharine stuck her lips out in a pout. "And now I've got so many things to worry about. Steve Ratoff, my first husband, is coming to New York. Besides that, I have a hangover."

Helen ignored that. "Are you going to see him?"

"Steve? I don't know. I *am* curious. My father would be livid if I did."

Helen's lips tightened. "Not for him to object—not after what he's been up to. . . ."

Katharine chuckled delightedly. "Isn't he shocking? Will he *ever* live it down?"

It was nothing as serious as full-fledged disgrace, what

had happened up on Madison the night of Leland Penton's sudden demise. Had it not been for an overtalkative doorman greedy for a fifty-dollar news tip, there wouldn't have been any sort of scandal. As it was, the *New York Post* had carried only an initial, mild, exploratory sort of story. Then Penton's retainer, Harvey, made the grand mistake of showing other downstairs staff the two G-strings he'd found behind the sofa in the living room. How was Harvey supposed to know what these things were? His life had been so sheltered at the Pentons'. The next day, the *Post* had a more lurid follow-up, going on about G-strings in the dead financier's flat and mentioning that the well-known retired investment banker and Penton-intimate Richard Darktower had been another visitor on that fateful night. Darktower had run for the hills, that is to say, the depths of Long Island.

"I've always said," Helen remarked dryly, "that men by themselves get up to no good."

"How would you know, Helen?"

Stubbornly, Helen insisted, "I know, that's all."

"You practically grew up in a convent, Helen."

Again Helen colored. "I know enough about men from what my mother told me. Just children, men are, always out for the women . . . women . . . women."

"That's what makes the world go around, Helen."

"Leave me off it then," Helen said stoutly. She stared at the hand in her lap and at the other linked to Katharine's. "I think too much of myself for that activity, Mrs. Moss."

"Helen, you've never had a lover?"

Helen sputtered. "What a question, Mrs. Moss!"

Katharine laughed lightly and stroked the backs of Helen's fingers. "I've never had a lover I've really enjoyed. I don't know why."

"You've had lovers?" Helen echoed disbelievingly. "Even though you're a married woman?"

"Of course," Katharine said complacently. But of course, it was not true. Oh, she'd looked around, thought about it during her marriage to Stefan Ratoff. But nothing had ever happened. She wasn't like her mother, not in that way, at least.

Helen's voice was tearful. "None of them are good enough for you, Mrs. Moss." Her hand gripped Katharine's urgently. "You're too good for any of them."

"Oh, no!" Katharine tossed her head vigorously. The discussion was waking her up. "They've been good enough for me. It's just . . . me." Her eyes teared with self-pity, for, unwittingly, she was getting to the heart of it. "I'm cold and frightened, Helen."

"Don't cry, Mrs. Moss. None of it's the end of the world."

"I know it's not the end of the world. It's just . . . I feel such a failure. I wish I was still a virgin—like you."

"Oh," Helen cried out. "And I wish I wasn't."

Helen's fingers squeezed so tightly, Katharine's hand began to ache. "Helen . . . please." She pulled, and, embarrassed, Helen let go. "It's nothing for you to worry about, Helen. I'll be all right."

"But you are going to lunch," Helen urged.

"What does it matter whether I go or not? Dolly Percy will have just as good a time without me, probably better."

"No, no," Helen exclaimed warmly, her cheeks glowing. "I want you to show yourself. Walk in proudly! You're so beautiful, all blonde and pretty with your fine features and lovely long legs."

"Helen! You're just trying to make me feel good."

Impulsively, Katharine pushed herself up and kissed Helen's cheek. Helen started but she smiled with such quick appreciation that it made Katharine put her lips quickly to Helen's mouth.

They hardly brushed lips, but Helen turned such a color red that Katharine chuckled.

"Mrs. Moss. . . ."

"Helen! You devilish girl, what are you trying to do to me?"

"Oh, Mrs. Moss," Helen repeated. "Please. You're just making fun of me, aren't you?"

"*You're* embarrassing me," Katharine teased, "talking about my long legs like that, lovely long legs. Sometimes I'm not so sure about you, Helen."

"What are you saying, Mrs. Moss?" Her eyes glistened.

"Oh, nothing, Helen, for heaven's sakes. I'm just joking. Ah," she sighed, "virginal Helen."

"And it's true that I am," Helen said primly. "Not that . . . if I wanted. . . ."

"I'm sure, dear," Katharine murmured. "But that would be a sin, wouldn't it?" Helen's face was set self-consciously straight. "Tell me, Helen, didn't you ever, just once, give my little brother a kiss?"

Helen stiffened, as if she'd been shocked. "No, Mrs. Moss, I never did."

"And never wanted to, little lass?"

Helen did not answer at once. "I wouldn't tell a lie," she finally said. "Conrad is a very handsome young man and I'm ready to admit it."

"One kiss?" She hesitated. "Tell me—didn't Conrad ever try to kiss you?"

"No," Helen said, "never."

"He's your age, Helen," Katharine pointed out. "A year or two younger, that's all."

Helen laughed, trying to sound merry or silly or both. "Too young for me, Mrs. Moss."

"I know. And not the right . . . religion, either, Helen." Katharine subsided gloomily in the bed. "Too bad for him, I couldn't imagine that anybody would be a better wife than you, Helen."

"Ah, Mrs. Moss. . . ." Helen looked at her hands. "Someday, maybe."

"Someday is right," Katharine said resignedly, "someday you'll be swept off your feet and that'll be the end of you—like me!" She laughed harshly.

"Don't belittle yourself, Mrs. Moss!"

"I'm not," Katharine retorted, just as quickly. "I know full well who I am and what I'm doing. Don't listen to them, Helen—I'm not going crazy. I am not a drunk or a dope addict. You do know that, don't you, my sweet?"

Helen nodded. "Of course I do. I never thought otherwise, Mrs. Moss."

"Good," Katharine said. "I'm better. You make me feel better, Helen." She paused, tasting recrimination. "So

. . . if I'm to meet the beautiful Mrs. Percy, Port London's leading adulteress, I guess I'd better start getting ready."

Helen's eyes jarred again. "You're saying that Mrs. Percy. . . ."

"I'm saying," Katharine said jocularly, "that Mrs. Percy by now has slept with every loose man in Port London, including my husband. . . ."

"The scoundrel!" Helen seemed to blanch. "You can't be serious."

"Helen," Katharine said maliciously, "if it was like in the old days, Mrs. Percy would be wearing a big red "A" sewn on her chest. My dear, she'd even be living in an A-frame house."

Helen gasped her outrage. "Mrs. Moss, it's not right. There is no justice, is there?"

"Well. . . ." Katharine shook her head. Energetically, she sat up, then swung her legs to the side of the bed to sit beside Helen. Again, not planning it, she kissed Helen on the cheek. It gave her a certain pleasure to touch such smooth skin with her lips, to feel life in another creature. "Actually, sweetie, I think there is justice. It just takes a while to arrive, like the quality of mercy. No, Helen, right now I definitely feel there is hope. You believe? Good! Well, come on, time to get dressed. . . ."

Seven

Katharine breezed through the revolving doors at *Le Cirque*,
unstrapped her trench coat and passed it into the checkroom.
Dolly had already taken possession; she was sitting with a
glass of wine at a table in the dead center of the room.
Katharine moved forward, nodding to several people she
knew. "Hello, Mrs. Percy," she whispered, bending to
kiss Dolly lightly on one cool-as-alabaster cheek.

"Darling! You look wonderful! How are you?"

"I am wonderful," Katharine gushed, aware, of course,
that Dolly, as perceptive as she was, couldn't make her
out. She gazed fondly at her oldest friend. "But it's you
who are the picture of health."

Primping extravagantly, Dolly patted the dark brown
ringlets which framed her unblemished pale oval face. Her
eyelashes fluttered, eyes flickered and short straight nose
flared at the nostrils. Dolly was a beautiful woman. People
said she looked—and acted—a lot like Cleopatra but Dolly
was surely taller and couldn't be quite so fully developed.
But developed enough—beneath the loose blouse she was
wearing just off the shoulder, a bit much for lunchtime,
the perfectly smooth neck and throat led to creamy breast,
in the cleavage of which dangled a piece of crimson
costume jewelry shaped like a serpent.

"Well. . . ." Dolly paused to smile at her patronizingly.
"You must have had your Wheaties this morning, darling."

"I feel marvelous . . . for a change."

"You haven't even mentioned a headache yet . . . *that*
makes for a change."

"I don't have a headache, smarty. I want a drink, though."

Dolly had scarcely to shift her head to bring a waiter scurrying. "My friend would like a drink."

"Vodka martini, straight up, with a twist," Katharine said briskly. "Make it a double."

"And another glass of white wine, *garcon*." When the waiter had gone, she added, *"Wine* at lunch, dummy, not vodka."

"Somes likes their wine, somes likes their vodka, honey."

"Yes," Dolly said acidly, "and *somes* gets plastered and falls on their ass."

Katharine shook her head. "Not today. I feel too good to get drunk. Only get drunk when I'm depressed."

"Dear me, we *are* full of piss and vinegar, aren't we?"

"Yes, indeed." Katharine studied Dolly's unlined face, the humorous, mocking eyes. Here was the woman she was sure had slept with Erik Moss. "What brings you to the big city?"

"Nothing much," Dolly shrugged. "It's been a long winter. I need a little city action."

"Of course you do," Katharine assured her. "Where are you staying? At Frank's place?"

"Yes, like always."

Frank Berliner was an interior designer of their acquaintance who kept open house for all his friends, domestic and international, in a luxurious apartment in the mid-sixties on Fifth Avenue. Reputations of out-of-town ladies who put up at Frank's remained untarnished. He was a wonderful escort, lively and attentive, a perfect "beard."

"Frank hasn't been well," Dolly said flippantly. "I think he caught a dose of herpes. It's running rampant among the *chic* set." She smiled coyly. "Maybe that's why I'm better off living in Port London. At least I haven't caught herpes yet. God knows if anybody's due to catch it, it's me. I'm so *terribly* disreputable, everyone is talking about me. Why, just the other day I laid a deckhand off a Russian whaling ship right on the front steps of Old Church."

Katharine flattered her with an exaggerated gasp. "Dolly!"

"Ain't I terrible, though?" Dolly sighed, then stared at her accusingly. "You look so good, if I didn't know better, I'd say you'd taken a lover."

She threw the word out suggestively, in a way that made Katharine sure Dolly was trying to get around to the subject of Erik.

"Heavens, Dolly, you're in a mood today! You know there's nobody for me but my own dear husband."

"Yes, I know," Dolly said tersely. "Speaking of whom, I suppose he's told you all about our project."

"Yes," she said, "the Smithers House. He's really thrilled. It gives him something to do. He gave up his job, you know."

"He told me," Dolly said, eyeing her carefully. "He said you needed more of his time. Is that so?"

"Yes, I suppose. I'm jealous of every minute he doesn't spend with me," Katharine murmured.

Yes, of course. Erik had resigned from the Darktower firm because she'd demanded it of him, because she insisted she couldn't bear being alone all day. Actually, the resignation had been his idea, this then transmitted to her, just as he continually suggested, so indirectly no one could ever say otherwise, that the tranquilizers, sleeping pills, a few aspirin now and then would not hurt a healthy woman. She felt like telling Dolly that it would be far better if Erik took two jobs and stayed away from her all the time. But she couldn't say that—she was not going to deliver him to Dolly on a platter. Dolly was going to have to work for it.

"Well," Dolly said warmly, "Captain Smithers will give him plenty to do. You'll have to come to Port London more often, once we've started the restoration."

"That'll be nice, honey."

"You know, darling," Dolly said archly, "Erik has a quite marvelous feeling for antiques and old things."

"I *do* know," Katharine smiled coolly. "He told me he can actually sense the presence of Captain Smithers in the house."

Dolly tittered and held up her glass. "I think he carries that ESP business a little too far . . . Here's to you, good-looking."

Katharine responded. "And to you, beautiful. How *do* you do it?"

Dolly chuckled self-satisfaction. "I'm still taking air baths, Kitty."

"Still?"

"Yes, definitely. I go outside in my robe early in the morning and I whip it off and run around the lawn stark naked . . . even when there's snow on the ground. It's so *co-old,* so delicious. Darling, it's sensational for the circulation."

"You *are* crazy, honey." Katharine laughed lightly at her, preparing, as she was, the news shock of the luncheon. Softly, she said, "Steve is coming to New York!"

"Oh?" Dolly might have said: so what? "I never liked Steve. I always thought he was a big fake. What are you going to do about him?"

"Why should I do anything? We're not married anymore."

"But he'll want to see you. You'll have things to talk about—like money, for instance. And—dare I mention it? Conrad? How is Conny?"

Icily, Katharine shrugged. "Fine. He's living down in the Village."

"And you've never even been to see him, have you?"

"Why should I? He's probably living with some . . . body. I don't want to embarrass him." Dolly's eyes were stern. "Really, Dolly! He hasn't invited me, after all." She squirmed, knowing what Dolly thought, that she was too sensitive. "I'll see Stefan if he wants to see me. We don't have any grudges. . . ." She smiled boldly. "He's coming with a good friend of his named Marco Fortuna. A very rich Sicilian."

Dolly's eyes twinkled. "Maybe I'd better not write Stefan off so fast. Does this Marco *person* own a castle near Lake Como, or is it *Lake Homo?*"

"Just because he's traveling with Steve. . . ."

"I know. It doesn't necessarily mean he's a fag," Dolly said with her usual directness. "So what, anyway? Was it so bad? I'm told it can be very convenient—a gay life, if you'll excuse the expression, and certainly more fun than being married to a man like my late husband."

Katharine nodded uncertainly, telling herself with some remorse that she was not, at the moment, in a position to pass sweeping judgments either way.

"Promise me," Dolly said, "that when Marco Fortuna shows up, you'll do your best to get him to Port London. Is he rich, really?"

"I hope so."

"Yes—for Steve's sake," Dolly said spitefully. "Okay—what are we going to eat?" She chuckled insipidly. "Don't say that hulk of a man sitting over there by himself."

"Dolly. . . ."

"I know . . . incorrigible."

Katharine followed Dolly's stare. The man was big, going bald, hawk-nosed, his skin sallow. He felt their attention and turned, smiling distantly, eyes coldly magnified behind heavy glasses.

Dolly leaned forward and put her fingers next to her mouth, a sure way of letting the man know they were talking about him. "I'm not positive," she whispered, "but I think he's Gene Francotti. He invents motors. I've seen him at Port London. You probably have too."

"I thought the motor had already been invented," Katharine murmured.

"Don't be an ass, Kitty. He does motors for ships. I think he's got a boat of his own up in Port London Harbor."

The man possibly named Gene Francotti was soon enough left on his own again. Dolly and Katharine ordered fish and green salad and proceeded to talk of other, unimportant things. Dolly had to be on her way by three; she had a date at the Metropolitan Museum with a curator in the American wing, getting ideas for the Smithers project, she explained.

"Is Erik meeting you there?"

Dolly eyed her sardonically. "Not that I know of. You think I've arranged a tryst with your hubby inside a Franklin stove?"

"Very funny. . . . He didn't say what he was up to today."

"Well, if we do meet, I can tell you, it'll be completely

accidental." Dolly grinned. "Although, I must say, I wouldn't mind. But—no, no, not with the husband of my best friend."

Sure. Katharine thought, *and so much for best friends.* She didn't believe Dolly for a second; she knew her too well. Dolly was an expert at dissembling, an astute and shameless liar. In character, Dolly changed the subject.

"He's staring at us," she muttered.

"Who is?"

"That man. God, Kitty, he's so ugly." She giggled. "If he is who I think he is, his nickname is Gizmo. Gene 'Gizmo' Francotti. That's because he's always playing with his little gizmos."

"God, you *are* awful. Don't you ever think of anything else?"

Waspishly, Dolly hissed, "About as much, I suspect, as you do, Miss Ivory Soap, ninety-nine and nine-tenths pure. You take after your father, that's what I think. Imagine! Arranging a little fun for poor Leland Penton and having it end like that."

"Really! Daddy said he had no idea—it was all Penton's doing."

"A likely story."

Katharine chuckled joyously. "My poor mother is in total shock."

"Your mother is?" Dolly repeated amusedly. "That's rich. The way *she* used to behave, probably still does."

"Why do you say that?"

"Don't be naive," Dolly murmured. "Everybody knows Margo got around a bit. She even raked my poor deceased husband across the coals before his surprise goodbye."

Coldly, Katharine said, "I was never given to understand that my mother fooled around."

"Okay, then," Dolly said evasively, "forget it." She looked at her watch. "I've got to go. Do forgive me for running," she said sarcastically. "By the way," she added, half out of her chair, "come by tomorrow night for drinks. Frank is having people in for me."

Katharine nodded. "Maybe."

Dolly made for the checkroom next to the revolving

front door, collected a long sable and slipped it across her impeccable shoulders. She lifted her hand and waved once; when Katharine smiled back, Dolly blew her a kiss over her fingertips. Katharine watched her exit, stage center, then waited for the air to clear.

The doorman was asking her if she needed a cab when she heard the deep, rumbly voice over her shoulder. Katharine turned and realized she was being accosted by the man whom Dolly believed to be Gene Francotti.

Dolly had been close to the truth when she'd said he was ugly. His face was not pretty, that was for sure. But his eyes lit the pallidness and, with the heavy smile lines that broke its length and spareness, it was a startling and perhaps even unforgettable face.

"Don't tell me," he said, chuckling deeply. "You're Katharine Moss. I thought I recognized you."

"How do you know me?"

He laughed and the laugh was good too. "I asked the woman in the checkroom."

"You're Mr. Francotti."

"Yes. I could see your friend telling you that. What's *her* name?"

"Dolly Percy," she said numbly.

"Where are you going?"

"Nowhere . . . I don't know. Just for a walk."

"I see." He stared straight into her eyes, making her feel weak in the knees. "I was watching you. You're beautiful. But bored. Don't deny it."

He tapped the toe of his shoe on the curb. The gesture was enough to draw a cab.

"Mr. Francotti. . . ." Her breath was coming erratically. She felt herself flushing.

"I'm getting in the cab," he said curtly. "Yes or no?"

She hesitated. "Why . . .?"

"Because I want to take you home and make love to you, that's why," he said softly. "I figured that out inside."

The words pierced her like darts, hitting every tender spot in her body. How could a man talk this way?

"Well?"

Slowly, she nodded. "All right."

Very easily, calmly, he helped her into the cab and told the driver his address. Katharine cowered beside him, feeling the bulk of him, the nervous energy, the animalness. "I'm afraid of you."

"Don't be." He smiled confidently at her. "I'm a very gentle Quasimodo."

"Why do you say that?"

He shrugged. "I'm *up-front*. I'm not exactly movie-star handsome, as you see. And don't try to tell me I am, otherwise I'll toss you out of the cab."

She slid away from him, very flustered. How *did* one agree that he was certainly not very good-looking? His skin was coarse, the nose imperious, chin jutting, the lips thick and almost cruelly set as he looked at her.

"What I said was that I'm very gentle," he repeated, chuckling throatily at her discomfort.

"Wonderful," she murmured.

In ten minutes, they reached his corner near Sutton Place. Francotti paid off the cab and led her to a side entrance. "I have my own elevator," he told her casually. "I'm a very private person. That way, when you come to see me, nobody need ever know."

Again, shock reverberated in her. He assumed she would visit him here again! Nonetheless, she followed him meekly into the elevator which shut with a hiss and thud and ascended to a large wood-paneled room, much too cluttered with chrome-and-leather furniture, books, pictures, and magazines scattered across all the tables. A large, tilted drawing board occupied one whole corner by the long window which afforded a full view of the East River.

"This," he said proudly, "is my home and my office. Would you like a drink?"

Katharine shook her head. "I'd like to use the bathroom."

He pointed. "Second door on the right. Let me take your coat."

She undid the belt of the trenchcoat. Plucking it from her shoulders, he said, "Ah, fur-lined. I might have known." But he hung it up respectfully before turning to her again. "Like I said, you are beautiful."

"Yes," she replied steadily, not frightened now, "and I know—you're not." She stared back at him as fearlessly as she could, in the circumstances. "But don't make yourself out worse than you are. You are *not* Quasimodo."

"I don't have a hunchback if that's what you mean. But I look like I got hit by a train. My nose isn't exactly what you'd call Wasp-straight. It's been broken four or five times."

"That's not my fault," she said.

His laugh followed her as she walked boldly down the dimly-lit hall. After all, using a bathroom in a strange house showed a certain recklessness. Katharine turned on the light and looked at herself in the mirror. What in the *hell* was she up to now? She must be crazy; things like this were not done. She put the palms of her hands on her shoulders, where his had been. The intensity of him was still there and she trembled, apprehensively, wishing she had turned him down, gone home, had a drink . . . anything. Did he expect her to undress in this cold, alien apartment? She couldn't go all the way with a man like this, as fascinating as he undoubtedly was, as magnetic as were his vibes, she couldn't take off her clothes and lie down alongside a man like this and open herself to him. No! Nervously, she did what she had to do, feeling her belly roil, hoping the noise would not reach through the walls, then patted her face lightly with powder and applied fresh lipstick to her mouth . . . intent, rigid mouth, lips set, stern face.

When she emerged, Francotti was perched on the high stool behind his board. He hardly looked up. "Just fiddling around," he said, as if she'd asked what he was doing. "Working on another gadget . . . *gizmo*, I mean. They call me 'Gizmo' Francotti."

"I know. Dolly told me." Now was the point at which Katharine should announce she was ready to leave. But he didn't seem receptive to farewell; suddenly, he seemed indifferent to whether she was there or not. Timidly, she walked to the window, telling herself there was no danger after all. She stared down at the river. The day had been gray in the morning and cold, as if preparing for snow. But later, the sun had appeared and, though it was no warmer ouside, the weather seemed more companionable. Below, in the river, choppy little waves danced with light.

Not turning, Katharine said, "Didn't we actually meet once? It seems I've known you. I can't remember . . . my memory is terrible. I think somebody pointed you out."

"Across a crowded room?" he took her up sardonically. "Yes, as a matter of fact, we did meet. In Port London a couple of summers ago. I was doing some work for a man with a big boat and a lousy motor. You were with your husband," he recalled precisely, "down on the dock. We talked and we all had a brunch-time drink together. . . . How could you forget me, for God's sake? I was all oily, in a pair of ripped pants. I know—you assumed I was a lowly deckhand and dismissed me with distaste."

"No, I wouldn't. Or did I? I'm sorry." She was stricken with shame.

"You *didn't* and anyway it doesn't matter. You were drinking a Bloody Mary and ignoring your husband. Why?"

She stared at him, rounding her eyes with puzzlement. "I can't remember why." She smiled at him. "He'd probably done something terrible."

"He was dressed like a fashion plate."

"Erik always dresses like a fashion plate. He loves good clothes."

Francotti winked at her, drooping a heavy eyelid. "Is that the kind of a man you like, dresses well and has nothing to say?"

"Nothing to say? He has enough to say."

"He sure as hell didn't that day. He didn't say a word. He seemed to me like an arrogant son-of-a-bitch."

"*Did* he?"

"Yes. I'm sorry . . . maybe I shouldn't say that. You love him."

She shook her head. "No, I don't . . . but I see what you think of me—that I'm an empty-headed idiot. That's all right, most people do."

Sharply, he retorted, "I didn't say that. But what do

you people actually *do* with yourself? Don't tell me—I know," he teased. "You have lunch every day, visit the hairdresser, go shopping and you serve on committees."

Hotly, she cried, "I seem to remember you were just at *Le Cirque* having lunch, Mr. Francotti."

"Right," he agreed, "I go there a lot. I can afford it, that's number one. I think the food is the best in town and I love to watch the Beautiful People at play. Also, don't forget: I work all morning and after lunch I come back here and work until dark, until I can't see anymore. I think I deserve a good meal, don't you?"

"No need to get hot under the collar about it—you want to have lunch at *Le Cirque*, Mr. Francotti, you just go ahead and have lunch at *Le Cirque*. You sound like a lonely man—are you a lonely man?"

Her attack set him back just enough to please her. "Why do you say that?"

"I didn't say it. I asked if you are. I'm like you—up-front."

He laughed amusedly. "Don't give me that—you've never been up-front in your life."

"Oh, I see. That's what you really think." Katharine whirled around, furiously, her legs trembling. Now was definitely the time to say good-bye; they'd reached an impasse of mutual dislike. She stared sadly at the river, watching the tugboats struggling against the current.

His voice intruded softly. "All right—sometimes I am lonely. At night. I make myself go out, to the theater, movies, opera, ballet . . . sometimes, when I'm feeling wildly anti-social, I just stay here and read, or work some more."

She shrugged and still couldn't summon the courage or will to say the niceties and to leave. Katharine studied the bookcases, aware of his eyes on her back, and was attracted by a rear corner of the room filled by a triangular, wooden table, bolted to which on a heavy steel plate was a gleaming object in intricate metal; it looked like modern art but she knew it had to be the model of a motor.

"What is it?" She put her fingers hesitantly on it.

"That's a scale prototype of the first commercial engine

I ever designed. It's chrome-plated. Beautiful, isn't it?"
He hopped off his stool and came to stand beside her.
"You see, it's a ship's engine." Long, muscled fingers,
scarred, here and there marred by black places where
grime had gotten under the skin, poked at components.
"Cylinders . . . drive shaft . . . propeller . . . cooling
systems. It was a marvel in its own time, fuel-efficient
before we absolutely had to be fuel-efficient. Most important of all, my dear," he said warmly, laying a hand on
her shoulder, touching, caressing, "it was easy to service
and to repair. That's the trouble with most goddamn boats—
you can't get at the engines." He smiled at her, like a
friendly lecturer. "That's why I was so dirty that day in
Port London."

"Will it run?" she asked.

He chuckled at her, tightening his grip on her shoulder.
"Will *you* run, Mrs. Moss?"

"I mean the motor, Mr. Francotti." She had gone all
faint again.

"I mean *you*, Mrs. Moss, and you can call me Gizmo if
you like."

"I think I prefer Gene," she said in a low voice. "I'm
Katharine . . . or Kate." She tried to creep away from him
but his hand held her shoulder. "You're hurting," she
whispered.

"Do you want to run? You can, if you want to. I was
serious about what I said outside the restaurant. But I don't
push. Do you want to go?"

His hand was so heavy, and each finger seemed to
address her, each padded joint to impart electricity. She
knew she *should* run. But she hadn't the force, the breath
in her body, the stamina. She couldn't move. Slowly, a
degree at a time, her body swung around until, at last, she
faced him humbly, her head hanging. "I want to run . . .
but I can't."

"Good." Right fingertip under her chin, he lifted her
head and kissed her lightly on one cheek, then the other.
He was not *that* sort of man, she realized. He was not
going to force her down and rip off her clothes and make
love to her whether she wanted it or not. But somehow, he

inched them away from the model motor and across the room to the leather couch.

"I'll call you Katharine," he said deliberately. "You say you don't love your husband. Why? He doesn't understand you?"

Indecisively, she put her head back, feeling his big arm. "He probably understands me too well."

"Or not at all."

"Could be," she admitted. "Look, you're leading me along . . . are you a psychiatrist? If you are, you shouldn't be sitting next to me. It wouldn't be ethical."

"I'm trying to understand you."

"What about me understanding you?"

"That'll come later."

She laughed. "This is crazy!"

"But you're not scared of me now, are you?"

"No, but I'm curious. Why did you really ask me to come here? I mean . . . why me? I'm not interesting. I have nothing to say, that's what Erik tells me."

"How nice. Does he always try to make you feel good about yourself?"

"Well," she exclaimed impatiently, "he's right, isn't he? What do I have to offer in the way of fascinating chit-chat? I've been married twice, both times failures. *Failures!*" she stressed defiantly. "I have one daughter, a house in Port London, an apartment in New York, and a second husband who doesn't work."

"I thought he was in the family company," Francotti observed.

"Not anymore." She stared up at the ceiling, rubbing her head against his arm. "It seems, according to the story circulating, that I didn't want him to work anymore, that I wanted him close to me all the time, at my beck and call."

"True?"

"*I don't know*. Sometimes . . . the way it happens, Erik begins discussing something with me and then all of a sudden I'm agreeing and an hour later it comes out it was my idea. Isn't that stupid?"

"Very."

"You see," she said blithely, "I'm dumb."

"You are *not* dumb."

"I drink too much," she said, acknowledging it freely, almost with relief. "So maybe I don't know what I am agreeing to half the time."

"I had that figured out too—that you drink too much," Francotti said irritably. "It's not something to be proud of."

"I certainly am not proud of it," she huffed.

"I offered you a drink. Why didn't you take it?"

"I didn't need it," she murmured. "One does not drink with one's psychiatrist."

"Oh? Doesn't *one?*" He mocked her gently. "Let's put it this way, Katharine Darktower Moss . . . I don't care if you have a little vino, but if you drink a vodka in front of me, I'll give you a kick right in the ass. Agreed?"

"Yes, Doctor."

"So, now," he continued comfortably, "tell me why you made this husband of yours quit his job."

"Am I just perverse?"

"Probably. You wanted him completely dependent on you. Very cruel, that."

"Sorry, Doctor," she said breezily. "But not so—he has money of his own."

"Oh, yeah? How much?" Francotti snorted. "Whatever he's got, it's nothing compared to what's in the Darktower vaults." Katharine nodded hesitantly and he continued, "All right. So you've got him dead to rights—now what?"

"A good question. I think, actually, I'd like to see him get another job. By the way," she added weightily, "he's having an affair with my best friend, Dolly. The woman I was having lunch with."

"Mrs. Percy." He laughed wryly. "If they're not having lunch at *Le Cirque*, out of boredom they're in bed with their best friend's husband. Why don't you do the same for her?"

"I would," Katharine said daringly, "but Dolly doesn't have a husband. He killed himself a few years ago."

He whistled, but quite indifferently. "Whew! But again, Katharine, I'm not surprised. She probably drove him ape-shit. You know something? Stick with me and you'll lead a nicer life. I'm simple-minded but simple in my simplicity, if you see what I mean.''

Katharine nodded, trying to be just as casual. "You're kind of sudden, Mr. Francotti. An hour ago, we were having lunch at separate tables and now, here I am in your apartment and there's not even a chaperon and. . . .''

"And what? My, my," he mocked. "You've sure got yourself into a compromising situation, Katharine Margaret. Nobody would believe nothing happened between us.''

She knew he could feel her body trembling. "This isn't what I expected from my psychiatrist—right here, on your couch.''

"Verily," he grunted, "right on my couch. You know, I tend to be very Italian and impulsive. Don't ask me to explain what I see in you, Katharine Margaret. There's really no good reason why I should particularly like you. You're not my kind.''

She lowered her eyes miserably. "I've already confessed there's nothing to me except the money and the real estate.''

"In neither of which I'm the least bit interested, especially the money part.''

"So?" she cried. "Good God, what's this all about, then? Let me go!''

"No. Defying all reason, I like you. Otherwise, I wouldn't have said a word to you. I'm too bright.''

She smarted from his logic, his arrogance—there was no other word for it. He was a chauvinist pig, no doubt of it. But she couldn't say that. "You're so goddamn Italian . . . macho, that's what! I don't have to listen to all this bullshit!''

She struggled to get away from his arm but, laughingly, he drew her closer. "You *do* have to listen. We're going to try each other out, see how we articulate. That's a mechanical term—the various parts of the machine have to articulate smoothly, otherwise it doesn't go *put-put*.''

"Just like that, Jesus!" she exclaimed. "I'm not part of a machine. How can you be so sure of yourself?''

He grinned. "I'm getting an enormous feeling that this

is my red-letter day, like I came around a corner and discovered the wheel.''

"Or a motor.''

"Whatever—I'll be good to myself. Because you're the opposite of me. You're blonde and I'm black-haired.''

"Like hell—you're going bald, Francotti,'' she contradicted him gently.

He paid no attention. "You're beautiful, but icy . . . I'm a warm person.''

"I am *not* icy. I'm emotional. I could be just as hot-blooded as you.''

"You'd have to prove to me that under the frozen crust there's not another two miles of ice.''

"Damn you! Why do I always have to prove myself? I'm sick and tired of people calling me cold and icy and withdrawn. I'm not that way, goddamn it!''

His eyes leapt. "Cool it, Katharine. You sound like an Italian.''

"And I'll be one too.''

She lifted her face and put her mouth against his full lips. Breathlessly, she kissed him, staring as far as she could get behind his glasses into yellow-speckled grayish-green eyes, then closing her own eyes and concentrating on the kiss, mouth open, tongue seeking, daring him. She did not recognize herself in such impetuosity . . . and *he* was not nearly as impulsive and bold as he made out. Francotti returned the kiss gravely, his right hand on her shoulder, then at the nape of her neck. He pressed her forward, against him. His body was hard, muscled; his hands rough and calloused. Under his blazer, she slipped her fingers between the buttons of his shirt into modest chest hair; the nipple tensed as she brushed it with a fingernail.

"My God,'' she sighed, as if she'd never noticed the phenomenon before, "your heart is beating.''

"Did you maybe expect chimes, Katharine?''

"Francotti,'' she whispered, "aren't you ever going to touch me?''

The steel frames of his glasses were in the way and she reached up to remove them.

"Wait, wait . . . I've got to put them where they don't break." He placed them on the coffee table, between two stacks of magazines. "Now I can't see a blasted thing."

"Can you see my face?"

His eyes ogled her defenselessly. "I can see your face. Just barely."

"Never mind—close your eyes and feel your way, Francotti."

Again his voice was soft, his mouth deeper into her bosom as he unbuttoned the Chanel suit top. "This is your last chance to run, Katharine Margaret. Last exit. . . ."

"Last exit, before what?" she murmured, only half-hearing what he said.

"Last exit . . . before entry, Katharine Margaret." He chuckled.

"Oh . . . yes, please, let's," she said, now wanting very badly to be undressed in this strange and alien place.

Very carefully he helped her out of the jacket and, focusing myopically, laid it on a nearby chair. Next, he stood her up and freed her of the tweed skirt. Underneath, she was wearing only black bra and panties—had she somehow known? Holding her fast between his knees, as if he were still half-sure she would run, he unsnapped the bra top and pulled it away from her breasts.

"Salute!" He kissed each nipple.

"Oh, Francotti, please," she whispered. "Take off your clothes . . . your socks too. I know what you Italians are like."

"Witch!" he said, "you are looking at a very sophisticated Wop, as you shall soon see."

Impatiently, she pulled the blazer from his shoulders and threw it on top of Madame Chanel, then unbuttoned his shirt. While he was undoing the cuffs, she solved trouser buckle and zipper and let his pants drop to the floor. "You're *embarrassed*! And I thought you were a big. . . ."

"Cocksman? Not me, lady." Blinking rapidly at her again, he lowered himself to the couch to extricate himself from shoes, pants and socks. And then, though he squirmed, he let her pull down his boxer shorts. Not taking her eyes off his body, the spareness of it, muscles, erection, Katharine slipped out of her black panties.

"Well," he laughed nervously. "Am I pointed in the right direction?"

Christ, she realized, he was so strong, but so vulnerable. Like he had said about coming around a corner, she was awed by such Fate.

She put her arms around him, pulling him to her, feeling the bulk of his erection. She flattened her breasts against his hard, muscular body and lifted her head again for the kiss. He held her firmly, hands running down her back to buttocks, thighs and then he pushed her away slightly to make room for his hand, which he inserted between them, kneading her belly, down to her loins, her crotch, fingers along her vagina, squeezing until she cried out and all but fell backward on the couch.

The leather was cool against her back, then warmer. He crouched over her, kissing her nipples, belly, between her legs, and she held on to him, softly caressing until she cried out. "Francotti! Please!"

He towered over her, his long frame, the bulk, bigger than Erik, much bigger than Stefan, and she held his hips, guiding him and felt the end of his erection against her; she reached between them and took it and gave it to herself. As he entered, her whole body seemed to cringe before him, out of wanting to please, then adapting to him, taking everything and wanting more, even as he filled her to capacity.

Why now? Why here? How had this happened, she asked herself, dimly aware with her logical mind of his measured stroking. She held him lightly by the hams, hooking ankles over his calves, wrapping legs around him, receiving all of him, taking it and then sensing inside herself the enormous growth of it as he worked himself to a frenzy of pushing and thrusting and she cried out at his force and then, with a hoarse cry, he loosed himself, his neck muscles stiff with the need and the torture of it and collapsed, his head in her throat. His hips continued to churn her like butter and having had his she began to climb again, straining against him with the hump of her crotch, moaning, she could hear herself doing that, groaning, then breathing so hard, so torturously, she began to understand that what was happening was rare, unusual, an almost forgotten sensation. She was actually . . . yes, actually, yes, she was . . . maybe, if she worked, pushed, strained, bore down, she was going finally to make it, it, the summit, pinnacle and for once in a blue moon she was going to come. And then, almost whooping, humping, she did . . . and did again . . . and again, ah, yes, sobbing now without restraint or shame.

"Christ Almighty," he gasped. "That must have been the beginning of the world."

"It was," she stammered, gasps choking her throat. "You've done me in, Francotti."

"I think you needed that, madame."

"I've needed that for a long time. I didn't know I needed that."

"Just shows to go you. . . ."

"What?"

"We articulate," he murmured. He stared down at her severely. "Just like I figured we would."

"You're so smart, so brilliant," she murmured, keeping her eyes closed. "How can I serve you whose wish is my command?"

He took the question seriously. "I don't know yet, Katharine Margaret. You must realize I'm a very self-centered man . . . I'm also a married one."

"What! Goddamn it! I never thought to ask." Her eyes flipped open and she glared at him. "Why didn't you tell me before."

He shrugged his bare shoulders. "It didn't occur to me. Besides, you're married too, so we're even."

"But you knew I was married," she quavered, suddenly, idiotically, near tears. "You should have told me!"

"She's far from here. Actually, Katharine Margaret, I'm not even sure I am still married. She's a marine biologist—we met over a barnacle. She's in Florida right now, I think, searching for Spanish treasure."

"Oh. . . ."

"Do you still want to serve me?"

Katharine nodded shyly. "I think so." He stretched against her, rocked his hips and the pressure aroused a tingle of vestigal orgasm. "Oh, yes," she said. "But I warn you, I can't cook."

"Do you want to think it over? Or do we have a deal?"

"A deal?" she muttered, her mind not fully on the subject matter.

"We try each other out? We enjoy life together a little?"

"Francotti, I'd like to send for some clothes and stay here, just like this, for a solid week."

"Yeah," he drawled, "you can if you want. What I'm saying, you can stay, leave, do whatever you please. You see, there's nothing anybody can do to hurt me, in revenge, or retaliation, if you like. People might try to blackmail me here or there but it only works once here, once in a while there, and never in both places at once. So, you could become talk-of-the-town, shameless wench, but there's no way anybody could hurt you. Do you see what I mean?"

Katharine nodded. "I understand, Francotti." She stared at him, still not believing it. "You're saying that—even though I have zilch to offer you."

"What'd I just say?" he demanded irascibly. "Gizmo Francotti has spoken."

"Let me ask you something else then," she murmured, still somewhat out of breath. "Did the motor go *put-put*?"

"*Put-put*, shit! It went *Var-oom!*"

Eight

They needn't have lingered so long at the museum. Dolly wasn't even sure why she'd wanted to go there in the first place except to meet him but, in any case, if she'd been quick about it, they could have had a couple of hours alone at Berliner's apartment before she had to dress for dinner. But Dolly fiddled around perversely and, in the end, there was only time for a couple of drinks in the Stanhope Hotel bar across Fifth Avenue.

Dumb ox that he was, he didn't realize until Dolly had engaged a second dry-martini that it was her lunch with Kathy which had thrown her off stride. Elbows on the little table, glass between her fingers and her eyes focused on the glass, Dolly muttered acidly, "Kitty seemed in a quite *marvelous* mood today, darling. I think she's snapped out of whatever was ailing her."

He drew in air. "Don't be misled. With her, it's a story of off-again, on-again. At this moment, I'd wager, she's home *resting*. You don't think she stopped with the vodka at lunch, do you?"

"I don't know," Dolly said levelly. "Why don't you take her to a doctor? Maybe she's a simple schizophrenic. Maybe a *cruise* would be the thing."

"Yes. . . ."

Sharply, Dolly said, "Why don't you buy a proper boat? Get rid of that stinkpot you run all summer."

Now he understood. Dolly was in a truly foul mood. "On the other hand," he murmured, "I wouldn't want to go away—I couldn't bear to leave you, my darling."

Dolly's eyes switched at him mockingly. "Really?" She sighed elaborately. "*On the other hand*, why couldn't we go to Europe together? Don't you think *we* could have a wonderful time? After all, I'm not neurotic and I'll tell you something else—the lads down at the Lobster Claw are rating me these days as among the top ten lays in Port London."

Her eyes were steady, defying him to say it wasn't true. He managed a groan. "*Dolly–chen.*"

Damnation, she was unrelenting. "You could leave her, you know. Why don't you?"

"I cannot, my darling," he said miserably. "I am responsible. I am her husband."

"Oh, Christ!" Dolly growled disgustedly. "You're much too honorable. It's bad for your health. You have a responsibility to yourself too, you know. And me! Yes, goddamn it, what about me?"

"Ah. . . ." He fixed his eyes on her fiery black pupils. "My darling, I am working it through, believe me. Going with you, alone to Europe, I am captivated by the idea of it, *Dolly–chen.*"

Her eyes blazed, a rosy color flushed out her cheeks. "Darling, we'd die of it—but what a way to go. Let me tell you, I ache from wanting it," she whispered. Good God, she knew how to arouse him. A flush of heat burned his bowels.

"*Dolly–chen,*" he murmured uneasily.

Eyes red-hot, she took the cigarette out of his hand and put it to her mouth, puffed insidiously, then slipped it back in his fingers. "I'm very possessive, darling," she whispered, so softly, her voice trickled under his skin. "I don't like it on the run like the other day in Port London. I want you all the time, so that I can reach and grab your pecker and kiss it and stick it in me."

"My darling," Erik gasped, "please. But why did we stay at the museum so long? Wasted time. Ah," he groaned.

"I lingered because I'm *mad* at you," she snapped. "You're going to have to do better."

"But I'm doing the best I can."

"You're not! We're getting nowhere. Maybe I'll go to

Europe with you and find me a new husband. I can't wait, *darling*," she muttered acridly. "I have hot pants. You know that! I should have them made out of asbestos." She laughed too loudly. Fortunately, the people closest to them were several tables away. "Buy a boat and take me sailing and I'll behave better," she promised.

"I sailed with my father on the Baltic," Erik said slowly. "I have not cared for it much since then."

She paid no attention. "Gibber Higgens has got a two-master he's selling. You could get it for two-fifty."

Two hundred and fifty thousand, she meant. "I'd have to mortgage myself."

She laughed raucously. "Like hell you would. Well. . . ." She reached under the table to pat his knee, then, seeing no one was in position to see anything, she slid her hand up his leg. "Too bad, old boy. Maybe another time." Cruelly, she grinned in his face, sticking her tongue out teasingly. "Got to go, darling. Will you take me home?"

"Of course," he said stolidly, not giving her the pleasure of knowing how high his lust was running.

Erik snapped his fingers for the check, paid in cash and tipped generously. "Ready, my darling?" he murmured, helping her on with the long sable. They went outside to wait for a cab down Fifth to Berliner's apartment. Perhaps, he was thinking, perhaps there might just be time. But she intercepted his thought.

"If you're thinking of slipping me a quickie, think again. You know about Lysistrata and the Trojan Women? Well. . . ." She laughed spitefully. "No more nooky until you shape up the future planning, Herr Mossberg. It's either . . . or."

"Darling," he protested, "Don't—make such an ultimatum. . . ."

Dolly gathered the sable around her, shivering. The cold made her cheeks so red and healthy, the lips so full, blooming, like roses, sweet like strawberries. *Verdamnt!* He could have eaten her down to the wishbone.

Glowering triumphantly, she announced, "If this be ultimatum, then make the most of it, sweetheart."

*   *   *

Katharine had still not gotten home by the time Erik arrived from dropping Dolly, then circling back up Park Avenue. Now, this was a departure from the norm. Especially as he had just finished assuring Dolly that for sure Kathy would already be here, with drink in hand or fast asleep.

"How strange," he muttered to Helen Ryan, "and she hasn't called either?"

Helen shook her head. "It's not like her, Mr. Moss, to be gone so long after lunch."

"Well, Helen, it's not *that* late. Six p.m. But nevertheless, I do wonder where she is."

Helen wrung her hands nervously. "There was a telephone call for you—from Mr. Steven Ratoff."

"For me? Even more strange—are you sure, Helen, he was not asking for Mrs. Moss?"

"He asked for you."

"For heaven's sake," Erik mused, "perhaps she's gone to see *him*."

"She wouldn't do that, would she?"

He shrugged. "Who knows? Where is he, this Mr. Ratoff?"

"He said to call him back at the Plaza Hotel," Helen said as she clapped her hands to her face and rushed from the room.

"Helen. . . ." But she was gone. Hell, he muttered to himself wearily, as if life were not already complicated enough. Erik took off his topcoat, went into the library and, without even considering an alternative, made himself a Scotch and soda.

Then he went to his desk, rang the Plaza and asked for Stefan Ratoff.

"Yes?" The voice was tired, the accent unidentifiable. Buried deeply in it was the staccatto Slavic nasalness, but French, German and Italian overtones had been laid on top. Erik had no doubt Ratoff spoke all those languages and more. Anybody born in such an unlikely place as Bulgaria or the Carpathians, had for his own good to speak a dozen languages.

"Is this Stefan Ratoff?"

"Yes . . . Ah! Moss?"

"Yes. You called me."

"I did," Ratoff murmured faintly. "So this is the voice of the present husband of my former wife."

"What is it I can help you with?" Erik asked, stiffly. Certainly, there was no reason to incline to pleasantries.

"I have no wish to disturb you. It is . . . simply. I am in New York for some weeks. There are people I would like to see—perhaps you could give me the whereabouts of Conrad Darktower, my former brother-in-law, a dear boy, as you know, Herr Mossberg."

Erik's lip curled. "My name is Erik Moss, Herr Ratoff. Surely, the number is in the book. Conrad lives in Greenwich Village."

"The number is not listed," Ratoff said.

"I. . . ." Erik paused, not knowing the most diplomatic way to say it. "Conrad mentioned you had written. I hope . . . you see."

"I know, I know," Ratoff said impatiently. "You need not fear I will corrupt the poor thing—this was the most untrue and unjust charge Richard Darktower made against me. Insulting . . . *if* I were not a tolerant, nay philosophical, man."

"You understand his feeling . . . his fear," Erik said sternly.

"Of course. There was never any basis for it. Please. . . ."

"I can give you the phone number," Erik sighed. "It seems fair. Conrad was looking forward. . . ."

"He is over twenty-one," Ratoff said wryly. "Tell me, though—in Zurich you were still known as Mossberg."

"Now *Moss*," Erik said gruffly. He opened his address book and found Conrad's number. After reading it, he asked, "And you will be in New York . . . how long?"

"Some weeks."

"I'm sure," Erik said softly, "*Kâh–ti* will be wishing to see you too. She speaks of you, you know, Herr Ratoff."

"Wonderful . . . and perhaps we too should have a meeting, we two."

"Why?" Erik demanded bluntly.

Ratoff lapsed into rapid but not totally grammatical

German, saying they did have something in common, namely that both of them had been or were married to Katharine Darktower, and then, of course, they could always talk about the *past*. Had they never met before, Ratoff wanted to know, say in the late forties as mere youths, or during the fifties in Paris or Berlin? Erik told him flatly, coldly, that they had never met before and there seemed no good reason why they should do so now. Ratoff heard him out, then casually asked, "How *is Kat*?"

"She is well."

"Ah, good," Ratoff muttered, as if he had suddenly lost interest. "You may call me, if you wish."

"Leave it at that, Mr. Ratoff," Erik said formally.

He hung up and quickly dialed the last number he had for Conrad, wanting to get through first to earn some credit with Kathy's aloof brother. It was in this accidental manner that he first became aware of the girl.

"I am Conrad's brother-in-law. *Who* is this?"

"I'm a friend. Lilly Royce. Conrad's told me about you."

"Yes? And what did he say?" Before she could answer, he asked. "And why have I not talked to you before, Miss Royce?"

"Call me Lilly if you want," she murmured. Erik could see her mind turning, wondering how old he was, what he looked like. "I guess you've never called before—and sometimes we're out."

Hell! She was frank enough about it. She was living with Conrad. Not that Erik gave a damn—but there were those who would be vastly relieved to hear Conrad was living with a girl. Richard Darktower would be most pleased of all.

"We were not," he murmured, "aware of Conrad's . . . friend."

This girl, this Lilly, chuckled wetly, almost derisively. "He wouldn't mention me, would he? Conrad is so straight-laced—he's a square, isn't he, Mr. Moss?"

Erik chuckled dryly. "Yes. Definitely." He was picturing her with a certain longing, thinking of carefree student life, Heidelberg, the *Student Prince*, all those things he had never experienced, despite his posturing. "And you, Miss Royce," he asked drolly, "what do you do?"

"I'm an artist, Mr. Moss."

"Oh? And what sort of pictures do you do? I'm very interested in art, Miss Royce."

"And history, according to Conrad."

"Yes—Conrad believes I have an umbilical cord attached to the Seventeenth Century. I am more interested in the past than the present or future."

"That *is* exactly what Conrad says," she laughed.

"Never mind—what do you paint? That was my question."

"A little of everything," she replied impulsively. "I just stand here and paint and paint."

"Well. . . ." Erik stopped to think. Still he had no clue to Lilly Royce. But her voice, all he had to go on, was timbred, deep, indicating a forceful woman, an energetic woman. "Well, maybe some day Conrad will let us see your work. Perhaps I could help. . . . You do sell?"

"Not yet . . . I'd like. . . ."

"I am not as dusty or rusty as Conrad makes me out, Miss Royce."

"I'm sure not," she cried enthusiastically. "I . . . is there some message for him?"

She was in a hurry. She wanted to hang up, get rid of him. Perhaps Conrad was there after all, motioning for her to get off the phone, to hang up on the old fool. At their age, with their spirit, anybody over the age of thirty-five was an old fool. *Verdamnt!*

"Nothing important. Someone will be telephoning him— but let it be a surprise. Good-bye, Miss Royce."

His hand was perspiring when he replaced the phone. For some reason, a mere voice had excited him, titillated him, her words like hands groping his leg.

Erik wasn't aware of Helen behind him until she spoke. "I . . . I have to go pick Margaret up from ballet, Mr. Moss."

"Yes," he said absently, "and Mrs. Moss is still not back. What on earth is she doing?"

He turned to look at Helen. Her hands fluttered embarrassedly at the buttons of her wool coat and he was astonished, not pleased, to see the expression of anxiety on her face.

"Mr. Moss. . . ." She stopped, flustered, blushing crimson.

"What?"

She couldn't speak. "I worry about her . . . You. . . ."

"What?" he demanded, more loudly than before. "What do you want to say?"

Miserably, Helen goggled at him. "I want to say . . . I want to say . . . I hope you are a good husband to her, Mr. Moss."

"What? What!" He jumped up and paced toward her, then furiously away. He stopped and glared. "Bitch! Is that any business of yours?"

"I want her to be happy, Mr. Moss!"

"For the sake of Christ!" he exclaimed. "Is that it? Are you saying something bad about me again? *You* want *her* to be happy, Helen? How sweet and wonderful of you," he sneered. "Do you want me to be happy as well, Helen?"

Nervously, she nodded. "All I want is to help."

Erik laughed without making any noise. "Then come here and let me bite your big Irish tits . . . cow!"

A growl, half-grunt, half-scream burst out of her throat.

He laughed aloud this time, patiently, he thought. "Go, Helen. Pick up Margaret, please. Some other day I will bite your milk tits."

Her heels clattered wildly on the parquet floor as she fled. The front door flew open and he heard a jumble of voices. He followed Helen and saw Katharine had just come in. Calmly, she looked from Helen to him.

"What's going on? Why is everybody so excited?"

Erik squalled, "For heaven's sake, darling, where have you been? Helen is about to die of worry."

"No," Helen cried softly, her face flaming, "I'm just going to pick up little Margaret."

Erik pushed past them and flung open the closet. He snatched out his coat and a hat. "No, *I* will go to fetch Margaret . . . I need some air, right away."

He stepped through the door and slammed it behind

him. This household was becoming too much for him—a neurotic wife and a delusional lunatic for a maid. Yes, it could easily be argued that Helen was too unstable to be responsible for Margaret, his daughter, and the only person in the whole world that Erik Moss cared anything about.

Nine

"Helen, what's happening here?" Katharine asked.

Helen shook her head. "Nothing—Mr. Moss said a very terrible thing to me."

"What? What did he say? Not about me?"

"No. Something terrible about me, Mrs. Moss, I don't know if I can stay here any longer."

"Nonsense, Helen," Katharine said briskly. She handed the girl her coat, then whirled into the living room. "If you won't tell me what he said, how can I deal with it?" she asked, reasonably enough, Katharine thought.

"It was a dirty thing he said, Mrs. Moss," Helen said.

Her face was so troubled. But, somehow, Katharine could not find it in herself to be very concerned. When you came right down to it, she didn't care what Erik had said to Helen or why.

"How do I look, Helen?"

Helen eyed her woefully. "You look fine. The cold weather agrees with you, Mrs. Moss."

Katharine smiled. She knew something that made her feel wonderfully well, something she was not going to tell anybody. It was strange and wondrous, wasn't it, that a bare hour ago she had been as intimate as one could be with another human being and it didn't even show. Nothing. Not a hint. She almost wished the fact of it could blink on her forehead like the Pepsi-Cola sign across the river from Francotti's small apartment.

"Well, Helen, I feel so good I'd like a drink. I'd like a vodka. . . . No! On second thought, open a bottle of white wine. We have one cold in the refrigerator, don't we? Open it and bring me a glass of nice cold wine. Is it Italian?"

Helen stared at her as though she were insane. "I don't know, Mrs. Moss."

"Dear Helen," Katharine murmured. "I'll tell you what—forget everything Erik Moss said. It doesn't matter. You're *you* and it doesn't matter what *he* thinks of you."

Helen drew a deep breath and hugged Katharine's trenchcoat to her bosom.

"You . . . I hope, Mrs. Moss, forgive me. You don't love Mr. Moss any more, do you?"

Katharine shook her head icily. "And I haven't for a while, Helen."

The girl frowned deeply, sorrowfully. "That is a poor lost man, Mrs. Moss."

"Tough, Helen." She grinned. "Maybe you'd like to save him."

Helen blushed. "No, I wouldn't. I couldn't, Mrs. Moss. It was a terrible and insulting thing he said to me."

"He can be a terrible and insulting man, Helen."

"You'll leave him . . . you'll divorce again, won't you?"

"Well. . . ." Really, this was getting a little too personal, wasn't it? "I think I'll go upstairs, Helen. I'm for a long, hot bath. You can bring me the wine up there, please."

"Yes, sure, but. . . ."

"No *buts*, Helen. Bring the wine upstairs."

"Yes, yes, all right."

Katharine didn't bother with the lift. She marched up the curved staircase connecting the living room with a graceful balcony overlooking the library, unimpressed by the climb although she was feeling dead-tired and aching wonderfully in all her limbs. Any concern for Helen fled her mind as she remembered Francotti. His passion had been very nearly too much for her and yet, though she was so unskilled and lately even so unpracticed, she had been able to respond in a way that she was sure had delighted him. *Him. He. Francotti.* His hands, his body, his legs, arms, mouth, all of him like an army on the march, ravaging the land, raiding the ice-pack in which she had been frozen. It was all so new to her, yet old as the hills, she knew. The difference between Erik, the fabled stud—everybody she had ever met said Erik Moss was a world-class stud—and Francotti, only a man, was profound.

Hastily, Katharine pulled her clothes off and went into her bathroom and turned on the water. She wanted solitude now so she could concentrate on him, because his heat still flushed her and she could feel him, still inside her, hurting her exquisitely.

Despite all her brave talk, of course, she had had to leave him, as much as she wanted to stay. But then, at last, he would not allow her to stay—she had a child, she had responsibilities. Francotti was a conservative and cautious man, she discovered, neat of mind. He was a logical and reasonable man and he disliked loose ends. He ran what was called a tidy ship, as much as it was within his power to do so on dry land.

But she would return to him, hurry to meet him and they would make more love in the afternoon.

When the water temperature was right, Katharine stepped into the tub. The hot water washed her, quickly made her sleepy and then she realized she was sated, body limp, breasts swimming lazily, yes, and marked from his mouth. There was a red blotch on her belly and bruises between her thighs from his hard body and her insides were tender. Katharine didn't care. She didn't care at all.

But she'd forgotten about Helen. Helen tapped at the half-open door and Katharine knew she could see the body in the bathtub.

Helen's voice was timid, frightened. "Shall I bring in the wine, Mrs. Moss?"

"Yes, bring it in, Helen," she said. No, she didn't care.

Helen put the glass into her right hand. Smiling, Katharine watched Helen's face, her eyes as she identified the marks of passion.

"Mrs. Moss, excuse me, I. . . ."

"It's all right, my dear," Katharine said. She began to feel proud of it now, of herself. These marks, they were honorably earned, medals of honor. "Helen, I shouldn't tell you. But I will, because I've decided I don't care. I was with one of my lovers." She chuckled brightly. "He became a little excited, you see."

Helen's gasp was labored. "You shouldn't tell me that, Mrs. Moss."

"I wouldn't tell you if it weren't true, Helen."

"Oh, my God! You'll need salve, Mrs. Moss. This . . . man. Man, no. Beast, he must be a beast."

"Hardly."

"Oh, God, it was when I asked Mr. Moss if he wouldn't be a good husband to you that he said the filthy thing to me, telling me to mind my own business. And now . . . I feel like, I don't know what."

"*Now*, you see I've been a bad wife, Helen," Katharine said firmly. "But, I said—I don't care. It's been a long time coming."

"Your revenge?"

"Yes, if you want to call it that."

"See the bruises," Helen marveled. "Is . . . that what happens?"

"Only if you're having fun, Helen."

"Oh, the saints! Merciful saints above, Mrs. Moss. I . . . I'll be praying about this."

"Helen. . . ." Katharine tried to think of appropriate words. "You think I'm going to go to hell now, don't you? Well, I don't—when you love, Helen, it's the greatest gift . . . an *un-sin*."

"I can't help the way I feel, the way I'm brought up, Mrs. Moss."

"I know." Katharine studied her tolerantly, feeling somehow sorry that the poor girl hadn't been lucky yet. "Well, dear, I don't think you should stand there staring at me like that . . . I'm finally going to get rather embarrassed, you know."

Helen began to laugh unsteadily. "Yes, you're right. I'm sorry. I'm just trying to think of you, like that, being with a man. I . . . what's it like, will you tell me?"

Katharine closed her eyes, still not able to make herself care.

"Merely wonderful, Helen. I couldn't explain . . . you'll find out."

Helen shook her head. "Maybe. I wonder."

Silently, the two women looked at each other. Then both heard the door open downstairs.

"They're back, Helen," Katharine muttered. "You're not to tell on me now, dear. And keep Margaret downstairs 'til I'm done with the bath."

"And dressed."

"Yes."

Erik's voice boomed heartily, announcing what they knew, that he and little Margaret were home.

"Mrs. Moss . . . mum . . . after what he said to me, I know what he's like," Helen murmured. "I'm glad for you . . . I told him all I wanted was for you to be happy."

"Thank you, dear."

When Helen had left, Katharine reached from the tub to throw the lock on the bathroom door. Wisely, for in a moment, Erik was there, outside, trying the door.

"Darling. . . ."

"Yes, Erik, I'll be out in a few moments."

"May I come in?"

"No." She said it bluntly enough. "I'm private right now."

"Oh." He didn't know, did he? And she didn't care. "You did give Helen a scare. Where were you all afternoon?"

Her shoulders moved comfortably in the hot water. She longed to tell him she'd been making love with an attentive man. But she could not tell him that, could she? Not now. Not yet. "I lingered with Dolly quite a while. . . ."

"*Did* you?"

Katharine was so acute, so tuned to a perfect intuitive pitch by Mr. Gene Francotti that she understood at once that Erik had met Dolly in the afternoon.

"Yes," she said, "we had so much to talk about. I guess we were together until four or so, maybe later. . . ."

No sound came from the other side of the door. So Katharine continued, taunting him. He would know she was lying but he could not charge her with it, not unless he wanted the rupture then and there.

"After Dolly, I walked down Madison all the way to Fifty-Seventh and then across to the Plaza. . . ."

"To the Plaza," he grunted.

"Yes. Why?"

His breathing was harsh. "I wonder if you ran into Stefan Ratoff. He's here, at the Plaza. He called late in the afternoon wanting Conrad's phone number."

"I didn't see him," she said calmly. "I had some tea and then I walked home."

"Darling, what a lot of exercise. You must be exhausted."

"I am," she said curtly. "By the way, Frank Berliner is having cocktails for Dolly tomorrow. I thought I'd go."

"Oh? *You* will? And shall I as well?"

"If you want to, of course. I thought you might be busy with something else."

"What else could there be, darling?" he said softly. "Am I not at your total service?"

"Are you?"

Lazily, Katharine lifted the fragile wine glass to her lips. Luxuriously, she sipped. She should have asked Helen to put it on ice. Nonetheless, it felt wonderful, lusciously viscous sliding down her gullet. She realized Erik was still standing, silently, on the other side of the door. Thoughtfully, Katharine cupped her right breast in her left hand and pushed it toward her chin. If she'd been able to reach, she'd have kissed the nipple. *Um*, pointy and red, tender now, used, suckled. Then, caressing her belly, tentatively stroking her thighs, yes, she was all present and accounted for.

"Darling. . . ." Katharine didn't answer. "Darling . . . are you all right in there?"

She smiled to herself. He thought, possibly, she was gulping pills, certainly vodka. Once more she lifted the wine glass.

"Kathy! Goddamn it! Are you all right?"

In a low voice, distantly, she said, "I'm fine, Erik, just fine."

Ten

Marco Fortuna, who had come to America with Stefan
Ratoff, was a tall and, on first impression, courtly man so
stiff about the waist that Katharine thought surely he'd
break in half when he bowed to kiss her hand.

"Charmed, so charmed," he stated, his voice roundly
cherubic like his face, in contrast to the rest of the body.
"Stefan has told me so much about you I feel you are my
very own."

He ignored Erik who was standing behind her staring
bemusedly at the Sicilian.

"This is my husband, Erik Moss."

"Ah, yes, ah, yes," Fortuna cried, showing dazzling
white teeth. "Erik Mossberg. We spent some months
together at the Sorbonne."

"Did we?" Erik said scornfully. "Very interesting, in
view of the fact I did not attend the Sorbonne."

"You did not? Well, you should have, and then we
would have been there at the same time." Fortuna laughed
merrily and turned his attention back to Katharine. "Of
course, you will be very anxious to see Stefan."

"Will I?"

"But, naturally. He is there. . . ." Fortuna gestured
toward the windows facing Central Park. Katharine picked
out the slim figure at once. Stefan was easily spotted in a
crowd and, once identified, he was not easily forgotten. His
light stoop had been so distinctive, so aristocratic. Now,
she noticed with a spasm of concern, the stoop was merely

more pronounced. Stefan stood with his hands clasped behind his back, staring across the city.

But Dolly was upon them before Katharine could move, even if she had been going to Stefan. "Darlings, you've met my count . . . isn't he lovely?"

"Dear lady," Fortuna gushed, his voice so wet she worried a spurt of saliva couldn't be far behind, "dear lady, I had no thought of being greeted so marvelously in New York. Such a beautiful flat Mr. Berliner has here."

As if he recognized one of his own, Fortuna took Erik's arm and drew him across the room to point out a picture spotlighted on the opposite wall. It was a work, he was saying, that had once belonged to the Prince of Naples.

"Darling," Dolly cried softly, "don't you love him? He's so absolutely decadent and European."

"He looks like he's wearing a corset," Katharine observed.

Dolly frowned. "Now, Kitty, tell me what you think—he doesn't have to be gay, does he, just because he's with Stefan? I'm inviting them out to Port London."

"Good luck," Katharine said. Glancing around, she did not see Gene Francotti in the room. She'd invited him, begged him to come, late that afternoon. "An interesting man might show up. A very interesting man."

"Who?"

"Somebody I met once up in Port London," Katharine said, openly smiling. "You'll be surprised . . . if he comes."

It would be just like him, however, not to come. She'd already learned that much about him, in just the two such short afternoons. He was so independent; he did exactly what he wanted, when he wanted to. Yet, curiosity might draw him here.

Dolly happened to be staring at the open door of the apartment. "Well, I'll be damned," she said, "there's that ugly guy we saw at the restaurant."

Katharine's spirits leapt with relief—God, if he hadn't come, she couldn't have stayed another minute. Her body seemed to surge forward although she did not move a step. She laughed breathlessly. "That's him, the interesting man. What happened was—when I was leaving *Le Cirque* that day, he came over and reminded me we'd been introduced a couple of years ago."

She waved at Francotti until he saw her. He looked surprised, nodded and came toward them.

"Gene Francotti," Katharine pronounced his name in such a way Dolly looked startled. "Meet Dolly Percy."

"Yes," he said gravely. He touched both their hands. "And how are you today?" he asked.

Katharine smiled. After all, they'd parted only two hours before. "I'm just fine," she said. "I'm feeling wonderful, just wonderful."

His eyes narrowed. "Well, that's good. I'm glad to hear it."

Marco Fortuna returned, still gripping Erik's arm. Erik was smiling coolly, listening to Fortuna's patter.

To Francotti, Katharine said, "I'd like you to meet my husband. Erik, Gene Francotti. We all had a drink together once in Port London Harbor."

"Oh? How do you do," Erik stated, studying Francotti's face. "I remember—you were working on the Higgens boat."

"Correct." Francotti's face was set severely. Katharine knew that right now he was not approving of himself.

Dolly couldn't be left out. "And Mr. Francotti, I'd like you to meet Count Marco Fortuna."

"So pleased," Fortuna said.

"Likewise," Francotti replied.

They shook hands perfunctorily.

Erik asked, "You're a marine engineer, isn't that right?"

"Yeah." Francotti nodded loosely, his big head bobbing. He glanced around idly. "Very nice place. Whose is it?"

"It belongs to Frank Berliner, the decorator," Dolly said.

One knew it was the home of a decorator, or at least that it had been done by a decorator. The main salon, where everybody was gathered, was brilliantly conceived. Shining hardwood floors ran to walls painted a bright but not shocking yellow and the furniture, from grand piano in one corner to groupings of silk upholstered chairs and sofas, mesmerizing little lacquered tables and the art hanging all

around them, invited coverage in the next issue of
Architectural Digest.

"Yes, yes," Francotti murmured and, not at all surprisingly, he added, "I've known Frank for some years.
We've worked together on a few projects, you know," he
told Katharine exclusively. "Frank does the cabins and I
do the boiler room. Where is he?"

"Here . . . somewhere," Dolly murmured. She was
staring at Kitty, then at Francotti, then back at Kitty.
"God, darlings, it's turning into an awful crush. Come
with me, Count." She took Fortuna's arm and firmly led
him away.

Francotti smiled at her, then Erik. "Well, never know
when you'll meet up with people again, do you?"

The way he phrased the pleasantry, the sardonic tone of
his voice made her shiver. He was angry. She knew
why—she hadn't told him Erik would be at the party. But
he might have guessed—she *was* still married. But obviously
he didn't want to be reminded of that.

Pompously, Erik said, "It's a cliche to say so but a
certain small group of people see each other over and over
again, in the most unlikely places."

"Yes," Francotti said, his lower lip jutting. "I hate to
think that might be true—there are certain people I'd just
as soon didn't see me again."

"Ha!" Erik laughed appreciatively. "I know what you
mean. Fortuna, for example, thinks he knows me from
Europe. He does not, thank God."

"The phenomenon you mention could make it convenient
for the historian," Francotti ventured. Erik smiled again;
he *would* agree with that. "Well, I'd best find Frank
Berliner."

"And," Katharine said listlessly, "I'd better do the
right thing and say hello to my first husband."

Francotti's thick eyebrows bucked. "The gang's all here."

Erik chuckled dryly. "We're very modern, Mr. Francotti."

"So I see," Francotti said ominously. "Modernity. I'm
not so crazy about it."

"Nor I," Erik said.

Katharine straightened her back. "Well, excuse me."
She didn't look at Francotti's face but she saw him bow
ironically. Now she hated herself. What a fool she was!
She'd thought she'd been so clever, getting him here, and
he only resented it.

Resolutely, she approached Ratoff. "Stefan? Hello."

His back stiffened and he turned quickly, a smile on his
face. "Hello, Kat," he cried, his voice clipped, a trick
he'd always used to cut his accent. It made him sound a bit
like Cary Grant. "I saw you come in. You're looking very
well."

"And you."

He shook his head. "No. Not good, I fear."

"Why?" she demanded. "What's wrong?"

"I'm ill," Stefan said calmly. "I will die soon."

"Stefan!"

"It's true, Kat." He nodded sorrowfully. "That's the
reason I've come over with Marco."

Gazing at him, she saw that possibly it *was* true. His
incredible good looks were gone. The once boyishly
handsome face was lined. There were deep black circles
under his eyes and folds of unhealthy skin sagged off his
chin line. All the dissipation showed now. Even the beautiful
nose was criss-crossed with lacy red veins. He was too
thin—his stoop was no longer an expression of aristocratic
ennui but of simple weariness.

"But, Stefan, my dear, my dear," Katharine whispered,
stricken, feeling doubly bad now, "what's wrong with
you?"

He tried to toss his emaciated shoulders. "As they've
always warned me, Kat—the liver. Too much of the good
life, cherie."

"Oh, hell!" She was not going to accept that. "Stefan,
you were always a hypochondriac. The liver—that's
nothing."

"Oh, yes?" He held up the glass that dangled in his
fingers. "See this—soda water," he said scornfully, "with
a little bit of lemon juice. Not too much, however. Even
lemon juice can be lethal."

"Oh, for God's sake!" she cried.

"Think kindly of me, cherie."

"I've never thought otherwise," she snapped. "Where are you living now, Stefan?"

"In *Geneve*, in beautiful, so exciting Switzerland. You have met my *patron*, Marco?" He smiled apologetically, then added, "It is not what I'm sure everybody is thinking. Our relationship is one of pure friendship . . . Marco's father was a *closer* friend. Marco is not one of us."

"Us?"

"I mean he is not like *some* of us, cherie. He is completely a ladies' man and indeed should have been named Casanova Fortuna." He smiled at her daringly. "You know, cherie, I've always understood you better than any other man, your dear father included. Better than your new husband, I'm sure. Is he here?"

Warily, not knowing what he was hinting at, not wanting to know, if the truth be known, she said, "He's over there, the man with the mass of gray hair."

"And the thick glasses?"

She almost laughed out loud. "No, that's somebody else. Erik is the one with the . . . eyes."

Stefan seemed to spring to attention. "I feared so. The eyes are those of a bird of prey. This Mossberg . . . Moss . . . one has heard of him."

"*What* has one heard? Tell me. I know so little about him, even after ten years."

"Yes," Stefan nodded tiredly, already bored with the subject. "He is supposedly quite brilliant. But an enigma. No one knows precisely where he came from—he appeared out of the ashes of Europe in the fifties." Ratoff shrugged. "It is said he beat his way into the service of James Merriwether, that he undertook various assignments, some as mysterious as Mossberg, or Merriwether, himself. People also say he was on his way to becoming a wealthy man— and then something happened."

"Yes. He met me," Katharine murmured.

Stefan grimaced. "No. Something else, I believe, which made you that much more important for Mossberg. Ha!" Ratoff chuckled acridly. "He plucked for himself the beautiful golden princess, Katharine Darktower Ratoff . . .

the *Ratoff* does not sound so well. But then, neither does Mossberg. I suppose that is why he shortened it. Well . . . dearest,'' Stefan went on philosophically, ''and that's the way it was. Too bad, no? We could have survived very nicely, the two of us. But your father, King Richard, would not have it. One foolish mistake and *basta*! I am practically deported from the land of the free and the home of the brave.''

Remembering, Katharine nodded distantly. ''Maybe . . . I think it would have been different if Conrad hadn't worshipped you so.''

''Bah! It was not my fault your beloved little brother lived with us. It was not my fault he was constantly underfoot,'' Ratoff responded more heatedly. ''The most unfair of all King Richard's indictments was that one. You know, my sweet, how scrupulously I kept Conrad at arm's length.'' He smiled. ''Not that he wasn't a beautiful boy.''

Katharine shook her head dismally. ''Come on, Stefan! You know what was going on then—my father and mother were divorcing. It was a terrible period for Conrad. Where was he going to go?''

''Quite!'' he exclaimed. ''But out of dire circumstance, it was unfair of Richard to condemn me.''

''He was wild in those days.''

''Yes, wildly neurotic,'' Ratoff grumbled. ''And then to make so much of the other . . . business. Something no one even knew about.''

''No one?''

The ''other business'' had been nasty business. To be caught in the men's room of Darktower's very own Princeton Club with the great professor Szigismund Sardo was a business that took a great deal of hushing up. So, therefore, *basta*, enough. But that hadn't been the last of Stefan's ''boyish pranks.'' During his terminal period of abandon in the big city he had taken to appearing at parties in makeup and then, drunkenly, to making passes at bankers and busboys alike, not that they all objected. But as Daddy Darktower had told her, enough was too much.

''Yes,'' Stefan mused disinterestedly, ''King Richard, blessed be he in Wall Street.''

"Well," Katharine said tartly, "whatever happened, you can lay the blame on your own good self, darling."

"It doesn't matter now. How *is* Conrad?"

"He's living in the Village," Katharine said uneasily. "Still going to school but he's a part-time instructor too, so all is not lost . . . I thought you were going to call him."

"I did," Stefan said amusedly. "But he was out. A girl answered. Can you imagine? A girl."

"He's living with a girl? I didn't know that."

"Too true, cherie." Stefan smiled mockingly. "Still, that's good, you know. It's not such an easy road the other way—as you know."

"A girl. . . ."

"Yes, Kat, a girl. Isn't that fine?"

Katharine felt herself blush. "Yes," she said doubtfully.

"You were always too fond of him," Stefan chided her delicately. "Actually, King Richard should have realized that it was not I with evil designs on his little son."

Katharine chuckled. "You dog, Stef. You always said that."

"And I was always right, wasn't I?"

"Don't be silly, darling."

"But we never lied to each other, did we, Kat?"

"No."

Slowly, he nodded, satisfied with her. "All right—now when am I to meet the famous Mossberg?"

"One thing," she said stiffly. "Please. When you see Conrad, try not to . . . confuse him."

"I won't flaunt my decadence—is that what you mean?"

"Conrad is still a very innocent boy, you know," Katharine pointed out. "He's still very immature."

Stefan nodded sardonically. "Innocent, yes. I know. The very worst kind, the innocent kind."

She led Stefan across to where Erik was still standing with Gene Francotti. She realized Francotti was deliberately attempting to rile her with this outward show of cordiality to Erik. She interrupted them swiftly. "Erik, I'd like you to meet Stefan Ratoff. Stefan, this is Gene Francotti."

Francotti shook hands with Stefan quickly, then began to duck away. "I've really got to say hello to Frank Berliner before I leave. Nice to meet *you*," he said to Stefan.

Stefan and Erik touched fingertips politely, Erik watching his predecessor in Kathy's couch with the deadly concentration of the bird of prey Stefan had mentioned. For his part, Stefan was quite unconcerned. He had surrendered much of his old haughtiness.

"My two men," Katharine murmured. "It's time you two met, if you never have before."

"We never have met before," Erik said sharply.

Stefan shook his head. "As strange as it might seem, I never before have laid eyes on Erik Mossberg."

"Erik Moss!"

"So American," Stefan said, "this land of equality, home sweet home and all that."

"But I *am* American now," Erik said. "And you?"

"I never foreswore Europe," Stefan said mildly. "These days I carry a Swiss residence permit."

"And what brings you to America?" Erik inquired.

"Nothing in particular. My friend Fortuna wished to visit New York and I thought I should come . . . once more."

"Of course."

"*And Dolly*," Katharine said emphatically. "She's inviting Stefan and Marco Fortuna to Port London."

"That promises to be dull." Stefan smirked cynically. "Dolly naturally has designs on the poor boy. He would be a catch of sorts, cherie. He has a beautiful house on the shores of Lake Geneva."

"Exactly what Dolly wants," Katharine said. "A man with a chateau."

Erik shook his head judicially. "Too boring for Dolly."

"Well, he also has a flat in Paris," Stefan said.

"That," Erik said irritably, "would be more like it."

Katharine could not resist taunting Erik a little. "If Dolly goes racing off to Europe, Erik, how ever are you going to fix up the Smithers house?"

"Precisely what I was thinking," he said grimly.

"Not to worry," Stefan said languidly, smiling secretively. Katharine realized he was so astute he would know without asking that she and Erik were on the rocks. "No," he went on, "Marco would make it a transatlantic marriage."

"Yes," Erik said icily, "so as never to be too far away from Dolly's money."

Stefan took the point with a sickly grin. "Marco, my friend, has a fortune of his own. Besides, fortune-hunting is passé since I retired." He smiled at Katharine. "Although I cannot agree that two million dollars separation pay is exactly the jackpot, cherie." He shook his head as Erik tried to interrupt. "Bad form, no? And it's no secret that I've spent it all . . . all of it, except for the jewelry."

"Sir," Erik said angrily, "it does not do to talk about such things in public."

"Bother!" Stefan said carelessly. To Katharine, he muttered, "Say hello to your mother. She is a true gem. I have no hope of seeing your father and do not really want to."

"Good-bye," Erik interrupted impatiently. "We must go."

"Yes, good-bye," Stefan smiled mockingly. "Perhaps one day you will invite me for lunch at the Princeton Club—I assume you did inherit my membership."

Eleven

Richard Darktower, the country squire in question, lord of much of what he surveyed, stood on the forest side of his house inspecting what was left of winter near the ocean and what of spring was being previewed, his mind occupied by the recent occurrence which had changed his thinking.

Poor old Lee Penton, it had been too much for him, hadn't it? At first, Darktower had been deeply shamed for Penton and himself to be caught out in the *Post,* thanks to Penton's "gem" Harvey; but then he had begun to receive notes, a few phone calls, from old friends at school and off the street, to the effect that You Old Dog You, Richard Darktower, We Didn't Know You Had It In You. Slowly, shame and promises to the Almighty of Future Virtue gave way to a certain pride.

Yes, by George, there was life in the old dog yet! And maybe life was not meant to be lived so close to the bone of respectability. Hadn't he earned the right to a bit of fun and frolic? Wife gone, children grown up—or sort of—and grandchildren not his responsibility, Richard Darktower was his own man now and what he did with the years left to him was his own goddamned business.

Once, in the month or so that had gone by since that fateful night on Madison Avenue, he had taken a quick trip up to Boston, a city where his every footstep would not be charted, and had tried himself out again, daringly, on a young and seemingly innocent whore, acquitting himself with honor, or, if that was not the right word, then

114

with a physical prowess that belied his age. But this second adventure had not been enough; it was not the same. Miss Teats, as he remembered her, had been one of a kind.

Now, standing very still for a survey of tentative buds on his rose bushes, he thought fondly of Clara as he put his hands in the pockets of his baggy tweed pants and stroked himself to a fair erection for the hundredth time.

Clara Riding had had a certain something, he assured himself. He was not deluding himself about that. Warmly, he remembered her breasts, the cupid mouth affixed to his penis.

Blast! Clara was in New Jersey and not here on Long Island when, not infrequently, late at night, Richard Darktower began to yearn for avoirdupois. And then in the morning, he'd have second thoughts and wouldn't make the phone call. Even if he called, even if Clara Riding came to Wainscott, what then? Could Richard Darktower get away with such a structuring in this backwater?

Morosely, he stared at his rosebushes, just poking fresh probes toward the cold sun, the ground, birds swooping more enthusiastically than they should have in the trees down the hill in the forest. The cycle of life and death went on . . . Did he dare to step off? From far away, he heard cow noises and the bellow of a bull. Had the mating season begun—surely it was well over by now with calves due to drop in late spring. Had his own mating season run its course? Surely not! He fingered his spike of erection. No, he was still virile enough to father another platoon of children. And, he told himself regretfully, had Margo, the present Mrs. Himmelmann, been less promiscuous and more fruitful, this new generation of Darktowers might have numbered a dozen rather than duo. Sperm was sperm, like the man said, and the best wine came out of old bottles.

Darktower kicked at the frosty ground with the toe of his boot. Soon, this earth would become fertile again, once more give itself to reproduction. Hell, he could be the same. With half a mind, he could take a young wife and plough himself another furrow, plant his seed and watch it sprout and grow. But there was a rub: by the time this seed reached its maturity, Richard Darktower would be gone. He could not bear the thought of leaving something behind he would never know. That was the reason he no longer bought tax-free municipals with a maturity date beyond nineteen-ninety. Oh, hell! Darktower picked up his feet and trudged toward the limit of his property. What the hell was he going to do? Life certainly was not meant to peter out like this.

Darktower had not been back in the city since the Penton scandal and his brief humiliation at the hands of the *Post*. And he was certainly not going back anytime in the foreseeable future. Kate had called to say Ratoff had indeed arrived in New York with a person called Marco Fortuna, supposedly a count. Why was it all these pretenders flocked to this last great bastion of all that was good? The answer was, of course, obvious. They were getting money, jewelry, pictures, anything of value out of a continent that was clearly on the way down and out.

Disgruntled, he continued walking, now through an open field that represented his territorial buffer, then over a swell in the earth's crust and downward again toward the spot where Rush Creek cut the corner of his estate. The going was rougher here. Clumps of frozen, unruly sod interfered with his boots. But he walked on to the slit in the earth which harbored the creek.

Kate . . . her voice had been worried, anxious. Ratoff, she'd told him, was sick. Supposedly, he was dying of liver or kidney disease. Darktower was not surprised to hear it—men of Ratoff's stamp always finished with that trouble. Ratoff was sick . . . and poor. Too bad.

It was like Kate that she should worry about such a wastrel. He stared glumly from his vantage point down at the creek, still solidly frozen in the middle but beginning to give to the current around the rocks along the bank. Faintly, he could hear the bubbling sound of riotous water. The creek would be high this spring for there had been a lot of snow. Darktower had once considered building a dam across the narrow downstream place where the creek ran out of the rocks and creating a bigger pool into which he might have cast a fly. But everybody in the vicinity complained when you fooled around with the water. Moodily, he stooped down, freed a stone from the frozen turf and tossed it on the ice.

Darktower turned and began to walk back to the house, thinking how drastically he had failed to settle the course of Kate's life more . . . what? Happily? Securely? He still didn't understand how she had managed to fall for two such men as Ratoff and Moss. Of course, Margo had been a strong influence. Margo had no doubt been more strongly attracted to the two men than Kate; she'd considered Steve Ratoff a darling even after he'd been exposed as a flaming fairy. And, even now, Margo began to steam when Moss came into the room. It would not have surprised him. . . . But no! Margo had some inhibition.

Whatever, Margo had talked Kate into it twice. The first time, for the "white" wedding, the Darktowers, still married then, had thrown the event of the year right here, on his lawn. Darktower had had his doubts but he'd gone along, like a good father, the good husband that he'd been.

Conrad, he'd been no more than ten years old then, Darktower morosely remembered, at the most formative age. And soon enough afterwards, too soon, Margo had gone her own way. Ratoff, strangely, not so strangely, that was the trouble, had treated Conrad almost like his own son, Kate's little brother. For a time, that had been a close-knit family and he, Darktower, had been none the wiser until Ratoff's outrageous behavior at the Princeton Club had scared the daylights out of everybody and served to write his ticket back to his bankrupt continent.

Then that horse-dung Erik Moss had jumped out of the scenery. He was not the sort to let a good thing pass him by. He'd met the Darktower heiress in Paris, having already earned his reputation as an international playboy and, so Darktower's European friends hinted, pimp for that international son of a bitch Jim Merriwether. Merriwether had such a reputation for ruthlessness that his competition pulled down the blinds and headed for the cellar when he headed their way. What had happened between Moss and Merriwether, Darktower didn't know and he had never asked. The one thing he would have liked to know was whether Moss had retained any clout with Merriwether—that was the only ticklish factor in the present situation.

For it was certain to Darktower that everything was wrong between Katharine and the Kraut. He was sure it was only a matter of time. And, as always, Darktower would wait it out. He was devoted to Kate, to the grandchild. To Conrad.

Having assured himself that the world was still somewhat in order, Darktower went in the kitchen door, climbed out of his duffel coat, parking it and his tweed hat on a hook behind the outside door.

"Now I'll have the coffee you mentioned," he told his matronly housekeeper Mrs. Glascock, "and read the paper."

Mrs. Glascock was a woman of snappy energy and if anyone had asked you where she came from, you'd quickly say, "Down East." Her legs were like sticks and her arms bony too but she moved through the house like lightning. Not that there was so much to do. Being alone, Darktower lived between bedroom and the downstairs sunporch, which was his library; by nature, he was an orderly man.

He was stuffing his feet into woolly slippers and collecting the morning's *New York Times* and *Wall Street Journal* off the kitchen table when Mrs. Glascock asked him the question which could not have served him better.

"Mr. Darktower, would you mind if I leave you for a couple of weeks?"

"How's that, Mrs. Glascock?"

She smiled proudly. "My daughter, the one in Florida, wants me to come down for a few days. She's having another baby, you see, and she said I could use some sunshine after our winter. She's sent me the ticket."

"Ah! Wonderful . . . for you. By all means, go! I can take care of myself. I know how to boil water."

"You wouldn't be annoyed with me?"

"Far from it."

"All right then. I'd be going on Friday." Today was Wednesday. Fine. "Oh," Mrs. Glascock exclaimed, "I shouldn't forget to tell you—*your* daughter called again while you were out.''

"Ah . . . daughters. God bless them!''

Smiling broadly, Darktower went into his library and opened his desk. The card she had given him was on top of his pile of things to do. Clara Riding. Yes. First he had to call Kate. The husky, heavy voice that answered in New York was that of their nursemaid, Helen Ryan.

"Richard Darktower, Helen. Mrs. Moss there?''

Kate sounded worried, busy, impatient. He reminded her that she'd called him.

"Oh, yes, I did.'' Her voice was cautious. Off phone, he heard her say, "Helen, just close the door.'' She was breathing hard when she came back to him.

"What's wrong?'' Darktower demanded.

"*Nothing,* nothing. I called to tell you I'll be driving out your way later today. Can I stop by?''

"Well, of course! You don't have to call.''

"We'll be there between three-thirty and four. Is that okay?''

"Didn't I say so? Who's we? Is Erik going to be with you?''

"No.'' He's already in Port London, working on the Smithers House with Dolly.''

"Christ!'' he grunted. "That goddamn house. You'd think it was the only tumble-down shack they ever built in Port London . . . Kate, is there *anything* wrong?'' He remembered what he'd been thinking.

"No, no! Everything is *right,*'' she said. She sounded so excited. "I'll see you this afternoon, Daddy!''

Hanging up, Darktower drummed his fingers on the desk. They were still a little stiff from the cold. God, when would he be granted the luxury of not worrying about his daughter?

Mrs. Glascock delivered him his coffee in a big mug— his only coffee of the day according to his own strict regimen and therefore beautifully presented—and headed for her appointed rounds upstairs. Only then did Darktower dial the New Jersey number.

A bell-like voice answered the ring. "Good morning." Such a cheerful greeting.

"Could I speak to Miss Clara Riding?"

"This is she, speaking."

Darktower laughed nervously but there was no backing out now. "I have your card here. My name is Richard Darktower. We . . . uh . . . met one night in New York."

"I'm afraid I don't recall," Miss Clara Riding cautiously replied.

Of course, she would be careful. One couldn't afford not to be, not if one were a clairvoyant of note.

"Well, I can refresh your memory." He paused. "In fact, it turned out to be an unfortunate evening. A death occurred."

"Oh, my God," she cried softly. "I had a premonition that day something bad was going to happen. I had another premonition not twenty-four hours ago that I'd be hearing more about it. Am I needed?"

"Yes, in a way. . . ."

"I knew we had made a terrible blunder, leaving those . . . paraphernalia . . . behind. You must understand— Gloria and I, we were so flustered."

"I understand perfectly," he said, "and anyway, that's all water under the bridge, as we say."

Her voice was timid. "There's no trouble then?"

"Oh, no. I called to ask you something."

"Ask away," she said happily, "Mr. . . . Darktower, isn't it?"

"Yes," he grunted. "I live out on the Island mostly. I can't remember if I told you that. An hour or so out of New York."

"How nice."

"Do you . . . ever . . . uh . . . come this far afield?"

"Long Island?" She sounded startled. "Well, I've been there, but not recently."

Boldly, he made his proposition. "Would you like to come?"

"Oh!" He could see her pudgy lips round in surprise. "Maybe . . . I don't understand. It's quite a distance and neither Gloria or I drive."

"But you could come by train, or bus. I'd mean it to be for more than a day—I was thinking in terms of a week or so."

"A whole week. I don't know. Our repertory is rather limited."

Swiftly, Darktower cut in. "I wasn't thinking of Gloria—just you. The house is actually quite small, you see."

"Heavens! I don't know what to say. I'm *very* flattered."

He pressed her. "You could consider it a vacation." He heard Mrs. Glascock on the stairs coming down. Hastily, he proposed, "You could take the Long Island train to Rockaway and I'd pick you up. I'd take care of the ticket, naturally. Think about it, Miss Riding. Here, I'll give you my number." He did so before she could make any objections. "Do you have that now?"

"Yes . . . all right, I will consider it," she said thoughtfully. "I'll call you back, later this afternoon."

He smiled in the direction of New Jersey. "Please say yes. I think you'd enjoy it."

Her laughter tinkled.

Darktower hung up just as Mrs. Glascock came into the room with the coffee pot. "Would you care for another *cuppa*?"

"Yes, thank you," he said jovially. "I think today I will."

He moved himself, coffee and newspapers to his comfortable chintz-covered armchair by the window, a window securely glazed against draft, and hooked his reading glasses over his nose. Before he started on the *Times,* he looked outside and goddamn if it didn't look like bad weather on the way again. He made sure to tell Mrs. Glascock she was certainly lucky to be heading south and, by God, she better hadn't change her mind.

"No fear," she sniffed, glaring at the darkened meadows. "March . . . in like a lion and out like a lamb. Not this year. This year it was in like a lamb and here it goes out like a lion. We're going to get another heavy snow. I should say *you* are. I'll be gone."

*   *   *

Mrs. Glascock made a platter of sandwiches before she left at two and, having finished the newspapers, Richard Darktower sat quietly watching the worsening weather and waiting for his daughter. The first snow flurries began at two-thirty; at three, relishing the deafening quiet of the impending storm, he went to the drinks cabinet and poured himself a Scotch, which he took neat. By now, a half-inch of fluffy snow covered the ground. Hopefully, the roses would not be frost-damaged, for it wasn't that cold. The temperature hovered on the border between snow and rain, in this changeable sea climate.

His thoughts quickly fled to New Jersey and Miss Clara Riding. The more he thought of her, the more svelte she became in his mind. That night, with Lee, he'd merely been thinking fat. No, quite possibly, Miss Clara was not fat at all. It was the big breasts that induced one to think of her as fat all over. Her face—so pleasant, he remembered— nicely creased with pleasure lines, the small mouth and lips that were so soft. The tongue he remembered best, of course, broad like a shoe horn. He wondered how they would get on here, in the quiet of the countryside, just he and she. For some reason, Darktower assumed she was an intellectual of sorts, that she read weighty books and loved to listen to broadcasts from the Metropolitan Opera.

Well, they would just have to see what transpired. He was not legally bound to her. If they didn't jell, zip, off she went, back to New Jersey. Wash the hands, and that was the end of it. He thought to himself, complacently, that never again would he commit himself in a binding, legal way.

Look at Kate, he thought grimly. Bound to Erik Moss, the bastard, working on his project with Dolly Percy. Oh, yes! Some project. Dolly Percy was a virulent little tart. He remembered her as a bright and spritely little girl, then as a pubescent, teasing creature and, if he'd been a nasty middle-aged man, she would have been the very little baggage he would have enticed into illegal embrace. Now, in her later thirties, Dolly Percy was more open in her pursuit of men. Poor Harrison Percy—something to do with the Securities and Exchange Commission—that's how it had ended for him. Percy had been indicted and convicted but he had chosen merciful death as the best alternative to a stretch in Sing-Sing.

Percy had departed quickly and with little fuss. Dolly, seemingly, had been untouched financially, her money being separate from his. But he wondered how much of a shove Dolly had given poor Percy, cruelly, unknowingly, toward embezzlement and malfeasance and mismanagement of trust accounts, and how much, therefore, his death tainted her in ways other than financial.

Like Darktower, Dolly seldom went into New York; she preferred a smaller pond, although there was no way her activities could be kept quiet there. Darktower gathered she was by now considered by many of the dowagers to be the scarlet woman of Port London.

He was moodily staring at the golden Scotch in its Baccarat glass when he heard the choking, muffled sound of a car in his driveway. Waving, Kate climbed out of the passenger side of a black Cadillac. Whoever was doing the driving cut the motor. The other door opened and a tall man wearing a floppy fedora hesitantly circled the car.

"Daddy!" Kate flung herself across the snowy gravel and into his arms. But Darktower was watching the tall stranger, noting, as he came closer, the big-featured face, the wire-framed glasses. "Daddy, I want you to meet Gene Francotti!" She laughed so excitedly and Darktower thus became aware that what he had expected to happen eventually was already in progress. "Gene is driving me to Port London."

"Gene" glanced at her, his face impassive. Was Darktower to assume the man she so enthusiastically introduced was somebody's chauffeur? Hardly, despite the Italian name. He was holding an expensive overcoat on his arm. No, no chauffeur.

"How do you do, Mr. Darktower?"

Darktower took the hand, felt its toughness, calluses, strength, all in that single grip. "Hello." There was something new in Katharine's expression. Maybe not new, exactly, but certainly unusual. He realized numbly that she was in love. Again! Good God! And, once more, Richard

Darktower was prohibited the opportunity to offer his judgment in advance of the fait accompli.

Leaving coats, hat, on the chair by the front door, Darktower led them into his library. As Kate flopped on the bright-colored sofa facing the fireplace, Darktower occupied his confused thoughts for a moment in pumping up the flames. He noticed that Francotti, in the most natural manner possible, sat down beside her.

"Well, then," Darktower mumbled, "you made it. What about a drink?" Francotti shrugged, neither yes nor no, and Kate, for once, didn't seem interested.

She was waiting to explain: "Gene has a job to do on a boat and he invited me to drive out with him. It seemed a convenient thing to do."

Darktower nodded tensely. "What sort of job is that?" He knew she was telling a lie; there was more to it than that. Boat? Francotti was more likely a Mafia hit-man or spaghetti salesman. With a name like that, what else?

Francotti stared at him so levelly that Darktower retracted his suspicion. "I'm an engine man. I've got to take a look at a boat there, in dry dock."

Joyfully, Kate declared, for his information, "Gene is an inventor. He invents marine engines."

"No, no," her friend said modestly. "Mainly, I fix engines."

"You're an inventor and don't try to deny it!"

Wryly, Darktower murmured, "We're having trouble with the vacuum cleaner. I wonder. . . ."

"Daddy!"

Francotti chuckled appreciatively. He was a wary creature, Darktower judged. "Your daughter exaggerates, Mr. Darktower. She shouldn't try to make me more than I am. I'm a grease monkey, that's about it."

Darktower spoke to Francotti directly. "No. If Kate decides you're an inventor, then, by George, that's what you are."

She frowned at him. "What my father is saying is: What Kate wants, Kate gets. Not especially true these days, though, is it, Daddy?"

He did not move away from the fire. "You do pretty

well, my dear. Well . . . you must be hungry. We have sandwiches. I'll open a bottle of Bordeaux. How does that sound?''

''Wonderful,'' Francotti grunted. ''I'll give you a hand.''

''All right.'' Darktower took the platter of sandwiches Mrs. Glascock had prepared out of the refrigerator and set it on the table. He kept a modest wine-cellar in one of the kitchen cabinets and from there he selected a Bordeaux, handed it wordlessly to Francotti along with a corkscrew. While Francotti very deliberately peeled the foil off the top of the bottle, then meticulously inserted the curl of corkscrew, Darktower assembled the rest of the makings of the snack.

Still, they did not speak. The cork exited the bottle with a healthy pop and Francotti put it to his generous nose. ''Smells okay to me.''

''It's okay,'' Darktower told him. ''There.'' Everything was on the tray. He glanced at Francotti and was somewhat surprised to see the man's amused smile.

Very quietly, so Kate could not hear in the next room, Francotti said, ''You're thinking. . . .''

Darktower nodded coolly. ''I surely am. Shall we. . . .'' He motioned with his head for Francotti to lead the way.

He put the tray with the sandwiches, plates, mustard, relish and all on the coffee table in front of her. ''Do the honors, Kate.''

''All right.'' She asked them which sort of sandwich they wanted, put it on the plate with mustard or whatever, and passed the plates around.

Darktower was touched. Whatever this man Francotti was, he seemed good for her. She looked like her old self, ten years younger, her smooth face clear and untroubled. Appreciatively, he studied her long legs, always so nimble and quick, the comfortable waist, neat bosom, the full throat, blonde hair that invited stroking. She appeared now so placid, at peace with the world.

Darktower knew instinctively—the fat was in the fire. It was already beyond him. What was he called upon to do next? Ask that question? Sir, are your intentions honorable?

Francotti beat him to it. "I'd better explain myself a little, Mr. Darktower," he said flatly. "You see, your daughter and I have developed a . . . relationship."

"I've already figured that out for myself."

Katharine gasped a laugh. "We're in love, Daddy."

Francotti moved his head reprovingly. "We *think* we're in love, sir. I should know better and it's against my better judgment."

"Why's that?" Darktower demanded. "There's nothing wrong with this girl that the right man couldn't cure."

"I'm getting a divorce," Katharine announced.

Darktower nodded sardonically. "That seems in order, in view of what you say. Does Moss know yet?"

"Not yet. But he will. I'm going to tell him today," she pledged, her eyes on Francotti.

"Are *you* sure of this?" he asked Francotti.

"As sure as I can be *now*. I almost cancelled her out."

She chuckled thrillingly. "He got mad at me. I invited him to a cocktail party—Erik and Stefan Ratoff were *both* there. Gene was *very* mad. He doesn't like people to play tricks on him."

Darktower nodded. "I can sympathize with that."

"He wouldn't see me for two weeks, then I called him. I have no shame."

Francotti made a gesture which told her to stop. Again, he turned to Darktower, and frankly said, "I want to clear the decks. I gather you get very nervous when it comes to your daughter's money. Well, I don't need her money and I don't want it. I have a thriving practice as an engine doctor."

Darktower responded with a frosty smile. "I'm not looking into your financial affairs."

"No, but you probably will," Francotti said, and of course he was right about that. "I want everything understood right now."

"What about Margaret?" Darktower demanded.

"We'll make whatever arrangements are necessary. Erik won't argue."

"He worships that child," Darktower reminded her.

Katharine shrugged. "I'll get custody."

Darktower nodded doubtfully. "Probably—but a divorce may not be without problems. You realize that, don't you?"

"Maybe," she said determinedly, "but I'm going to do it. I want my life back."

Later, the snow began blowing and drifting against the house and it became evident the drive to the main road was blocked. It was decided, with welcome, mature logic, that Kate and Francotti would stay the night. Later still, as naturally as if they'd been married a dozen years, Kate took Francotti's hand and led him upstairs. Richard Darktower was left with his brandy before the wintry fire. What should he have done? Forbid them this? Hardly. A few months before, he might have felt differently about everything.

But now Richard Darktower was not in a prudish mood.

Twelve

"I'm thinking the chances are I'll end up marrying Marco Fortuna," Dolly Percy muttered drearily, "lacking any better solution to my widowhood."

"My darling, of course you can't! The man is. . . ."

"What? A fag? A fortune-hunter? What difference can that make? He'd be a good companion."

"If you take him," Erik said stonily, "you buy the package, Marco *and* Stefan Ratoff."

Dolly moved her head against his shoulder, caressing with her hair. "I'll take Marco . . . and throw Steve back in the water."

"You can't be serious." But he understood what Dolly was trying to do. She was inciting him to a promise he could not make. She wanted him to leave Kathy and he couldn't, not yet.

"I am serious," she said tensely, "absolutely serious. After all, this, as pleasant as it is, isn't getting me anywhere. You're not going to leave Kitty. You can't afford to."

He absorbed the remark indifferently, then yawned. "I can *afford* to do anything I wish. But it's problematic, don't you see—what would happen to my child?"

"Why should that be a problem? You'd see her. After all, we're civilized, aren't we?"

"Oh, yes," he said sarcastically, "so very civilized." He jumped back to the matter of Marco Fortuna. "So, did you become engaged to Marco last week when they were here?"

"In a manner of speaking," she chortled.

Erik groaned elaborately. "You are more decadent than any of us Europeans. How can you make me suffer so?"

"Jealous, are you? Good."

Erik turned his head to kiss her flushed cheek. Under the silk sheets, her soft body was warm as a furnace. He put his hand to her emboldened breasts, nuzzled the nipples so red and serrated with hardness. Her ivory-toned body was always so taut, ready, her sensuality shattering. A man had to be strong, a man needed stamina to match lust with Dolly Percy.

She murmured appreciatively as he handled her, "Ah, you see," she moaned, half of her abandoned already to ecstasy, "whomever I married, it would never interfere with . . . this."

"But it's foolish," he protested, increasing the pressures of his fingers.

"I can afford to be foolish." She scratched at his chest and belly, her hips rocking, thighs trembling. Erik ran his right hand down the length of her to the tips of her toes, squeezing the big toe at the place determined to be the lowest passion point, then kneading her upwards. Breathing fiercely through inflamed lips, she gripped him with both hands. "I can afford you too," she muttered feverishly. "This endowment, like the whole faculty of a university. Shall I eat you up now?"

"Yes, a little please."

She swung around quickly, roughly, butting him with her head and fixing her soft lips on his engorgement, chewing him thoughtfully. For his part, Erik kissed her thighs and moved his mouth to the center of her being. Whatever had transpired, Dolly still managed to smell of the great outdoors. With the tip of his tongue, he parted the velvety lips of her vagina and carefully searched for the center of the universe. Her mouth jerked on him when he found it and she whimpered. "Oh, God, I'll come!" She did, abruptly, her thighs thumping his head desperately. But this was only the preliminary. Muttering to herself, she reversed position, rolled him over her and pulled him quickly inside her, puffing hoarsely and trapping him in her legs. "Oh, yes, God! Fast . . . fast!"

She kicked the covers back, letting the chill air upon them. Arms stiffly at her sides, merely the pelvis gyrating at him, her ripe lips parted and she panted. Erik held back expertly, waiting for the levels of excitement to merge, then as she began to crest again, he let himself go, at the same time rolling her pouty white breasts.

"*Gott!*" he gasped gutturally. They always enjoyed hearing a few German exclamations at the time of orgasm. It made the whole thing, somehow, seem more legitimate.

Dolly cried out, as if in pain, a strangled groan. "Christ, I can feel it, all through me!"

He continued, still fully extended within her, sensing the return of his erection. This was his god-given ability. He could go on forever and they all loved him for it. This was his reputation, his career, his ambition, his life. Crazy thoughts ran through his head. His million, yes, he deserved it. He kept at Dolly, aware that her nerves were jangling. Soon, he would deliver himself of the second coming—that pleased them beyond all else, making them think they were so desirable and wonderful doing it that they could make the stud of all time come, and come again, and again. Few men were capable of it. A seventeen-year-old, yes, once in a while, but it was unusual in a man of forty-five. Cruelty went with it, a pinch of sadism. He was hurting her now and she declined into stifled sobs of pain and joy. Stretched flat, pushing her down, he felt her body go slack.

"Oh, darling, I'll die. Please. . . ." A smile of painful pleasure gorged her face. He felt the thumping of her heart against his chest as he ripped her apart with his strength. Yes, some day, one of them *could* die of it. But such a thing, he knew realistically, could never happen. However mighty the master, she, Woman, had the greater power of recuperation and rebirthing of desire. In the end, they were always the conquerors, as submissive as they might seem to be.

Her final lunge was desperate. She wailed as he released himself again, muttering anger in her ear. "*Gott! Donnerwetter!*"

"I quit! Enough, man, enough!" Her voice was almost inaudible.

"My darling, *Dolly–chen*. . . ." He gently bit her ear lobe. The postcoital tenderness was very important to them. "*Herzchen . . .* my own little heart."

"Yes," she muttered petulantly, "like that—you're better at this than anyone. And I love it most. So why don't you come with me? You have to make the break, goddamn it!"

"*But I cannot. . . .*"

"You're so goddamned honorable! What about Kitty? Does she love it at all?"

He shifted uneasily. "Every woman is different, as you know, just as is every man."

"Bullshit," she grunted crudely. "I know she doesn't like it as much as me."

Erik shrugged. "True," he admitted. "I will tell you she doesn't find much joy in lovemaking anymore."

"You mean . . . what?"

He was embarrassed by the question. "We . . . I . . . at times, she has told me she does not care what I do, so long as I am discreet."

"Christ! She's told you to go get it outside—is that it?"

Glumly, he stared into her eyes. "*C'est ca, herzchen.*"

She was instantly all over him, covering his chest with little kisses. "You poor darling. What the hell could be wrong with her? Don't you see? It's an invitation. Leave her, darling!"

"I cannot."

"Jesus!" she snorted in disgust. "Then, I promise you I'll marry Marco Shitface and take off to Europe with him and fuck everything that moves! You'll never get another shot at this candy box and that's that." She pounded his chest with her fist. "You'll be good and sorry, darling!"

"I know I will," he said soberly. He reached for cigarette, lighter and ashtray on the bedside table. In a moment, drawing in smoke, he murmured, "We've always gotten along so well. Whatever happens, do not be angry with me. I must do what I have to do."

"Then do it and be damned," she grunted, her face

turned to the mattress. One steady downward push, he thought, thirty or forty seconds, and she would be out of her misery. "How come you're here anyway? I thought Kitty was coming up from the city today."

"She was delayed by the snow."

"Well," Dolly said nastily, rolling over to stare at him discontentedly, "you'd better get going. She's probably there by now, your sweet little wife."

"Dolly, *please* don't be angry. You know that I love you very much."

"Huh! Love! An easy word, meaningless."

"Please. . . ."

"Bull," she snorted. "I know you don't love me. You just adore my ass and the fact I'm in the top ten." She smiled acridly. "*Say* I'm a good lay, darling."

Erik smiled patiently. Women! How he adored and despised them. "You are the best possible lay. You are a marvel, your every movement a concerto, every twitch and tingle of your muscles and nerves a whole sonata. I can feel you to my backbone and backbone to brain."

She tittered, her lowdown laugh. "The pliant little snatch, firm and snug around your great long jolly roger."

"Exactly." He sighed. "Such a connection."

Dolly closed her eyes wistfully. "A merger," she whispered. "That's what Harrison always said: such a merger. Two asses in tango-time."

"So it often seems," Erik agreed.

"Yes." Now she glared at him maliciously. "But you're odd man out."

"My darling. . . ."

"*My darling*," she mocked. "I ought to reach down there and tear it right off. How would you like that?"

"I wouldn't, not in the least," he said stoically. "My life would be ended."

"Tell me something," she asked sourly. "Did you work as a gigolo in Europe? Is that how you learned your trade?"

He laughed patiently. "You know otherwise."

"No, I really don't. All I know is what you've told me."

"Or what Kathy has told you."

"Hell, *she* doesn't know anything about you either," Dolly snapped.

"She does!" he said stiffly. "All there is to know. A child of the war, displaced from his homeland, adrift on the winds of change, tossed in the turbulence of the century. And here now, in my place of refuge, so grateful."

Dolly made a facetious face and pointed at her center. "There's your place of refuge, right there."

"A sweet harbor, yes."

"Yes. Yes." she whispered, then dolefully added, "Well, you'd better go. If I'm not going to be damned for an adulteress all the way, then there's no sense in getting caught halfway."

"I will say good night," Erik murmured regretfully.

Dolly sat up on the edge of the bed. "At least, don't forget we've got to talk seriously tomorrow about the project. By the way," she said, "did you read in all the background material that during the war the Smithers dump was a whorehouse?"

"I did not see that." He chuckled, tucking his arm around her bare waist, inclining his head to kiss her shoulder. "Old houses have their own histories, like people, their good times and their bad times."

"Yes." She was unimpressed by the dialectical argument. "Then, after that, for a while it was a funeral parlor."

"No!" He pulled her closer. "Why, my darling, that is wonderful. Such irony—from the act of procreation to death, all in one house."

Dolly shivered against him. "Not so wonderful to me. Walking through there now I'll imagine the smell of dead people."

"Like the stench of rats, even though long gone," Erik recalled.

"Jesus!" She jumped up. "That's disgusting too. Come on, I'll walk downstairs with you."

"Not necessary," he said.

But she paid no heed. She ran water in the bathroom for a moment, then came out wearing a sweater and pair of slacks. "You're ready?"

Quietly, they walked down the steps to the main hall. Dolly put her fingertip across her lips. It was only nine P.M. and the Donovans, her couple, would still be up, though dozing in front of the TV. She opened the front door and stepped outside with him on the flagstones of the driveway.

"My darling," Erik protested, "your feet are bare. You'll catch your death."

"I love the feeling of cold." Oblivious of the ice and frost, of new snow still drifting down on a light wind, she put her hand in his arm. "I'll walk you as far as the end of the drive and then run back."

"But you cannot—you'll freeze."

"I tell you, I won't!" Laughing, she let go of his arm and pranced ahead of him, lifting her feet high, gasping at the coldness.

Erik followed her quickly, cursing to himself. Dolly was trying to prove something to him that didn't need proving. He already knew she was headstrong, childish, impulsive. All these women were childish to an astonishing degree—Kathy, Dolly, Margo, all the women of their silver-spooned circle.

When she was ten yards ahead of him, Dolly darted off to the side toward a clump of pines, their branches dropping beneath the weight of ice and snow. Softly, she called, "Erik... . Er–ik. . . ." Hating it, he stepped off the firmness of the driveway into the wet mush. When he caught up, Dolly was under an umbrella of pine branches, standing, shaking. Sweater and slacks lay beside her, in the snow.

"Please," Erik said sternly, "this is silly!"

"No, no! If I have to be cold as death to possess you, then I'll be cold!" Daringly, she lowered herself into the snow.

"When have I suggested such a thing?" he demanded angrily. "I will not! Get up—at once!"

But she only giggled mockingly. "It's soft."

"Dolly! I insist! Get up!"

She laughed like a fiend. "I'm in cold storage!" She

challenged him, humping her hips toward him. "You could put it in cold storage and keep it for hot days."

"You are a little fool!"

"Take off your pants," she cried, "or I'll scream!"

"*I* will not," he said stubbornly.

"Just unzip, if you're so afraid, and come aboard."

"This is the most stupid thing I've ever heard of," he grumbled. Nonetheless, he knelt between her legs.

Dolly fumbled with his trouser front. Her hands were icy. "You're hard! Come on! Tell me if this is what you've been wanting."

Her thighs were cold too but inside she pulsed with heat.

"This is weird," Dolly exclaimed. "Oh, my God." He could not stop her from crying out loudly, not caring that her voice would surely carry to the main road and a passerby would think that, hidden in the forest, a bobcat was mating with a mountain lion. The snow melted under her and she was drenched in perspiration and wetness, shaking in her anguish, teeth chattering. Aroused by her excitement, Erik ground down on her. Dolly climaxed suddenly, loosing a scream that pierced the silence. Erik pulled quickly away.

"There, now," he said grimly. "I'll carry you back to the house."

"You'll have to," she moaned, shivering. "I can feel icicles on my ass."

"Dolly, what am I to do with you?"

"Nothing," she muttered. "Let me get my pants on."

Erik adjusted his clothing and, when she was ready, lifted her and carried her back to the driveway and toward the house. She clung to him, her arms around his neck, her face very cold. She was crying, but laughing at the same time.

"Now, tell me," she whispered in his ear, "do I possess you?"

"Yes, yes," he said. "But you really are mad."

He opened the front door and, treading lightly, bore her light body back up the curving staircase to her bedroom.

He set about massaging warmth back into her frozen feet.

"My toes are numb, darling . . . and my ass. It's quite numb with the cold."

"I'm not surprised," he said stiffly. "You'd best take a very hot bath."

"Will you run the water?" she asked forlornly. "Don't leave poor me, Erik." When he returned, she moaned, "You won't. . . ."

"No," he muttered. "You're a little fool."

Tears came to her eyes and she allowed herself to tremble convulsively. "Erik, don't hate me. I promise I'll be good. I love you so much and you don't give a damn for me."

"Stop talking like that! You are not amusing."

"You don't love me," she bawled.

He didn't answer. He picked her up again and carried her into the tub. She gasped. It was as hot as he could reasonably make it; her body blotched red spots with the heat. Erik reached into the water for her toes.

"Can you feel them now?"

Dolly sighed. "Yes, thank you ever so . . . but you *don't* love me."

He felt like slapping her. "Am I bound to love you just because you pull a foolish stunt like this?"

"*I did it for you.*" Her eyes were so wide, so innocent, yet they seemed to sparkle with mockery, maybe worse.

Erik smiled at her from over a great distance. He cupped her firm, round chin in his thumb and forefinger, twisted her head sharply on her spinal column. "Not for me," he drawled. "You did it for yourself."

"No! I did it because I get hysterical just thinking about you. What must I do to have you?"

"Behave like a sensible human being."

"And if I do, will you come with me?"

Irritably, he said, "You know I'm in no position to promise anything, not now."

"Shall I give you money?"

He tapped her lightly on the cheek with his fingertips.

Money. Why did it always come down to money? Money, yes, he loved it but there were things one did not do in order to have money.

"I'll give you money," Dolly said slyly, "because we're friends. Not to buy you—I *know* I couldn't buy you." He merely looked at her, watched her lips move, her face change expression, grow petulant again as he did not answer. Casually, she splashed water at him. "Goddamn it, we could have such fun!"

"Yes. Possibly," he agreed glumly.

"Then why be so goddamn gloomy all the time?"

He smiled wearily at her. "See—you are already criticizing me for being gloomy."

Fiercely, Dolly growled, "You're that way because of *her*. She's such a goddamn depressing woman!"

Soberly, he nodded. "She is not a happy person. Sometimes, she is a trial."

"There! You admit it! A few days ago, you wouldn't even talk to me about her."

"We're friends," he explained simply.

"More! I just froze my snatch to a pudding for you. I'd do *anything* for you."

"Please. Don't embarrass me. I am not worth it."

"Oh. . . ." Dolly expelled a frustrated burst of air. "I see. The fact is you're not capable of loving. Isn't that it?"

He smiled sadly. "Love is such an illusory thing."

"Not to me, it's not," Dolly snarled. "I'm all for it. I believe in it. But not you. You can't love—or won't!"

"No," he said sharply.

"Well, then?"

"I . . . yearn for love."

Dolly thrashed impatiently in the water, her body temperature now well back toward normal. "I'm getting out," she said. "I've had it." He offered his hand, then wrapped her in a giant white towel and rubbed her vigorously, her buttocks, her limp breasts. Dolly closed her eyes and moaned tremulously.

"Darling, please stay. Can you? Please stay with me tonight. You don't have to go home."

''No.'' He realized he did not have to. Even if Kathy had finally reached Port London in this snowstorm, what difference would it make? She wouldn't know or care whether he'd arrived. Why shouldn't he begin to make the break? Dolly was very possessive, yes, to an extreme, but perhaps it was not so bad to be possessed.

Thirteen

Erik left Dolly's side at six the next morning. He washed and dressed and, ready to leave the house, sat down next to her on the bed. Dolly emerged from a deep sleep as he put his face next to her ear, drawing in her musky scent. *Sans* make-up, perfume, all the trappings of great beauty— her face was childlike in its innocence, a sleepy smile lighting her cheeks. The contradictions in Dolly were forceful enough to make him wince.

She turned with a wide yawn and held her arms up to him, drawing his head down for a kiss. "Now, I know you're mine, you great long pecker-face." She chuckled softly, feeling his mouth tense. "A quickie before you go?"

All he could do was murmur, "Hertzchen. . . ."

"I know, I know," she grumbled pettishly, "image, image. I am going to see you later. And maybe Kitty will be delayed again."

"Later, yes," he agreed. There was to be a lecture that afternoon at the Heritage Assembly's headquarters and all members had promised to attend.

"Darling," she asked in a tiny voice, "didn't I make you happy last night? Aren't I accomplished?" Her lips parted in a faint, self-assured smile, and she ran her tongue over her dry lips. "Did I thrill you with my mouth?"

"Oh, my darling. . . ."

"When will you tell her?"

"Soon," he lied.

She said simply, "I'm counting on you."

"Then Marco Fortuna is on the back burner?" he asked, as if playfully.

"Of course! Marco isn't up to this. He doesn't have the stamina."

Erik frowned at her. "Yes, I forgot. You gave yourself to him, didn't you?"

Her face assumed a babyish pout. "Well, you'll admit I have to exercise all my options . . . as Harrison used to say."

Very casually, Erik laid his hand on her smooth throat. He knew his eyes were as expressionless as closed windows. "I am a very possessive and jealous man."

Dolly smiled at him, then giggled. "I'm possessive too."

"You know," he muttered blackly, "it's not beyond me to kill."

"Me too," Dolly hissed sweetly. "I catch you with anybody else, I'll scalp you and cut your nuts off."

He relaxed his hand, patted her cheek. "I must go."

Dolly went back to sleep even as he stood there watching her, the coy little smile still on her lips.

Erik slid out the front door and back into the snow, making no sound. Their footprints from the night before were obliterated. He marched confidently through the gate at the end of Dolly's property and picked up his stride. It was a mile down the road to Maples. Snow still fell as lightly as dust and he was quite alone. Even the trucks wouldn't be out until later to sand the roads. The morning was misty and he remembered the foggy plains of Northern Germany, farm animals wreathed in breath fumes, warmly bundled men going about their morning work and the uniformed overseers on their horses with whips, the sound of hoarse, crude voices breaking the freezing cold.

Despite these nightmarish memories, those horrendous mental landscapes after the manner of Hieronymus Bosch, Erik's step became lighter. It was good to be alone in a peaceful place, in the early morning. Life was under control. Dolly was mad . . . insane . . . for him and, to a lesser degree, Kathy was tamed; but she had become so elusive he could not be sure of her any longer. Perhaps he should do as Dolly wished: make the break and take his chances with Richard Darktower.

It was nearly seven by the time he reached Maples. Their housekeeper, Mrs. Rogers, was up and about. He was knocking the snow off his feet as she opened the front door.

"My sakes, Mr. Moss, you're up early."

"I couldn't sleep, Mrs. Rogers. I went out for a walk."

"And it's still snowing," she observed, with displeasure. "I thought we were done with the snow for this year."

Erik shrugged resignation. "Evidently not." He was struck anew by the pointlessness of discussing the weather and the fact it was the central thread of most Port London conversations . . . raining out there, yep . . . looks like rain, sure does . . . it's really comin' down, ain't it? Up to our ass in snow, ain't we?

"I guess Mrs. Moss is really snowbound," Mrs. Rogers muttered.

There was no sign of the car but, nevertheless, he could have had no way of knowing whether or not Kathy had arrived during the night.

"I'm sure the roads will be fine this morning," he murmured tactfully.

"Yes, for sure she'll be here in time for lunch, Mr. Moss."

Ah, so she hadn't arrived yet. "Probably," he said.

"Breakfast now, Mr. Moss?"

He told her bacon and eggs and coffee would be wonderful on such a morning as this, then wandered into the living room, which was light and airy even on such a murky morning. The sofas and armchairs were covered in cream-colored fabric, Eighteenth Century French antiques were positively ethereal in gleaming wax and with the horsey pictures on the dead white walls and the occasional piece of Chinese export porcelain, the ambiance was one of optimism, good faith and celebration of the world.

Erik picked up last evening's newspaper and proceeded

to the wide-windowed breakfast room next to the kitchen. He opened the paper and lit a cigarette. Nothing new, aside from the usual international tension, border skirmishes, detente crisis, worry about recession. Nothing gripping. It seemed Richard Darktower had provided the eastern seaboard with its last good scandal. Erik chuckled to himself. Darktower was such a hypocrite, the very image of breeding and grace; behind the image, however, lay a personality whose piratical potential nearly equalled that of his former employer James Merriwether.

How brutally Darktower had dealt with Stefan Ratoff, how ruthlessly he would deal with anyone who tampered with his family and good name. Mercilessly. This realization lent deep misgivings to Erik's half-hearted decision to say goodbye to Kathy and hello to Dolly.

It did not do to trifle with Richard Darktower. It amazed him even now that Darktower had apparently not run a minute check on the affairs and financial status of one Erik Moss. The only explanation was that Darktower had been so pleased to have Kathy free of Ratoff that he'd have accepted King Kong as husband number two.

Everyone, Erik reminded himself, had something in their past and so did he. His past dated to well before his employment by tycoon James Merriwether. It went back to the sordid war and post-war years in Germany when Erik had been no more than a boy. Remembering was nearly enough to give him a migraine headache. No, his mother had not been English, nor had he gone to an English school. His mother had been Austrian—like Hitler.

But Erik speaks such a perfect English, they said. Of course, he told himself scornfully, he had a gift for languages and he spoke French as well as he did German, and English as colloquially as both. His English could even have been accent-free but he cherished the accent—the accent was all the reminder he wanted of the past.

Goddamn it! He swore to himself in English and put out his cigarette as Mrs. Rogers appeared. Past *was* past, he would not dwell upon it because doing so made him gloomy, more than gloomy, morbid, so morbid that when he gave himself to it for more than a few moments at a time he was ready for suicide.

"Here's your breakfast, Mr. Moss," said Mrs. Rogers as he made no move to let her slide the tray in front of him.

"Oh, yes!" He glanced up and smiled. "Thank you."

"Still snowing out there," she mentioned, turning, placing her hands on her hips to stare with displeasure at the weather.

"It'll stop soon," he muttered. She *must* leave him alone. Get out, Mrs. Rogers. Get out of here!

"I'm going upstairs now," she said.

She would see that his bed had not been slept in. And he didn't care. How could it have been slept in, after all, if he'd spent the night in a chair in front of the fire in the living room?

Erik grinned to himself: a clever man had an answer for everything. *School in England?* Well, you know how it is, he hadn't actually stuck it long enough to graduate. *English mother?* Well, you know how it is, she was actually born in India. *The world is topsy-turvy?* Sure, you know how it is.

Erik ate his breakfast hurriedly, hardly tasting the food. Yes, it was that way. People were always slinging mud. Was it his fault that young Millicent Fairclough, sweet Millie, had jumped out of a window in Monte Carlo? Poor infatuated girl. Try telling that to Jim Merriwether.

With a last cup of coffee, Erik returned to the living room for another look at the paper.

In an hour, Mrs. Rogers was back downstairs. "Did you make your own bed this morning, Mr. Moss?" she asked inquisitively.

"No, oh, no. I didn't sleep in it, Mrs. Rogers." He presented her a tired smile. "I stayed downstairs too late last night, reading and I fell asleep. That's why I was up so early."

"Oh, Mr. Moss," she tutted, "you could catch your death doing that."

* * *

Katharine arrived practically on the dot of eleven. The car crunched in the driveway and stopped. The front door opened and he heard voices. The door closed and there was the sound of car retreating.

"My snowbound darling," Erik called from the living room.

Katharine walked in. She looked wonderful, cheeks flushed and rosy. But she paused indecisively. "Hello."

"Someone delivered you," Erik said.

Katharine nodded, her face set. "I drove up with Gene Francotti. You remember him—from Dolly's party."

"Oh, yes." He waited for more.

"I thought I might as well come with him as drive myself. He's doing another job at the boatyard."

"That was convenient, yes," Erik murmured. "But my dear," he joked clumsily, "what will the neighbors say, the two of you snowbound?"

She was unflustered by the hint. "We stopped at Daddy's in the afternoon, then got snowed in there."

"Oh, I see. That was convenient too."

"Erik. . . ." Katharine started on a new thought, then stopped.

"Yes? What is it?"

"I want a divorce."

Erik smiled broadly. "Ah, *that* is not quite so convenient, darling!"

Katharine advanced into the room and sat down tensely on the arm of one of the overstuffed chairs. "Convenient or not, I've decided. You and I. . . ." Again, she stopped.

He smiled, ever so patiently. "You and I what?"

"You know," she stumbled, falling over words, "it hasn't been good. I haven't been a good wife. I . . . well . . . I probably should have stayed with Stefan."

He registered shock. "On the contrary, you've been a *perfect* little wife."

"No, no!" She shook her head stubbornly. "Stop mocking. I'm a burden to everybody." He didn't try to answer. He stared at her, his head tilted to the side in fascination. "You know something is wrong. I'm uneasy, insecure," she went on, words tripping. "That's why I've been so nervous. You know it's true! Erik . . . you *do* know that's true. Let's part . . . before it's too late."

He said coldly, "What Kathy wants, Kathy gets."

Her eyes flattened. "All right, yes." She twisted her fingers in a handkerchief in her lap. "I know what I'm saying, Erik. This is my salvation. I want to *survive*."

"And you stopped at your father's for his approval of this rash move, isn't that so?"

"Not necessarily," she faltered. "I've not been a good mother either, because of the tension. I need to spend more time with Margaret. Seeing Stefan again reminded me how unhappy Conrad was in those years when. . . ."

"The prince," Erik interrupted. "The little prince, heir to all things Darktower, him whom we must all worship. Conrad, sniveling, sneering Hamlet."

"He's not bad," Katharine cried.

Erik crossed his arms and regarded her coldly. "Don't endeavor to fool me, darling," he said. *"Who is it?"*

She looked startled, even ashamed, he judged.

"Yes—the man you've fallen in love with. Don't talk to me about Prince Conrad. Is it Francotti? *Yes, it is,* I see that. You spent the night with him at your father's. I can't believe it—adultery under Richard Darktower's roof!" Erik loosed a searing laugh.

"We were trapped by the snow," Katharine exclaimed angrily. "I said we stayed there, not that we slept together. Don't jump to conclusions."

Calmly, he said, "I know you're lying. I also know that your father would confirm anything you chose to say. However, don't forget, my lily-white little darling, you were already having it off with me whilst still you were married to poor Stefan. So, you see, there is no reason for me to believe you are not cuckolding me with Mr. Francotti—well in advance of even a legal separation. Correct?"

Her face grew stonily distant, blue eyes uncommunicative. He hoped he was not miscalculating. As confused and neurotic as she was, she was still capable of terrible obstinacy, a wild horse to be brought back under the whip.

Tersely, she said, "Don't make everything sound so filthy."

"Confess you're in love with Francotti!"

"I don't know if I am or not. Don't push me."

Icily, Erik defined the situation. "It is *not* Stefan or Conrad or Margaret you're concerned about. It is yourself—as always."

"Goddamn you!" she cried in frustration. "I am worried about them, all of them. That's true! *And* I am concerned about myself too!"

As if he had rehearsed all morning for this moment, Erik very deliberately stood up. "I have the most awful headache. I did not sleep well last night out of worry. I must have a nap."

"Erik!" Her voice rose.

"My darling," he said soothingly, "I simply cannot discuss a thing like this now . . . if ever. I am totally shattered. Distraught. I must rest. This afternoon, remember, we have tickets for a lecture at Assembly House—at two."

"I'm not going."

"But you must, my darling. It's intended to be very interesting—on the subject of interior decorating in colonial and modern times."

"I'm not going!" she spat. "Why won't you discuss *this* with me now?"

"I told you, did I not, that I have a terrible headache?" He shot the barb. "You do understand what it is to have a headache, don't you?"

She scowled at him hatefully. "I don't intend to have any more headaches." She said it in such a way he knew it was supposed to have special significance.

"Oh? Wonderful. You will be very healthy. I am so pleased. In that case, as we've already agreed, there is no point in further discussion."

"I didn't agree to anything."

He stopped at the door and turned. Kathy's hands were pressed anxiously against her cheeks. She looked so attractively miserable, he thought. He hoped she *was* miserable. He would do his best to make her miserable. "Be ready at a quarter of two," he ordered curtly.

"No!"

"You must. I insist. We must keep up the pretense. You *will* come with me because you are my wife and will remain so." His teeth bared at the logic of his argument. "Besides, Dolly is looking forward to seeing you."

Fourteen

By the time she reached the Heritage Assembly's headquarters on Plymouth Avenue, Dolly Percy was feeling very pleased with the world. She had walked the mile and a half from her house, warmly dressed for the weather in thermal tights, tweed slacks, and a vicuna turtleneck beneath a rough Donegal hacking jacket. A wide-brimmed Irish fishing hat covered her sleek black hair and fur-lined gloves protected her fingers from the tingling, lovely cold.

Dolly kicked wet snow off her boots and went inside the big, old Victorian house that they had taken over some ten or fifteen years before, quite possibly the first property to come the assembly's way since it had accepted the task of preserving what was best of the Port London heritage, colonial and modern. Assembly House was now the focal point of many local activities and through its days served as lecture hall, picture gallery, bookstore, library and, among Port London's older set, a comfortable place in which to loiter.

The uneven oak-strip floor creaked under her boots as Dolly walked to the rickety table set up outside the bookstore section of the ground floor and helped herself to a cup of steaming tea.

Several of the assembly stalwarts were already there, those long-time Port London residents who enjoyed nothing on a snowbound Saturday afternoon as much as nodding through a lecture on their glorious past. It was so cozy, being part of tradition, gathering here to discuss what really mattered: restoration, preservation, acquisition, or groggily to listen to an expert come all the way from Boston or New York to assure them they were the custodians of American history.

Dolly nodded to Mrs. Boone, who was said to be descended from the family of famous Daniel, then to a distant cousin of the Cabots or the Lodges or both; to Mrs. Champlain, of the family of Samuel de Champlain, after whom the lake had been named. Dolly said hello and retreated. They were ancient stiffs, a caucus of gray old ladies, thin-faced old dowagers all, crouching in their woolies, huddling in their ratty furs, clattering their tea cups, chatting.

They didn't gossip, did they? They didn't have to; everything they knew was true. Dolly was aware of what they must say about her—she was the scarlet woman from New York City; she'd been chased out of Manhattan. She couldn't have cared any less. Ostentatiously, Dolly took a compact out of her soft leather shoulder bag, stroked it with her forefingers, then opened it to inspect her face in the mirror. Shamelessly, she treated herself to fresh lipstick. After all, ladies, she muttered to herself, don't want to get our lips chapped, do we?

As she was prettying herself, Dolly was overtaken by an unexpected *ka–choo*!

"Oh, Mrs. Percy!" Mrs. Boone cried, as if the roof had fallen in, "I knew when you came in you hadn't dressed warmly."

"No, no," Dolly said, "I'm fine."

"Cold coming on," said Mrs. Champlain dogmatically, "everyone in town's got a cold coming on."

But not you, Mrs. Champlain, Dolly advised herself spitefully, because a cold or the flu would take off like a bat out of hell when it got a look up your nose.

"No," Dolly replied breezily, "I don't think it's a cold. I've an allergy."

"An allergy?" Mrs. Champlain gasped. "How could a person be allergic to anything in the wintertime?"

Dolly chuckled. "I think I'm allergic to snow."

They couldn't see she was trying to make a modest joke. "Snow!" barked Mrs. Boone. "How could anybody be allergic to snow? No, dear, you've got a cold coming on. Better go straight home and have a whisky by the fire and some aspirin. The aspirin will take it out of you . . . and it speeds up the blood too. Everyone should take an aspirin a day.''

"Yes . . . most likely," Dolly murmured. Her attention was already straying.

Erik and Kitty had not arrived yet and chances were, she thought, that Kitty wouldn't come at all. Not if Erik had told her. Glancing archly at the ladies who were still staring at her with huge incomprehension, Dolly helped herself to more tea. It was weak—they'd probably been pouring hot water on these same tired old leaves since last week.

Studying examples of original local art taped to the walls of the corridor leading to the lecture hall, Dolly meandered away. Grandma Moses they ain't—how wonderful if there *had* been a local to match the Moses ejaculation of color . . . ejaculation, yes, Dolly thought, on this gray New England afternoon. Jesus, she moped, the pilgrims must have been bored out of their wits besides freezing their asses off that first winter.

Thinking of frozen asses, Dolly surreptiously felt her behind. It was still smarting from exposure to that snowbank. But elsewhere she was warm, bathed in the heat of the night before, her crotch trembling when she remembered. Every nerve and nerve ending and every tiny capillary in her body was alive and well. Hello, ass, how you feeling? Hello, legs, there you are, working, and hello, tits, you got fondled enough, and hello little snatch, quivering, slavering, pulling on the dork of her imagination and feeling it throbbing.

She would faint if she kept it up. Instead, Dolly returned to the tea table and put her cup down. No use fantasizing now. She went back down the corridor to the lecture room and chose a chair near the front, but not too near the slide projector.

The ladies began to trickle in as the time closed on two P.M., and a few older men, some bearing canes, all silver-haired. They didn't have anything to do, either on a day like this.

Somebody behind her said, "Well, hello, Mrs. Moss . . . Mr. Moss. . . ."

His voice came, grave, calm. "Good afternoon, ladies."

Shit! Dolly turned her head and, despite everything she had feared, she was shocked to her toes. Kitty looked horrible! *He had* told her. And, still, she had come along?

Dolly did not know what to do. She turned her head, to stare straight ahead. Kitty would not want to sit with her, not now. But she was surprised again. Kitty's voice, a whisper in her ear. "I'll sit next to you, sweetheart."

"Oh!" Dolly spun. "Darling! How are you?" Whatever he had told her, Dolly realized her name had not been mentioned after all—just as well. "You look like you've lost your best friend."

Katharine didn't answer at once. She stared at her hands, then twisted her head toward Erik who was still talking to someone in the aisle. "It's a bad day," she whispered. "I feel terrible."

"Darling," Dolly said, not able to banish sarcasm from her voice, "not another headache, I hope."

She shook her head. "No. Erik's the one with the headache."

"Oh?" That was a peculiar construction to put on it. He *must* have said something to her. Dolly's speculation was fractured by another sneeze. She rummaged in her bag for a handkerchief. "Shit! It *is* a cold coming on."

"You don't dress right for the weather," Katharine said.

"The *ladies* have already told me that fourteen times, darling," Dolly said irritably. "Actually, I feel wonderful. I walked all the way here."

Katharine shrugged indifferently. "How healthy of you."

Now, pressing against Dolly's shoulder, Erik's hip. "Hello," he said. "May I sit?"

Dolly glanced up at him, a secret signal in her eyes. "Well, sure, sit between me and Kitty. I'll move over one," she said, reaching into her bag again and drawing out an envelope. "Here's that material you wanted on the Smithers house. Remember what I was telling you?"

"Oh, yes, thank you." But he didn't fully understand until he had pulled the envelope open and looked inside. His eyes leapt, he seemed to turn white, then quickly he stuffed it into his pocket. Dolly chortled to herself—how daring of her! And what was in there should convince him, if he needed convincing, that she was very serious about him . . . about them. "Thanks," he repeated, and dropped into the chair. Katharine did not look at him; rather, her body seemed to quail.

Recklessly, Dolly picked up the slack. "Should start any minute now. If not, we give him ten minutes, then take off. Personally, I'd rather be down at the Lobster Claw having a stiff one."

She spoke too loudly. Ahead of them, shoulders jerked and necks tensed. Erik glanced at her quickly, a flicker of amusement at the corner of his pursed lips. He hissed, "Not so loud, my darling."

Dolly chuckled and shoved the tip of her tongue out at him. She crossed her arms over her tender breasts—and shifted on the hard chair. Still, her bottom burned, as if she'd been whipped, which, she admitted, she deserved to be. She acknowledged all the charges—she was, yes, possessive, cruel and mischievous. Kitty didn't know it yet, Dolly told herself cockily, but she had just lost herself a husband.

Once the lecture did begin, Dolly scarcely heard it, and when the lecturer, a droning bore from Yale, turned from words to blurry slides, Dolly gratefully closed her eyes. Even then, it seemed the light-show would never end. But, of course, it did.

"My, wasn't that interesting?" she murmured politely. Dolly knew Kitty hadn't heard a word of it either. Coldly, she gathered her fur around her and stood up. "Let's you and I go for a drink, sweetheart. Erik has something else he wants to do this afternoon, don't you . . . *darling*?"

Erik was proofed against sarcasm. "I have some appointments, yes."

His aplomb never failed to impress Dolly but today it seemed to ricochet off Kitty. "I'll take the car and drive Dolly home."

"Please be careful on these roads," he said solemnly.

Katharine didn't reveal any more of her trouble until she and Dolly were at a window at the Claw, overlooking the wintry wharfs. They were not well known here and Kitty irritably had to repeat her order for a double vodka martini with a twist and on the rocks. Dolly ordered her usual, a chilled Chablis.

The Lobster Claw was frequented mainly by "townies"— the local merchants, mechanics, fishermen, and, during the summer months, tourists. The Plymouth Avenue residents seldom came here and when they did, like Dolly and Katharine, they were treated with a mix of condescension and envy, and not very politely.

"These people make me tired," Katharine growled, eyeing Dolly so malevolently that she thought, oh, oh, here it comes, the blast of condemnation. "People, Christ, they *all* make me tired!" Katharine's usually placid face became so miserable Dolly almost regretted her role as destroyer. But, she warned herself, the road to hell was paved with regrets.

"Come on, now," she said carefully, "we're pals— remember?"

Katharine nodded, then angrily said, "My goddamn marriage is a shambles. You realize that, don't you?"

"Shambles? Is that how you'd describe it?"

"Erik is very unhappy," Katharine said bluntly. Dolly held her breath—waiting for the rest of it. "I've not been good for him. He knows it. I know it. This business of him not working—that's so destructive, Dolly."

"Bound to be," she said tersely.

"Well. . . ." Katharine drew in a deep breath, shaking her head. The drinks arrived and she took a pull on her martini before continuing. "I offered him a divorce—and he won't even discuss it. Damn it, Dolly—*he won't give me a divorce!*"

Dolly would have been knocked reeling, if she'd been

standing up. As it was, her wine glass, halfway to her mouth, stopped in midflight and she gasped. "My God! You asked *him* for a divorce!"

"Yes." Katharine was so occupied with herself she didn't detect the disbelief, shock, Dolly's gathering fury. "I don't know what the hell I'm going to do about it either."

"Uh. . . ." Dolly heard her own hoarse exclamation. "Christ . . . darling . . . an awful . . . dilemma," she faltered.

"I even told him I might be in love with somebody else," Katharine said sorrowfully. Dolly teetered on the edge of a scream. "But he won't let me go. He's determined to make me suffer, even if it's bad for *him*. I can't stand the sight of him anymore. And he can't bear me."

Dolly sat stiffly, feeling the numbness spread through her body like paralysis. Finally, raspingly, she was able to say, "Of course . . . what do you expect? He's not going to let go of your money."

Oh, the rotten bastard! Dolly's rage, the sense of injustice, of being used, tricked, lied to, choked her. She had just given him an envelope with ten one-thousand dollar bills inside it! One-thousand dollar bills were not easy to come by; she kept just enough of them near her to buy what she unexpectedly wanted or needed.

"What the hell am I going to do?" Katharine cried. Hand shaking, she lifted her martini.

Viciously, Dolly said, "Well, to start with, don't get drunk. I'll tell you what to do—you walk out on him. Come with me . . . to Europe. Marco Fortuna proposed to me . . . and maybe I'll marry the dirty little son-of-a-bitch. You know what they say. . . ." Dolly smiled caustically. "Living well is the best revenge!"

A faraway look crossed Katharine's face. "Dolly—the point is, if I walk out I already have somewhere to go."

"What!" Dolly was rattled. Poor Kitty? Kitty wasn't so poor, was she? No, she seemed to be in full control of her destiny. For an instant, Dolly hated her. Then she remembered—Dolly had somewhere to go too: A chateau outside Geneva. That was *okay* for starters. Erik Moss could goddamn well rot! "Slut! You *do* have another man?"

"You know him. He came to your party at Frank's."

"Gene Francotti? Holy shit!" Dolly's chin wobbled. She was almost in tears. Black envy all but curled her toes.

"Why are you mad at me?" Katharine asked timidly.

"I'm not, ninny! I'm. . . ." Dolly paused to cool down. Talk about life's ironies. "You're in love with him? And he's in love with you?"

Katharine nodded, as if it were all too good to be true. "I think so."

"Then do it, darling," Dolly urged. "Walk out!"

Had she no pride? Was she thinking now that she'd accept Erik Moss by default? Would she? Christ, she thought, she'd hate herself forever if she did. She'd see him castrated first.

"Walk out?" Katharine repeated doubtfully. "Then what?"

"Then . . . nothing," Dolly snarled. "Get your father to handle him—Richard Darktower will make him wish he'd never been born. Richard Darktower is a *man*! He'll twist Erik's nuts off. Miserable man, miserable son-of-a-bitch! He'd deny *you* happiness, make you live like this? Erik thinks he's back in feudal Germany. Goddamn it, you didn't sign on as a slave, did you?"

Katharine put her hand on Dolly's. "Relax, honey. Not so loud. I agree with everything you say—don't carry on so!"

Dolly made fists of her dimpled hands and hit the table. "I know, I know, it just makes me so mad when I hear about somebody misusing my friend."

"I have to make him see reason," Katharine said hopefully. "We'd both be better off."

"No doubt! No fucking doubt about it." Dolly waved for their waiter. "Darling, I'm going to join you in a vodka martini. Let's get fried."

But Kitty, blast her, didn't want to. One more, she told Dolly, and then she'd drive her home. "I've got to see Gene."

"He's here?" Dolly gaped at her.

"I drove up with him," Katharine confessed. "He's doing some work at the boatyard. I'll see him tonight . . . somehow."

"Tell him to come to my house. He can join you there." Dolly squinted severely. "Would you carry on your illicit romance under my roof, you slut?" She delivered her lowdown chuckle. "Well, of course you would, if that's what you wanted to do."

"Yes," Katharine said wanly. "What Kate wants, Kate gets."

"Exactly!"

But, to herself, Dolly was promising something else—confrontation with Erik Moss would be like the meeting of fire and dynamite. She'd have her ten thousand back; either he was going to divorce Kitty and come to her, or she was going to make him suffer the tortures of the damned. There wasn't any man who could treat her like this . . . especially after everything she had done for him, surrendering herself as she had in the most erotic ways she could devise.

And now this? Oh no!

Fifteen

Vaguely, they heard the sirens a few blocks west of the sea front as they climbed into the Moss's Mercedes. Then, reaching Plymouth and turning right in the direction of Dolly's house, a speeding police car cut through the traffic in front of them.

Peevishly, Dolly said, "Somebody must've held up a liquor store. We're getting it up here too, your big-city crime."

Katharine drove carefully, aware of the two vodkas under her belt, but the buzz of the alcohol was far in the back of her mind. What she was trying to decide was how she could arrange her evening, after she'd dropped Dolly off. Directness was probably the best approach—she would simply drive down to the docks again, park near Johannson's Bar and go to meet him at the boat. Or, should she go back to Maples and wait for Erik and have it out with him once and for all? The third alternative was to do what Dolly suggested—hole up at Dolly House and wait for Francotti there and to hell with everything. She could leave a message for him at the yard office, or get somebody from Johannson's to deliver it. He'd drive over to Dolly's and then. . . .

Then what? She had to settle things with Erik. Francotti was not going to accept anything less than that. But the prospect of facing up to it, as always, depressed her.

"It is a question of *me*, isn't it?" she mused aloud.

Dolly knew precisely what she meant. "You are damned right it is." Her normally pert, vivacious face was drawn.

157

All this talk of Erik, Katharine realized, irritated Dolly vastly and she had to wonder what there was, or had been, between them. Perhaps nothing; maybe she was all wrong about Dolly.

Dolly sneezed irritably, if it was possible to produce an irritable sneeze, and cried, "Oh, shit! I really am catching a cold."

"How'd you do that, sweetheart?" Katharine asked idly, concentrating on the road.

"How *should* I explain?" She laughed sardonically. "Actually, you see, I was jacking-off a snowman and he came all over me."

"Dolly! You are just terrible." Katharine grinned primly.

"Nothing worse than a slushy, mushy snowman, darling." Abruptly, she coughed. "What the hell's so funny about that? Nothing." Dolly stared out the car window. "I'll probably have a joke when the world is ending."

"It's not ending, though," Katharine said. "It's just beginning." She told herself this must be true. Her life was about to begin. All she had to do was to be strong and firm. She must not allow Erik to intimidate her; he was so good at intimidating people.

Moodily, Dolly agreed. "I guess marrying Marco would be a beginning."

"But you don't have to do that, sweetheart. You could buy your own villa in Geneva."

"By myself?" Dolly hooted. "I'd get ripped off and what the hell's the good of a villa without a count or duke or something in it?"

Calmly, Katharine assured her, "You could get anybody you wanted. You don't need Marco Fortuna."

Dolly shook her head. "He's probably all I can get, if the truth be known. Anyway, I'd take him—just out of spite to get back at all those Port London hags who look down on me, Dolly Percy, the fallen woman."

"Hell, they don't matter." Katharine turned the Mercedes into the driveway an acre away from the house, shielded from the main road by a picketline of evergreen trees, now laden so heavily with ice and snow it seemed it would take a month of springtime to melt it away. Behind the trees,

Dolly's doll house squatted in the hard ground, a trickle of smoke rising from one of the chimneys into the gray sky. "Sweetheart, your house always looks so peaceful and quiet. I don't see your snowman, though. Where is he?"

"I knocked him down, the bastard. After all the loving I gave him," Dolly said morosely, "Why do you ask? You know there never was a snowman."

"Oh—I thought there was. You were only kidding?" Katharine sounded disappointed.

"Come in the house. I want another drink and so do you. I don't want to be alone—Francotti can really come and meet you here, can't he?" Opening the front door, Dolly looked at Kitty over her shoulder. "I'm so goddamn jealous of you. Why in hell can't I have somebody to be in love with?"

"You will, sweetheart."

Inside, Dolly started grumbling about her housekeeper, Mrs. Donovan, who never heard the door. She opened a closet and shoved her jacket inside, then grabbed Katharine's fur.

"There!"

Dolly turned and they faced each other, a bit wanly. They had been through the mill, hadn't they, the "sisters," the twins. Katharine was almost a head taller than Dolly, her blondeness in sharp contrast to Dolly's dark hair and the gypsy sallowness of her skin tone. Somewhere, Dolly did have a smidgen of Mediterranean or Latin blood in her veins, she thought.

Warmly, Dolly put her arm around Katharine's waist, snuggling close and kissing her cheek. Through her turtleneck, Katharine could feel Dolly's breasts, limpidly rising; she realized with a start that Dolly was not wearing a bra.

"Whatever I say, I'm happy for you."

Katharine caught Dolly's scent, strong and steamy and instinctively bent her head to return the kiss on Dolly lips, so soft and yielding. Dolly giggled and surprised Katharine by thrusting the tip of her tongue teasingly into her mouth. Hastily, laughing disarmingly, she pulled away.

"Come on! Into the den!" The couch faced a crackling

fire. Katharine sat down contentedly while Dolly made the drinks, then perched beside her, drawing her legs up under her and also staring at the fire. "Now—isn't this nice? Old friends—we've known each other forever. We have no secrets, do we?"

"Not that I know of."

Disgruntled, Dolly asked, "About men, though, we do. Women always have secrets about their men. It's too bad we need the bastards at all."

"We don't, not really," Katharine said. "For children, I suppose. Aren't you ever going to have any, sweetheart?"

"I'm just about past it, wouldn't you say?" Dolly asked wryly.

"You still could, if you wanted to. It's not so dangerous now. They have those tests older women take to make sure the baby is okay."

Dolly grimaced. "What! You want me to go off the pill—I'd lose my tits, what there is of them."

"There's nothing wrong with your tits."

"They're not like yours. You've got good, big ones—and they don't sag, do they?"

"A little."

"Well, I wouldn't have thought so. Does he like them?"

"Francotti?" Katharine didn't look up. She remembered his big hands and said shyly, "He seems to."

"He better, goddamn it!" Dolly stared insistently. "Do you realize we haven't even seen each others tits since we were sixteen or seventeen?"

Confusedly, not wanting to be reminded of it, Katharine remembered their girlish love. Once, it was true, they hadn't had any secrets. They'd shared beds on weekends, cuddling and hugging each other in the innocence of youth, not knowing what they were doing but never going too far . . . held back, by what?

"That's long ago, sweetheart. We're old now."

"Too goddamn old," Dolly grunted, "and I don't like getting old, not one bit! Think of all the things we've missed. We could've been screwing a long time before we started, if we'd known any better. And what did we do? We waited."

Katharine tried the vodka. "Honey, you didn't wait long—you were married when you were eighteen."

"True," Dolly acknowledged, then grinned slyly. "I never told you one secret, darling. I lost my virginity when I was sixteen—long before you did."

"How was that?" Katharine asked. She only asked because Dolly seemed anxious to tell her.

"Don't you remember? I fucked a boy scout that summer. That's how it happened."

She did remember. Dolly in those days had been a little chubby with baby fat, but her face had been the same as it was now, eager, intrepid.

"An Eagle scout?"

"No," Dolly joked, "but he was first-class. Actually I was scared to death and for months afterward I was sure I was pregnant. Maybe I should have been, but it wouldn't have been a great first marriage, would it, me sixteen and him fourteen?"

"What did Harrison say? Wasn't he expecting a lily-white virgin?"

Dolly huffed disgustedly. "Harrison was so drunk the night we got married, he didn't know what was happening. I played dismal damsel for him and I suppose forever after he was guilty in his own mind of vile defloration. Then, of course," she sneered, "he had to blow his brains out. That made a lot of sense, didn't it?"

"He didn't want to go to jail," Katharine pointed out.

"Christ, the idiot would have been out in three months! The Republicans wouldn't let one of their own rot in the cooler."

Katharine made a sympathetic sound. "So tragic, sweetheart."

Dolly shrugged. "Well, it did serve to remove Harrison from my life—not that I've made so much of it since then. We probably wouldn't have lasted another year together anyway." Dolly shook her shoulders and turned on the couch, her voice jittery. "What about you, darling? Let's talk about you—I know *you* weren't a virgin when you found Steve and don't try to tell me any different."

Katharine frowned. "Mine wasn't half as romantic as yours."

"Romantic! You must be joking!"

Katharine shook her head darkly. "What happened to me was a carload of us were out one night and they got me drunk. That was the first time I ever got drunk in my life and I don't even remember which one of them did it to me in the back seat." She shook her head perplexedly. "I think maybe it was more than one of them."

"What!" Dolly's face sharpened in amazement. "You mean you were gang-banged?"

"I can't remember."

"Gang-banged!" Dolly tittered. "How wonderful. That's always been my dream—to get gang-banged by a whole shipload of pirates. Imagine the dirty things—all sweaty and horny after months out of sight of land."

Katharine stretched her legs toward the fire. She couldn't take Dolly seriously. "It probably wouldn't be as much fun as you think, sweetheart. You're liable to get one with a great wart on the end of it. . . ."

"Wouldn't that make it better, though?"

"Dolly . . . all you think about is men. Am I like that?"

"I don't know," Dolly said coolly, "but I can't think of much else worth thinking about. You want to talk about politics, for instance?" She took Katharine's empty glass. "I'll make another."

"One more."

"Sure, one more, famous last words. Look," Dolly said from the other side of the room, "I happen to believe women think about sex even more than men do. Else, why spend so much time and money on clothes and makeup and face-lifts and tit-lifts?"

"Remember, it's the male bird with the brightest plumage."

Dolly shook her head. "I know all that old stuff about the birds and the bees. I'm talking about human beings. In our species, the mating game is a woman's game. We just ain't like the birds, darling."

Dreamily, Katharine said, "It'd be fun to be a bird for a while."

"Like hell! I like being a predator," Dolly said fiercely. "You know, sometimes I even wish I was double-gaited, so I could enjoy everything."

"Dolly!"

"I'm telling you, it's true." Gleefully, she slid closer to Katharine. "If I was, I'd go after you."

"You wouldn't!"

"Yes, I would! I'd throw you down and kiss you . . . all over."

"Dolly!" Katharine protested languidly, holding her eyes to the fire.

"Yeah, it'd shock the living daylights out of you, I know. You're so goddamn pure of heart."

"Aren't I though?" Katharine said faintly. Lazily, she shifted her legs. Poor Dolly, she had no idea. "Maybe I'm not entirely what you think I am, sweetheart." She put her hand on the smooth arm of Dolly's turtleneck and caressed it for a second. Not wanting to, she imagined what was underneath, ripe breasts with the dusky nipples. She could reach out and take one—but she and Dolly weren't like that. They joked—they always had.

The phone rang, deflecting her thoughts. Dolly jumped up. "Yes, hello. Yes. Oh . . . you. Yes, she's here." She turned, her hand over the mouthpiece. "It's Mr. Asshole himself."

Erik's voice was muffled. "I'm calling you because I don't want you to think badly . . . there's been an accident down here."

"What?" What was he talking about? "What accident? Where?"

"At the boatyard—where your friend Francotti is working. It was not my fault."

Her heart faltered. "I don't understand . . . what's wrong with your voice?"

"Nothing. My mouth is cut. There was an accident."

"He's hurt?"

"Listen to me!" he cried. "He's hurt a little, and also the boy working with him. A winch slipped. They're in the hospital."

"What happened?" she cried loudly. "Tell me what happened, for God's sake."

Erik's accent turned harsher, guttural. "I came down here, to talk to him."

"Why, goddamn it?"

"For obvious reasons."

Naturally, she was supposed to understand that. Her anger blazed at him, with added strength. "What right did you have. . . ."

He cut her off gruffly. "Wait at home for me, I tell you."

"No!"

"Kathy—I am commanding you to wait for me."

"And I'm telling you. . . ." She stopped breathlessly, searching for words. "I'm telling you . . . no!"

She slammed down the phone.

"What happened, for God's sake?" Dolly turned from the window.

"There was an accident at the boatyard," Katharine said, her eyes glued to Dolly's face. "He was hurt . . . somehow . . . Francotti was hurt."

Dolly swept up to her. "Darling . . . it'll be all right."

She began to cry, then to laugh. "Can you believe . . . the miserable son-of-a-bitch went down there to *talk* to Francotti? That's when whatever happened."

"To talk to Francotti? Why?" Dolly's eyes cleared and she laughed sardonically. "To talk him out of it? Jesus Christ," she snarled, "he wants very badly, very badly, indeed, to keep you."

"Maybe," Katharine said bitterly, "but he's not going to."

She pulled away from Dolly and went to the fire, thrusting her freezing hands at the heat, laying her fingers on the top of the brass screen, aware that it was very hot.

"Get your hands off there, for Christ's sake!"

"Yes, oh!" Katharine jerked her fingers away and licked them with her tongue. She turned around. "Why does everything have to be so complicated? Francotti would *hate* Erik going to him, talking. . . ."

"More like *begging*," Dolly sputtered scornfully.

"Yes." She nodded nervously. "Begging. God, he'd hate it. He'll hate me for letting it happen to him. I think he *socked* Erik."

"I hope he socked him, the fucking bastard! I hope he knocked out all his fucking teeth!"

"Dolly, Dolly!" Katharine laughed anxiously. "I'm afraid—is he going to hate me now?"

"No, he's not, for God's sake," Dolly barked. "Don't be such a goddamn baby . . . he's going to understand."

"I'm going down to the hospital," Katharine told her. "I must, mustn't I?"

"I would think so."

"Erik's coming here. Don't tell him where I've gone. I don't want to see him." Katharine hurried into the hallway but Dolly was ahead of her, taking her fur off the hanger and putting it over her shoulders.

Katharine hugged Dolly tightly for an instant, then opened the front door.

"Good luck!" Dolly yelled after her. "And don't worry. I'll take care of Mr. Asshole."

Sixteen

No one had ever advised going to the Port London Colonial Hospital for anything more serious than sunburn or toenail trouble but in times of emergency there was no choice.

Both Francotti and the boy working with him at the boatyard had been extremely lucky. They'd got the engine hanging free over its bay while installing new piping or something. Then Francotti had gone back up on deck to talk to somebody and, accidentally, probably due to the crummy weather, the winch handle had let go and damned if the engine didn't fall straight through the hull of the boat. Fortunately, the boy had not been directly underneath it at the time but nonetheless it had hit his work boot a glancing blow and he had suffered a badly twisted ankle. Francotti himself had a broken left forearm, where he'd been struck by the spinning winch handle, and bruised and broken fingers on his right hand, evidently from slamming them against a bulkhead in anger.

And, yes, the lady would be able to have a word with him in a few minutes, after the forearm had been properly set and other tests had been made. Francotti's pulse showed some irregularity, no doubt because of pain and anger, but they were going to give him an electrocardiograph just to be sure.

"The boy is all right?"

"Him? He's fine. He'll be out this afternoon."

"And Mr. Francotti?"

"We'll probably keep him until morning. We want to

sedate him. Wait a minute. I don't know who you are—
who wants to see him?''

Katharine didn't know what to say. A friend? A Mrs.
Moss?

''Tell him it's his mistress.''

''Oh.'' The doctor's eyebrows waggled. They didn't get
many mistresses calling at the hospital in Port London.
''All right. I'll tell him that. Just take a seat over there for
a little while.''

As she waited, Katharine worried. Surely, he was all
right. It couldn't be counted as significant that his pulse
raced after a nasty accident.

When she was finally given entrance to Francotti's room,
she knew she was in for it. He lay stiffly, his long, hard
body coiled to strike, and, behind his glasses, the eyes
flat, deadly. His face was pinched white with anger.

''Hello,'' she murmured nervously. ''I'm sorry . . .
I. . . .''

He lifted his bandaged right hand. ''Don't speak. What
do you mean telling them you're my mistress?''

She moved closer to him but again he stopped her with
his hand.

''What *should* I say? I *am* your mistress.''

''No, you're not. Not at all. I don't like the word.
Mistress—very amusing word to use here in Port London.''

''Look,'' she said hurriedly, ''I said I'm sorry. I didn't
know he was going down there to see you. I'm very
embarrassed.'' She looked around. ''Is there any place
to sit?''

''No,'' he barked. ''You're leaving anyway. That Moss
. . . he almost caused a complete disaster.''

Katharine nodded speechlessly. She stood, keeping the
space between them, as he bid, holding her fur around her
fraily.

He went on, indictingly. ''If Ben had been under that
thing when it fell, he'd be dead as a goddamn doornail.
What the hell is it with you people, for Christ's sake?''

''Us people?'' she muttered. ''It was *him*, not me.''

''Bullshit! Listen, honey, where the hell does he get off
coming down there and bothering me? Telling me, like

some fucking cavalier, that I positively cannot, simply cannot, you see, carry on with his wife. Well. . . ." He breathed hoarsely. "I'm not carrying on with his *wife*, goddamn it. I'm carrying on with a *woman* who's divorcing him—aren't I? Numbly, she nodded. "Oh yeah? Well, I've got a feeling I'm not going to carry on with either one of those broads!"

"No! Listen, I told him this morning just after we got here that I want a divorce," she whispered.

"And?"

"He said it was out of the question," she admitted.

"Wonderful," Francotti sneered. "And then he comes down to see me and gives me this line of bullshit—you're supposed to be a very disturbed woman, did you know that? You're neurotic, high-strung, hysterical. What about it? You don't know what you're doing. You're always throwing yourself at men. You live in a fantasy world. He even told me you're a nymphomaniac. What about that?"

"No," she denied. "It's all lies. How can he say these things?"

"I don't know," he said bitterly, "but it makes me sick. It's not my kind of thing. I don't want anything to do with your kind of people."

She could not believe he could be so cruel. "You think I'm insane, that I put him up to this?"

"I don't know what to think," he growled. "All I know is the son-of-a-bitch almost did me in. Goddamn it, I don't want anything to do with any of you. Go stew in your own circle, Mrs. Moss."

She couldn't stand his voice, the words. She backed toward the door.

"Wait!" He held up his hand again. "Go in that closet. My shirt's in there. There's an envelope full of money in one of the pockets. Take it and give it back to the son-of-a-bitch. 'Oh, yes, Mr. Francotti,' " he hissed, capturing Erik's Teutonic accent, " 'please, for your trouble, please take this small sum.' That's when I slugged him in the mouth, broke my finger, hit the winch handle." His voice rose to a bellow. "Take that goddamn money and tell him to shove it up his ass! You got that, Mrs. Moss?"

*   *   *

When Mrs. Donovan finally got back from the shopping, she burst into the den where Dolly had put herself again, in front of the fire, and announced there had been some kind of accident at the boatyard.

"I know," Dolly said. "Bad news travels fast."

"Shall I bring you some tea?"

"No. Make me a drink. A big vodka with ice, please."

Dolly did not take her eyes off the leaping flames, not even when Mrs. Donovan came back with the drink. Then the older woman left the room, having deposited on the desk a grocery list and receipts for money spent. Dolly heard her footsteps across the marble of the foyer and the sound of a door being closed, far away.

Doors closed, didn't they? Katharine was right—everything was so complicated. Life was a cheat. *Her* life was a good example of that. Nothing went smoothly; she didn't ever get what she really wanted. Tears of self-pity smeared her makeup. Katharine had said they were at only the beginning . . . how could she be so sure it wasn't the bitter end?

Hearing the sound of another car in the driveway and a door slamming, she realized Erik Moss had arrived. The bell rang and Mrs. Donovan retraced her slow footsteps from the kitchen. In a moment, Erik came hesitantly into the den.

"Dolly . . . where's Kathy?"

"Gone." She stared at him. "What happened to your face?"

His hand rose to his cheek, which was swollen, next to his cut lip. There was a goose-egg-sized bump on his jaw line.

"I bumped into something," he said.

"Like hell! Francotti thumped you, didn't he?"

He shrugged angrily. "Where is she?"

"Gone. She wouldn't stay."

"Then where did she go?"

Dolly lifted her glass again. "Look, *darling*, I just told you I don't know. Don't come into my own house to interrogate me—you're not the Gestapo."

His lips pulled away from his teeth in a semblance of a smile. "Hardly . . . I am disturbed. . . ."

"You sure are."

"I asked her to wait for me. Why did she leave?"

"I should think, *asshole*, because you called and told her Francotti got hurt."

"Of course! She has gone to the hospital!"

Such a revelation! Christ, she told herself, he was sometimes amazingly dense. "She's in love with Francotti, you know."

He laughed shakily. "Ridiculous. She couldn't love him."

"No? Then. . . ." Dolly inhaled slowly for the showdown. "Then why did she ask you for a divorce—which *you* refused." She paused to allow anger to gather full force. "You are a perfect son-of-a-bitch!"

"Dolly!"

She made the classic gesture of dismissal with the back of her hand. "Yes . . . Kitty came to *you* asking you for a divorce. And you turned her down. You lied to me. You never intended to leave her. Never!"

His hand dropped from his cheek. Combined with bruises and bumps, his look of dismay was grotesque. "Nonsense, my darling! Yes, I refused her because it was in her own good interest. She does not *love* this man." He strained with sincerity. "It would have been a cruel thing to let her go to him. But I did *not* refuse a divorce in principle. You should know that."

"Like shit! You're a liar, and a rotten liar at that! Give me that money back!"

Erik bowed stiffly from the waist. "Certainly. You will get it," he said coolly.

"I'd better!"

He shrugged deprecatingly. "There is no way you could prove you gave me money."

Slowly, understanding and hating it, Dolly nodded. "You're right. But there are other ways."

"Of course. Now, may I please use your phone for a moment?"

She shrugged coldly. Erik dialed information for the

hospital number, then the Colonial Hospital. Was there a Mrs. Moss there visiting a patient named Francotti? No? Well, had Mr. Francotti had any visitors? Yes, a woman in a fur coat, but she had not given a name and she had just left. Was Mr. Francotti resting well? Yes. And the woman in the fur coat, had she had a pleasant visit with Mr. Francotti? Yes, most likely, but maybe not so pleasant . . . chuckle, chuckle . . . judging from the shouting in Francotti's private room disturbing the whole floor of the Colonial Hospital.

Smiling, Erik hung up. "It seems my message has gotten through," he murmured, not in particular to Dolly.

"Wonderful," she snipped.

Remembering, he rushed from the telephone and sank to his knees in front of her. "Now, darling, you *must* tell me you understand nothing changes between us. You know that I love you."

"For Christ-sake!"

"Darling, I am just so bewildered."

Dolly shook her head violently. "You're not bewildered— you're an *asshole*, like I said. Why in hell did you go down to that dock anyway?"

"I went to speak to him, to make him realize he was not dealing with a normal woman, but with a woman of fantasies. Kathy is the victim of a sexual fantasy, my darling!"

Dolly made a distasteful sound, feeling sick. "You're crazy. There's *nothing* wrong with her. Kitty is *not* insane. She'd been to bed with the man. She loves him!"

"No!" Erik exclaimed emotionally, leaping up. "Please, it is not possible for me to think of Kathy and another."

Her eyes snapped. "I don't believe you. You can say that—after *you've* made love to me?"

He nodded. "And will again."

"Oh, no! Like hell. Never again with me!"

His hopeful smile crashed on his chin. He dropped back to his knees. "*Hertzchen*, please."

"Get up. You're not an honest man, Erik."

He jerked backward, his lips hardened lopsidedly around the bruises and cut. Tension jolted the focus of his expression. "Please do not insult me. Above all, I am an honest man."

"Oh no." Dolly disagreed coolly. "Above all, you're a fucking liar. Get out of my house. I don't want to see you anymore."

He grew distant, face narrowing. "If a man said words to me like that, I would kill him."

"Don't make me laugh."

A change came over his· face. A frown, then a scowl twisted his lips. He stared haughtily. "*Killing* is not so difficult," he said softly. "You have enjoyed yourself well enough with me. Satisfied your appetites and begged for more. Honest? Did *you* confess to Kathy that you have slept with me? No, I thought not. Who then is so dishonest? A man who tries to protect people he loves or a woman who deceives her best friend with her best friend's husband?"

Dolly didn't bother to answer. Casually, as if it were the most natural thing in the world to do, she drew her hand back and lashed out—catching him across the cheek. Erik did not budge or condescend to touch the spot. His face went absolutely dead. He extended his right hand and put the knuckle of the forefinger under her chin, nudging her gently. "I could snap your spine with a single pressure," he whispered. "No. . . ." He pulled his hand away. "You will change your mind, my darling. Tonight, tomorrow, you will remember the way it was." Slowly, he climbed to his feet.

For once, she put him down with her look. He stammered, "I am not a bad man. You should be more understanding of me."

"No doubt!" Dolly brushed past him to stand at the window, her back to the room. If he was going to kill her, now was his chance. She stood quite still until he left the room and she heard the front door open and close.

Seventeen

They kept a big Ford station wagon permanently in Port London, along with a vintage Rolls Royce Richard Darktower had bought them for very formal occasions during the summer and, walking home from Dolly's for the second time on this day, this time in anxious and an embarrassed frame of mind, Erik decided that he'd use that to get back to the city. Even if Kathy returned to Maples after her visit to the hospital, it was not possible they could share the same car for the two-hour drive to New York.

Damnation, he told himself, it was such an unbelievable, inconceivable mess. How could people land themselves in such situations? It was natural, of course, that all concerned were going to be upset—Kathy because he had forbade her this man Francotti and Dolly because she could not fathom the depth of his emotions toward herself *and* Kathy. Goodness, he thought, he could not simply discard his wife, could he? That would not be an honorable thing to do. And Francotti? How did Erik Moss or anybody else know what Francotti's real intentions were?

Dolly, of course, he accepted, was more bothered by his putting off the divorce than by any sympathy for Kathy's predicament. With Dolly, Dolly always came first.

Francotti himself had been no more tolerant, or willing to talk it through, and then, to Erik's amazement, Francotti had hit him. Erik trudged along, head down, his swollen chin and cheek buried in the afghan collar of his loden coat, hands deep in the pockets, his fingers clenching and unclenching. Thinking of Francotti made him nervous. His shoes were soaking wet when he reached Maples. Of course, he reminded himself irritably, he hadn't known the day was going to turn out like this. Hearing him at the door, Mrs. Rogers fluttered out of the kitchen.

"Has Mrs. Moss been here?"

"No, Mr. Moss." She stared in wonder at his face.

"Hell!" he cried, as if this was the worst thing that could happen. "We got our signals crossed . . . an accident . . . and now I think she's driven back to the city alone."

"Oh. . . ." She chittered like a simian. "Wouldn't you know?"

Erik went immediately upstairs and threw what little he'd brought with him back into his overnight bag. He put the wet shoes in the vicinity of the radiator but not so close they'd crack.

Before leaving, he made a last phone call to Dolly.

"My darling. . . ."

"My darling . . . *my ass*," she snapped.

"Please," he whispered, "if Kathy calls, tell her I'm on my way back to the city."

"Okay. Good-bye."

Erik smiled to himself. He was wise to have called; she'd known he would. She'd been thinking about him. Her anger would cool and she would realize remorsefully that she had been unreasonable and then, again, later, in the night, in the cold bed, alone, she would yearn for him.

Erik pulled up at Park Towers a little after nine; in a moment, the ever-alert weekend doorman popped out.

"Hello, Peter," he said easily, "did Mrs. Moss get in yet?"

"No, sir. Is she on the way by herself?"

"Yes," he dissembled smoothly, "perhaps she's stopped somewhere. Can you take care of the car, please? It won't be in long. I'll be driving back to Port London in a day or two."

"No problem, Mr. Moss."

Helen Ryan seemed to have been poised by the door of the duplex. Theoretically, Saturday was her night off. But spare time was meaningless to Helen; she hardly ever left the premises except for a walk to the park every afternoon.

She peered past him. "Where's Mrs. Moss? Didn't she come with you?"

"Does it look like it? Close the door!"

"Yes, sir." She pushed the door shut with the palm of her hand. "She stayed in Port London?"

Erik looked at her patiently, aware that she'd seen the bruises. "She's either there or on her way back in the Mercedes. We had a problem today."

"Oh!" Helen's face reddened.

"A little accident." He indicated his cheek.

"She's not been hurt?" Helen's eyes flew wildly in every direction.

"No, no, just a problem with the brakes. She'll probably be calling soon. I'm going in the library for a drink. Where's my daughter?"

"Why, with Mrs. Himmelmann, Mr. Moss."

"Yes. Naturally," he said unpleasantly. "She can't wait for us to go away so she'll get her hands on Margaret."

"She loves the child, Mr. Moss."

"And so do I, Helen, *verdamnt*!"

"Yes, sir. Tell me if you want anything, Mr. Moss."

Want anything? What would he want of her? The look in Helen's eyes was so lonely and woeful he wondered what she might want of him.

His first phone call was to Port London.

"My darling? Has Kathy called? I am so worried. She hasn't arrived home."

Dolly's voice was rough, uneven. "Nope. No calls."

"What's the trouble?"

"I'm drunk, *my darling*," she jeered.

"Dolly, *liebchen*, I will talk to you tomorrow. I have so many things to say."

"Fuck that, Mr. Hitler, put it in writing. I don't trust you Krauts. Don't call me anymore—and *I want that money back*."

"You shall have it," he muttered. Money? Didn't she think about anything else? Damn! He should have retrieved the envelope from blasted Francotti's pocket—why had he made such a tasteless gesture anyway? By trying to test the man's reactions, he had only made things worse. Francotti had been insulted and, at that moment, it was all too late.

Money, money, money. He was reminded that the time had come for him to call Herman Himmelmann, to make his pitch. He needed income, quickly. The vipers were closing in.

Herman, his very favorite father-in-law, picked up the phone on the first ring. "Erik, my boy," he said gently. He was so different from Darktower, willing to accept a person without putting an overload on suspicion and wariness. "You're checking on Margaret? The gang's all here, Erik. Conrad too. They're in the other room, playing Monopoly. I'm doing the real thing."

"Which is?" Erik inquired faintly.

"Studying the IBM quarterly report," Himmelmann boomed jovially.

"Herman," Erik said carefully, "speaking of that, I'd like to talk to you. Would you have a moment early in the week? Business, not personal."

"Sure, Erik. Call my secretary first thing Monday. We'll have lunch." Erik was about to say good-bye when Himmelmann went off again, on a surprising tangent. "Erik," he said, lowering his voice, almost whispering. "I want to ask your opinion about something. Conrad came over to ask me . . ." He laughed embarrassedly. "He wanted to know if I could see my way clear to helping out Stefan Ratoff whom, you know, I've never met."

Deliberately, Erik repeated, "Help him out? I don't understand."

"Ratoff is broke, flat busted," Himmelmann muttered. "Conrad says his health is bad. I know the boy was very attached to Ratoff. But Erik, I can't see my way clear to loaning him . . . *giving him* money. I think he might even be insulted if he knew Conrad came here . . . begging for him."

"Insulted?" Erik chuckled dryly. "I doubt it."

"You think not?" Himmelmann said slowly. "Well,

still, I can't think of any reason why it should be *me* to give him money—as much as I'd like to please Conrad."

Erik weighed the odds before saying, "I think, sir, that Conrad has some lessons to learn—nobody *owes* anybody anything, that's the hard fact. Ratoff made his own life and Conrad shouldn't expect anybody to bail him out."

"I know . . . I know," Himmelmann sighed. "Charity never works, Erik."

"If anybody . . ." Erik paused. "If anybody, Richard Darktower should be called on . . . not you. And, I can assure you Richard Darktower won't come up with a farthing, Herman."

"I . . . uh . . . more or less said the same thing to Conrad."

A sour wave of desolation swept in after they hung up. Conrad, he thought, the prince. He would never grow up. Erik wondered what had happened when he'd seen Ratoff again. Something, yes, something must have happened. How else could Conrad have left his Greenwich Village girlfriend of a Saturday night to travel uptown to plead Ratoff's case? Was it possible that Ratoff, even in his invalid state, still possessed such force of personality, such power over this foolish boy?

Verdamnt! Disgusting, yes. He remembered the sound of that girl, Lilly's voice. Poor stupid boy. . . .

Erik poured himself a fresh Scotch while he considered the matter of Lilly. Forget about Kathy and Francotti and Port London . . . and the golden prince. Think of the girl.

He decided finally there was only one honorable thing to do. He dialed the number, fingering the push-buttons as if they were little nipples. He paused before hitting the last figure, then punched it hard. The voice answered, breathless.

"My Lilly, my Lilly," he sighed into the phone.

"Who is this? Roberto?"

"No, not Roberto." He realized the injury Francotti had inflicted on him served to disguise his voice. "Will you talk to *me*?"

"Who, for Christ's sake? How do you know my name?"

"We have talked before," he whispered. "I know you."

Lilly laughed harshly. "Well . . . I don't know you."

She paused, debating with herself, he knew, whether to hang up or shout deafeningly in his ear and then hang up. "What do you want to talk about?"

"Love, Lilly."

"Christ," she muttered, "It's an obscene phone call. I don't believe it."

He chuckled deeply. "Lilly, will you meet me tonight?"

She laughed, flustered. "I wouldn't meet a stranger. I'm not crazy, for God's sake."

"I know a small hotel . . ."

"Oh, no, buster. None of that."

Erik sighed. *"If* you knew me . . . *would* you?"

She hesitated, as if looking around the room. But Conrad could not be there. "I don't know. . . ." she stammered. "I . . . it depends. . . ."

"You are in love with another?" This would tell the tale, if she answered honestly.

"Are you a friend of his?" she demanded.

"No, no," he said quickly. "Would you—if I tell you who I am?"

Cleverly, she said, "Tell me who you are and then I'll answer."

"All right," he said. Life itself was a lottery. "Erik Moss."

"My God!" She chuckled incredulously. "I'm surprised, Mr. Moss. I didn't recognize *your* voice."

"Well?"

"I . . . really . . . you want me to meet *you*?"

"Conrad would not know, would he?"

Her voice hardened. "You think I'm some kind of a tramp, don't you?"

"Never. Not at all."

"Jesus!" Her breathing rushed.

"This is your chance, Lilly. Listen, we'll just . . . talk. Whatever you want. I'm not a dangerous man."

He waited as she decided, which she quickly did. "All right. When?"

"In an hour."

He told her the name of the hotel and the address and after putting the phone down, vented a loud laugh. Only then, he realized he was not alone. Helen Ryan was standing in the doorway.

"I heard!" she accused him angrily. "You arranged to meet a whore."

His eyelids came down like riot screens. Mouth tight, he said, "You heard what! You're fantasizing."

"No! I heard!"

"My heavens, Helen, you eavesdrop like this? I was talking to a friend, joking."

Helen pressed her fingertips to her temples. "No, no, I know better. Poor Mrs. Moss."

Damn, of all people, he was not going to be destroyed by Helen Ryan. "You are hysterical, Helen. What on earth ails you?"

Wailing, she cried, "I love this family and this family is coming apart at the seams."

"You love this family?" He smiled sadly.

"Yes!"

"Well, Helen," he said reassuringly, "we love you too and you must not imagine bad things about us. Come here, Helen. Approach me."

He held out his hand. Fearfully she sidled toward his desk. Beckoning her closer with his eyes, when he could reach her, he touched her fingers, then held them in his own. She was trembling violently.

"Dear Helen, we worry about you, you know. You *are* such a beautiful young woman."

"No, no, I'm not, Mr. Moss."

"Yes, yes, you are," he mocked gently, nevertheless, he knew, flattering her. "You have beautiful skin, soulful eyes. Perhaps we do not love you enough."

Her mouth fell open and she began to breathe quickly as he stroked her fingers, ran his thumb across her wrist, along a pounding vein. He took her other hand too and gripped it tightly, pulling her closer to him, between his legs, so that her breasts were level with his face. He smiled encouragingly at her.

"Dear Helen. . . ." His voice was a caress and more than trembling she began to shake. He touched her chest with his forehead, as if in obeisance, then put his face between her breasts. She gulped feverishly and would have recoiled had he not been holding her so fast. "Helen, dear Helen. . . ."

Her lips drew back from her teeth in a grimace of pure pain. He kissed the place where her breasts converged beneath white blouse.

"No! You shouldn't. . . ."

Soothingly, he murmured, "See, dear Helen, it is not such a bad thing to be a woman."

Now, trying her, he dropped her hands. And she did not budge. Possibly, she didn't have the strength to run, even to crawl from him. Yes, possibly, he thought, and continued, very deliberately, to unfasten her blouse. When all the buttons were undone, he slipped the blouse away from her shoulders, stroking her arms and thus infiltrating his hands behind her to unsnap the metal tabs of her brassiere and pull it forward. At this, she cowered but Erik firmly pushed her arms out of the way to reveal milky white breasts, drooping a little; he smiled at them, then at her in compliment, thinking that for a woman of her build they were very respectable. He ran his swollen mouth across them, from nipple, across valley to nipple. Helen shuddered and groaned resonantly. And now the skirt. Kissing her breasts still, he ran his hands behind her again.

"Mr. Moss . . . you're not to. . . ." She cringed when he pulled the skirt down and let it drop to the floor. "Oh, no! Mr. Moss, you're the devil!"

But she was not convincing. Her mouth opened and a look of hope replaced what had been a frown. When he yanked white panties below her knees and slid his hand to the bulb of her crotch, she bleated, "I can't believe it's happening . . . don't laugh. I'm a virgin, Mr. Moss."

"All the better then, dear Helen."

Quickly, he lifted one foot, then the other to get the panties free and there she was, presto!, stark naked and positioned for the plucking.

Helen groaned piteously. "I'm so scared, Mr. Moss. What do you want me to do?" As if she didn't know.

"Whatever pleases you, Helen," Erik said placidly.

Her eyes bulged. "You know I don't want a baby."

"I know. Nor do I. That wouldn't do, would it?"

What was going on? This was not his style. His intention had been only to shut her trap by seducing her, cruelly, and, perhaps, if he enjoyed that, then sadistically too, for she was a true interfering bitch, this Helen Ryan. Now, revoltingly and so unlike him, he allowed himself to be traduced by the ritual of seduction; the seducer was falling under the stupefying influence of his victim. Helen's face remained widely ingenuous but her eyes turned, somehow, provocative. He realized, and wasn't surprised, since this was so often the case, that Helen was not nearly as unschooled as she pretended. You couldn't take anything at face value anymore. Were there no more untouched Irish-Catholic lasses left?

He laughed. "Dear Helen. A trollop true, that's you!"

"*Joking*, aren't we?" she said. Suspicion took her, then distrust. He must not make fun of her, no. He had to make her trust him. He could not draw back; he wanted her now, very much. Wanted her tamed.

"Would you come with me?"

"Where? Tell me where."

"Upstairs."

Instantly, she took his hands, pulling him out of the chair. Feeling foolish, Erik put his arm around Helen's bare waist and walked her from the study into the living room.

"We ride," he murmured.

"Yes, let's ride," she agreed.

Like the fabled bicycle, the elevator was built for two. Helen pressed against him, pushing with her breasts. The coffin-like box shuddered and began its slow ascent, then, without warning, stopped.

Helen yelled. "Mother of God, it's stuck!" As quickly, she realized what that meant. "We'll have to ring the alarm and what will they see? Me! In here, with you, and no clothes on. Mr. Moss, what will I say?"

He couldn't help himself. He laughed. "I don't know, dear Helen. *In flagranti, in elevatorum?*"

"It's not funny!"

"Helen, let the beast catch its breath." But she was

right—if he couldn't get the goddamn thing going, they were in for a very embarrassing time. Delicately, Erik touched the *DOWN* button. The elevator thudded to the floor.

"Oh, thank God, sir!"

"Dear Helen, shall we walk up?"

She held his perspiring hand as he led her up the curved staircase and into Kathy's bedroom. There, while she watched, fascinated, he discarded his clothes. Helen's eyes gleamed. Again, timidly, she asked, "What *am* I supposed to do?"

"To receive me," he said simply. "Are you a good hostess?"

"I don't know. I've never practiced being a hostess. How do the hostesses do it?"

He thought for a moment. "They make silly remarks and they flirt and then they fall on their backs and spread their legs . . . and hope their guest enjoys himself."

"All right," she said doubtfully, trying to absorb the spirit of things. "I can do that. How *well* you look today, Mr. Moss. Do come in and enjoy me . . . I mean the party."

He laughed, so heartily. She was trying too hard to please him, Erik wasn't quite sure how to proceed; he was out of practice with the peasantry.

"I'm afraid, Mr. Moss." But her eyes glistened at the sight of him.

"Don't be silly," he said loftily. "You know, I have made love to many women in my lifetime."

Abjectly, she nodded. "I'm sure you have. And now me—the last of the lot. I wouldn't do it unless. . . ."

"The last? *Unless what*?"

"The last is best." Her voice was assured. "The best for last." He looked askance and she added, "The devil has to get his comeuppance. Mrs. Moss told me that," she whispered.

"I don't understand what you're saying, dear Helen. Rule One—no talking."

Mutely, she nodded, backed against the bed and sprawled. In repose, her body softened, and she spread her legs, as a good hostess should. Erik walked the miles between them, wondering how he would prevail. And, of a sudden, it was gone, all his desire, all his determination to subject her.

"What's wrong?" she cried. "Am I ugly?"

It was that remark she'd made, so casually but fearsomely, that put him off—he was *not* the devil. "What did my bitch-wife say? Tell me!"

Helen smiled at him then, so wickedly he was flabbergasted. Satan *was* loose, he thought. "Here, now," she urged, reaching for his waxen rapier, and pulling him toward her.

"Tell me what she said about me!"

"Nothing—that I was to pay no attention when you insulted me, that I should always do what you said."

It was now, he told himself, or never. He had brought her this far and he must complete the job. Helen regarded him challengingly. Roughly, therefore, he placed his hands on her thighs, pushed them apart and lowered himself, presenting himself at the portal, so to speak, doing everything but knocking.

Her eyes danced. "You *are* going to do this?"

"Isn't it what you want?"

Helen clamped her lower lip between her teeth, as if preparing for torture. He entered her very slowly, but surely intruding into a clammy climate.

The way was difficult, often impassable, it seemed, but he pressed bravely forward. She bucked reflexively each time he bested a fleshy obstacle, resisting, trying to draw away but at the same time luring him ahead. She folded her hands over his back, digging in her nails, venting virtuous protest.

So carefully he thrust that her belly collapsed with joy. She held him tightly with her arms. Her legs swung free and the heels came down on the small of his back.

Helen panted, "Don't do it inside me, please. Pull out before you do it."

All of her was directed to the place of union; her body reached at him so beseechingly that, not being able to pull out, he ejaculated painfully. Helen did not notice, only punished herself more, whimpering as she reached a form of climax, a minuscule orgasm.

Seconds later, she cried out. Her eyes rocked and he knew she had achieved fulfillment, that is, total guilt. She began crying hysterically.

"You've done it to me now. Do you know what that means?"

"What does it mean?" He felt like a fool.

"I've commited a mortal sin. And so have you!"

"I'm not a Catholic."

"It doesn't matter," she whimpered. "You don't have to be a Roman Catholic in order to go to hell."

"Oh, nonsense, Helen! I know all about mortal sin— you're already damned a thousand times, for every time you masturbated."

"Oh, no!" she cried frantically. "I was a virgin, Mr. Moss, until this very minute. And now you've ruined me."

"Really? I don't see any blood on the sheet."

Her eyes flickered at him. "It doesn't matter. I did it *for you*, though you treat me so badly."

"Don't talk nonsense, Helen." Trying to avoid her smoldering eyes, he said, "Stop being such a blessed saint."

"Because I love you and have. . . ."

"Love, no!" he exclaimed. "I don't believe in love, darling Helen." Her body leapt as he pronounced the word *darling*. "I believe in lust, that's all."

Her face was wretched. "You'd have us be like the animals, Mr. Moss."

"*We are* animals, after all."

"Oh, no, oh, no. . . ." She struggled underneath him, but he had kept her there, pinned to the bed, his steel fragilely extended within her, slowly recovering temper. "Why did you make me do it then, Mr. Moss, if you think I'm nothing but an animal? And didn't you call me darling?"

"I call everybody 'darling,' " he grunted, holding her shoulders flat. "I love everybody, Helen. Like God does— not personally and individually. I love the human—or animal—race but only in general."

"That's impossible. Oh, what's happening now?" He had resumed a slow beat, hardly moving his hips. "Oh, God save me!"

"It'll be all right, Helen," he whispered. "Just go to confession."

"No, it's no good now. The priest . . . he'd ask me if I'm truly sorry, truly contrite . . . and I'm not. Oh, Mr. Moss! I'll be damned. If I died right now, where would I go?"

"To hell, of course."

At that, she began to cry freely, but nonetheless tugging him forward with her muscular arms, hugging him tightly in her young, nubile arms and legs.

"We'll both go to hell," he pledged.

"Damn you! You don't believe in God, do you?"

He impaled her decisively at each word. "Am . . . I . . . required . . . to?"

She jerked convulsively, for he had pushed her to the limit, to the very edge of the cliff. "I require . . . . you . . . to!"

"And who," he demanded furiously, "might you be . . . to require . . . that . . . of me?"

Helen groaned from far within. Her eyes opened but she didn't see him. She couldn't see anything except blazing scarlet orgasm floating across her vision. She belted out a desperate screech, burst into new tears, gasping hopelessly. "I know it now. You *are* the devil, Mr. Moss. And you've ruined me for the second time."

Darkly, he said, "A person cannot be any more ruined than just plain ruined. It's a definitive state, my darling."

"*My darling!*" she repeated hauntingly. "My darling? What are you saying, Mr. Moss? That word means nothing to you."

"Merely a word, dear, sweet, lovable, adorable Helen." He strung the meaningless endearments together like fish.

"Ah, ah," she sighed, "and here. . . . ." She patted the bed. "Doing it right on your wife's bed, Mr. Moss. Shameless."

"A bed is a bed."

"I won't tell on us. . . . ."

He laughed gently. "No, I wouldn't think you would."

"Now," she said scorchingly, "you're going out to meet a whore, are you? After this? That's why you ruined me, isn't it? So I wouldn't be able to tell?"

"Don't be childish. I . . . ruined you because I desired you."

"No, Mr. Moss, I know better." She squirmed. "Get off me now, please. You're so heavy and your . . . thing—what do you call it anyway?—it's hurting."

"Call it the staff of life," he muttered. "Helen, you were marvelous . . . for a former virgin."

Her body sagged as he stood up and away from her. "You're just saying that."

"Of course I'm just saying it. I just said it, didn't I?"

Agonizingly, she said, "And no love. No love."

"No . . . no love, Helen."

She studied him woefully. "I feel *so guilty*. I could kill myself, Mr. Moss."

He shook his head. "That would be an even worse sin, Helen. Face it—you're in a no-win situation."

Eighteen

It was well past the hour he'd promised Lilly by the time Erik reached the Hotel Eros, a stone's throw from Times Square, New York City. The Eros was appropriately sordid, a truly filthy place but, for its uses, perfect, better than the Plaza or the Pierre, not to speak of the Warwick or Regency. Cracked linoleum paved the way into a dingy lobby and, beneath a flickering neon ceiling fixture, to a front desk more like a bullet-proof post office cubicle than anything else, glass-enclosed with a grated hole for conversation, at face level, with a bald-headed *concierge* whose face had never seen the light of day.

"How're you tonight?" Erik asked evenly.

"Huh? Oh. Haven't seen you in a while."

"I'm meeting somebody."

"She's upstairs." Erik nodded and turned toward the hallway which contained elevator and stairs. "Wanna buy some rubbers?"

"No, thanks. Not tonight."

The elevator door clanged like prison bars. On the fifth floor, down a long, dim corridor, Erik tapped at the door. Her familiar voice was small, frightened. Not surprisingly, for this was not Sunnybrook Farm.

"My darling. . . ." He breathed the passwords into the crack of the door. The chain rattled inside as she removed it and a pale face appeared . . . good God, topped by a growth of wild red hair. "Lilly, *it is you*!"

She smiled so shyly, her eyes bright, bright blue, perhaps not as transparently, at the same time opaquely, blue

187

as his, but a cloudless sky-blue. Even the eyelids were blue-tinted, paper-thin. Her white skin was almost albino-pallid, as if she had been bleached by the electricity he felt jump between them.

Lilly showed no sign of moving, so he pushed inside and closed the door, locking it again securely. "I am so sorry to be late," he whispered. "There was a phone call of the greatest importance."

"I . . . uh . . . was getting ready to leave, Mr. Moss." Her voice was reedy, like that which trickled from crybaby dolls.

"*Erik . . . Erik . . .*" He stepped close to her, put a hand on each of her skinny shoulders and looked into her eyes, unblinkingly forcing his virility on her. "You are lovely, yes, precisely as I imagined you." He kissed her forehead. "And I?"

"You're like your voice," she admitted. But she was thinking of something else. "The man downstairs is awful. He knows you."

"Ah!" Erik chuckled carelessly. "Yes, I have been here before. Now and then, one meets a splendid woman at a party or dinner, in a museum or restaurant, a woman of such abandon she won't rest until she has been possessed in such a place as this. In women, not all women, but some, there is a great appetite for the sordid."

"Me?"

"No, no, not you, I mean older women whose only outlet is sex."

Lilly's eyes fluttered and she showed small white teeth. "I'm amazed that you. . . ."

Erik chuckled. "You mean that Conrad's relative could be such a devil, eh?" He remembered what Helen had said. "Well, I try to be nice to the ladies, you see." He didn't think he was impressing her very much. "And Conrad—where is *Conrad* tonight?" he asked heavily.

Lilly shrugged. "I don't know—out making a bomb with Roberto, I suppose."

"A bomb?" Erik smiled, not quite understanding.

"They're terrorists, didn't you know?"

"Conrad, the little prince, a terrorist? That's hard to believe."

"Yes, it is. Why do you call him the little prince?"

Erik winked at her elaborately, telling her this must be their private joke. "Crown-prince to all that is Darktower."

Mention of Conrad troubled her. She was a little bit loyal, he realized, enough so she looked around worriedly, crossing her arms over her blue sweatshirt. She certainly had not dressed formally for their date. Below the sweatshirt, she was wearing tight corduroy slacks and brown boots.

"I really don't like this place . . . Erik. Maybe we could go someplace for a drink?"

He smiled comfortingly. "My darling, this won't be our permanent place. I have something else in mind. No, for you, this is too awful, an ugly place. I see that and I humbly beg your pardon. But for now what does it matter, when two people are drawn so irresistibly to each other as well, my darling Lilly?"

"Are we?"

"Are we not? Please. . . ." He lifted his hands to her shoulders again, feeling the youthful energy under the sweatshirt. Her body was tense because she wasn't sure what he was going to do. Erik was not sure either. With a generous gesture, he fondled her spare neck, her back, noting the absence of bra-strap, and kissed her forehead, each of her pale cheeks. So close to her, he felt a warm— flurry of breath. "I adore your red hair—I mean, in the sense of wanting to possess a woman with red hair."

"To possess?" Her eyes dimmed.

"Yes, in the sense of wanting someday to make love to a woman with red hair." He brushed her cheek again with his swollen lip. "Later, Lilly, if you like, I will lease a studio, a secret place where you can work and where now and then I will be able to come to talk to you."

"A studio? But I don't need a studio. Conrad's. . . ."

He stopped her before she could expand that thought. "Perhaps *you* don't. But *we* might."

Her doubt, indecision, remained. "Maybe we ought to get out of here . . . Erik." Her narrow face shadowed enough to jeopardize his strategy. "I'm not sure we're talking on the same wave-length, Erik. You know, of course, I'm living with Conrad.''

"God! Don't remind me," he exclaimed superciliously. "Remember, Prince Conrad is nothing more to me than a stranger in the night.''

She bit her lip. Her blue eyes flamed with remorse.

"Why are you looking at me like that? Ah, you noticed my bruises—I stopped suddenly yesterday in the car. If I had not been wearing a safety belt, I would have gone through the windshield.''

"I hardly noticed it," she said embarrassedly. "A cut. . . .''

"And bruise. A very close call, Lilly. Not everyone has a pretty face all the time, you see.''

"Should we go?''

"No, we should not. I would like to kiss you now.''

She closed her mouth tightly. "I'm not sure about this. I don't think. . . .''

But she had no choice in the matter. He put his mouth to her soft lips, forcing his tongue between them, against her teeth. She gasped and began to struggle, but he held her tightly. She was so light it was no job at all. He laughed gruffly, the sound muffled in her flesh.

He moved his face away from her, staring into her eyes, now alight with concern. "I won't hurt you, Lilly, I promise," he hissed.

"You better not.''

"Please. . . .'' He softened his expression. "I'm so tired. I need a place . . . a person . . . somehow to give me respite. May I not worship you a little, Lilly?''

She didn't know what to say. A problem like Erik Moss had never been hers to handle. "I don't understand you," she said unsteadily. "I don't know if you want to rape me or just fuck me . . . Erik.''

"Ah! Do not use such language, please, Lilly!''

"I'm sorry. It's the way we talk.''

"I can't stand it!" he exclaimed. "You are not afraid of me, are you?''

"I don't know. It's so strange. Your eyes scare me. They're like *hidden* in those cavities.''

"Bags!" He laughed gleefully. "That's because I am old, Lilly."

"You're not *old*," she disagreed.

"Lilly, have mercy on me, please."

"I've never. . . ." She almost didn't say it. "I've never made love to an older man." Her bravery revived at his seeming indecision and her eyes twinkled. "The guy at the desk thinks I'm a hooker—maybe you should pay me, mister."

"Pay you?"

"Sure, lovey." Her eyes narrowed shrewdly. "A fifty ought to do it."

He muttered weakly. "What do I get for the fifty?"

"I'll French you," she said daringly.

"Lilly!"

"That's the way us hookers talk, mister."

Firmly, he said, "Now, Lilly, no more play acting." He glanced at the bed. It was a sickly affair, sagging, covered with a thin blanket. Two flat pillows lay against the headboard. "Come. Lie down beside me."

She took a deep breath and nodded. "All right, See if you can get me hot." She let him kiss her tenderly, very carefully, closing her eyes, responding to his tongue with a light pressure of her own.

"Ah, Lilly," he whispered, "it will be you who will save me."

"You think so?" She was not very impressed with saving. Perhaps that was more in Helen's line. Erik slipped his hand under her sweatshirt and, encouragingly, she moved her arm so he'd have space to palm her breast, so tiny, the nipple hardly bigger than a pimple. She breathed more easily now, with more assurance. "Oh, . . . you're succeeding. You're getting me hot!"

"Good."

As he kissed her passionately, sucking on her mouth, thrusting tongue, she began to feel for him, first hesitantly, then more boldly, leading him on demandingly. Abruptly, Lilly jerked her body to attention and pulled her sweatshirt over her head. As swiftly, she kicked off the brown boots and then made him unzip her jeans and slip them down.

"Ah, Lilly! So beautiful, all of you."

"Get undressed."

When he was naked, she lay on top of him, massaging his body with her own scarecrow frame, all hips and sharp ribs but nevertheless tantalizing. He oozed pleasure. She was the most lovely thing he had ever experienced. Was that possible? Better than Dolly even? Yes, better than Dolly.

"Suck my tits," Lilly commanded and he did. "I'm going to sit on your face now." She did and he lapped her like an orgiaste until she screamed thinly at the ceiling. "It's nice I found you. I'm glad you made that obscene phone call."

"Lilly, you are so wonderful and my weekend was so trying. I was out in Port London."

"Of course. With your wife." But she said it without rancor.

"Conrad told you," he assumed. Yes, true. "But you don't know her."

"I feel I do," she said absently. She perched over him, meeting his gigantic erection and slowly accepting it, lowering herself until, unbelievably, it was entirely part of her, as tiny as she was. "Whew," she whistled, "full up . . . yes, your wife," she sighed. "Conrad talks about his wonderful sister all the time—so I feel I know her. And now I know you, don't I—in the biblical sense, as they say." She grinned, gritting her teeth and swaying.

"Don't talk. I don't want to hear about him. Prince Conrad has never accepted me—he has always hated me, I think."

Lilly's eyes closed, her small face pointed upwards ecstatically. "He'd hate you the more now, wouldn't he?"

Erik lay back luxuriously as she used him, relishing the violation—for, yes, she was violating *him* now, not the other way around. She'd had nothing to fear, had she? Silently, fiercely, she increased the urgency of her movement, bearing down, asking for more, more, more. She didn't make any bones about it, this lovely flower child. She braced her long fingers on his belly, as if balancing, hiked herself up to the point of losing contact, then with a release of air, thumping down . . . up. . . .

As she approached her moment, he helped, forcing himself far into her, grinding, hurting, until she climaxed shrilly, dropping forward to kiss him hungrily, angrily, careless of his bruised mouth. Erik let himself come at last, gushing, thankful he had not spent everything on Helen.

"Lilly, you drive me. . . ."

"Bananas?" she grunted joyfully. "Is that so? How can that be? I'm only a kid."

"No, no, I know you, Lilly, you're an old soul."

"I understand," she teased, her mouth fastened to the side of his neck, "you just like little girls, lovey."

He smiled happily. "And I will eat your toes, little one."

"And the hairy red pussy, don't forget about that."

He put his hand between them, at the joining, feeling the sharp angles of her pelvis. Lilly seemed undernourished, like a prisoner in a camp, those creatures starved and whipped and bestialized into submission. But of course she was not subdued. She had power, he felt, great power. Incredible, Erik thought, the strange shapes and dimensions life could assume.

"I know what else you like," she murmured, "you like the sensation of splitting me in half. You think you are, but you're not, you know. I'll tell you a secret, that's impossible."

"I know," he said. Smugly, he went on, "And you admit now, don't you, that we first met several incarnations ago, probably in ancient Babylon. Even with my eyes closed, I know you from the past."

"It'd be nice to think so—keep talking." Lilly was indifferent to such speculation. Something more relevant occurred to her. "There's no way Conrad can find out about this, is there?"

"How could he? I'm certainly not going to tell him."

"You know," she muttered, "I wouldn't want to hurt him. You've got to understand—he's a good kid."

"Whatever you say, my darling." He allowed himself

to think about it, then expressed the obvious. "He resents me because of Ratoff, you see," he said brusquely. "Have you met the Ratoff creature yet, my darling?"

"Yes—before Mr. Ratoff went to California." Lilly hesitated. "Conrad adores him."

Erik made a *hrumphing* noise. "Yes . . . unfortunately."

"He says Mr. Ratoff was like a father—years ago."

"A father?" Erik chuckled.

"Yes! No more than that," Lilly said sternly. "And no less! He swore to me . . . anyway, Mr. Ratoff is very sick."

"Yes," Erik murmured. "And he's also ill."

Nineteen

After they'd finished loving each other to stupefaction, they dressed and left the awful place, walking up Sixth Avenue, called the Avenue of the Americas, to the Algonquin Hotel. In the little bar to the right of the entrance, he ordered Lilly brandy and for himself a Scotch and soda. They sat at a little table-for-two and he talked to her about love. But the longer, the more eagerly and persuasively he talked, the less sure Lilly was about anything.

"Would it be so outrageous?" Erik demanded softly.

Lilly shrugged. "I don't know. You surprise me. You scare me. I mean—it shouldn't go too far, should it?"

Stiffly, wounded, he said, "If I love you. . . ."

"Oh, Christ! You couldn't. You don't! It wouldn't work."

"It would," he declared so seriously. "Think about it. Don't be frightened; it's the most natural thing in the world."

She agreed to that much and no more. Then it was time to go. Erik put her in a taxi and gave her a twenty-dollar bill, not the fifty she'd asked for, smiled, and sent her on her way.

It was after midnight by the time Lilly got back to the Village. She hadn't counted on a reception committee. Sourly, she surveyed the unlikely foursome. As curious a figure as Roberto was, the two characters Lilly had never seen before were much more so.

Roberto affected tailored suits with vests; he was clean-shaven and well-barbered. But his two friends—for they had to be his friends, not Conrad's—were positively raunchy. One was long-haired and unkempt from head to foot. Maybe thirty years old, probably a lot younger than he looked, he sat slouched against the wall, scratching at one of those filthy army fatigue jackets much favored by the alienated. The second stranger was fat, dull-eyed, his bulk contained in a soiled jogging suit. A padded black wind- breaker with Mao collar lay on the floor beside him.

Roberto, spread out on the couch, had obviously been doing most of the talking; long fingers pressed together under his nose, he scowled, obviously annoyed at her interruption.

"What's this? A meeting of the cell?" Lilly demanded.

The unkempt one sneered. "Who's the cunt?"

Conrad looked pained but remained silent. He didn't try to defend her.

"Shut up," Roberto growled. "This is Lilly . . . Lilly, meet Carl."

Lilly looked at him scornfully. "Fuck you, Carl."

Blackly, Roberto added, "And Dork." He waved at the fat one.

Lilly didn't even bother to say hello to Dork. He looked too stupid to answer. Christ, she thought, and now this—a bunch of dumb asses talking bullshit.

"Lilly," Conrad said, "you're late. Where have you been?"

She had her answer all prepared. "I went out to the movies . . . what the hell's going on? Besides name- calling?"

"We've just been talking," Conrad muttered.

"What about?"

"Lilly . . . please," Conrad said. "Nothing important."

The one called Carl snarled, "What? Nothing important!"

"I said shut up," Roberto snapped. Dejectedly, Carl dropped his chin on his chest but didn't look any the less vicious. Roberto smiled at Lilly now, his black eyes so liquid and soft you might have been deceived about him. Nervously, she looked at Conrad. She'd been sort of in love with Roberto for a few months before meeting Conrad, and Roberto had kind of handed her over to Conrad, his idea being that Conrad might prove to be very important to them what with his connections and all that money. And so, not happily, not unhappily either, she had come to live with Conrad Darktower. And now, she reminded herself, she had met—met, yes, the very word—Erik Moss, whom Conrad despised. Irony, that's what it was and irony delighted her.

"This is a meeting of the disloyal opposition," Roberto stated proudly.

The dumb-looking one called Dork drawled, "Somebody like you, cunt, wouldn't understand what that means."

"No, I wouldn't," she said.

Disgustedly, Carl snarled, "Some big social consciousness you got here, Roberto."

"Yeah, fuck," Dork grumbled, "friends like this, who needs enemies?"

Lilly glared at one, then the other. "Okay, scumbags, meeting's over. Buzz off!"

Carl and Dork both turned to Roberto for guidance. He nodded. "Yeah, you might as well go."

"Suits me," Carl grunted. He assembled his bones and pushed them off the floor, scratching his ass. Dork did the same, slipping on his Mao winter uniform. "So long, *cunt*," Carl said.

Lilly moved out of the doorway to make way. "Don't come back," she said. "It hasn't been nice meeting you."

"Jesus," Roberto sighed, "do you have to be so rude, Lilly? They're not bad, just a little highstrung."

Conrad stared at his hands, his smooth face troubled. Lilly remembered what Erik had called him: "the Prince." "This kind of stuff, Roberto," he stammered, "I don't want anything more to do with it."

"Like what stuff?" Lilly interrupted. He was such a baby—twenty-four years old and he needed twenty-four-hour protection.

Roberto grinned at her, over his fingertips. "The kind of stuff I'm into, Lilly."

"Revolution! Shit! Don't make me laugh."

Roberto's eyes turned beady. "Those two guys are fighters. They don't like what's going on in this country."

"Oh yeah? And what are they going to do about it?"

His answer was simple, calmly delivered. "They're most likely going to start killing people."

Lilly froze. She knew it was all sham, this fixation of Roberto's on violence, terror, killing. Yet, he never stopped talking about it.

"You're a stupid ass!" She swung her eyes to Conrad. "His big hero is that nut-assassin, that Venezuelan."

"Yes! Carlos!" Roberto cried. "And? So? What's wrong with that? He *is* a hero. They've never caught him. He goes into the jaws of death and comes out unscathed."

"Bullshit!" Lilly exclaimed just as excitedly. "He's a coward. He hits from the back. You told me so yourself."

Roberto smirked. "So? This is not a gentleman's war, Lilly. If you can hit from the back and get away, then you hit from the back."

Lilly kept her eye on Conrad. "Enough! I don't want *you* playing around with it." But curiosity drew her back to what Roberto had said. "Just who is it they're going to start killing?"

Indifferently, he shrugged. "Cops most likely. The pigs. They're easiest—you just catch 'em alone on a side street."

Conrad spoke hesitantly. "That *is* a coward's way of doing it, Roberto."

"Yeah? How would you do it, pretty boy? There's no such thing as bravery or cowardice in a war like this."

"You're crazy," Lilly stormed. "And that one you call Dork? You should rename him *stupid*. I wouldn't go to a *war* with a *moron* like him."

Roberto grimaced. "It so happens, Lilly, that Dork is an expert at making pipebombs. Don't get him mad at you." Gracefully, he slid off the couch, buttoning his form-fitting jacket. "Well, time for me to go, comrades."

Christ, she could not bear it! "Comrades? Jesus! You're some revolutionary, aren't you? Where'd you get that suit? It's a Pierre Cardin, isn't it? At least your two buddies dress the part, *Roberto*."

He was unperturbed. "Don't talk foolishly—behind the lines dressed like this, I can go anywhere. I could walk right into the Princeton Club and they wouldn't blink an eye . . . sit right down and have a drink with that pig of a father of yours or your bloated Eric Moss. . . . Right, *Con*?''

Lilly drew a careful breath, calming herself, pacing him. "The object being?"

"Simple. I gather information about which of the pigs is worth the trouble."

"*What* do you mean?

Pompously, like an ego-inflated attorney working his jury, Roberto gripped the lapels of his suitcoat and sneered at Lilly as if she were completely stupid. "We need money for our cause, Lilly. You've read the newspapers. How do the fighters in Italy get their money? They kidnap important people and hold them for ransom."

She snorted. "In this country, you hold up Brinks' trucks, *Roberto*. Somebody ought to ask the police to protect you from yourselves."

Hotly, Roberto said, "I'd advise you not to think like that, Lilly."

"And you?" she demanded of Conrad, "what do *you* advise?"

He shook his head and grinned. "I'm just listening."

"*Con* is with us, honey, whatever you say about him," Roberto smirked. "He hates his class, don't you, *Con*?"

Conrad, to her dismay, stammered, "I don't know . . . it's just that. . . ."

Roberto stopped him. "It's *just* . . . they stink. The fish starts stinking from the head down. Lenin said that."

"Lenin was an asshole," Lilly said. "Anybody who reads the papers can see that."

Roberto's body shook in anger. Lilly smiled, pleased to get at him. He shook his finger at her. "You're not a political person, Lilly, goddamn it. You're nothing but a goddamn artist, a parasite on the ass of society!"

"Thank God!" She glared at Conrad. "And you? You want to change things too? Careful, they might stop giving you an allowance . . . you might have to go to work."

"Lilly!" Conrad protested. At least, he could manage a

little irritability, if not anger. "I'm not like that and you know it."

"What? Not a hypocrite, like *him*?" She pointed at Roberto. "His parents send him money so he can go to school—and the asshole is going to *law* school."

Roberto began to hop up and down. "Lilly, you don't understand the fucking dialectic. Jesus!"

She bawled at him, "And what *is* the fucking dialectic?"

"I couldn't even explain it to somebody like you!"

Once more she challenged Conrad. "How long are you going to listen to this? Tell him to go!"

"We're not *hurting* anybody. We're only discussing . . . This is interesting for me."

"You're wasting your time," Lilly said coldly. "If that's what you want, go ahead. Thanks—not me."

Roberto glared at her vindictively. "You *love* this society, don't you? I know why—because you think the assholes are going to buy your shitty pictures, use the money they've stolen from the peasants and workers to support you as a parasite."

"Parasite?" she hollered. "Thief? And where did you steal that suit? I know you didn't pay for it."

"At Barney's, goddamn it! It's not stealing. We call it expropriation."

She laughed wickedly. "Calling all men to Bar—ney's, is that it?"

Conrad finally began to smile and Lilly wound up, like a baseball hero, to throw her curveball. "Your name isn't even Roberto, you fake!"

"How in the hell do you know that?" Roberto yelped.

"I used to see letters addressed to you, asshole. Your real name is Charley Underwood. You're no more god-damn Latino than I am."

Charley Underwood paled. "You bitch! You looked at my mail? How dare you look at *my mail*?"

She shrugged. "That's the dialectic, Charley. Nothing is bad if it helps my cause. It's just a matter of definition."

"Roberto" grabbed up his lambswool topcoat. "It doesn't matter what my real name is. I may be Charley Under-wood but I *think* Roberto."

"You do not know a single word of Spanish, Charley. You're a phony," Lilly accused.

He compressed his lips angrily. "You two are a pair of swine."

Conrad, at last, stood up. "Hey!" He was taller than Charley Underwood. Charley shrank from Conrad, Lilly noticed with something close to rapture. "Roberto . . . Charley . . . you better hit the road."

Roberto moved toward the door. "I'm going because I want to, not because you're telling me to leave. You don't scare me, you know."

They were such children. Lilly had made her break with Roberto by moving in with Conrad. Perhaps the time was approaching for the next break. Listening to Roberto make his final declamations before slamming out of Conrad's apartment, she remembered Erik, his hard body; her own body still ached from him.

"Lilly," Conrad said, when Charley Underwood could be heard thumping down the stairs, "you know he can't stand anybody making fun of him."

"That's because he's a child," she murmured. "And it's stupid for you to waste your time on these guys."

"Probably," he agreed mildly. He usually did agree with her.

"Come on," she urged, "you can't hate. You're a lover, not a hater."

"Am I? I don't know."

She felt motherly now as she made him sit down beside her on the couch. Lilly had had a surfeit of love for one night but nonetheless she had to comfort him, hold his blond head against her bosom.

"I don't know, Lilly. I feel very depressed."

"Why should you be depressed?"

His head burrowed into her scant bosom. "Seeing Stefan again. . . . He's so sick . . . it's sad. They ruined him, they sent him away. For that, I *can* hate them and I can agree with Roberto."

"But you don't know everything that happened. Or how. . . ."

"I know it was cruel."

"What did . . . Stefan say about it?"

He moved his head negatively. "Nothing. He wouldn't talk about it," he murmured. "Katharine could have saved him. It was my father's decision, Richard Darktower's," he said bitterly. "He was too strong for all of them . . . including my mother—she's never had an original thought. She buys clothes and goes to lunch—that's her whole life. Think about it—they sent Stefan away because he was a playboy—a dilettante. And they're *all* dilettantes. That's what Roberto is talking about—and that's where I could agree with him. Not with the killing and all but I can agree they're not socially . . . what? Worthy? Worth preserving?"

"No." She shook her head stubbornly. "Don't get it wrong. Remember that Roberto is a dilettante too. He's just as fake and boring as all the people he'd like to kill."

Conrad smiled playfully. "You're not a revolutionary, Lilly."

"And neither are you, lovey."

Twenty

It was getting on toward midnight and Darktower was feeling cold and stiff and tired. He was also worried that his "relative" from New Jersey would be arriving Wednesday. He hoped Kate was going to pull herself together before then.

"I think," he murmured, "that we need some sleep."

There was nothing more he could say to convince her that this Gene Francotti, who seemed a very solid, determined sort of citizen would, if it were a matter of simple fate, change his mind and have her back. What would be, would be; there was not a hell of a lot anybody could do about it.

Katherine curled in the chair opposite him, her long legs tucked up under her, staring morosely at the fire, which he'd been feeding and poking the whole night long. Finally, she asked the question he'd known was bound to come.

"Why did you make Steve leave?"

Stolidly, he said, "He wasn't good for you . . . for any of us."

"He was as good for me as Erik Moss. He was kinder than Erik Moss. Why did you ever let me marry Erik Moss?"

"Ratoff was no good, Kate. You know that. He was a mess. He shamed us."

"Shamed *you*, not me. But you made me leave him and then I had to marry Erik."

"You didn't *have* to marry anybody."

"You were uncomfortable with me not married," Kate charged.

Darktower decided he was not going to be dragged over the coals again on this, not just because Kate had lost her grip on a man. "Listen," he said, "*I* was not uncomfortable about anything. If you remember, it was your mother who wanted you to marry him. I *never* cared for Moss." She tossed her head so disdainfully that Darktower went on sharply, "My mistake was not getting the son-of-a-bitch checked out. I remember telling myself: get him checked, get him checked! But then, everybody was so eager, I figured, well, if the son-of-a-bitch worked for Merriwether, he couldn't be all bad. No," he summed it up, "I was perfectly willing for you to wait until a good American came along."

She laughed bitterly. "Like Harrison Percy, maybe."

"Harrison Percy was a goddamn fool, and especially a goddamn fool because he married your friend Dolly."

She turned her head to peer at him in the dimness. "What's so bad about Dolly?"

"What do you suppose?" he demanded irritably. "She's man-crazy, and always was. 'Hot-pants,' we used to call what she's got."

Kathy laughed caustically. "Well, *she* has fun, Daddy. Tell me, what am *I* supposed to do?"

"Carry on!" Darktower said quickly. "Get your divorce—never mind about this Italian guy. Get the divorce anyway."

"There wouldn't seem to be any particular hurry about it now," she said desolately.

"You're wrong. The guy could change his mind tomorrow. Sounds to me as if he doesn't like being dangled, doesn't like guys coming to bribe him."

She shrugged. "I think I'll change *my* mind and let Erik *dangle*. He's made me suffer enough."

Darktower stiffened. "In what way? How has he made you suffer?"

"It's hard to explain. He's perfectly proper and polite and everything. But he looms, and lurks. He can be cruel in a dozen small things an outsider cannot notice."

"The son-of-a-bitch," Darktower rasped. "I've always thought he was creepy. But you're right, he *is* very proper."

"And propriety is everything, *isn't* it?"

He chuckled at her sarcasm. "I haven't done too well in that department lately, have I?"

"Dolly is convinced the hookers were *your* idea."

Darktower felt his blush even in the shielding darkness of the library. "That little tramp! She would say that! The truth is, those two women surprised the life out of me when they showed up."

"But you didn't flee, did you?"

"No, I didn't. I'm sorry if you were embarrassed, Kate."

"Hardly," she cried lightly. "I was thrilled and pleased for you. Why *shouldn't* you have some fun too?" Her profile sharpened in the soft firelight. "Is it true that your former wife played around?"

"What? Why would you ask *me* that? That is not a nice thing to suggest about your mother."

"But is it true?" she insisted. "Dolly said so."

Darktower was highly insulted, not so much for Mrs. Himmelmann as for himself. "That goddamn Dolly! What makes her an expert on my family? Why don't you ask Mrs. Himmelmann if it's true?"

"Because I'm asking you—very nicely too. It doesn't matter to me, even if it is true. Is that why you divorced her?"

Slowly, biting the words like bullets, he said, "No, divorce was merely the last act of a long epic. Whatever happened, it started happening a lot earlier. You never knew any of it." Or had she, blast it? "Anyway, it's nothing for you to brood about."

"I won't, believe me," Katharine said. "I don't intend to brood about anything anymore."

"Good. Don't. Those spells of yours, it's not worth it—just because this Italian guy is difficult is no reason for you to get desperate."

"I slept with him, you know."

He was embarrassed. "I know that," he snapped,

"including right here, which was not the most judicious thing."

"I'm sorry," she said, but she wasn't thinking sorry. She was thinking about her Italian. "I'm going to get him back." Saying it, she stared at him, her face determined.

"Good. You do that."

She held up her hand. "Don't say—what Kate wants, Kate gets."

"I wouldn't dream of it." Darktower hit his knees with his fists and stood up. "Well, what about drinking to it? To the capture of your Italian! A brandy and then we turn in?"

"Francotti told me if I ever drank anything again but wine he was going to beat the shit out of me."

"Good God . . . he is forceful, isn't he? Never mind—brandy is but the further career of good wine." Darktower held the decanter up to the faint light and poured two moderate drinks. Then he sat down closer to her. "Shall I tell you something?"

"If it's cheerful."

"Well, you know those two women who came to . . . entertain us at Penton's? One of them is named Clara Riding—she's a nice person. Dolly was wrong about them being hookers. They're not."

"I hope not." Darktower could see the glitter of a smile on her face.

He blurted it out. "I invited her up for a few days. She'll be arriving Wednesday. You don't need to tell anybody about that."

"Who would I tell?" she demanded, surprised.

"I'm sure your mother, Mrs. Himmelmann, would be astonished to hear about it."

"You *want* me to tell her! To make her jealous."

"No, not jealous, pray not that. I would like her to be aware that the world didn't stop turning when she married Mr. Himmelmann."

Kathy nodded somberly. "You've invited a shady lady here to Wainscott? You'll get run out of town."

"Bull," he retorted stoutly. "She's not a hooker and she doesn't look shady. She's a clairvoyant. Besides, don't talk about women of shady reputation—half the society hostesses in New York started life as whores in Paris or Rome.''

"Everybody talks about them too, don't they?"

"Let 'em talk," Darktower said. "Why shouldn't I enjoy myself? You just said so. Besides, I really admire Miss Riding."

"I hope you'll be careful."

He dismissed the caution. "That's easy to say. I hope *you'll* be very careful too . . . but let me tell you something, Katharine Margaret Darktower . . . I don't intend to worry about you. I worried myself enough over Ratoff and Moss. You're on your own now."

She drew a contrite breath. "Poor Daddy. You're always picking up the pieces, aren't you?"

"Not anymore," he said harshly. But, more thoughtfully, for there was no way he was not going to be involved in her financial affairs, Darktower added, "Moss won't come cheap." He was thinking of the trusts. She was protected. The family was protected. But the trusts were not foolproof either.

"We'll see," she said gloomily. "Maybe he'll just walk away."

"And what are you going to do about the Italian?" Darktower asked patiently.

She shook her head. "I guess I'll just have to throw myself on his mercy."

Twenty-One

"I'm not asking you for anything," Katharine told Erik
coldly. "When I'm ready for the divorce I'll have it. I'm
not telling you to move out. I just don't want to see very
much of you anymore, that's all."

He faced her across the living room of the Park Avenue
apartment. She had just arrived from the Island after spending most of a leisurely Sunday with her father, not appre-
hensive about confronting Erik but at the same time not
eager for the meeting.

With that annoying, dogged little smile on his lips, he
stared at her, placing two fingers on his jagged chin.

"This," he mused, not speaking to her but around her,
"this is a strange specimen of womanhood with which I
am not familiar."

"Naturally," she replied sharply, "you would have to
diagnose me, wouldn't you? Didn't you hear anything I
said to you in Port London? I *told you* I was in love with
someone else."

Erik nodded, unimpressed. "Yes, you said something
like that. But I paid little attention. I thought it impossible—
when I love you so much—that you could fall in love with
another."

What he'd said was a lie, like everything else. "Make
me a drink."

This was something he did understand. "My darling—
should you?"

"Yes, I should and don't try anymore to make me out
an alcoholic," she said angrily. "I'm not and you needn't

try to persuade me that I am. I simply want a drink. A vodka, please."

"Kah-ti. . . ." He endeavored to look very troubled.

"Make the goddamn drink!"

He shrugged and walked to the chrome-and-glass trolley. It was then that Helen Ryan moved into focus in the doorway.

"What is it, Helen?" Katharine asked.

"Is there . . . anything . . . I can get you?" Helen faltered.

Erik didn't look up. "No, nothing. Thank you. Please close the door."

Helen stared at his back, then plaintively tried to smile at Katharine, who flicked her eyes, dismissing her.

Erik handed her the vodka. He had made himself a Scotch.

"So," she said flatly, "I think we understand each other now, don't we?"

His little bow was ironic and his accent heavier, as it was when he became nervous. "Am I to understand that you forbid me your bed?"

"Yes. Definitely. You needn't click your heels either. This isn't out of some German operetta."

"No, I see—now we have Italian *opera buffe*, a comic opera with Mr. Francotti as the baritone. The dream lover? Yes? My darling?"

Her face was stiff. "Not necessarily. You disgusted him so much he sent me away. I'm sure that will give you *some* satisfaction."

"Ah ha! Then my visit did have some effect."

"You told him a bunch of lies about me."

"Never! I told him merely that I love you very much and, were I to lose you, heavens knows what desperate action I might take."

"You bastard! You told him I was insane, a drunk, a dope addict . . . that I was a sexual hysteric!"

He smiled distantly, wanly. "But you *are*, my darling. Only I know these things about you . . . your fantasies, good God! How many times have you told me of them?"

She stared at him blankly. She did not really understand him. "I don't know what you mean."

He shook his head patiently, trying to take her arm but she pulled away violently. "My darling, in your moments of drunkenness, you would not remember." He turned away, shaking his head. "I am so happy Mr. Francotti saw the light of reason and logic. I told him *nothing* specific, you know. I generalized."

"I don't believe you," she said slowly. She would not give in to him, never again. "Whatever happens now between Francotti and me, it won't matter to our relationship. We're finished. The way I feel now. . . ." She hesitated, searching for the proper words. "I look at you. Reptilian . . . yes. I think a reptile would be preferable to your company now, *my darling*!"

His body stiffened. His eyes seemed to crawl away, retracting beneath their heavy hoods. "A reptile?" He repeated the description with relish and Katharine realized how close to the mark it was. "What a charming metaphor to use upon your own husband. Was I always a reptile? If so, then you must have been attracted to me for some reason. Perhaps you are a female reptile."

"Maybe so. No, I was thinking of it in another way—a reptile lies there, coldly, motionlessly."

"Yes!" he sneered. "Preferably in the sun to warm his ugly scales. A reptile needs warmth. He crawls out of the shadows toward warmth, the sun . . . and toward moisture. He has no moisture. He needs it like life's blood. Notice, sometime, since you are talking of reptiles, how they lie against the wall. If you spit on the tiles, in a moment they will be there, their forked tongues darting for the moisture you have made for them. It is then," he stated so coldly she could not stop from flinching, "it is then you step on them and kill them. No other way can you trap and kill them—only when they come to suck your moisture."

She gasped for breath. "Yes! You've described our relationship."

"Described the way you feel about me, is that it?"

Her heart was pounding but she could be as cruel as he, this tanned torturer. "Yes."

"Very well." He moved backward and dropped very casually into the easy chair by the fireplace. "What you suggest suits me very well. For your information, I am meeting with Herman Himmelmann. I want to go back to my career." Katharine merely shrugged. "I have my income," he continued, "but I will need more. I will look for a place to live, something small, and I will begin to spend time there."

"Good!" She had wondered how to introduce the subject of money. "You have the money for a down payment. . . ." His eyebrows hopped haughtily. "The ten thousand you left with Francotti," she added.

Kathy opened her purse and took out the envelope of money. She tossed it but it fell on the carpet between them. Erik glanced down, but did not deign to stoop. He went on as though she'd said nothing.

"In due course," he continued pedantically, staring into the golden whisky he was twisting in front of his eyes, "in due course, when I am settled and when the child has become accustomed to this rupture—for *her*," he murmured, "it must be painless, natural and for *her*, outwardly, we must remain *friends*. Friends, yes." His mouth circled the word and transformed it for Katharine into a hateful word. "I think only of the child. For myself, I care nothing." The mouth drew down. "Then in a year or so, I will withdraw. I think I shall return to Europe. I hate it here."

"Do you? I thought you enjoyed playing country squire and preservation buff and man-about-town."

He shook his head severely. "I despise this country. I do not admire Americans. I did not before and I like them less now, having lived with them."

Katharine was unimpressed. "Except for James Merriwether, that is. Don't forget about him. You worshipped him, *my darling*."

"Did I?" he responded coldly.

"I thought you did. He was very good to you, wasn't he?"

His chin cocked off-center. He nodded reluctantly. "He was good to me, but I was good to him as well. It was not overpaid, I can assure you. Merriwether had his dirty laundry, like everybody else.''

"Not you, though,'' she pointed out acridly. "You're clean as a whistle, aren't you?''

Erik nodded coolly. "Yes, relatively so.''

"Why are you going to Herman? Why don't you go back to Merriwether? Everyone says he holds you in such high esteem.''

"He does, yes, I believe so. But I could not, not after leaving him so abruptly. He never forgives that. You see what I sacrificed, my darling?'' he drawled.

"I'm *so* sorry.''

"That I had the misfortune to fall in love with you?'' He shrugged and laughed. "I regret nothing.''

"You and Edith Piaf,'' she said laconically.

"Yes.'' Erik chuckled. "And all the time, you and your father, the redoubtable Darktower, thought I was interested only in your money. Not true! I am here because of you. Everything is because of you. The child . . . my lost career . . . everything. And only because I fell in love with you—when *you*, as I have discovered, are incapable of loving anyone.''

"That is not true!''

"No,'' he said briskly, "it is true. I know that. I told Francotti—men fall in love with Kathy and Kathy does not reciprocate..''

Angrily, violently she shook her head. "It's a lie! How do you dare tell anyone a thing like that about me? I *can* love. I *am* in love . . . right now!''

"With him?'' Erik shook his head stubbornly. "I know you are not, even as you sit there telling me you are. You fantasize. Love is beyond you, true love. You are capable only of fantasy love.''

Resistant, she watched him, remembering she must not believe anything he said. "Think what you want.''

"I will. I have an opinion and I know I am right.''

"Well, then, let me tell you I will feel no pain whatsoever when I see the last of you.''

"I am sure that is so.''

"Then why delay your departure? You hate it here so much, go back to Europe immediately."

He studied her in his deadly calm. "I have just explained to you what is involved. When all is prepared, I will go. Obviously, I must prepare. I cannot hurl myself into the unknown."

She closed her eyes for a second. "This is boring." She finished the vodka and got to her feet. On her way to the drinks trolley, she kicked the envelope of money closer to him, but still he did not move to retrieve it.

Quietly, but with hostility in his voice, he said, "You are drinking too much. Don't deny it. Personally, I care not at all if you are distraught because of this Francotti."

She kept going. "I'm not distraught. You've managed to screw it up pretty well but I see things clearly now. I am in love with him. I know it now."

"Whatever. What I am trying to say is not easy to express, but I must say it. With your drinking, custody of a child would be a problem. I would be . . . unwilling . . . for Margaret to live with a person who is constantly soaked in vodka."

Unperturbed, Katharine put ice in her glass and poured more of the drink he had just mentioned. Hardly raising her voice, she said, "You son-of-a-bitch, don't think I don't understand what you're doing."

"What might that be?"

She shrugged. "Setting us up for the payoff. Why don't you just tell me right now, *my darling*, how much?"

Erik blushed bright, furious red from white forehead to throat, where tie met skin. He put his glass down and eased out of the chair. He paced across the room. "That is very insulting to me."

"No more than you are to me. Don't think you're going to blackmail me."

His mouth tightened, making wrinkles at the corners. "You *are* a drunk."

"And you. . . ." Wildly, she sought words that would hurt him. "You are a reptile—stand there so I can spit and then you can crawl for it . . . and I'll step on you."

His eyes dropped balefully, as if he were taking aim.

"No one will step on me, my darling. Have no fear of that."

She lifted her glass shakily. "I know what my feeling about you is now—I hate you! I'll divorce you right away if that's what you're angling for. You'll get your money." He flushed again. "Why don't you get it off the floor to start with, get down on your knees and crawl for it."

The slap was unexpected. It was not a powerful blow but it was smartly delivered and it stung and projected her several feet backward. His eyes dug at her. "Call it mental cruelty, if you wish."

"Or physical. Battery." She put her hand to her cheek. "You actually hit me. At least that's an emotion."

"I did not want to bruise your fair skin," he grunted. "If I had wished, I could have knocked you unconscious. The force of the blow was quite calculated."

"I'm sure," she mocked. "Like with Francotti? You're a bully. He knocked you on your ass, didn't he?"

His eyes jumped furiously. "I was not prepared for the cowardly blow. He is an emotional, impulsive man."

"Exactly," Katharine exclaimed. "And you—no, *nothing* out of passion!"

"Correct, my darling," he said bitingly, "it will never be said that Erik Moss was involved in a crime of passion."

"Your face is still swollen," she observed, not kindly. Then, before he could stop her, or move out of the way, her hand flashed and she threw her drink at him.

"Ah ha!" he cried, almost joyously. He caught her arms and held them fast, pinned to her sides. The glass fell on the floor. "Now, my little brave one," he muttered, "please for you to pick the envelope from the floor and give it to me."

"No!"

"Yes!" Laughing nastily, he put his knee behind her legs and buckled them. She went down. He released her right arm. "Pick it up, my darling."

"No!"

His hand gripped the back of her neck and he shook her head roughly, his fingers digging into her other arm. She braced her right hand against the floor, trying to resist but it was no use. Grabbing the envelope, she tossed it in the armchair.

Still shaking her, he yanked her back to her feet and pushed her toward the couch, turning sideways as she tried to kick him.

"Miss Katharine lashes out," he snarled. "My spoiled darling, not quite so violently, please."

He placed his left knee beside her on the couch and then, still holding her with one hand by the throat, his face jerking and crimson with anger, he put the other hand to the top of her blouse and tore it from her in shreds. Tucking his forefinger under her bra, he rended it too, baring her breasts.

"Stop it! Stop it right now!"

"Shut up!" Palm of his hand against her chest, he pressed her into the couch. "So I am forbidden your bed and you are in love with Francotti—is that it? You're a drunken slut!" he roared, "a whore, a whore with money. Francotti is too good for you."

She had never seen him lose control so completely. "Let me up!"

His face was contorted. "I will soil you so that you'll be ashamed to go to another man."

She heard the door open and looked to the side, hoping for rescue. Helen Ryan's face froze fearfully when she saw what was happening. Erik glanced at her briefly. "Get out!"

"Oh, God. What are you doing?" Helen exclaimed.

"Nothing. I am teaching your mistress some manners. Come here and hold her arms. She's gone mad. I must call a doctor. We need a straitjacket."

Her eyes anguished, Helen edged across the room.

"Helen, don't you dare touch me," Katharine said.

"Mrs. Moss . . . please . . . stop fighting!"

"Yes, indeed," Erik jeered, "please do stop fighting. We need a sedative. Don't we have anything in the house?"

"Upstairs . . . I don't know." Helen's voice shook.

Katharine realized she had lost. She stopped struggling, indifferent to her exposed breasts. Let him do his worst— she glared at him, then at Helen.

"Ah, *better*, Miss Katharine," Erik sighed. "Helen, you are a witness to your mistress behaving like a mad dog."

Katharine said nothing. Nothing now. Let him do what he wanted. Perhaps he could soil her, ruin her and what then? She could kill herself; that was always a way out. She closed her eyes and turned her head, then opened them a crack to see him put his hand on Helen's shoulder. "Your mistress, Helen, has said very naughty things, as she does when she is so disturbed. She builds such a great neurotic fire and one must put out the fire."

Helen began to whimper when Erik dropped his hand to his trousers and unzipped his fly; she blinked fearfully when he pulled out the limp thing. Katharine didn't know what to expect now; talk about straitjackets and committal, Erik was the candidate. He aimed his penis at Kathy and quite calmly urinated on her chest, then, extending his aim, on her face. She closed her eyes, feeling it on her eyelids, nose, throat, and despite herself the flavor—acrid, it seemed to eat at her face like acid.

Erik chuckled and Katharine heard Helen's hoarse, horrified breathing. "You see, Helen, there are people in this world who are calmed by such a . . . sensation . . . which would be so distressing to anyone else. You see how quietly she lies now? At peace, aren't you, my darling."

Dully, Katharine said, "Nothing you do changes anything."

He laughed falsely. "Don't you see—I have once again established my territorial integrity. It is how animals and barbarians say this property is *mine*. By pissing on it."

Helen began to gag and stumble toward the door. Erik shouted at her, "Come back here at once."

Helen spun around in fright, as if the devil had been about to let her go, then changed his mind. "Oh . . . please. . . ."

He laughed again. "Now what shall we devise for little Helen to bind her into our triangle?"

Her voice anxious, Helen muttered, "I have no wish to be pee'ed upon, Mr. Moss. All I do . . . all I want to do is help."

"Of course. But Helen likes other things, methinks."
There was the sound of rustling clothes and a cry of protest
from Helen.

Katharine watched, only half-aware of what was happening and only half-caring. Maybe he was right—everything *was* all over. There was no hope for her. Everything was so godawful. A man like Francotti didn't belong in such a mess as this and she could not get free of Erik Moss. He was diseased—no one knew what was wrong with him, but at night, sometimes, as she remembered, she could almost smell the disease festering within him. Katharine closed her eyes again and wished she were dead.

Why, she asked herself desperately, was everything coming so abruptly to climax now, at this particular time? In a matter of weeks the world had blown up in her face. She had never wanted to be forced into a decision.

Ignoring Helen's labored breathing and what was happening to her, Katharine scrambled off the couch and across to the drinks trolley. She picked up the knife, razor sharp for dealing with lemons.

She held the knife in her hand, meaning at first simply to ram it into her stomach. She was soiled, as he said, clothes torn, half-naked, and before her eyes he was humping Helen from behind, sadistically, the more so each time Helen whimpered.

He did not see or hear Katharine. Her intention was to reach between these two squirming animals and to sever the connection. No! Neither did she plunge the knife into him. Rather, she drew the sharp blade down his back, cutting his shirt and drawing a line of blood on his skin. At first, he did not even feel the blade, so honed that its cut was painless. But at last the sting of it impacted his spinal column and Erik howled, thinking he had somehow been mortally wounded.

He wrenched himself out of Helen and stumbled away, eyes shocked and frightened. Katharine held the bloody tip of blade before him.

"My darling," he gasped, "what are you doing?"

Katharine smiled at him. "Don't come near me or I'll destroy your face." She knew if he came one step closer she'd use it on him. He realized that too, backing away, tripping over Helen's legs.

She pointed the knife at him and he recoiled as if the knife had been a cross and he an evil spirit.

"Don't *ever* come near me again," she said fiercely.

Twenty-Two

It was by no means tragic news that Mrs. Glascock had decided she'd better stay in Florida until her daughter's baby had been born. After two weeks in the sunny clime, she called to let him know she wasn't sure she'd come back north at all. "What I'm saying, Mr. Darktower, is that I wouldn't expect you to hold my job for me now. You understand?"

Darktower grinned across the telephone at Clara Riding. She was sitting, quietly facing him, behind a fold-up cardtable upon which she was deploying a pack of tarot cards. "Of course I understand, Mrs. Glascock. You just do what you think best and don't bother about me. I'll make do. I may be going to Europe anyway in the next month or so."

Clara Riding, she whom he had come to know first as Miss Teats in the apartment of his dead friend, Leland Penton, didn't look up from the cards. A pair of reading glasses parked on the tip of her pert little nose, she studied the cards as he talked, laying them down, one after the next. Her chubby chin rested comfortably on another, second chin. She was double-chinned, not triple. She was not that fat, he told himself again. She was generously proportioned, built more for comfort than speed, as the boys said.

"Does that mean you'll be asking me to stay a bit longer?" she asked after he'd hung up.

"That's exactly what it means, Clara. I hope you can stay."

"I can, Richard."

They didn't need many words, the two of them. Darktower had little interest in her clairvoyant talents and paid no great attention to the cards, or the tea leaves or palmistry. He had managed to put off the Ouija board. Attention to the occult was Clara's preoccupation—that is, when she wasn't in the kitchen cooking. The kitchen had been her first stop as Darktower had been showing her around ten days ago; she'd been absolutely delighted at its size and range of appliances, so carelessly assembled. Since then she had hardly ceased cooking and, with a familiarity that surprised both of them, she insisted he eat well and more sensibly than he ever had. As a result, in only the ten days, Darktower had gained weight. His trousers were tight around his belly and he began having trouble with the top button of his shirt.

"Gloria won't be angry if you stay, will she?"

Clara lifted her eyes and looked at him over the arc of reading glasses. "You're speaking of Miss Ass?" He nodded and she laughed merrily. She had a pretty laugh, a lively laugh, a laugh that was so full of life and quite without artifice. "What in the world did you ever think of us that night, Dickie?"

He shook his head, as he'd done when she'd asked the same question before. "Sure surprised me, honey. I didn't know what to think."

She appraised his expression. "Did you think we were *bad*?"

He said what she wanted to hear. "Yes, I did. I must say I did."

Clara tinkled laughter again. "And we were, weren't we?" She paused to consider how bad. "Two shocking-pink ladies like us, we always have such a good time, though, doing what we do. It never *seems* bad, you know, Richard, and Gloria will never accept a date at anything but the best addresses: Park, Fifth and Madison and only between Fifty-Seventh and Seventieth. And, gee willikers, Dickie, a girl does have to eat." She punched herself in the belly with both thumbs. "Gosh knows, since I've been here, though, I seem to've lost weight. It must be the weather."

"*Ducks*," Darktower sighed, for Miss Clara did like being called Ducks, "I'm gaining it off you, then."

"Good," she said comfortably. "I like a man with some meat on him. Skinny runts don't do me any good. Besides, you know what they say?" She giggled, joyousness rampant in her chest. "You can't drive a railroad spike with a tack-hammer."

Darktower chuckled. She was not really a coarse person, however. She said things like that for his benefit. "The thing about that night," he recalled, "is I couldn't make out how such *cultivated* women got into that sort of . . . trade."

"Richard," she explained once more, "it's not a trade. Gloria and I always considered it show business, which it really is, except for the part when we perform fellatio—and in its own way, that's show biz too, don't you think?"

"Yes." He was delighted to agree. "I do think so."

"Which doesn't mean, of course," she said thoughtfully, "that one performs it any way but very semi-public." He nodded and winked at her and she screamed immoderately, "Richard, you have no shame, you know! You're a very naughty boy."

"Naughty old man, you mean. And you know what? I don't give a damn."

"Enjoy!" she cried.

"Yes, goddamn it, enjoy!"

She lowered her eyes back to the cards. "Were you serious about Europe, what you said on the phone?"

"Sure. We discussed it, didn't we?"

"The cards are in favor," she murmured, "and so are the signs."

That was the one thing he hadn't been able to avoid. Clara had insisted on doing his astrological chart the very first night, demanding to know of him the date, time and place of his birth, and then after a lengthy analysis, declaring they were compatible.

"We're coming up roses, ducks," he said.

Clara beamed at him, her chubby lips drawn to a prideful smirk and her eyes sparkling in pudgy cheeks. "Richard, I don't want you to get me wrong. It would be a *presumption* for me to force myself on you. It's expensive in Europe and you know I don't have that kind of money. My pittance *is* a pittance, from the cards and now and then when Gloria and I go show biz."

He hummed pleasantly and winked again. She meant what she said, he knew. He'd been around too long to be fooled. "Don't worry about it. You'd be my guest and a welcome one. One thing, though—Gloria wouldn't expect to come with us, would she?"

"Gloria? Oh, no. We're free agents."

Jovially, he said, "And if we run out of money, you could go show biz over in Europe."

She frowned reprovingly. "Oh, no, not if I were with such an upright person as you, Richard. I'd be Miss Straight Arrow."

He smiled at her fondly. "Goddamn it," he said, "we are going to enjoy!"

Vivaciously, she agreed. "We can no more than *try our best*!" She brushed the tarot cards together. "How would you like me to make a batch of brownies?"

She lifted the table out of her way and pushed herself out of the folding chair she favored when dealing. Standing, she was a formidable and handsome figure, not very tall, true, no more than five-six or -seven. But her bosom stood out like a shelf and below that, her stomach was actually quite tucked in, giving in to hips that were, yes, muscular to say the least, and thigh and calves like good strong saplings. But she was not fat. She was stalwart.

He followed her into the kitchen and took a beer out of the refrigerator while she assembled the ingredients for her brownies.

Clara hummed and whistled to herself as she rinsed a mixing bowl and the shallow glass pan in which she would do the baking.

"Miss Clara," he mentioned thankfully, "you're such a happy person." Wistfully, since she agreed, he added, "I wish I could transfer a little of that asset to my daughter.

She's got the miseries these days. Love-sick . . . a guy threw her over.''

"Poor child . . . I thought she was married.''

"That's done.''

"Poor child,'' Clara repeated vaguely, carefully measuring the flour, even though making brownies was second nature to her.

Clara was forty-two, not really old enough to call Kate a poor child. Clara, however, did seem older, wiser and more secure in her ways. She knew who she was. Clara was aware that her "business" was not quite reputable but he could imagine her, nevertheless, having close-up relations with a thousand men and yet remaining utterly untouched.

"What if we took her with us to Europe?" he asked.

Clara seemed stunned. "Wouldn't she be terribly shocked?''

"Why should she be?'' he demanded. "Aren't we upfront?'' Actually, he realized, they hadn't had any call yet to be upfront. "We're babies compared to the people she travels with.''

"Yes,'' Clara said, "but what would you say if she did object?''

A good question. "I just wouldn't tolerate any objections,'' he said. "It's *my* life, isn't it?''

"And mine . . . yes.'' Silently, she turned back to her brownies.

Darktower set down the beer can and impulsively put his arms around her waist, pressing her against him, gripping her breasts in his hands, so strong and big through her cable-knit sweater. She jogged her buttocks against his thighs and he made her feel the swell of his railroad spike.

"Dickie! Heavens! You're such a tiger!''

"My second childhood, ducks.''

"Heavens, Dick! Let me finish this first, can't you?''

He continued to hold her casually from the rear as she added a few more bits of this and that to the bowl, turning a wooden spoon energetically the while and, finally, pouring the gooey mixture into the baking pan and popping it into the oven. Finished, she pushed his hands from her breasts and turned away from his grasp, facing him challengingly. Not to be stopped, Darktower dropped his face, all of it, into her sweatered cleavage. Clara gasped.

"Such a tiger!"

"I can't get enough of these, ducks."

"And at your age! I always thought men got past it, but I see I was wrong about that. The brownies, Richard, the brownies—they'll be all done in about twenty-two and a half minutes."

"It'll turn off automatically."

Clara kissed his mouth with the puckered little lips he so admired. She out-Clara Bow'ed Clara Bow. "Cupid," he murmured.

"Cupid, with his little bow and arrow?"

"With his little arrow, anyway."

"Oh, Dickie. Umm. All right. Let's go upstairs."

She glided ahead of him as though she were mounted on ballbearings, across the light-mapled floor into the living room, treading lightly on his Oriental carpets, and up the narrow stairway to the second floor. Boyishly, Darktower held his hands under her cheeky rear, supporting each upward lift of her feet. On the upper floor, Clara, kicking off her fuzzy slippers, jumped up on the bed and covered herself with a plaid blanket.

"Here we are, Dickie," she coo'ed.

Boisterously, he jumped in behind her and ducked under the blanket, grabbing indiscriminately at flesh. Again, Clara fastened her suction-cup lips to his face and made enthusiastic smacking sounds on his flesh. He had not decided yet whether she actually enjoyed his avid attentions or merely acted as though she did out of the long practice of simulation. Not worrying about it, he tackled the sweater, pushing it clear of her bosom so he could apply mouth-to-skin intimacy. Clara's nipples were, by themselves, bigger than a lot of women's entire tits, he told himself, stupefied. His former wife, the present Mrs. Himmelmann, had always been so antsy about having them played with. Come to think of it, he had probably made his mistake by treating Margo too much the lady. If he'd put her down once in a while to take a pull on his spike, she might not have gone elsewhere to do it, namely, for example, in the backseat of Len Libby's car where, by all accounts, she'd explored Len's roots like he was from the Amazon delta. Yes, Darktower growled to himself, his life with Margo had been altogether too proper, not fun. Now, it was. Clara made it so. Playing with her was a jolly experience.

"Oh, Dickie-dick!"

Clara lowered her chin so she could watch him, so sweetly, so gratefully, while he did everything to her upper structure but salute. Moaning and oozing delight at his kisses, she thrashed around, but carefully, so as not to throw him off the bed, and finally allowed him to tug down her shiny black chino pajama bottoms. Her rosy, roughed cheeks puffed in what would pass for passion, as he stroked and squeezed her; he reciprocated with a snort of lust when Clara undid the buttons on his tweed walking britches and wiggled her fingers inside.

"Richard, what have we here in your knickerbockers?"

"It's my charley, you know that, ducks."

She purred, suggesting softly, "Should I give him face?"

He had never completely understood what this phrase of hers meant. He was aware of the vapid, and semantically meaningless slang words, "give head," and he supposed that "give face" was Clara's way of saying the same thing in more genteel fashion.

As she delicately made at him, he was reminded, as always, of that traumatic evening at Lee Penton's when this whole wonderful adventure had begun. It seemed like a million years ago and Lee a million years dead. He was, actually, dead enough so it didn't matter whether it was one year *or* a million. Dead was dead.

Just as she pursued life itself, Clara gave Richard Darktower her all. She smacked her lips, licked her chops, chomped, sucked, spit and even seemed to burp out her intake of excess air. A hell of a service, he considered, all in all, especially as Clara absolutely *knew* when he was ready to pop and at that point pulled teasingly away, gasped, and wiped her mouth on his shirt-tail.

"Dickie, come on top, please," she pleaded, her voice

petite. "I want it in me, Dickie, please, I do, yes I do, Dickie."

She grunted pleasurably when he sank it in. For such a bulky woman, her movements were most refined and the whole maneuver worked very smoothly. Clara held him, faster than the ice pack of the Antarctic, clamped to her bosom and scissored between her legs, pummeling his spike with what seemed like a boxing glove.

Her face twisted in unlikely, high-operatic expressions. But then, as he progressed, she began to giggle. The more he tore himself up, and her, the more fun she had and it was all he could do to keep himself from chortling and thus losing control. But why shouldn't this be a merry experience, like eating? He repeated the question in his head and in the end, before he finally did pop, he decided a federal regulation was needed to decree that climaxes *would* be fun: this deposit guaranteed by the Federal Humping Corporation.

Another of his now possibly numbered ejaculations thundered—not exactly thundered, more *whispered*—into her and Miss Clara whimpered appreciation, tenderly stroking his back. "Oh, Dickie," she breathed, so nicely, so flatteringly, "it's like as if Boulder Dam gave way and all into me. I wish I could put it in the brownies."

She didn't elaborate, commencing to shimmy under him like a car with loose bolts. He understood, dummy that he was, that Clara, out of the blue, was experiencing her own climax.

She gulped and squealed. "Keep big-red pounding, Dickie, for I am approaching *minerva*." He knew she meant *nirvana* but it didn't matter. He pressed forward, feeling, almost hearing, the discs clicking in his lower back, giving her the best he had. "Dickie!" she crooned, "Oh, Dickie! Dickie, oh! Umm! Good! Dickie! Oh, God, yes, yes, Dickie! Oh, please! Oh, my! Oh, Dickie!"

Her efficiently trimmed fingernails raked his back and beneath Darktower's still comparatively frail body, her bottom *whumped* with elan.

"Ducks . . . are you all right?"

"Dickie," she gurgled, "Does a bear do do-do in the forest? I am, I am!" She screamed and violently bucked.

As impetuously as she crested, just as abruptly she subsided, her eyes fixed on him in a stare which mystified, but also worried, him a little. Adoringly, she whispered, "I've never met a man who thrilled me so."

"Come on, ducks, don't hyperbolize."

"*Am* I breathing erratically? God, Dickie, it's because I love you so!"

If he had seen it coming, he might have been able to maneuver out of the way. Love was not what he'd had in mind when he'd invited Miss Clara Riding to Wainscott, Long Island. He had been thinking in terms of nothing more serious than Fun, with a capital *F*.

"That's good," he muttered into a pocket he'd made for his nose beside her left breast.

"Oh," she said generously, "you don't have to feel obliged to reciprocate, Dickie. I know you've made fools of many women before me, women more sophisticated and worldly than I. But for me . . . I . . . you see, it's a new experience to be treated so gently . . . so tenderly . . . so royally."

"Come on, Clara," he said heartily, "you're in love with Wainscott, not me."

"That too, but mainly you, I promise you!"

"Another week and you'll be fed up, bored."

She shook her head, disagreeing vigorously. "No, another week and you'll probably sweep away from me for a rendezvous with some femme fatale."

Modestly, he laughed again. "Clara, don't make me out to be the cocksman of the Eastern Seaboard 'cause I'm not. I've had enough of femme fatales, I can assure you."

The fact was he had never had anything to do with a femme fatale unless her name was Margo, the present Mrs. Himmelmann.

The telephone interrupted whatever he was prepared to reveal.

"Is this Richard Darktower, *Esquire*?" It was a male voice, heavily larded with class envy.

"Yes," he said pleasantly, for he was feeling warm and pleasant.

"Speaking," said the man, "is somebody to whom you gave a card on Madison Avenue some two months ago, or maybe a little longer than that, along with some money. Do you recall that night?"

A chill swept across his expanse of well-being. Clara felt him shiver and hugged him. "Yes, I do."

"Well?"

"Well, what?" he demanded.

Disgust boiled into his ear. "Don't you know that half that money was phony?"

"Phony?" Darktower cried, sounding genuinely amazed. "How could that have been?"

"*I* have no idea. Very possibly, somebody slipped you some counterfeit money and you, sir, inadvertently, or stupidly, or . . . *deliberately*, passed it on to me. Do you not realize, sir, that I could have gotten my ass in a sling if I tried to pass that at a bank?"

"I'm so sorry. I had no idea." Darktower bit his knuckle to keep from laughing.

"That's all very well for you to be sorry. But where does it leave me? You owe me about eighty dollars, sir, if you'll look at it from my point of view."

Darktower smiled at Clara. "I don't quite *get* your point of view."

"Restitution, that's the word, Dad. You got to make it good."

Darktower had let him go far enough. "Now, look," he snapped, "let's not talk nonsense! That was a heist, a stickup and it's not my fault, my friend, that you got some funnymoney from me. It's obvious that the weight of establishing the authenticity of a monetary instrument falls on the stickup man, not the victim."

"What? What the hell are you talking about?"

"Legally, the stick-up-ee is not responsible to the stick-up-or for the legitimacy of the cash he's carrying."

"Look, Mr. Darktower," the man said patiently, a little wearily now, "I've got your address right here on this card. Should I make a trip out there to collect?"

"It'd cost you more than eighty dollars to rent a car," Darktower told him. He had a bright idea. "I'll be over in New York in the next week or so." He nodded at Clara; yes, that was so. "Why don't we meet for lunch?"

"Are you out of your mind or something, Dad? I wouldn't trust you . . . you'd have the cops waiting at the front door."

"For eighty dollars? Bullshit," Darktower growled. "No, I guarantee no cops. I'll tell you where—at *Le Cirque*. That's a place in the Sixties, near where we met the first time . . . that's *Le*, 'l' as in *love*, 'e' as in *Edsel*. Second word, *Cirque*: 'c' as in *Charley*, 'i' as in *idiot*, 'r' as in *ratshit*, 'q' as in *queer* or *queen* or *quixotic* or *Quasimodo* . . . yes, yes, or as in *quirk*. Then 'u' as in *usury*, yes, yes, and the final 'e' as in *Edsel* again or *esteem*, or *eccentric*. Like me, yes, if you'd like to think so." The stranger sputtered indignation and Darktower cut in impatiently, "You'll remember me, most likely. Anyway I'll be with a *beautiful blonde lady*. Now, I'll tell you what you do—you eyeball us from the door and if the set-up doesn't look on the up-and-up, you can scarper."

"*Scarper*? What the fuck is that supposed to mean? How about talking English, Dad?"

Quickly, Darktower said, "*Scarper* is an English term and what it means is, if the coast isn't clear, you scarper, that is take off, *scrambolo*. Get it?"

"You're fucking crazy," the man said doubtfully. "What day?"

"A week from this Friday. Fifteen minutes before one in the afternoon. Okay?"

Hesitantly, the man said, "I'll eyeball it, like you said. You'd better show up because I'll be making the trip in from my estate in Connecticut."

"I'll be there, don't worry."

After he'd hung up, laughing uproariously, Clara asked, "Dickie, what in the world was that all about?"

Darktower didn't know the full story either. "I have a feeling I'm going to hire a desperado."

"To do what?"

"I don't know yet, doll. But I'm sure there's always something a desperado is good for."

He went on laughing until she put her round face close to his and licked his nose.

"My God, darling," Darktower cried exultantly. "I haven't had so much fun since I retired from the firm."

And *by George*, Clara didn't miss a trick. "Richard, oh, Richard," she purred, "do you know what you just did? You called me *darling*." She patted his face fondly with the soft palm of her hand, her eyes beaming out of their padded recesses. "Don't move. I'm going downstairs for a minute and I'm going to bring you up a brownie."

Twenty-Three

Just about everybody she knew was in New York that weekend. Steve Ratoff with his protegé Marco Fortuna had come back from California; Frank Berliner was up and about—he had taken Dolly to dinner at Trader Vic's at the Plaza Thursday night. And Kitty had told her Richard Darktower might well be in town with this new lady friend of his. Goodness! A lady friend for Richard Darktower! Dolly had always assumed Darktower had given up ladies for Lent some years ago and forgotten to resume the habit.

Erik—well, they weren't talking about him, were they? Erik Moss was strictly *persona non grata* these days. Katharine was in a foul state of mind. As determined as she was to work herself back in with Gene Francotti, Francotti resisted. He refused to see Katharine and now, so it seemed, he had gone off *incommunicado* on some sort of hush-hush Navy job. It was probably bullshit, Dolly told herself. But, whatever, it served to keep Kitty in a miserable mood—she had not been eager to do lunch, but Dolly, using the old stick-in-the-mud routine, had forced her into it.

The question now, Dolly mused that morning over her light breakfast of a half grapefruit, small bowl of crunchy cereal—fiber, they said, was good for bowel movement—a cup of black coffee and three cigarettes, the question was whether she and Katharine had the joint nerve to include Steve and Marco in their luncheon plan. They would be seen if they did, by all, Dolly with the vapid Sicilian and Katharine in the company of her ex-husband, Stefan Ratoff.

There would be talk, lots of it, lots of beautiful, wonderful gossip.

"Darling," she mentioned to Frank Berliner who was sitting on the other side of the round glass breakfast table, scanning the *Times*, "I'll give you a morning truism—it's better to be gossiped about than not to be noticed at all."

Berliner turned down the corner of the paper to look at her. He was smoking one of his Dunhills, from which he flipped an ash into a Mexican ceramic. "Darling Dolly, I think it's already been said."

"By Noel Coward, no doubt."

Berliner quipped, "No. Actually by his brother, *Base* Coward."

"Ta!" Dolly cried. "So fast in the ayem, aren't you? Thanks for putting up with me again, darling."

"I wouldn't have you stay anywhere else, porcelain face. I hope you weren't disturbed to find Freddie here last night when we got back."

"Perish the thought," she murmured. "I think Freddie was disturbed to see me, though. He's such a tight-ass."

"God, yes!" Berliner drawled, "I knew there was something I liked about him." Dolly barked joyful disgust. "Hoo, hoo, darling! Anyway, piss on Freddie. You can bring anybody here you like, you know? Feel free. You are among friends, as I'm sure you know."

Dolly shrugged petulantly. "Who have *I* got? Nobody."

"Poor baby." Wetly, licking his lips and puffing the cigarette, he said, "Tell me about Katharine."

Dolly frowned. "Well, you know that for all practical purposes they're split. Erik, the bastard, has gotten an apartment somewhere downtown."

Berliner squinted over his nose. "Tacky."

"Yes. I always thought Erik had loot but apparently not as much as everybody figured. If he wants a divorce, he'll just have to walk away, and without a pot to pee in. He owes *me* money—did you know that?"

"How could I know if you've never told me?"

"Well, he does. And I intend to get it back."

"Sweet Erik . . . not so sweet," Berliner mused. "Bittersweet. . . ."

"He's definitely not your type."

Berliner puckered his lips as if he were going to apply makeup. "You don't know my type, sweetie. Erik is big and strong. I have a feeling a person could get into a heavy s-m scene with him."

"Uh-uh," Dolly said. "He doesn't have the imagination."

"I'll bet he likes little boys," Berliner said shrewdly, "because just looking at him, sweetie, I can tell he's into *something*. He's got a kink loose somewhere."

"Darling," Dolly cautioned, "You know very well you should beware the sado-masochism route."

"True, true," Berliner bubbled, "it was almost the death of me last time."

"Poor dear," she said absently, lighting another cigarette and pouring more coffee. "I suppose I could still take Erik for myself if he wasn't such a swine about everything. Kitty sure as hell wouldn't care, not now. But her beau, that Francotti—an old friend of yours, isn't he—he's tough. He puts up with absolutely no shit whatsoever. Kitty's not used to that. She doesn't know what to make of it—usually, she crooks a finger and all the men come running."

"For the money, sure," Berliner said. "Francotti doesn't give a goddamn for money. I know him well enough to know that. Besides, he's got a lot of his own. He's been doing very well for years by being a good engineer."

"He's ugly."

Berliner nodded. "Ugly as sin. But he's probably hung like an Italian salami." He cleared his throat. "Not that I'd know. He's so fucking masculine he doesn't know that half the world is bent."

"Hung?" Dolly contemplated anatomy for a moment. "Marco Fortuna's not."

"Good God!" Berliner gasped. "Don't tell me you've already *succumbed*."

She smiled engagingly. "Naturally. One does want to know what one's buying, doesn't one?"

"One supposes," Berliner said sardonically. "And?"

"Like a *spaghetti*. The point is, darling, should I *marry* him? He hasn't exactly proposed yet. Tell me, do Swiss-domiciled Sicilians propose or just slip you the jewelry?"

Acridly, he commented, "I think what they try to slip you is a little boff first. But you've already done that. Has he mentioned jewelry?" he asked, with more interest. "I've heard around town that he's got some of his mother's stuff stashed away and he's *not* poor. But he'd still be after your money. It's a matter of honor for the Europeans to swindle American heiresses. Henry James discovered that a long time ago."

"What's his mother's stuff like?"

He shrugged airily. "Probably three or four tiaras, an Indian ruby or two and a moderate-sized diamond. It'd all have to be re–set, you know."

"What a challenge for an American girl," Dolly trilled. "But what the hell, darling, I need something to do. Not that I'm holding out any exaggerated hopes for Marco."

"Well," Berliner said flippantly. "He's *not* gay. I know that for a fact."

"He is traveling with Steve," she pointed out.

Berliner glared at her. "It is possible you know, sweetie, that a gay person can simply be liked for *himself*. I mean, you do have a *few* men friends, don't you, who just like you for yourself and not only because you're known world-wide as such a wonderful *fuck*?"

Dolly laughed. "No. I don't have any men friends like that."

"What about me?"

"I don't count gays," she said.

"Well, there you are," he pouted, "just what I'm telling you. Don't be such a bitch! Anyway, I've heard other . . . menacing . . . things about dear Marco," Berliner peevishly muttered.

"So?"

"He was in love with his mother, that's *so*! They slept in a single bed in the old *palazzo* until she died. I gather from circles who should know that she was a painted *virago*, a true witch in awful Sicilian style."

"Incest," Dolly surmised. "I'm not impressed. It happens in the best of European families."

"Ha!" Berliner yelped, "so clever, aren't we! So jaded! You think that's all? Not by half a cup, sweetie. The story goes on that Marco *continued* to sleep beside his mother in the narrow bed for several days *after* she died. You have the word for *that* at your fingertips, darling?''

Dolly grinned her filthy grin and shrugged nonchalantly. ''Zut! From incest to necrophilia? *Of course*, darling. The one follows the other as surely as sweaty socks after tennis.''

She sounded flippant but actually, Dolly was thinking they were all falling through a bottomless pit. There was no ending it, except, possibly, some place far out in infinity.

''God! You *are* a bitch, Dolly. You're so blasé.''

''I'm not really,'' she said. ''I might sound that way. Believe me, I will check out necrophilia. I don't think *Good Housekeeping* has put the seal of approval on that yet.''

Screaming merrily, Berliner jumped to his feet, clapping his hands to his cheeks. ''You know what they say, sweetie. Some like it cold, ha!'' He dissolved to tears for a second before pulling himself together. ''I've got to go. I have an appointment with Mrs. Throttlebottom at Bloomie's. She wants to change the wallpaper in the john at her house in Palm Springs.''

''There is *no* Mrs. Throttlebottom!''

''I couldn't tell you her real name, Miss Clever Pussy. Farewell.''

Berliner buttoned the jacket of his double-breasted blue pin-striped suit, adjusted a club tie into the notch of a stiff white shirt and, in the hallway, took a formal Homburg hat and also a double-breasted wool overcoat out of the closet.

Turning to Dolly again, he intoned, ''Good-bye, my dear. I'll see you later.'' He opened the front door, with all the gravity of a Wall Street banker, just as the phone rang. ''God, it might be her!'' He jumped back inside and grabbed the hall phone. ''Oh, yes, good morning. Oh, yes, how are *you*?'' he asked listlessly. ''Just a minute. . . .'' He cupped his hand over the speaking end of the instrument. ''It's Mr. Erik Moss.''

''Oh, shit!''

''Shall I say you've gone out?'' he whispered urgently.

"I can remember the day when he could cream your Gloria Vanderbilt jeans."

"I'll take it, I'll take it!"

Berliner pressed the *HOLD* button, waved and left. Taking her time, Dolly lit another cigarette. Let the son-of-a-bitch wait. She tightened her robe around her waist and went into the sunflower decor of the living room to take the call. She sat down in one of the antique Chinese chairs. "Yes?" Her voice was icy, frigid, distant, speaking from the moon.

His, on the other hand, was warm, eager, ingratiating. "My darling. I heard you'd be in town."

"Who told you?"

He paused. "As a matter of fact, Stefan Ratoff. You are *seeing* him and this Fortuna?"

"Why should Steve call you?"

Again, he hesitated, no doubt, she thought sourly, thinking up a good lie. "He called about Conrad. We talked a bit. He also wants money."

"Don't we all?" Dolly sneered. "You don't have any money to give him—except the ten thousand you owe me. Where is it?"

His voice was aggrieved. "It will be returned. How *can* I return it when I am never permitted to see you?"

"Put it in the mail."

"No, no, I would wish to return it personally. Would you. . . ." His tone became sepulchral. "Would you really mind so much if I did give it to Stefan Ratoff? He is very ill, you know."

"That's his problem." Dolly said bitingly. "If he wants money, let him ask his Marco or go to Darktower—on the other hand, don't tell him that—old Richard has got to pay you off next."

Erik laughed gruffly. "No, I think not, my darling. I am working again. I have an arrangement with Herman Himmelmann." He ignored her snort. "It has to do with family financial planning, the creation of tax-proof trusts. Herman appears to think I know many wealthy people and will bring the firm bluechip business. In truth, I am almost friendless. Still, I am paid a retainer, plus expenses, and a commission. Not bad, all things considered." He chuckled dryly. "My darling, could I interest *you* in a portfolio of tax shelters?"

Dolly found herself laughing mockingly. "Sorry, darling. *My* portfolio is already stuffed. I'm not interested in family planning anyway. I'm spending it all."

"I know you are," he sighed. "Very improvident of you, my darling."

"You had your chance."

"Is it really too late?" She hissed a bad word but he chose not to hear it. "When can I see you? Don't forget—we still have our Smithers House project."

"Yes." Dolly studied her cuticles. "But the wheels of preservation grind very slowly. Whether it's done this year or next, it's all the same. Right now, I'm thinking of reversing my *rigor mortis* by taking a trip to Europe."

"Oh, God," he groaned sorrowfully. "How I wish I could be with you in Europe."

"You've said that before. But, somehow, I don't think it's going to work out that way."

"But . . . *surely*, my darling, some hope?" he begged. "You're at Berliner's, yes?"

"That's the number you called," she grated. "You want to come to visit me here, is that it? You wouldn't care if Frank knew?"

"No, I would not care!"

"All right. Come here at five o'clock this afternoon." Why, why was she doing this? "Bring the money you owe me."

"I will be there!"

Dolly hung up the phone, not believing herself . . . or him. She puffed thoughtfully on another cigarette. She had considered herself in such total control of the situation, then, somehow, he had turned the tables on her. She had been so calm, so sure of herself. Now she was anything but. Under her robe, she brushed her bare thighs together, crossing and recrossing her legs. He was a rotten man, a man without honor, and she knew that.

Twenty-Four

The luncheon crowd was still thin when Katharine arrived at *Le Cirque*. She'd made the date for twelve-thirty but allowed herself time for a drink before Dolly arrived.

"*Bon jour*, madame." The maitre d' fussed, placing her in a corner banquette and passing along her request for a vodka martini, twist . . . rocks.

She was feeling fine and the drink, the fresh aroma of lemon, the bite of the vodka, made her feel that much better. Wasn't it exceedingly strange that she could be in such good spirits after all that had happened? Perhaps it was a simple function of thinking about Francotti. She could be amused now at how infuriated he had been that day in Port London, and in anticipating their renewal. For her marriage was truly over except for the legalities. Katharine had nothing more to do with Erik, certainly not after that final scene, the disgusting finale; he had revealed everything about himself: the depth his fury reached, the despair, frustration and hate. He came and went, scarcely ever seeing her and then, when he did, by accident, nodding distantly as if they were meeting in a public corridor. Katharine had no idea where he went, save that he was doing something with Herman Himmelmann . . . or when he left the apartment or when he came home, if he did, in the evening.

She did not smile to think of Helen, the poor thing, violated right before the eyes of her mistress. They had not mentioned it—what could they say about something too awful to discuss? So radically did relationships alter! And, everything, as bad as it was, contributed to Katharine's liberation. She mustn't forget that, must she, or that she had had a sort of revenge: the incision of knife wound, running like the bloody cut of surgery alongside his spinal artery. Katharine shivered, but the feeling of dread quickly passed. Fastidiously, she opened her pocketbook and took out a menthol cigarette. She had not smoked for some years now. Something had made her buy the cigarettes that morning—some defiance, a signal of independence.

Dolly bounced in just as Katharine stamped the cigarette out, after only four or five puffs. Enviously, she considered Dolly's energy level. It was like a slap in the face.

"*Joie de vivre*," she murmured. Her oldest friend sat down next to her on the banquette. "You've got it and I wish I had some."

"Don't be silly. You can buy it by the pound. All you need is a good poke once in a while." Katharine smiled; Dolly was a hopeless case. "*What's your complaint*? That shade of red makes your hair look good." She petted the sleeve of Kitty's suit, by Pauline Trigere.

"Sweetheart, *you* must have had a . . . nice poke recently," Katharine suggested.

"As a matter of fact, I haven't, but my memory is good," Dolly whispered. "Another of those awful vodkas? I'm having a glass of cold Chablis," she told the waiter.

Dolly asked at once how everything was going—between herself and Erik, naturally. Katharine tried another of her cigarettes. "It's just a question of when—and how we end it. Some drastic things have happened—I wouldn't tell you what. He wants money, of course, and Daddy is not very willing."

"All you need are airtight grounds," Dolly said slyly. "Then you can throw him to the wolves."

"I know," Katharine said wearily. "But that's so tacky . . . so cheap."

"*Not* very cheap if you have to fork over a million or two." Dolly was not a forgiving sort of person. "Doesn't he ever hit you, or anything?

Katharine's laugh sounded pathetic in her own ears. "I said I wouldn't tell." No, as case hardened as she was to his affronts, what had happened that day in the apartment was so weird and revolting it couldn't be mentioned anywhere but in the privacy of a judge's chambers.

"But you need some kind of grounds for divorcing the bastard," Dolly grunted. "Mental cruelty or incompatibility won't do."

"We'll try to make it . . . amicable, for Margaret's sake." It hurt to say the word.

"Amicability, I'm told, costs a lot of money." Dolly looked at Katharine sharply. "Why don't you try adultery? That's always good in New York State."

Katharine smiled calmly. "With you?"

Dolly nodded tentatively. "If you like. I don't mind. My reputation is so besmirched, a little more mud isn't going to hurt."

Katharine was not shocked. Dolly obviously wouldn't be lying, and looking into her mind, even into her soul, Katharine found herself not caring at all. Voice steady, she said, "Don't tell me you'll make this great sacrifice just to help me—I know it's your way of telling me you *have* slept with Erik. Don't bother to deny it. It's of no interest to me, of absolutely no consequence."

Nonchalantly Dolly lit one of her own long cigarettes. "All I'm offering is to play the *role* of co-respondent, darling—not to burn myself at the stake." Her dark eyes danced. "You know I don't give a goddamn for him. I'm *your* friend!"

"He'd deny it," Katharine said.

"He could try. All you've got to do," Dolly puffed contemplatively, "is tell your lawyer to have a little talk with me."

Even then, Katharine felt no tug of jealousy. The green-eyed monster must be locked in the men's room. "We wouldn't want to invent adultery," she said slowly, watching Dolly's volatile face. "You *did* screw him, didn't you?"

Dolly nodded abruptly. "Yes, a couple of times. But there was never much to it."

"I'm saying: I don't care—but the fact is you did do it to me, didn't you?"

"I wasn't doing *anything* to you," Dolly said. "I laid him because I thought it might be exciting. That's all there was to it."

Despite what should have been great anger, Katharine chuckled, and, what was more amazing, she felt fondly toward incorrigible Dolly.

There was one thing, though. "Keep your hands off Francotti," Katharine warned. "You lay a finger on him and I'll rip off your head."

Dolly's response to this dire threat was to laugh merrily. "Darling, you know I don't touch boyfriends. I promise not to make a move until after you're married. Anyway, what right do you have to warn me off? Francotti *ditched* you," Dolly pointed out harshly.

"He *thinks* he did! He's got another think coming, though."

"But he's *gone*," Dolly cried. "He ran! He's supposed to be off building a motor or something for the CIA, isn't he? Isn't that his story?"

"That's what he said the last time I talked to him," Katharine agreed grimly. "The last time he read me out. He wouldn't let me come to see him, him in New York alone, in a cast, practically not even able to open a door."

Dolly sneered. "He sounds stupid to me—why should he get mad at you just because Erik went to talk to him? It's not your fault, for Christ's sake!"

Katharine nodded sadly. "He blames me, though—the boy he was working with could've been killed. Then Erik offered him money and that's when all hell broke loose. You see," she added bitterly, "that's *our* style, supposedly, to give the *peasants* money so they don't make trouble."

Dolly's face tightened. "Money? No shit. How much?"

"I don't know, sweetheart," Katharine said patiently. "An envelope full of it."

"An envelope full of it?" Dolly exclaimed, as if somebody had stuck a knife in her.

"Yes, yes," Katharine said, growing annoyed. "The *point* is that was the last straw. Francotti is a proud man."

"And a pain in the ass," Dolly added crudely. "It

wasn't *your* idea to give him money. What's wrong with him?''

Katharine shook her head. ''He's very prickly.''

''Pricky, you mean,'' Dolly said, then qualified herself more good-naturedly. ''I suppose it's a novelty for you to meet a man who *isn't* ga-ga about money. That sure would be nice,'' she went on wistfully, her thoughts obviously drifting. ''Well, we'll just see about that, won't we? Christ . . . we are best friends, aren't we?''

''Who else but your very best pal would let you hump her husband?''

''So true,'' Dolly agreed, ''and I promise to let you hump mine as soon as I find one. Christ,'' she swore again, ''splendid tramps, ain't we?''

''Yes.'' Katharine paused. ''A little jaded. It must be the gentility of our class,'' she added sarcastically, ''that which my *lover* finds so fascinating.''

''Your lover?'' Dolly echoed her slyly. ''You better move fast.''

''I repeat,'' Katharine said, ''hands off, sweetheart.'' She glanced toward the revolving door, exclaiming softly. ''Oh my God!''

Richard Darktower was making an entrance. Close to him stood a blonde woman of medium height, her considerable width enclosed in a shiny mink. Darktower very solicitously helped this woman out of the coat and gave it, with his dark raincoat and hat, into the checkroom.

The woman had to be the friend he had told Katharine about in Wainscott. She glanced casually around the dining room, an expression of amused tolerance on her face. Katharine thought, and knew Dolly would agree, that she was wearing too much powder, her lipstick too bright. Black satin trousers accentuated the roundness of her waist, rather than de-emphasizing it, and she topped herself with a gold-embroidered black sweater too tight for her prominent upper story.

Her father caught Katharine in mid-stare. Smiling proudly, he took his lady's hand, led her past the beaming maitre d', who was standing beside the appointed Darktower table, to Katharine and Dolly.

"Clara," he said distinctly enough so that just about everybody in the room could hear him if they so wished, "I'd like you to meet my daughter: Katharine—Kate—Moss. And this lady is Mrs. Dolly Percy. Girls, I want you to meet Miss Clara Riding, a good friend of mine."

Miss Riding extended her hand to Kate, then Dolly. "I'm so very pleased to meet you both," she said, as if pledging to them this was so.

"How do you do?" Katharine responded vapidly.

"Very pleased to make your acquaintance," Dolly muttered, her face bland and controlled.

Before nightfall, Katharine told herself, it would be all over town, especially within the circle Richard Darktower and Mrs. Himmelmann had inhabited, that Richard Darktower was forsaken no longer.

When the two were as far out of earshot as they were likely to get this particular lunch hour, Dolly whispered in a hushed voice, "Christ Almighty, can he be serious about her?"

Katharine nodded. But it didn't matter whether he was serious—even though her father and mother had been parted for years, Katharine quivered at the social slap, guaranteed to sting her mother for months to come.

"Where does she come from?" Dolly asked. "I've never heard of her."

"I don't know," Katharine said. "Out of the woodwork? But that's all right, sweetheart. I wish him luck . . . love . . . whatever he wants."

"Well, *me* too," Dolly affirmed, her eyes fixed on the Darktower table. "There's another setting—who *else* is Richard having to lunch?" Sourly, she added, "One thing's for sure—he still doesn't like me for beans."

"He doesn't approve of your lifestyle, sweetheart," Katharine told her wryly. "And neither do I. After all, sleeping with my husband is not in good taste."

"Touché," Dolly drawled callously. "Shall we have another drink, or shall we order?"

"Both."

Katharine tried not to stare at Darktower and Miss Riding. A faint, patient smile remained in place on her round and complacent face—it said that she wasn't put out by their curiosity, that she understood that Kate, in particular, would be very curious about her.

"Wait 'til my mother hears about this!"

"And there's no way in the world she's *not* going to hear about it," Dolly forecast. Then, "Whoops! I think the third party's arrived." A ferret-faced man, medium tall, almost crouching, slipped across the restaurant and said something to Darktower. Her father stood up and eagerly shook his hand. The man looked over his shoulder, into the corners of the room, nodded warily at Miss Riding, and sat down in the empty chair facing the door.

"Now he looks really strange," Katharine mused. "I wonder what Daddy is up to now."

Dolly shrugged. "He's probably somebody's accountant. Who is it he looks like, Humphrey Bogart? Yes, he looks like Bogart."

"Bogart didn't look slippery and . . . so evil."

"He could when he wanted. It's the hair that's like Bogart," Dolly decreed. "He's got a very pronounced widow's peak. Oh, shit, what does it matter?"

"What matters," Katharine said quietly, "is that Daddy is rowing with one oar."

"Never happened!" Dolly said decidedly.

Katharine was fascinated to watch Darktower, the way he handled this, to her anyway, very unusual social situation. Her father sat, smiling distantly but poised expectantly, holding what Katharine knew would be a Scotch and soda between his fingers. He was not nervous or at all jittery. But why would he be? He never had been. The mystery man appeared to be doing the talking, making his points, whatever they were, by poking the tip of his right forefinger at a nosegay of flowers in a white vase in the center of the table. When his drink came—a little darker in color than Scotch, it must have been a bourbon and water—he nodded, without acknowledging the waiter. All the while, the same bemused look held Miss Riding's face, framing her cupid's bow of lipstick.

"What in the world could they be talking about?" Katharine wondered aloud.

Finally, ending one phase of whatever was going on, Darktower raised his glass, first to Miss Riding and then to the third man. Softly, Darktower said something that must have been of landmark nature, for the black-haired man's body jolted backward; again his eyes furtively hopped about the room. Darktower showed his teeth; he must, Katharine assumed, be introducing his famed wry chuckle. The man was reassured enough, however, to put his glass to his lips.

"Come on—let's order. Forget *them*. When are *we* going to Europe?"

"I dunno," Dolly muttered. "Well, darling—fish or salad?"

"I'm dieting," Katharine said. "A piece of sole and glass of Chablis."

"Some diet," Dolly sniffed. "Vodka, wine and a piece of fish."

"Better than lots of bread, sweetheart."

Dolly, surreptitiously watching Darktower's table, wasn't listening to her. "I've never seen him before . . . anywhere. Have you?"

"Nope. But this place isn't the whole world, is it?"

"Everybody comes to *Le Cirque*, darling, at one time or another. Didn't you meet *Gizmo* here?"

Katharine frowned. "I wish you'd stop calling him *Gizmo*. That's really a lousy nickname. It doesn't fit him at all."

"What should I call him? Gene-baby? His real name is probably Gino."

"Then call him Gino," Katharine ordered.

"Okay, I'm easy. You know, nobody said hello to that man when he came in, did they?"

"Some people think it's better not to be known."

Dolly frowned. "Don't be crazy, darling. It's marvelous to be known—for your misdeeds *and* good works."

"Good works?"

Dolly smirked. "*Of course*, good works. You know what my good deeds are? They're the bad deeds I haven't yet managed to perpetrate."

"Cynical. . . ."

"I guess." Dolly paused to collect her thoughts. "When we go to Europe, if we ever do, we *will* spend time with Stefan and Marco, won't we?"

"Why not?" As she'd told her father, Katharine had nothing against Stefan. Rather, the opposite. "I've always felt guilty about Steve. He was a victim of the establishment."

"You sound flip enough about it," Dolly snipped. "Whatever, he's certainly living well enough."

"Living? *He says he's dying.* And I'm *not* flip about it."

Dolly paused thoughtfully. "I don't mind Steve so much this time around. He's a lot nicer. Better than your present husband. You did love him a lot, didn't you? And you're right—he did get a bum rap from your *daddy*." Dolly tossed her eyebrows in Darktower's direction. "Look," she went on rapidly, "have dinner with us tonight. Come to the Plaza, at eight. *Don't* bring Erik."

"Why would I bring him?" Katharine asked indifferently. "Why don't we talk about something else?"

"About *Gino*? Well, all right. How are you going to recapture him?"

"I need a plan," Katharine agreed.

"He'll be in Port London this summer, you know," Dolly informed her. "He's got the boat—and from what I've been able to find out about him he comes to Port London for most of the summer. He lives on the boat."

Katharine glared at her suspiciously. "You *have* been snooping! Goddamn it, Dolly. . . ."

"Cool it, darling," Dolly cried. "I was just snooping for you, in your interest. I'll invite him to my marvelous Memorial Weekend party. Maybe I'll even rent his boat, instead of Gibber's."

"Dolly!"

"Trust me, darling!"

"Trust *you*?" Are you out of your mind?"

Dolly laughed self-indulgently. She was so pleased with herself. "If you don't find me a new man, I'll steal *Gino* away from you, I promise."

"You little bitch," Katharine hissed. But she realized

Dolly had issued her fair warning, even though in jocular terms. "Take the guy there with my father."

Dolly snorted delicately. "Him, with whom I'm not even acquainted? Whose name is unknown to me?"

But, in due course, they were able to find out who he was. By the time their grilled sole arrived, Richard Darktower and his companions had finished lunch. The stranger escorted Miss Riding to the door while Katharine's father came back to their table.

"Who's *he*?" Katharine asked at once.

Darktower smiled cagily. "His name is Sam Merchant—he says. He's a crook, a friend of mine."

Dolly chuckled caustically. "Not from your usual circle of crooks, Uncle Richard," she said boldly. "We've never seen him."

"Why would you? He's not of *your* circle for sure, Mrs. Percy."

"He's handsome," Dolly observed, knowing she was annoying him.

"So was Bugsy Siegel," Darktower grunted. Katharine hoped he was not going to insult Dolly with the Miss Hotpants appellation. "Sorry—I can't tell you how to get in touch with him. . . ." Watching them closely, he asked, "What do you think of Miss Riding?"

"She's . . . interesting," Katharine replied haltingly. "Are . . . you going to be in the city long?"

"A couple of days. Clara wants to go to the library and the Met."

Dolly declared, "She seems like a most pleasant woman."

Katharine leaned forward. "I must see you, Daddy." He raised his eyebrows. "Can I come tonight, around six or six-thirty?"

"All right. I'm staying at the Carlyle. Ring from downstairs when you get there." He smiled innocently. "How's your mother?"

Katharine understood him. "Fine," she said calmly. "I don't know how she'll be after she hears . . . you've been here today."

He nodded, not anxiously. "I'm free, white, and twenty-one and I can do what I want." Complacently, Darktower flashed a rare grin. "As a matter of fact, Clara and I are talking about making a trip to Europe."

"So are Kitty and I," Dolly said.

"Wonderful," Darktower said sardonically. "Don't bring back any more European bums."

Dolly retorted, "Why, Uncle Richard, I haven't even had mine yet."

"I'm amazed you haven't. You know," he growled, "you two puzzle the life out of me. What makes you tick—besides men?"

"Whatever are you saying, Uncle Dickie?" Dolly teased.

Katharine's father frowned but not fiercely. Astonished, Katharine realized Dolly was flirting with him and that Richard Darktower was falling for it. But he shook his head, trying to show he was immune.

"You," he muttered to Katharine, "I'll be seeing tonight. *You*," he said to Dolly, "I'll never understand."

Dolly trilled a laugh at him. As Darktower joined the other two at the door, she turned to Katharine. "Darling, your *daddy* is a positive trick." She giggled naughtily. "I could make Richard very happy."

Katharine exaggerated a frown. "And you leave my father alone, too."

"All right, darling, if you say so," Dolly agreed lightly. "I'll just have to make do with your husband. When shall I do the co-responding, darling?"

"The sooner the better—*but* you've already done it."

"I never got pictures," Dolly cried daringly. "Don't thank me—for what are friends?"

Twenty-Five

"It's over for you, you know . . . Kitty does want her divorce." Idly, enjoying it, Dolly watched Erik's discomfort. The two were sitting in the ocre-colored drawing room of Frank Berliner's Fifth Avenue apartment, late-afternoon martinis in hand. "It seems like we've been over this before, darling," Dolly continued, making an airy gesture, "but when she asked you the first time in Port London, why didn't you say yes? Why did you lie to me?"

Erik lifted his wide-lipped glass to a petulant mouth. He swallowed almost half the martini before gravely answering, "I did not lie to you, my darling. I did explain—remember? It was not the time to discuss a divorce. Kathy was overwrought, imagining things about this man Francotti. She was doing herself great harm."

"Oh, yes?" Dolly doubted. "Great harm? Well . . . *you* did great harm to *our* relationship and now I think it's too late for us."

Did he have any idea how she was toying with him, leading him on? Dolly wondered. Her tactics had changed. She had been so very confused about Erik; damn it, she had been prepared to buy him—and had bought him, it seemed. Where was the money? She hadn't dared ask Katharine what had happened to the envelope.

Erik put his thumb and forefinger together to pinch the bridge of his nose, closing his eyes as if in pain, frowning wearily into the deep lines in his chin.

"Sometimes life is more than I can bear," he muttered.

"Oh, come now! Surely it's not that bad."

"No? You are saying that it is too late for us—that you do not love me anymore. And I am supposed to bear *that* with a smile?"

"But I don't know that I ever did love you," Dolly said casually. "I don't think it was ever anything more than pure lust."

And it wasn't any different now except that, despite the physical attraction, she was able to control herself. Why not? Dolly knew she could have him any time she was ready.

Erik stared at her as if she had said the most despicable thing imaginable. "Oh, God! *How can* I love you with all my heart?"

"Come now," Dolly mocked again. "Don't overdo it. Tell me, do you want to go to bed with me?"

"Yes, yes. Of course I do."

"I'll have one more cigarette first." She wondered whether Berliner was already here. If not, he had better be arriving soon, for she was setting the scene for Madame Co-Respondent, a drama in one act, possibly one climax.

Erik jumped up and lit her cigarette, positively fawning on her, eyes hopeful now, still not understanding what she was doing. "Oh, my darling!"

"Oh, *shit*, my darling. Don't look tragic. Lust will do."

"How *can* you be so cruel to me?"

Dolly shrugged negligently. "It's a class thing. I don't know . . . maybe you're just odd man out."

"Oh, God!" He clutched his forehead with his fingertips. "It is ruination here in this country for a foreigner."

Dolly inhaled smoke, struck again by her bright new understanding that Erik Moss was something of a clod, behind the European sophistication, the haughtiness—or was it simple arrogance—and the manners.

"I hate this country," he said bitterly.

"Then you ought to leave it."

"I intend to." He breathed fitfully. "When things are arranged."

"Tell me something: aren't you entitled to some sort of a settlement when you and Kitty divorce?"

He shrugged morosely. "I do not know."

"You signed an agreement, didn't you?" she insisted. "Of course you did. Richard Darktower will come up with some loot—he did for Steve."

"I am not Stefan Ratoff," he said loftily. "More than for money, I care for my daughter. I would not willingly concede custody to Kathy who, as you know all too well, is a drunkard and I suspect also takes dope."

Dolly smiled bitingly. "You *suspect*? Surely you'd know if she did, wouldn't you?"

"It is not something I care to investigate," he muttered.

"Bullshit! Don't give me that!"

"Not bullshit. I am sure she injects herself with it."

Dolly shook her head emphatically. "No. I never had any reason to think so. With what? Coke? Heroin? I've never seen a mark on her."

"I *do not* know," he repeated stubbornly. "But you can understand why I stopped loving her. She spends whole days in her room, the door locked. And thus, I began to love you so hopelessly, my darling."

Dolly drew calmly, a nibbling inhalation of her cigarette, wondering if it was not barely possible he was telling the truth. Kitty had always had her mental ups and downs, black despair followed by euphoria, those moods of the schizoid personality. God, if Erik were by some quirk telling even half the truth, then maybe he *was* a much misunderstood husband.

"I've never seen any evidence of dope," she repeated slowly.

He shook his head dumbly, mournfully glowering at the floor, his empty glass dangling between his knees. "My darling, if you forsake me now, I will perish."

Unsympathetically, for she was not going to surrender so quickly, Dolly said, "Easy to say, darling. Just one important question—*where the hell's my money*?"

He slumped even more abjectly. "I hoped you would not bring *that* up. It is in my safe deposit. I hadn't time to pick it up."

"Oh, shit," she groaned, "face it, Erik. It's all sham. You're not for real." Using the cigarette as a prop, for she was nervous and upset, fiddling with it, she drawled, "I don't know anything about you, not for sure. Was your life so troubled and painful that you have to be this devious?''

She appeared to have hit a responsive nerve; his eyes dilated and for once, in that instant, were vulnerable, as if he had pulled back a black silk screen and opened a thousand-mile tunnel to his soul. The change of expression was so fast, she could not isolate its ingredients. But even with such slight insight, Dolly turned cold, very cold, as if she had walked into a dungeon.

Erik pulled his eyes away. ''You do not know my story! The early years were horrible, horrible, my darling! There were things I could never relate.''

She tried to trap his eyes again but he evaded her. ''That's what Kitty told me at lunch—there were things between you she wouldn't ever discuss.''

He scowled contemptuously. ''She *would* say such a thing, would she not. Ha! Yes, she is right. There are things I would not discuss either. I think, my darling,'' he said waspily, ''you would not recognize the true innards of your dear friend.''

''Your war years? I've heard they were horrible for a lot of people,'' she pressed.

''Oh, yes,'' he whispered, ''to be shunted . . . a good word. A railroad expression, and very appropriate. Shunted here, there, everywhere . . . and nowhere.''

He fell on his knees in front of her, pressing her hand to his cheek. ''Please be kind to me.'' His eyes closed tightly, he shoved his face into her lap and his heavy hot breath through the wool of her dress scorched her thighs. Dolly was about to caress the heavy gray hair, but instead she took a handful and pulled his head up.

''Don't expect me to cry for you, Erik Moss,'' she said pointedly. ''The past is spilt milk.''

''Spilt milk, yes.'' Erik laughed tragically. ''More than that, my darling . . . blood. When you speak of spilling, speak of blood, not milk.''

Archly, she said, ''Don't make yourself out raped by history.''

"It *is* more than I can bear!" He put his forehead on her knee. "Please, come, let us go to your bedroom, yes?"

"Berliner might come back. Do you care?"

"No, no!"

"All right, then, come on."

After all, this was not going to hurt her awfully, was it? Giving him a little piece didn't represent any kind of legal commitment—*and* hadn't she promised her best friend she *would* establish grounds so firm they'd support a million legal torts? But where was Berliner?

Dolly had a strategy of sorts. In this fashion, she would make damn good and sure Erik was free of Kitty, free and loose and available. Then, later, if she, Dolly, decided to forgive Erik for all his sins, he'd be there waiting, eager, grateful. That was *if* she so decided and right now the *if* was goddamn *iffy*.

Dolly's assigned room at Frank Berliner's was a big sunny one, with windows facing Central Park. It was into this private, feminine place that she led the former Erik Mossberg, favored prey to the likes of the predatory American female. He closed the door, not even pausing to see if it would lock, which it did not. Without breaking stride, Erik gathered her in his arms and pressed her to him so that she could feel, without even straining, the muscled outline of his belly, thighs, ribs, and clotted mass of erection.

"My darling," he growled like a horny bear, "I have needed you so much."

Despite her fresh-found wariness of him, better understanding of her own sensuality, Dolly nearly collapsed when he put his thick lips on her neck, kissing the life out of her, then her mouth, the heavy tongue jabbing between her teeth.

"Easy. . . ." Dolly murmured, "Easy does it."

But he was not going to take her easily. He *was* desperate, like that beast she'd seen in the cave of his eyes. With a sweep of his arms, he snatched her off the floor and covered three long steps to the bed to throw her down upon it. She tried to smile; Erik didn't see her.

He undressed her impatiently, unbuttoning the wool

jersey dress with fidgeting fingers, slipping her out of her underwear with no sentimentality and casting it on the floor. He dropped to his knees at the side of the bed and pulled her toward him.

"Hey!" Dolly didn't like making love to a man who hadn't undressed. "You could take off your suit."

"Shut up!"

He *was* acting so differently Dolly couldn't formulate an objection. Erik buried his face in her mound, pushing her legs apart. His tongue, rough and as raw as sandpaper, found its way into her. Dolly gasped dizzily, feeling it swabbing her this way and that.

"Darling," she sighed, forgetting the money, Kitty, everything, "that's super. . . ."

The violence, near-brutality, aroused her but she didn't want to encourage too much of it. But at once, her body leapt, and impatiently, not caring now about anything, including whether or not he was undressed, she grabbed his ears and dragged him up to eye level. "Put it inside me—now!"

He threw his suit coat at a chair and missed, then dropped his trousers. Dolly was ready and she could play just as rough as he did. She grabbed at his articles and pushed him inside her with a piercing cry, relishing his force, his hips forcing her thighs apart and the hugeness pressing her into the earth, she imagining the vivid crimson slashes of her nail polish against the white of his ass. Loathsome, lovely, yes, and she would take him in or out of clothes, whether he was an honest man or a liar and cheat. Lust had outrun caution.

She had even forgotten about Berliner. Neither of them heard the door open and Dolly was as surprised as Erik Moss to hear Berliner's boyishly enthusiastic voice.

"Hi, ho! Hi, ho! Hold it!"

Erik vented dismay, alarm. His beard scratched her chest as his head whirled. Dolly flashed consternation. And the Polaroid went click!

Abruptly, Erik wrenched out of her and she gasped in pain. His feet hit the floor and he bounded awkwardly across the room before the frightened Berliner could make his escape. Erik's hand swept the camera out of Berliner's fingers. Even as the automatic mechanism was developing the picture, Erik kicked the camera across the floor.

He seized Berliner by the throat. "What is this?"

"Let go, man!" Berliner struggled to get free of Erik's large hands. "Let me go, goddamn it! Stop it! This is my house. You fuck in my house, you do it at your own risk."

Erik's voice was bloodcurdling. "I will finish you now!"

"Erik! Leave him alone, he's my friend!"

"By what right . . . ?"

"It doesn't matter," Dolly cried. Berliner stared at her nakedness, her quivering midsection, so distraught by surprise and coitus-interruptus.

Berliner's eyes bulged. "It's just a joke, for Christ's sake. Let go of me!"

"It is a joke I do not understand," Erik thundered. "The man is a voyeur of some kind."

Berliner swore violently. "I'm not interested in this shit. I'm nothing but a simple fag."

Erik bellowed laughter. "A simple fag? No doubt. Very amusing." He snarled at Dolly. "Maybe Frank would like to watch."

"Don't be disgusting," she said angrily.

"Disgusting? What is disgusting about it?" There was a pitying look on his face. "You people do not understand the meaning of the word *disgusting*."

Dolly hiked herself up on her elbows and tried to smile. But she could not help feeling very peevish. "Don't bother to be so outraged, darling . . . I don't mind. We're all friends. Besides, I like to have pictures of myself with my lovers, don't I, Frank?"

Berliner was smoothing his feathers. Bitchily, he jeered, "I'd sooner look at his ass than yours, darling!"

"Then look!"

Too late. Erik had zipped his pants, though his shirttail was still hanging out.

Berliner winced. "Quiff is not one of my favorite things, darling."

Dolly grabbed a pillow and covered herself from breast to knee. "All right. What now?"

Erik said stiffly, "I will be leaving."

Berliner felt confident enough to quip, "Don't go away mad, sweetheart."

Erik stooped, ignoring Berliner, and picked up the broken camera and the half-developed picture. "It did not come out," he announced.

"Never mind," Dolly said, "we don't need the picture. Frank can testify he saw us making it, if he's called upon."

"You would do that?" Erik demanded of Berliner.

Berliner shrugged. "I wouldn't enjoy it. But you know what they say, we Americans have got to stick together."

Erik grimaced. "You *Americans* are dishonest and corrupt. I see what the intent of this is—to compromise me in court, to make me the failed party of my marriage, and I am amazed at you, my darling. You would thusly blacken yourself . . . for the sake of your friend?"

Dolly said carelessly, "Why not? I have nothing to lose. You'll be lucky to get a penny out of Richard Darktower now. You won't get even as much as Steve Ratoff."

Berliner laughed, rather too hysterically. "But Steve got paid off for going down on a guy. You'd never get paid as much for a straightforward fuck."

Erik rubbed his face with one big hand. "This is repulsive." He looked blackly at Berliner. "I should throttle you." But he didn't sound convinced.

"Cut it out, darling!"

Erik was perspiring angrily. "I would have many things to say too."

"He's right," Berliner told her. "There's plenty of dirt on both sides of the fence. Starting with Steve."

"I am pleased you understand that much," Erik said.

Crossly, Dolly said, "Don't think I don't. We all speak the same language."

"Which is?" Erik demanded.

"The language of love, darling."

Twenty-Six

"We're going to the museum, Fred," Darktower told his driver, "but I want you to drive up Park and make the left at Eighty-First. . . ."

Naturally, Darktower had his reasons for taking this circuitous route north. Saying nothing—*his* not to wonder why but only to do and die—Fred helped Clara into the back seat of the long black limo Darktower customarily ordered when he had many business stops to make in the big city.

Clara didn't comment either. She was, in fact, not very interested in life's whys and wherefores, which, she held, served mainly to clutter the mind or divert it from more important endeavor.

Darktower put his head next to hers and whispered, "I want to have a look-see whether Sam is on station." She nodded vaguely so he explained, "It's been a couple of days now, ducks, and he still hasn't reported in. You don't think he'd just take the money and run?"

Clara shook her head. "No, Dickie. He likes you and respects you too much." Darktower made a scoffing noise. "But he does, Dick," she insisted, "though I don't understand why you're doing this. From what you've told me, your Katharine is a much mistreated little doe. But everybody knows it, don't they? Why do *you* have to go to all this trouble to prove it?"

She was right. He already had the goods on Moss. Dolly, according to Katharine, was prepared to testify she'd slept with the dastardly Kraut and she'd better stand

257

by her promise too, because Darktower knew things about the Percy trust funds that would blow them apart and ruin Dolly's life.

The thing was, he wanted *everything* on Moss. He wanted to rub Moss's Germanic nose in it. "You don't understand," he told Clara. "I'm going to take Moss right by the nuts."

She gasped, flatteringly. "Dickie, you're a vindictive monster!"

Through the intercom Darktower ordered Fred to take the Sixties very slowly. But, along the crucial block, neither Darktower nor Clara saw any sign of Sam Merchant on either side of the street.

"Surely he's lurking somewhere."

"I suppose," he grunted. "Okay, Fred, head for the museum."

The unexpected and ugly little incident occurred just as they were pulling away from the red light outside Park Towers. Two uncouth, unshaven, filthy young ruffians dashed in front of the limo, causing Fred to slam on the brakes. One of them, his eyes inflamed, thumped the front fender with his fist and screamed so loudly they could hear him through the locked doors and sealed windows. "Capitalist asshole!" Stoically Fred, looking neither right nor left, drove forward; the raging face flashed past the windows and the swinish young man spit at the car and hoisted his arm in an obscene gesture. "Fuck you! Capitalist pigs!"

Darktower's innards coiled. "Sons-of-bitches! Stop the car, Fred."

"*No, sir.*" Fred accelerated through the crossing.

Looking back, Darktower saw the young man standing in the middle of the street, still screaming after them and poking his finger at the sky. "Fred, I wish you'd go around the block and run that son-of-a-bitch over."

"I know," Fred said calmly. "But there wouldn't be much point to it."

Darktower groaned to himself. "You're right." To Clara he muttered, "How much do you think Sam Merchant would charge me for killing somebody like that?"

"Oh, Dickie. . . ." She smiled. "Probably about a thousand dollars."

The reason Darktower and Clara Riding hadn't spotted Sam Merchant on the street was that he was still sitting over coffee in his tiny *pied a terre* on First Avenue, smoking an unfiltered Camel and casually leafing his *Wall Street Journal*.

Sam was in no hurry. The Moss's maid, Helen Ryan, whom he'd made a point of meeting and charming the life out of only the day before, had called briefly to inform him that he couldn't come over yet. Moss hadn't left the apartment; she would call again the instant he was in the elevator.

Done! Well done! Merchant congratulated himself, glancing complacently around his studio apartment—one room, and a kitchen just about big enough to cook a mouse in, shower stall built for a midget and crapper to match.

He lit a fresh Camel off the old one. Despite all the cancer scares, Merchant kept on smoking unfiltered Camels, mainly, he understood, because the cigarette fit his image of himself: of cynical modern-day buccaneer, hands in his pants pockets, Camel hanging out of the corner of his mouth, smoke curling into the right eye, which he kept closed in the downside of a blink. Shit, he was *something*— and a half. Never mind the slim gauntness—Merchant weighed in at a measly one hundred and thirty. But what little he had, he knew how to use effectively. In a fight to the finish, he was as lethal as a three-hundred-pounder, plus a hell of a lot smarter.

He whistled to himself and at his good fortune. This Richard Darktower was one hell of a guy to come up with a thousand a week, plus expenses; and the work was easy. Merchant had never dreamt, obviously, of *promoting* a deal like this on the basis of a not very successful stickup. But, in fact, he'd stumbled on a gold mine that night on Madison Avenue. Merchant frowned thoughtfully—he had to keep reminding himself that the old man was ruthless; he'd just as soon get you knocked off as look at you. And better be *very* respectful of the popsie Darktower traveled with. She was something else, indeed, but Darktower doted on her.

Sam Merchant had very seriously contemplated his options upon payment of his first week's retainer of ten one hundred dollar bills. He could play square with Darktower; or he could stiff him. Remembering the cold eyes, he decided it would be best to play it very straight. Besides, if he came up with the goods on this Erik Moss, the chances were fifty-fifty he'd get a bonus of a trip to Paris, France— Darktower and the blonde-bomber were planning a trip over there, a place Merchant had never been, and the old man had hinted Merchant might do as driver-bodyguard. First, however, he had to come through on this low-life creep Erik Moss.

And so, using the old noodle, how better to get started than by cozying up to the maid at the Moss establishment on Park Avenue? At least, it *seemed* so to Sam Merchant, for he'd had no actual experience as a gumshoe; what he'd told Mr. Darktower about being a mini-electronics genius was a little stretched too, unless you believed a salesman of computer printout paper fell in that category.

Anyhow, if a creep like this Moss *was* a player, chances were he'd started by playing around with the housemaid. In Sam Merchant's experience, the maid was the first place a guy like Moss would go for a little extra ass. After that, he'd roam farther from the master bedroom.

Right on! Puff, puff on the Camel. Mission Helen Ryan!

Merchant picked up the pad he'd been using the night before to list his cast of characters. At the top of the page: Erik Moss, then Katharine Moss. Next, the kids involved: First, Conrad Darktower, the old man's son by his marriage to a woman now named Himmelmann: Second, Margaret Moss, eight years old, the daughter of the two principals. Helen Ryan's name jumped at him from the opposite side of the paper, circled and underlined for emphasis, because she was the key to the whole imbroglio, according to Sam Merchant's way of thinking. Linked by a diagonal line to Moss was the name Mrs. Dolly Percy. Darktower had insistently jogged at Merchant's memory until out of weariness he remembered her and Mrs. Moss together at that restaurant. He was to keep his eyes peeled for Mrs. Percy, a hot little number, who evidently had confessed to laying the defendant, Moss, the one time and maybe there would be a repeat.

Merchant could not easily understand such goings-on— how, for instance, Darktower's daughter had the gall to put her best friend up to fucking her husband. Suppose this Mrs. Percy, presently the witness for the plaintiff, as Katharine Moss would be described, got to like the defendant so much she refused to testify against him? Suppose, on the other hand, Mrs. Percy actually wanted to get her paws on the defendant so much that she fabricated the whole business about fucking him?

Worriedly, Merchant shook his head and drew morosely on the Camel, feeling the irritation of the smoke in his right eye. He winced and wished it were later, about noon, so he could have a shot of bourbon. Bourbon helped a guy like him think straight. *Suppose* . . . and no supposing about it, he, Sam Merchant, *Numero Uno*, Mr. Number One and a walking *Sine Qua Non* of himself, was getting his ass into a sling? Suppose the old man was using him as a patsy in some strategy much too devious for Sam Merchant to decipher, having not been brought up personally in the world of rich and not very nice people?

But, things being what they were, what the hell? There was no doubt working for Darktower was preferable to sticking people up in alleys. All things considered, he was sitting pretty. Five of the hundred dollar bills were still in his pants pocket and a secondary plan was developing in his head—maybe opening an account at the Bowery Savings. Darktower had also hinted now was the time to buy common stock. But Merchant thought he tended to be more careful than a man like Darktower, who'd had plenty to start with and could afford to believe the old Wall Street saying: Nothing ventured, nothing gained. Or, a successful squirrel risks his nuts.

The phone rang. "Hello . . . baby," Sam Merchant murmured toothily.

* * *

"There he comes, the fucker," Dork hissed.

"Oh, shit, the son-of-a-bitch is taking a cab," Mark growled.

"How in fuck can we follow him if we can't afford a cab?" Dork whined.

"Scumbag, shut up! We know he's going downtown. We take the bus down there and wait for him to come out to lunch. It's ten o'clock. Write that down, asshole. We got to know his schedule."

"Roberto's got to give us money to tail a guy like this," Dork grumbled. "He never goes on a bus, not him."

"Never mind. We take the bus downtown and wait for him. Next time, Roberto gives us money."

"Why, anyway?" Dork complained. "Conrad says this Moss don't have any money."

Mark shrugged. "I dunno. Roberto says follow him around, find out exactly where he goes, what time, who he sees. He don't see anybody but lots of rich people. He sells them stocks and bonds."

"Prick!" Dork yelled aloud.

"Yeah, all of them, that's right!" Mark agreed at the top of his voice. "All of them living off the backs of the poor people. Goddamn capitalists!" He screamed so noisily that a woman in a mink coat halfway down the block turned in alarm. Mark bawled at her, "Whatayou lookin' at, cunt?"

The woman hurried away, ducking in a moment under the canopy that sheltered the entrance of the building Erik Moss had just left.

"Shit," Mark muttered angrily, "cunt's goin' in there. I wonder—can we follow her?"

"Never get by that door guy. Looka him. Big motherfucker."

"We'd stick *him* with a knife."

"Cut off his balls."

"Carve his asshole . . . catch her in the elevator. . . ."

Dork chuffed merrily. "Make her eat it, rich cunt!"

"Mr. Hopkins," said Mrs. Himmelmann, "do you see those two frightening men down the street?"

"Yes, Mrs. Himmelmann, I've been watching 'em all the morning. They're loitering."

"I wish you'd call the police," she said. "Did you hear what they said?"

Despite his knowledgeability, Mr. Hopkins was a mild man and his heavy face flushed. "I couldn't help hearing, Mrs. Himmelmann."

"Trouble is we don't have the right anymore even to complain about such behavior to the police. All *they* do is shrug," she complained bitterly.

"True, Mrs. Himmelmann, the police can't be bothered hardly."

"Well. . . ." Margo Himmelmann shook her head resignedly, preparing to go inside. "In a way, you can't blame them. They're so busy with all the murder and rape, they can't worry about bad language and whether or not a person shaves his face."

Mr. Hopkins was gazing at her in such comradely agreement, you'd have thought they'd been on the Long March together. Instantly, Mrs. Himmelmann wondered if his eyes were so warm and reassuring because he too had heard about Richard Darktower's defiant appearance at *Le Cirque* with a blonde of uncertain age. Everybody else in town had and *all* of them had been on the phone in the past couple of days, whether to commiserate or to enjoy her embarrassment, she couldn't be sure. Was Mr. Hopkins trying to make her feel better about it?

She hesitated. "Nice . . . uh . . . to chat with you, Mr. Hopkins."

"Likewise, Mrs. Himmelmann." He smiled comfortably. For a moment, she thought, he looked like he'd plant a sympathetic kiss on her forehead.

"See you later . . . Hoppy. . . ." She shot him a glittering smile.

Did he seem stunned? Mrs. Himmelmann waved playfully, passing through the door he was holding open and into the lobby, across the inlaid oak floor to the elevator. As the door *shushed*, he was still staring after her. She tasted her lipstick with the tip of her tongue. Hopkins would lay down his life for her now! One thing about

Margo Himmelmann, she never threw in the towel and by all means would never say die! She was crazy about men, all shapes and sizes, and even at the age of fifty-eight— correction: fifty-two—even at that ripe age, she enjoyed a steady diet of love. Fifty-two, ha! That made her about fourteen when Kate had been born.

Nevertheless, one took life as it came. Poor Himmelmann, it was about to happen to him again. Margo didn't know how or when, but Herman was soon to have a new set of imaginary cuckold horns fitted to his bald dome.

"Lovey." Lilly's eyes widened with pleasure when Erik came in. "I didn't expect you 'til later."

"Lil . . . lovely Lil."

"Careful. I'm all painty, lovey."

"So I see." Not touching her sweatshirt or corduroys, he bent his head solemnly to kiss her thin lips.

"I'm happy you came this morning. I've been feeling kind of down." ,

"Down? You're never down, Lil. *Are* you pleased to see me?

She blinked childishly, nodding. Erik stood back and stared at her. She was such a waif, like a being from the war years, a starved Jew. Goddamn it! Why must he continually make these comparisons? He hated his memories. . . .

He *had* starved too in those months right after war's end, and, worse than the starvation, had felt the hate and scorn, even at his age, not only of the victor but of his countrymen, the vanquished. Why? Was it his fault he'd been born to such a woman? Softly, even as he stood gazing so soulfully at Lilly Royce, he cursed himself in German, lashing the spine of his memory with hateful words.

Just as swiftly, he shook himself, breaking the despairing mood, and moved his eyes to her easel. "May I look?"

"Sure," Lilly said quickly, as if relieved to divert his attention.

In their early days, she had been uneasy when he'd

looked at her work but by now his appreciation was so total that she liked him to inspect the paintings, even to watch from behind as she laid down the oils. One day, Erik had become convinced, Lilly was going to be a famous artist. She could not fathom what he saw in the pictures or in her—that the driving force of her innocent enthusiasm was extreme insecurity, the opening expression of a terrible black fear, which, he was sure, would lead her somehow, later, to tragedy. Knowing this, he was drawn toward her even more strongly; he related to inevitability, the black curse, for it would be the mate of his own. When she grew older, could she escape, a person digging herself out of an avalanche of defeat, destruction or would it smother her? Had it already smothered him?

Studying the painting, Erik limply nodded. It was so derivative of Rothko: dark shadings of color descending toward noncolor, black at the edges, but all linked by diiagonals of pencil-thin white, like lightning bolts across the vision of a blind man. People would say, Erik told himself, that the white streaks represented the human spirit's struggle to prevail, not understanding, as he did, that the marks were merely the last shock waves of ruination.

"It's the best, Lil."

"It's for you, lovey." Her voice pitched scarlet, like her hair. "I've never done better than in the last month!"

"Ah!" He knew it and she would learn. "We're like-souls, Lil. We belong together. Will you come to Europe with me to live forever?"

She thrust her pointed face toward him. "What do you mean?"

"Simply that we go to Europe together, you and I."

Her face reverted to a tremulous smile. "I don't know anything about Europe. I don't speak any of the languages."

"The better to learn." He straightened his shoulders. "I *do* know Europe and I do speak the languages. What I suggest is we settle quietly, perhaps in the mountains in Austria, or in Tuscany, close to Florence. You would do your art. . . ."

"And you?"

He smiled hopefully, dreaming. "I would watch you

paint. I would be your manager. I would arrange your exhibitions and send out your bills. I am a very good salesman.''

She laughed, not believing any of it. "I don't think you'd like it. You've got to be in the mainstream."

He shook his head irritably. "I am sick to death of the mainstream, my darling! I want to be far away. I want to slow down time." She didn't understand—how could she? "Here everything is too fast, too furious, and it all makes time travel faster than it should. In the mountains or in ancient Tuscany, the world does not spin so fast."

She nodded; he *was* very serious. Avoiding his eyes, she gazed stolidly at the canvas. "I *have* been thinking of pulling up stakes at Conrad's."

Did his heart leap? Possibly. "And?"

She shrugged, still not looking at him. "I'd just move in here if you're going to keep the place."

"Would you be comfortable? It's very Spartan," Erik murmured.

"No!" Fiercely, she turned. "Why not? I'm sick of Conrad and especially his so-called friends. Conrad is a child. And *those others*—they talk about *you*, you know. They keep asking Conrad about you."

Erik smiled fleetingly. "And what does the little prince say?"

"He says there's nothing they can get out of you, that you have no money." She lowered her eyes, embarrassed by her own words.

"Ah ha!" he exclaimed angrily. "So you, therefore, don't believe we could remove ourselves to Europe. *You* think I could not afford it!"

"That's not what I said," she protested shakily. "What I'm trying to tell you is I'm worried. For some reason, they have a fixation on you. They talk about following you, using you somehow."

"I won't stand still for that! How dare they?" he demanded angrily.

"They dare," she said. "I've told you—they think of themselves as terrorists. They're stupid but that's what they think. And that's what they've been talking about."

"I see," he said slowly. "But Conrad does not encourage them—that is a relief of sorts. Would they follow me here?"

"I suppose it's possible."

"If they did, they would find you—and Conrad would know about us, Lil." He touched her lightly on the shoulders with his fingertips, then ground his hands against each other, feeling the tension in the muscles of his arms. "Would you care?"

"I wouldn't want to hurt him."

"Tell me then, what do these creatures look like?"

Even describing them was distasteful. Her nose wrinkled. "They're dirty. One is tall and thin and dirty and the other one is shorter and fatter and dirtier."

"Their names?"

"The fat one is Dork. The thin one is Mark."

"Terrorists?" Erik chuckled disbelievingly.

"They worship that man . . . Carlos. Don't ask me why."

"Ah, yes, Carlos." Erik stroked the name with his voice. Careless now of the paint blotches on her sweatshirt, he put his arm around Lilly's waist and kissed her forehead. "My darling, I think in any case you should say farewell to Conrad."

"Yes, I know. It's not nice cheating on him. I'd rather he knew."

"It would complicate things needlessly." Lilly, he was aware, did not harbor a complete artistic scorn of money. "It might compromise my search for financial independence, you understand."

"Lovey," she said soberly, "I know. I'm patient."

"We must be honorable," he added thoughtfully, musing. "Perhaps the time *has* come to return to Europe." He looked at her. "Do these creatures actually mean me harm?"

"What they've got in mind, as far as I can tell, is to kidnap somebody rich for ransom to finance their goddamn *cause*."

Erik snorted contemptuous laughter. "Stupid! Still, I will begin to take care. There must be a different access to this building.'' For a second, mind clicking over checkpoints, he forgot her, then remembered and kissed the soft white skin of her neck. ''Oh, Lil, we are a pair of clever rascals! Before anybody knows it, my financial affairs will be restructured and we will be gone.''

With a small voice, Lilly picked out the one fly in the ointment. ''What about your daughter?''

''*Ach! Ja, die kleine Margarete.*'' He flashed a brave smile. ''Have no fear. *That will be solved along with all else,* my darling.''

To himself, he laughed even more boisterously, thinking of the inevitable negotiations with Richard Darktower. God, yes, Darktower would be overjoyed to see the back of Erik Moss. Most difficult, he calculated, would be the division of the community property Katharine and he had assembled—the house in Port London and the apartment. Together, the two would be worth at least four or five million dollars in today's market . . . half of that, taxes paid—yes, he would insist his money be free and clear— would fit neatly into a Swiss account.

When everything was settled, money being of paramount importance, then progeny, they would work out an amicable arrangement for the joint custody of little Margaret. Darktower would insist she go to school in America—very well. Erik Moss would insist she be exposed to Europe on her holidays—and Richard Darktower would have no choice but to agree to that reasonable request.

He kissed Lilly's red hair, smelling her freshness behind the heavy scent of oil paint. ''Yes, all will be arranged. *Lovey* will take care of everything because he loves you.''

''Oh,'' she sighed, closing her eyes tightly under his embrace, a small grin of self-satisfaction, or was it possessiveness, pursing her lips, ''you make it all sound so wonderful . . . so easy. It would be such a change, though, wouldn't it?''

''But not for the worse, Lil.''

''Eventually, do you think. . . .'' She paused coyly, her eyelashes fluttering, ''. . . would we be married?''

The shy question shocked him. ''You?'' He mocked her

distantly. "Liberated youth? I am confused—I was afraid to mention such a thing to you. But Lilly—*of course!*"

Her eyes swept him. She might, as he believed, be an old soul but women, eternal or not, never stopped, did they, wanting certain specific things?

"When do you think that would be?"

"When?"

"Yes, when. What month? Before we left, I'd hope."

"When?" he repeated, almost flinching beneath her stare. "Well, it's May now; everything should be settled by October. I hope."

"October? Okay," Lilly cried pleasurably. "My birthday is in October." She chuckled, too excitedly, he thought. "I didn't expect anything like this today, you know." She struggled up to kiss the cleft of his chin. "Lovey, will you buy me silver and pearls?"

Erik joked awkwardly. "Are you one of *them* girls?"

Twenty-Seven

Helen Ryan was surprised, then embarrassed to open the door to Margo Himmelmann. Dark eyes blinked anxiously, and her hand twitched at the top of her white blouse. "Oh! Mrs. Himmelmann."

"In the flesh, Helen," Mrs. Himmelmann said good-humoredly. "Where's my daughter? Upstairs?"

"Oh, no, oh, no! She went out hours ago, Mrs. Himmelmann, to the exercise and for her hair. Then luncheon."

"Drat! Since when on Tuesdays? I thought it was Monday, Wednesday and Friday. Who's she having lunch with?"

Helen ducked before the volley of questions, then answered, almost evasively, it occurred to her. "She's speeded up her schedule, ma'am. She rushes around all day . . . and every night too, it seems like."

"Lunch?" Mrs. Himmelmann reminded her.

"Probably Mrs. Percy, since they're thick as thieves these days. Or maybe that man. . . ."

Mrs. Himmelmann came to red alert, her eyes hammering Helen. "Man? What man? Not Erik Moss, I believe?" she said severely.

Helen shrugged, not as indifferently as she let on. "No, not Mr. Moss."

"Who, for heaven's sakes?"

"I don't know," Helen muttered.

"Is it none of my blessed business, then, Helen? Whose side are you on?"

"The family's, of course."

Mrs. Himmelmann was not so sure of that. As she walked into the living room and sat down carefully in the armchair by the fireplace, she remarked, "Well, Helen, I hope there *is* another man. It serves Mr. Erik Moss right—he's not to be trusted, is he?" she egged Helen on.

"Isn't he, Mrs. Himmelmann?" Helen asked anxiously.

"Of course not!" Mrs. Himmelmann spoke briskly, asking now for the truth and nothing but the truth. "Tell me, when my daughter is out of the house . . . was there ever anything untoward?" Helen shook her head speechlessly. "Did he ever . . . you *know*, Helen . . . did he ever make a *pass* at you?"

Helen looked ready to collapse. "Oh, Mrs. Himmelmann!" She cracked her knuckles loudly, like firecrackers going off. "Such a question!"

Blast if she wasn't on to something! "It's *not* a silly question, though, Helen. Such stuff happens every day. I'm asking, did he ever try to have his way with you?"

Helen's discomfort heightened astonishingly. She began to cry, pressing her fingers to her face, covering her eyes. "Yes," she muttered shamefully, "he did."

Mrs. Himmelmann gasped. She wanted to know but now was dismayed to hear it. "My God! I don't believe you!"

"You asked me," Helen wailed. "It's true. He did!"

"Impossible!" It would be incredibly stupid of Erik to fool around at home, in blatant violation of the eleventh commandment. "So, Helen," she muttered, "I suppose you let him . . . *silly goose*?"

Surely not. A fine Irish-Catholic girl like Helen Ryan would rebuff such a scoundrel. Again, Helen defied all reason. "Yes, ma'am, I did."

Mrs. Himmelmann felt herself shrink. "You did?"

"Yes, I did," Helen Ryan said firmly, though her head was hanging. "I thought maybe I could help—maybe I could save the marriage." Helen perched fingertips on the back of the sofa, next looking Mrs. Himmelmann in the eye.

Faintly, Mrs. Himmelmann observed, "That's not very
. . . believable, Helen. Or loyal."

Helen's grimace was ghastly. "Loyal it was! The man is
so broken up he'd just go out for a whore, Mrs. Himmelmann, and bring God knows what terrible disease into the
house. I call that loyalty—if you like a healthful house."
She gained courage as she spoke. "Besides," she added,
her face composed, "*you* shouldn't be lecturing *me* now,
should you?"

Margo Himmelmann opened her mouth, preparatory to a
harsh cry of insult and anger, but nothing came out. Her
back set rigidly against the chair. "Am I lecturing you?"
She chuckled nervously. "I wouldn't, oh, no, Helen . . .
you've been with my daughter a long time, haven't you?"

"The eight years since little Margaret was born, Mrs.
Himmelmann," Helen stated carefully, her eyes critical.
"I'm very observant too."

"Yes, I'm sure you are." Margo Himmelmann clucked
confusedly. She began to fear what Helen would pour out
about them all, if the dam were breached, things Margo
Himmelmann had either forgotten or had never wished to
know. "Well, Helen," she muttered, "what's happened
has happened, that's all. But. . . ." She hesitated. "Forgive
me, but I still don't understand really why you let him."

Helen spoke bluntly, as if she'd memorized the words.
"Why, he seduced me, Mrs. Himmelmann, as men usually do to poor women—they seduce them and bend them
to their will and do with them things that make sure
they're never the same again."

Mrs. Himmelmann nodded, breathing erratically, wondering just what it was had been done to Helen so remarkably that she'd never be the same again. This was emphatically not the way *she*, Margo Himmelmann, operated. No
man had ever seduced *her*. No, rather the other way
around, even though the man might have thought otherwise.

"Poor Helen," she murmured thoughtlessly.

"I know he doesn't love me and I don't care! The fact
of the matter is, ma'am, I'm ruined now."

Mrs. Himmelmann was shocked. "Good God! How
many times, did he . . . did you . . . ?"

"How many times did he do the ugly thing? Two times, maybe thrice. I can't remember."

"You can't remember? How could you *forget*?"

Helen confessed glumly, "I admit I just went crazy, Mrs. Himmelmann, and I'm not sure how much of it I dreamt about and how much of it really happened. It was so . . . ruinous. And it hurt and it was humiliating too. Were you ever humiliated by it, Mrs. Himmelmann?"

"What? I! Helen, I. . . ." Surely, Helen did not think she would answer such a question. Margo Himmelmann shook her head doggedly, as if trying her memory of long ago. "No, I never was humiliated, Helen. If you were seduced, why feel so humiliated?"

"But in front of somebody, Mrs. Himmelmann," Helen cried, despairingly. "He done it in front of somebody."

"What? Who? Helen, stop it! I think I'm going to faint."

Helen didn't spare the barbs. "In front of your daughter Katharine, Mrs. Himmelmann!"

Mrs. Himmelmann shrieked softly and closed her eyes. Never, never, had she, even she, heard of such a thing. "Oh, my God," she moaned.

"Yes . . . Oh, my God is correct, Mrs. Himmelmann."

Helen was enjoying this very much, wasn't she? "Helen," Mrs. Himmelmann said firmly, "I cannot believe that, willingly, you did it with him in front of my daughter."

"He did force me, don't you understand? And what he did to her. . . ."

"Don't tell me, Helen," Mrs. Himmelmann pleaded.

"I won't."

Again, Margo Himmelmann pressed her eyes shut. "He is a terrible and evil man, I see it now." She envisioned all terrible and evil things. "The man deserves to be hung."

Hung, she thought, hung, yes, like a stallion, a satyr.

"That he does." Helen agreed smugly but one sensed it wouldn't be her say-so that would hang him. "And I can tell you there's a man snooping around right now about him—I think Mr. Moss will end his days in prison for the evil man that he is, Mrs. Himmelmann."

"A snooping man?" It was difficult to bear, all of it, and yet another revelation.

"I think he's a detective, Mrs. Himmelmann, and he'll be here any minute. He asked me to call him when Mr. Moss had left. Mind you, he didn't tell me he's a detective—he played up to me yesterday as I was out for my afternoon stroll."

"He's playing up to you?" Of course! The maneuver was transparent; the truth thundered, like the tumblers of a lock. "Richard!" Mrs. Himmelmann shrieked. "He has hired a detective to get evidence on Erik! Good God—don't tell him of your experiences, will you, Helen? Not in front of my poor daughter?"

Helen shook her head doubtfully. "If asked, Mrs. Himmelmann. . . ."

"But, Helen, you'd have to take the witness stand. You'd be so embarrassed."

Sullenly, Helen said, "I'm ruined now so what does it matter? The both of them have ruined me, Mrs. Himmelmann." The both of them? Margo Himmelmann didn't ask the question but Helen saw it lurking in her eyes. "Yes, Mrs. Himmelmann, Katharine by confiding in me of her adultery. She has told me about all her lovers, no doubt to break down my virginal defenses . . . for *him*!"

Mrs. Himmelmann's face was beginning to fail, she knew it, the powder moistening with perspiration, swelling, cracking. Another five minutes of this and she'd have to go back to the beauty shop. She hardly dared repeat the word. "*Adultery*. . . ."

"You can believe it, Mrs. Himmelmann," Helen said, her tone implacable. "So, in court, if they asked me about *him*, then it would have to come out, wouldn't it, about *her*. With all else *I'm* guilty of, I do know it's a sin to tell a lie."

Margo Himmelmann groaned piteously to herself, her throat crawling as if she'd swallowed a poisonous bug but, thankfully, before she had to deliver her reply, the faraway *whooshing* sound of the elevator caused Helen to raise her hand.

"That'll be him—Mr. Merchant, I'll bet."

"Helen—what should I do?" She heard the panic in her voice. Mrs. Himmelmann had no wish to meet a private detective ever again—suppose it was Herman Himmelmann who had hired this detective to spy on *her*?

Helen marched away, motioning for her to sit still, strong hips grinding like mill wheels. A door opened, there were voices and, in a moment, Helen led a slender, slightly stooping young man into the salon. He was extravagantly black-haired, as if he had brushed himself out with shoe polish. His eyes roamed the room shiftily.

"Mrs. Himmelmann," Helen said formally, "this is Mr. Sam Merchant. He's just happened by to say hello— we're old school friends." Behind his back, Helen winked.

"I see," Mrs. Himmelmann whispered, "you were in school in Dublin?"

The man called Sam Merchant shook his head. "No . . . Queens." His voice was harsh, burred with a New York borough accent Mrs. Himmelmann couldn't place, yet it possessed a certain quality. What really impressed her was the look of his face, not so much sneer as a cynical setting that twisted one side of his mouth like the after-effects of a stroke. His teeth showed only yellowed tips. "Helen and I are old friends, Mrs. Himmelmann."

He didn't have any trouble with her name, did he? "You'd be about the same age, I suppose," she murmured.

"That's right. Just under thirty years of age."

Helen's eyes were bright, dancing with fun. Quite a joke, wasn't it? Yes, some joke, Mrs. Himmelmann thought. It was one thing to put a detective on Erik Moss, clearly a world-class rascal, but what if equivalent dirt should surface about poor Kate? God, such depravity! The divorce court, if it came to that, would hear the most dreadful things, stories her poor daughter would never, never live down if they reached the newspapers—which they would, following Richard Darktower's exploits.

Mrs. Himmelmann's attention wandered. Helen would have to be taken care of—she was no fool. Helen would have to go on a pension too, as Stefan Ratoff had, as Erik Moss most likely would, all these eyewitnesses to Kate's misfortunes.

"You were saying . . .?"

"I was saying, Mrs. Himmelmann," Merchant replied sardonically, his yellow teeth naked to mid-smirk, "how pleasant it is to meet you." He eyed her patronizingly. "You'd be the former wife of Mr. Richard Darktower."

"Yes." It wasn't a question, but a statement. "How would you know that?" It was obvious how he knew—he had been briefed by either Richard or Herman.

"I read the society columns, Mrs. Himmelmann, and the financial sections too." Merchant turned his spare body to grin familiarly at Helen Ryan. "You remember, Helen, how I was always a nut about the stock market." Helen nodded, gawking with suppressed amusement. At the same time, Merchant glanced significantly at Mrs. Himmelmann, letting her know, she realized, that he was not at liberty to speak openly in front of Helen.

Margo Himmelmann took the hint. "Helen, would you mind? I'd love some tea, or coffee, whatever you have on the stove. Mr. Merchant? Something cool . . . something hot?"

Merchant glanced at his watch. "It's going on noon," he said. A lie—it was just after eleven. "If I might, I wouldn't turn down a bourbon and water. Mind if I smoke?"

Helen began her passage to the kitchen as Sam Merchant pulled a pack of Camels out of the breast pocket of his shirt, with precision tapped one free, put it between his lips and lit it with the flick of a Zippo lighter. Mrs. Himmelmann watched the smoke trickle up his face.

"What do you do, Mr. Merchant?"

Helen was out of earshot. "I'm a private eye." Mrs. Himmelmann didn't register any response. "I was hired by your former—"

"Mr. Darktower?" she interrupted, relieved.

"Yes. To get the straight poop on Erik Moss, your son-in-law."

"For the purpose of?" she demanded crisply, even knowing what she did, pitying Erik.

He moved his shoulders disparagingly. "To the end of a divorce settlement without unnecessary hassle between him, the defendant, and the person who's the plaintiff, namely your daughter, Katharine.''

Margo Himmelmann breathed quickly, impressed by his syntax. ''I see. As usual, Mr. Darktower is not to be trifled with.''

Merchant nodded vigorously. ''It is a definite fact that Mr. Darktower is not to be trifled with, Mrs. Himmelmann. I would hate to be his enemy. He is a tough customer.''

''I know,'' she grunted acidly.

''But he is definitely *my man*, Mrs. Himmelmann.''

''Wonderful,'' she drawled. ''Since we're on the subject, when you spoke to him did you by any chance meet the blonde lady who everybody says is his new mistress?''

''*New* mistress?'' Merchant took her up cautiously. He moved his head away from the smoke but finally had to rub the corner of his eye. ''I wouldn't know about new or old mistresses, Mrs. Himmelmann. I did meet a blonde lady. The three of us had lunch together.''

''At *Le Cirque*, I know. Who is she?''

''He introduced us but I forgot.''

She smiled at him seductively and ran her tongue over her lipstick, fortunately, still intact. ''I admire your reticence, Mr. Merchant. Of course, you couldn't tell me, could you? After all, I'm not your client. It wouldn't be ethical, would it?''

''Definitely not,'' he said, apparently glad she'd reminded him of ethics.

Mrs. Himmelmann shifted her legs, still shapely, she knew, crossing the left one over the right knee so he couldn't miss the slice of thigh, all the while eyeing him frankly. ''We could talk business, Mr. Merchant. Out of curiosity, that's all, I'd like to know who she is. I'm going away for the weekend.''

Warily, he nodded.

''I'm going to the Plaza Hotel,'' she said.

He didn't get the humor implied. ''Hell, Mrs. Himmelmann, that's not going away. The Plaza is only about twenty blocks from here.''

''I know. That doesn't matter. I go away from home . . . at home. Call me from downstairs about five-thirty

Friday afternoon. I'll be waiting. Bring your toothbrush,'' she added daringly.

Merchant's sly eyes whip-lashed. Slowly, hand inching upward, he took the cigarette out of his mouth and whistled. "You don't beat around the bush, do you . . . baby?"

"No, I don't." She manufactured a wink with her left eye.

Merchant grinned, again, obviously, not believing his good fortune. "Say . . . baby . . . it'll be a pleasure."

Twenty-Eight

Katharine found out in the most obvious way possible that Francotti was back in town—from the maitre d' at *Le Cirque*—then cursed herself remorsefully that she hadn't had the sense to be there for lunch on the Monday and Tuesday, for Francotti had come in both days. Yes, the maitre d' reported, Mr. Francotti looked just fine and there was no sign of a cast on his arm.

She was prepared to stoop now, to throw herself at his feet. Whatever was necessary, she would do. But she had to be careful. Early Thursday Katharine called Conrad at his apartment and invited him to meet her Friday at *Le Cirque*. It would be the most natural thing, wouldn't it, brother and sister lunching together at their favorite restaurant, accidentally running into Gene Francotti who appeared there most Fridays if he happened to be in town.

She arrived twenty minutes early, her heart beating awkwardly and got her favored place at the banquette against the far wall, the place from which to see everything and still be private.

A second vodka martini was in place by the time Conrad arrived. Intensely, she watched his entrance, for a moment forgetting why they were here. Conrad was so handsome, his blondness a shining gift, even shinier than hers. He smiled broadly when he saw her and walked lightly across the room.

Katharine absorbed his features at close range. His skin was so clean, so fine, so translucently porcelain. Every woman she knew would have killed for such wonderful skin. He sat down and ordered wine.

"You could have brought your girl," she said in a low voice.

He grinned. "My girl? Where'd you hear about her . . . you didn't invite her."

"Stefan mentioned her."

"She works all day. She'd never come up here."

Katharine shrugged. "I wouldn't want to embarrass you . . . *have* you seen Stefan?"

Conrad nodded. "Yes. When he got back from California. We had lunch together a couple days ago."

"How is he?" Her voice dropped embarrassedly.

Conrad shook his head, avoiding her eyes. He took a long sip of wine. "He's sick. He looks horrible."

Katharine stroked his knuckles. "Darling, I don't know what anybody can do. I don't even know how sick he is."

"It's bad, Kate" he said blackly. "You can tell when you talk to him. He starts to say something, then drifts away. He's like on another planet. I don't know—should I go back to Europe with him?"

Katharine shook her head uneasily. "Darling, I don't know what to tell you. You've got this . . . girl friend. Could you leave her? Isn't she living with you in the Village?"

His eyes lifted crushingly. "You could help him, if you wanted to."

"How?" she asked weakly. "Conny. . . ."

"*You* could be with him."

"But we're not married anymore, Conny. I don't think he wants me around. He's with that man."

Gripping the wine glass tensely in his fingers, Conrad continued to stare at her. "That's right, Kate. Dodge reality. You're not *really* married anymore to Moss either—so what's the difference?"

"Conny, please. . . ."

"You could have saved him, Kate. He told me he's always loved you."

With a great effort, she reversed a rush of tears. "I don't want to hear it!"

"Right! You'd *never* want to hear it," he said coldly. "You're more spoiled than I am, Kate. The old man had the last word." He passed sentence on her. "And you caved in."

"Jesus," Katharine swore, "you are a little bastard!"

"You could have helped him."

"No, you're wrong, Conny. Nobody could save him. And nobody can save him now. What makes you think he even wants to be saved?" she demanded bitterly. "You lecture me? You were part of the reason Daddy sent him off!" Suddenly the tears broke past her defenses.

"I'm sorry—I shouldn't mention that—you were blameless," Katharine apologized.

He looked away from her, eyes wounded, nodding. "I can't stand that part of it."

Oh, Christ, she thought desperately, where the hell was Francotti? She needed him so much now, needed him quickly to stand between her and Conrad. But she realized it then—he was not coming.

Mournfully, hardly speaking, they ordered lunch and just as silently finished it.

"Do you want coffee?"

Conrad shook his head. "I've got to go uptown."

"Friday afternoon? No," she said, telling herself if this was the only way she could do it, break out of this emotional tangle, then she would do it this way. "I want you to come with me to meet somebody . . . a friend of mine. He broke his arm a few weeks ago and I want to see how he is."

He regarded her steadily, eyes flat, almost hostile. "A friend?"

"Yes." She squirmed, trying to smile. "A friend. You'll like him. He's a marine engineer, an interesting man."

"All right, if you want," he said, unwillingly.

"Let's go, right now!"

Quickly, Katharine signed the bill, leaving a recklessly large tip for the waiter. Outside, she hugged Conrad's arm, pressed against him, as they waited on the curb, then excitedly jumped into the cab when it pulled up. By now, she was laughing, breathlessly, eagerly. If the mountain didn't come to Kate, then Kate went to the mountain.

The cab seemed to take hours to get through the crosstown traffic but finally they reached the corner where she and Francotti had disembarked that first time.

"Pay him, darling," she said.

Katharine jumped impatiently out of the cab and almost ran to the door which opened to Francotti's private elevator.

When Conrad joined her, he said, "I don't know what this is all about. How do you know he's here? Why didn't you call first? You're a child, Kate."

"Shut up, darling," she said crossly. She punched the button which summoned Francotti to the intercom.

The electronics buzzed, then hummed. "Yes?"

She could hardly speak. "Hello, Gene. It's. . . ."

His voice crackled dispassionately. "That figures. . . ." She was aware of Conrad's expression. "Okay, come on up." The door buzzed open and they stepped inside.

"I don't get it," Conrad mumbled. "He didn't sound very eager."

"Oh! For heaven's sakes, Conny, come along for the ride, and don't mope so much."

Like the cab, the elevator took hours, it seemed, to reach Francotti's floor. But finally it stopped and the door swung free.

He was standing there, hands anchored imperiously on his hips. The surprise for him was seeing Conrad. He'd been prepared to shoot her down again. But she had finessed him by bringing a stranger.

"Hi!" Katharine exclaimed, soaking up his stare. He could not mask his memory, his admiration, no matter how hard he tried. "Stopped by to see if you were back in town. This is my little brother, Conrad. Conrad, Gene Francotti."

She did everything but shove Conrad forward, everything but push them together. Shaking hands, Francotti drew Conrad out of the elevator and into his living room-office.

"Whataya say," Francotti murmured.

"How do you do?" Conrad responded stiffly.

"Not too bad," Francotti murmured. "This nut is really your sister? Yes. I see. Look-alikes."

Katharine laughed hilariously. "Conny, some people call Gene *Gizmo*. That's his nickname."

Francotti nodded at her, his face amused: but his expression was reserved, and watchful because he couldn't figure out what she was up to.

"You were at *Le Cirque* today?" he asked, in search of something better to say.

"Oh, yes. They said you'd been in. So I realized you were back. Where *have* you been?" Katharine realized she was gushing too passionately in front of Conrad. Obviously, this man would be more than a mere "friend." But she didn't care. She was ready to take the jump. She couldn't help herself now.

"I've been in San Francisco, Hawaii, and a couple of weeks in Taiwan . . . Formosa, whatever you want to call it," he said calmly.

"Doing something for the government, that's what he's been up to, Conny," she warbled stupidly.

Francotti put a long, heavy forefinger to his lips. "Quiet—the walls have ears!" He nudged his wire-frame spectacles with the same finger, then dropped the hand into the pocket of a beige cardigan sweater. "I was coming over for lunch—then I got too involved to leave."

"You're working!" Katharine cried. "How marvelous!"

Again, he studied her quietly, as if she were really going crazy, then glanced at Conrad. He shrugged slightly. "Yes, Mrs. Moss, I'm working. I usually do. Come here," he mentioned to Conrad, "you might be interested. Are you into engines, that kind of stuff?"

Conrad, not knowing how to react, stammered, "I—I don't know. I'm interested, yes. But. . . ."

"What are you studying?"

Conrad straightened. "I . . . uh . . . teach. American Lit., eighteenth century."

"Oh . . . that. You look too young. Still—I'll show you anyway."

"Yes, show him," she cried, "and then the model motor. It's so *interesting*, darling!"

Now they both stared at her, the hysterical woman. She smiled back at them, inanely, she was sure, but she couldn't help it. She was trembling so violently that she rushed to the window to focus herself on the river while Francotti explained his drawings to Conrad. Surreptitiously, she watched them over her shoulder—they looked so *nice* together, she thought. God, if it could only work, she'd do anything, give anything. . . .

Francotti addressed himself to her after a moment. "Are you people going to the island for the holiday?"

"Memorial Day? Yes!" she cried. "Will you be there, Gene? I forgot to ask—how is your arm? Is it all right now?" She could have burst into tears of concern. Senselessly, she bawled at Conrad, "Mr. Francotti hurt his arm at the dock—working on a motor."

"It's *all right* now," Francotti declared evenly. "I've gotten over it. We almost had a disaster," he muttered to Conrad.

"Gotten over it? Oh, good! Good!" Gotten over it? Did that mean he wasn't angry with her anymore, that he'd forgiven her? "Will *you* be up for the holiday too?" she asked again.

Steadily, he nodded. "I'll be there, but not in harbor. I'm planning to take my boat out for a run." He laughed sardonically. "Your friend, Mrs. Percy, wanted her for a rental over the weekend." His shoulders moved stubbornly, "I don't rent out my tub."

"Didn't she invite you to her party?"

"Sure, but I'm not going. I don't like parties. You guys are all too sophisticated for me. *You know that*, Mrs. Moss," he said frostily, reminding her of the spike still planted in her heart. "What about you, young man? You like these hotsy-totsy parties?"

She protested. "*Why* do you keep saying those things?"

Francotti shrugged, winking at Conrad who, by now, was totally perplexed by the to'ing and fro'ing of obviously loaded words and expressions.

"*Say what*? I don't like parties, that's all."

Speechlessly, she nodded. He didn't rub it in. He acted,

instead, coldly neutral, indifferent, as if what had been love, or close to love, was now only an accident.

"Would you two like some coffee . . . or a drink?"

Conrad shook his head. "No, thanks. I guess we'd better be going, Mr. Francotti." He had recognized the brush-off and he was going to take his sister protectively out of the heat. Francotti wanted them gone! Katharine wanted to rush at him and knock him down to make him pay attention. Her eyes sought him on the other side of his drawing table. But his eyes did not reciprocate; they were blank, as opaque as a wall.

The game was up. She'd lost. Francotti was telling her, so long, Mrs. Moss. Good-bye. Farewell. Good luck.

"Yes," she muttered. "I think maybe we'd best be going. I'm sorry we won't be seeing you in Port London." She had some pride, after all.

He smiled confidently. He had prevailed. He had survived his surprise. The son-of-a-bitch, Katharine told herself dully. She was ashamed of herself now for having done this childish thing.

The fact of the matter was, Francotti was just not interested in her. He'd made love to her, laid her, yes, fucked her . . . and she had come up wanting. She was just not good enough. She felt his eyes on her sympathetically when she and Conrad got into the elevator.

As the door was closing, he winked, and her knees buckled—what was that supposed to mean?

She wanted to scream at him: I don't understand you! *I do not understand you!*

Twenty-Nine

Richard Darktower and his Clara Riding were just coming into the Carlyle suite after an evening downstairs with Bobby Short when the telephone began to ring.

"I'll go in the bathroom, Richard," Clara said.

"Don't be long, ducks. I've got to take a tremendous leak."

That was one way of saying there was nothing wrong with his sixty-five-year-old prostate, and even less wrong since he'd known Miss Clara. When he had to take a leak, Richard Darktower really had to take a leak.

"Yes?"

"*Chief?*"

"Yes. . . ." He recognized the voice of his hireling.

"It's me, Sam," Merchant said softly. "Are you alone, Chief? Can you take a report?"

"Goddamn it," Darktower cursed, feeling a little impatience was in order, "I've been waiting to hear from you. What's up?"

Pompously, full of himself, Sam Merchant boasted, "Chief, I got the stuff."

"Shoot, Sam."

Merchant commenced. "I followed subject from his place of work on Lower Manhattan at approximately five P.M. yesterday and again today. Subject grabs cab in a side street and fortunately at this time of day I am able to get another, instructing cabbie to follow that cab. Subject did not return to Park Avenue but instead de-cabs on First Avenue at Fortieth Street. I follow suit. Subject walks down Fortieth toward Second Avenue and then, near the corner, ducks into a cigar store and while in the act of purchasing a panatela carefully cases the street outside the window, as if sensing he has a tail.''

"For Christ's sake," Darktower growled, "did he spot you?''

"No, no, Chief! I, in the meantime, conclude he is being tailed by somebody else.''

"Who else, for Christ's sake?''

"Easy, Chief. I spot them soonest—a couple of skulkers, dirty punks, obviously snatch-and-run guys.''

"Who are they?''

"I dunno, Chief. What happens next is subject farts around in the cigar store for a few minutes, makes a phone call, then exits, walking north on Second. Between him and me are these two thugs . . . reaching the corner of Forty-First and Second, subject takes a fast right, the two punks close behind. As I discover right away, they are in for a big surprise. Subject is a big man, Chief . . . I make the corner, and observe with some surprise that subject has got the both of these two punks against the wall, each by the throat with one hand. Since he don't suspect that I am also tailing him, I approach and ask if I may be of any assistance. Subject sneers and snarls in a guttural tone of voice that these two low-life little swine, as he calls 'em, have been following him and he proposes to knock their fuckin' brains to pieces. One, a fat slob, is practically puking with fright; subject dispatches him to the sidewalk with a slap to the face and knee to the solar plexus. The other, taller, one is cringing and whining. Subject demands to know why they are on his tail and he had better confess or subject is going to bash him against the side of the building.''

"He's a tough customer, isn't he, Sam?" Darktower asked softly. Too bad Moss didn't play for the right team, wasn't it?

"He is a *very* tough customer," Merchant intoned, as if perparing to ask for a bigger retainer.

"Weren't there any police around at five-thirty in the afternoon?''

With dignity, Merchant replied, ''Do you ever know the police to be around when you need them? To the point, Chief, the second punk by now is shrieking that they're not following anybody and that subject had better take his hands off. Subject slaps him around a little and issues warning that if he ever catches sight of them again, it's gonna be some busted bones. To make his point, he gently *karates* this slime and knees him on his way down. Those two guys are not going to forget this confrontation very soon, I can tell you, Chief.''

''So . . . so?'' Darktower demanded impatiently. ''Get on with it.''

''Okay, okay, Chief. Subject notices I am still standing there and asks me again what the hell I want—I note his eyes are really scary, Chief, like two burning coals. Again, I reiterate I'm only stopping to see if he needs any help which obviously he does not. So I quickly say good-bye and look to be on my merry way.''

''Listen,'' Darktower said angrily, ''it was stupid of you to let him see you. He's not going to forget your face.''

''Chief,'' Merchant lisped, ''I am a man of many faces. Anyway, don't think I didn't see where subject went next.''

''*Where* did he go?''

''He went around the corner, doubled back and into an old brownstone on the block between First and Second. I duck into the house facing, run up to the fifth floor and ring a bell on a street-side apartment, yelling Special Delivery. A woman opens the door and I barge in saying ''Police'' and thus scaring the living shit out of her as in the front room I see some lines of coke on a piece of paper and obviously she is going to be entertaining. I tell her I'll go easy on her as I am really surveilling across the street. I carefully part the curtains and opposite is a studio with a big window. Here I easily make out object standing there with his arms wrapped around a slight figure, of a woman, I assume . . . hope.''

''But you couldn't see who it was?''

''No, chief. They were in silhouette.''

''Balls,'' Darktower barked. ''Could it have been that Mrs. Dolly Percy?''

"I don't think so, Chief. But now, since I know the whereabouts of subject's love nest, tomorrow I can stake it out and get the name of the woman . . . I hope."

"Okay, good work, Sam," Darktower said. It always paid to pat the hireling on the back. "So now we know he's got a place and where it is. All we've got to find out is *who* it is—woman . . . or man. It'd be more convenient if he turned out to be a fag, Sam."

"Uh, uh, Chief, not the way he handled those two guys."

"Sam, let me tell you something—Tarzan of the Apes was a fag."

"Yeah, I get you, Chief. Very deeply . . . Tomorrow morning, I perform another stake-out."

"Keep up the good work."

"Thanks, Chief," Merchant said cheerfully. "I'll say good-bye now. Say hello to the missus for me."

"The missus?"

"Your beautiful lady," Merchant explained.

"That's not the missus, Sam. That lady is a friend of mine."

"Oh, yeah? Well, say hello to Miss . . . I seem to have forgot the introduction."

Darktower smiled to himself. Merchant was surely inquisitive, wasn't he? "You mean Miss Berger, Sam . . . Henrietta Berger, that's the name of my beautiful friend."

"Say hello to Miss Henrietta Berger for me."

Clara returned just as he was pronouncing her fictitious name. When Darktower hung up, she asked, "Who's Miss Henrietta Berger, Dickie?"

"*You*, ducks. That was our Sam. He's curious about your name, so I told him."

Clara shook her head. "Dickie, so secretive! There can be no doubt that you are a Scorpio!"

Darktower put his arm all the way around her waist. "Yes, ducks—secretive, and rotten." He pulled her against him. "Clara, we've got him!"

"*Whom* have we, Dickie?"

"Moss . . . and right by the nuts. Sam found his love nest and all's left is to identify the woman . . . or man."

"But, Dickie, you already know about the one woman. Isn't one enough?"

"No, I want the goods on him with five or six or a dozen. I don't want to pay him a red cent. I want him over a barrel, plucked clean."

"Oh, Dickie, so vengeful! Scorpios never forget . . . or forgive!"

Thirty

With a few exceptions due to death and indictment, everyone Katharine and Dolly knew would be in Port London for the Memorial Day weekend and, being the flamboyant person she was, Mrs. Percy had determined to celebrate all day Sunday with the first, and perhaps last, of her annual "horror parties." In simple terms, she would invite all the local monsters, to whom she owed party invitations, and all the creeps from New York, most particularly those she knew to be on mutually hostile terms.

There was to be sailing Sunday morning for the very hardy aboard Gibber Higgins' schooner *Seaworthy*, still for sale and leased at every opportunity to help Gibber pay his mooring fees. These hardies, and the weak, would next gather in a big tent to be erected in back of Doll House on the bluff falling into Long Island Sound for a riotous luncheon to span the afternoon, with tennis for anyone who wanted it, croquet, swimming in the pool, dancing and, still later, snacks, continuous drinks and intense merriment to culminate somehow in the coronation of a Memorial Day king and queen.

Dolly was not concerned that this was something of a contradiction in terms or, really, when the party began and ended, for she was in a restless, reckless state of mind. The very best of the local caterers had been signed up, *Pies 'n Stuff by Grandma Marnes*, nowhere near as elaborate, or expensive, as the same operation would have been in Westchester County or Connecticut or New Hope, Pennsylvania. Hot dogs, beans, hamburgers, potato salad, cole slaw, corn on the cob and lots and lots of beer, that was the Port London ticket . . . rather, menu.

In the formal sense, invitation-wise, as they said, the Dolly Percy party, Memorial Day bash or blow-out, was intended to honor those two well-known foreigners Stefan Ratoff and Marco Fortuna, European sophisticates soon to return to their native habitat of Marbella, St. Tropez, Costa Smeralda, you name it. It might also serve, the way things were looking, to mark the temporary departure from these shores of those two New York sophisticates, Dolly Percy and her best friend Katharine Moss.

As announced, the redoubtable Richard Darktower had been persuaded by Mrs. Percy to stay at Doll House over the weekend and Dolly hoped fervently he would have the courage to bring along his blonde girlfriend. Strangely, though, Katharine reported, Mrs. Himmelmann had it on good authority now that the buxom lady's real name was not Clara Riding, as introduced at *Le Cirque*, but Mme. Henrietta Berger. *So* devious was Richard Darktower, Mrs. Percy reminded herself. Margo Himmelmann and her husband, Herman, would also, mercifully, be in Port London for the big weekend as guests of Kitty and her about-to-be-ex-husband Erik Moss at their tacky estate Maples.

Of course, as always, inconvenience was endemic—with Darktower and friend at Doll House, Stefan and Marco had to be removed to safer ground. They happily chose to spend the weekend on the *Seaworthy*.

With a maliciousness worthy of the angry gods, Dolly congratulated herself that it would be quite a party—*horror party*, indeed. The locals would be properly shocked, as they deserved to be, all those gossipy biddies from the Heritage Assembly; and if all else failed, if all her plans came to naught, Dolly promised herself that she, personally, would make it a red-letter party in Port London annals. After all, hadn't she already slept with most of the men not bolted down? Not even mentioning the locals, she had had poor bird-brained Erik; Stefan, all those years ago when he'd been married to Katharine and despite the fact he was queer as a kumquat; and Marco, of course, she'd been screwing to a frazzle since the two lads had come back from California. Katharine had warned her: it was looking *serious*. With Marco, yes. But not Kitty with her coarse Italian. He had brushed her off again and then, of all the nerve, had had the bad manners to brush Dolly off too. No, *Gizmo* would not lease his boat to her and no, he would not be coming to her glorious, immemorial party.

On the Friday, before the mob began to arrive, the four ringleaders of the affair were, in the late morning, sitting in the airy, now shaded, sunroom to the rear of Doll House drinking transfusions of Bloody Marys.

Marco and Stefan were all in white—shirts, shorts, socks, shoes and Dolly had no doubt, with white peonies stuck up their pissers. Marco was tanned to proper Sicilian olive brown, showing not even a whiff of Texas red-neck. Stefan, ill, as they all were aware, and along with that nervous and irritable, thin, dyspeptic, looked nonetheless still so distinguished. He sat wearily in one of the cushioned white wicker chairs, Katharine kneeling behind him, the very picture of devotion, her forearms dangling on his shoulders. Stefan was *so* tired—but Katharine all of a sudden so kind, so compassionate, as if somebody had sent an orphan to her care. Dolly herself was dressed in a brief tennis costume, she and Katharine having summoned the force for a set of singles in the early morning cool. Having taken off her sweaty tennis shoes, Dolly sat, flexing her bare toes.

Altogether, they looked, the four of them, arranged as they were in summer tableau, like a scene out of the Great Gatsby, a camera glimpse of the Beautiful People, a long shot of the Jet Set living it up on one of their four continents. Dolly wondered briefly what would become of them all.

"Here's to my Horror Party!" Dolly lifted her glass.

"Hurrah!" Marco shouted as loud as he could. He was stretched out on the second wicker couch. Draining his glass, he heaved it through the open door, to shatter on the brick walk outside.

"Hey!" Dolly exclaimed, "that was Baccarat!"

"So?" Marco jeered. "Fuck Baccarat, *cara*. I will buy you a dozen new ones. Two dozen!"

"Bullshit! I don't like to see nice things broken, just for the fun of it."

Marco howled joyously. "You broke your cherry, sweetheart. That was fun, wasn't it?"

Dolly glared at him, not knowing whether to laugh or cry. Marco was funny sometimes; hilarious even, if you were in that kind of devil-may-care mood. But he was awful too.

"You know," Dolly mused, "I don't know whether I love you or hate you. You're such an Italian *asshole*."

Again, he spewed laughter. "Sicilian, sweetheart, not Italian."

"Jesus, Texas—Sicilian—what a combination. They ought to label you and preserve you in formaldehyde."

He totally ignored her. To Katharine and Stefan, he chortled, "She was *wonderful* last night. It is like her whole being becomes her pussy. Shattering. Marco is in love again!"

"Pig!"

"*Cara*," he persisted, and she wanted to throw something at him, her Baccarat glass for instance. "I want the world to know it—your ass is mounted on ball-bearings."

Stefan's face was bored. "Together again," he languished. "Marco—*basta*, all right?"

Sullenly, Marco closed his mouth. The fact was that Stefan seemed to be the only person alive who had any kind of control over him. The two of them used each other well, Dolly thought. Stefan kept Marco from killing himself with excess and Marco, from what they could gather, provided Stefan with an existence. Marco had more money than he knew what to do with, thanks to a distant and fortuitously discovered relative of his mother's who had had the wit to tumble onto a cache of offshore oil in Nigeria.

Speaking softly, ironically, Stefan muttered, "Marco, my dear, you can be extremely rude, you know?"

"Yes," Marco giggled, "but *Marco* owns a private airplane."

"And boisterous. . . ."

"Yes, Marco drinks too much . . . but he's thinking about buying a house in Acapulco."

"Marco is not very handsome," Stefan observed coldly. "He is overweight, pendulous, and often breathless."

"But Marco's Swiss bank account atones for much." Marco chuckled moistly.

Dolly laughed raucously. "Marco sounds perfect for Dolly."

"Oh, God," Stefan groaned exaggeratedly, "it is too much. I have seen Marco through two marriages now, the last to a Serbian-born woman with breasts as big as hammocks. I will not survive the next."

"Quiet!" Marco screamed. "No morbid talk."

Dolly scowled. "You've been married before? Why didn't you tell me? I don't like worn-out merchandise."

"I am *not* worn out," Marco pouted, his smooth brown cheeks puffing. "Women love me and I love them back."

Testily, Dolly said, "You're not so great, *meat*-balls."

Marco gasped ecstatically. "*Sweet-slit*—you make fun of Marco."

In reply, Dolly reached for the ship's bell she used to rouse Mrs. Donovan out of the kitchen. It clanged, the sound ringing and echoing and ringing again against the bare walls, the dense afternoon.

"Cut the clapper!" Marco screeched, pressing his hands over his ears. "You will turn us deaf, you little snot!"

The sound had been enough to bring Mrs. Donovan. "Yes?" In Mrs. Donovan's voice was all the disapproval of old Long Island. But Dolly couldn't feel bad about her sensitivities. Mrs. D could always quit if she didn't like what went on upstairs. No, the recession-proof money was too good.

"Darling," Dolly said to her in high hauteur, "could you see your way clear to bringing us another pitcher of Bloody Marys . . . and what about a big platter of sandwiches?"

When Mrs. Donovan had ambled away, Marco hissed, "That woman is an old hag, sweet-slit. Why do you keep her around?"

"Shut up, Marco . . . because I need *somebody*."

He giggled again. "Sweetheart, I would willingly be your chief cook and pussy-washer."

Stefan groaned once more. "*Basta! Dio!* Idiot! You will truly be the death of me, fat little man!"

"Yes," Dolly sniffed, "Enough is enough!"

Marco chortled himself toward another huffing explosion. "Sweet-slit, *enough* is only a finger of speech."

Having finished the Bloody Marys and the sandwiches, it seemed, very briefly, like a good idea to take a short walk toward the water. Woozily, dizzy from the battering of the overhead sun, the four got only as far as the place in the lawn where Dolly was going to have the tent pitched. Defeated, they stumbled back toward the looming house. From here, it was incongruous in its seaside location— Harrison Percy had meant it to be an impressive pile, a monument to summer-time, good times. He'd been in love with Dolly in those days and as stable as the securities he handled. Then Harrison had been out of luck, *out of love* . . . and he'd blown his brains out, splattered them across this very lawn, so the story went. Perhaps that was why it possessed the deep shade of greenbacks.

Inside again, in the wicker seats, Dolly was fading. "What do you want to do now, gang? Another drink?"

Stefan answered for them. "No. It's time for a nap."

"Yes, let's," Dolly said. "Upstairs, everybody!"

Marco cried out—brilliantly, he thought, "We have so much fun together, let's have our nap together."

Dolly didn't know what to say, nor did Katharine. Again, Stefan had the answer. "As long as there is a pillow for my head. . . ."

"Me too," Katharine yawned elaborately. "Bloody Marys will do it every time."

The four, hand-in-hand, were up the steps and into Dolly's blue-and-white Delft rooms before she realized what had happened. What! All sleep in her bed! What a rare idea, but not what she'd had in mind. Marco, the lout, bounced up and down, then tossed off his white shoes and stretched out, closing his eyes. Thinking what the hell did it matter, Dolly slid in beside him; next to her in the middle of the bed, Kitty, so unconcerned Dolly was startled, settled placidly and Stefan sighed and said, "Good night, all."

"Nighty-night," Marco rumbled, a sly and stupid smile on his face. Turning, idly, as if sneaking up on her, Marco dropped his hand across her breast, inserting one finger shamelessly in the bra-top of Dolly's tennis dress.

She didn't care. Why should she? Why should any of them care? They'd all been *there* and back. They might think they had secrets from each other, but they didn't. They were *all* ruined, equally, no more and no less the one than the other.

Kitty's face was quiet, the long eyelashed recumbent on her cheeks. She breathed evenly, but Dolly knew she was not asleep; she was waiting to see what would happen. Very well, she could play the game.

Quietly, Dolly dropped her hand on the hump in Marco's shorts. His body leapt and he moaned deeply. Dolly made up her mind then and there. Cautiously, she pulled her panties down off her behind and turned so it butted his erection. Marco giggled, so loudly no one could be asleep now, except perhaps for Stefan, and the next riveting sound was that of a scratching zipper. He had it out of his shorts and up against her, between her thighs and instantly, it seemed, slipping into her and Christ! from this angle he was without end. Dolly's mouth gaped from the dull, blunt-object force and saliva dribbled down her chin; she inhaled so sharply that Kitty was bound to know.

Dolly pulsed with the act and Kitty shifted beside her. Forcing her eyes open, for doing so pained her mightily, Dolly saw Kitty's head was turned; she was staring, wide-eyed, astonished. In a second, she smiled deeply, wistfully, perhaps sadly, and the next instant, Dolly realized Kitty was fondling her breasts. Yes! No, it could not be and, yes, she remembered it happening so long ago during the night. But she couldn't give a *damn*! Let it happen, let it go on, she the love-machine. Dolly gushed warmly when she felt Kitty's slim hand on her belly, Kitty's long fingers groping between her thighs, searching for the place where his ram entered, departed, entered, and placing two fingers there like a buttonhole, pressing and caressing. God, Dolly whimpered, the two of them were raping her and she couldn't budge because she loved it so. Nothing, but nothing like this, had ever happened to her.

Marco began to strain, to grunt, to whine, stimulated by Kitty's fingers and with a movement like collision, he climaxed. The difference was the stuff shot past Kitty's fingers into *her*.

Dolly thought that surely she would pass out from a heat stroke, so intense was her own cresting. She let go in an uninhibited scream, like murder committed, not caring a damn, not a good goddamn. Wake the angels, and the devils! Tears rushed out of her eyes and she sobbed at them. "You got me every which way but up, you sons-of-bitches."

"We do that next, sweet buns," Marco exclaimed.

Don't tell me Stefan hasn't heard all this, Dolly screamed at herself, the phony, the orgy-master. Kitty's body was shaking, her hand stroking Dolly's cheek.

"*You*! I never knew you were queer!"

"I'm not, darling. I just enjoyed it for you."

"Hah!" Dolly retreated. She pushed Marco away and flipped over on her back. "That's the last of this nonsense, I can tell you. If it's going to be this way, I'm definitely not going to Europe."

She could almost see Kitty's mouth curl. "All of a sudden so righteous."

Angrily, Dolly cried, "I don't believe all this bullshit about share and share-alike."

"Except when it's somebody else's husband. . . ." Kitty's voice was so distant she might have left the bedroom. Dolly was prepared to launch a tirade when she realized Kitty had started to cry.

Stefan's weary pronouncement only made it worse. "Children, children—enough!"

"God!" Katharine exclaimed brokenly. "It's so sad. Why is it so sad, Stefan?"

"Is it?" Of course it was, he was saying, but the point was that it didn't matter much either way, whether they

were sad or happy. The end was in sight. His, anyway,
Dolly understood.

"Stefan," Katharine demanded, again with a shattering
plea, "why hasn't it turned out better?"

"Because. . . ." What he's saying *right now*, that's the
truth, Dolly told herself.

"But it's so . . . goddamn . . . sad."

Stefan's laugh was dry, like something blowing in the
wind. "No, it's only the reality of life, darling."

Thirty-One

It was such a beautiful day. It *might* have been a marvelous day, Erik decided, had he been driving anywhere but to Port London. Even with that, it was a wonderful day—how could it be otherwise when his daughter was sitting beside him in the front seat of the Mercedes? Conrad had insisted he would ride in the back even though his long legs would be twisted in the jumpseat. But no, the prince would not sit beside Erik, this man he *resented*, not realizing, Erik told himself, that there was good reason, if he'd known it, to exchange resentment for hate.

So it was. People invariably resented or hated each other for the wrong reasons.

Glancing into the rear-view mirror, Erik saw Conrad was hunched up uncomfortably, his raw, gangly wrists and arms hanging off his knees. Eyes half-closed, a moody frown distorting his sensitive lips. Yes, Conrad might be feeling as depressed as Erik for leaving Lilly by herself in the city.

Flatly, Erik changed the object of their thoughts. "What are your plans for the summer, Conny?"

The boy's expression lightened just a little. "I was thinking of going to Europe."

"A good plan! You'll enjoy that," Erik said enthusiastically. Naturally, a *wonderful* plan to get him away from Lilly. But it was not a plan Richard Darktower would approve of. The prince intended to pay a visit to those two wastrels in Geneva. But he would not dream of saying so.

Conrad's eyes switched toward little Margaret. "What's the brat doing this summer?"

Erik hesitated angrily. "It is not decided. There may be . . . complications."

"Complications? Isn't she going to the old man?"

Erik shook his head in the mirror. It would not do to talk about Richard Darktower in front of Margaret who tended to repeat everything she heard. She was looking at him, the eyes so blue, so innocent, so trusting and, for the millionth time, Erik's chest seem to flood, threatening to choke him. But why shouldn't his daughter trust him, think well of *him*?

"Why couldn't I go with Conrad if I wanted?" Margaret asked.

Erik chuckled so lovingly that even Conrad's face softened. "Europe is no place for small girls. .. ."

Conrad *had* to disagree. "She could come with me. I'd just beat her up when she didn't obey."

"What?" Erik tried to sound light-hearted. "Beat up Margaret? You brute!"

"Brute! I'm going to Grandfather Richard."

"It's just," Erik muttered, "your Grandfather Darktower might be making a trip of his own. He may not be here the whole summer."

"I'll be with Helen," Margaret said. "Or Mrs. Himmelmann. . . ." She knew instantly this was a faux-pas. "No, Mrs. Himmelmann wouldn't go to Wainscott, would she?"

"I don't think so, my darling."

"And what about my mother . . . Mrs. Kathy Moss. . . ." She joked coyly.

Erik groaned to himself. Conrad watched somberly. "Of course, she'll be there."

"And you. . . ."

"Oh, yes." No point in defining everything—agree for the sake of peace of mind. If Kathy was going off to Europe with Dolly, did Conrad know about it? Weren't the fools all traveling together? Damnation, everything had to be so complicated, too much for a middle-aged man. Perhaps he should break with Lilly and make a gigantic new effort with Kathy to reconstruct their marriage for the sake of the child . . . and peace of mind. Or was it too late?

Dolly had said it was too late.

Erik had determined that the weekend would be the perfect time for a showdown with Richard Darktower. First, he would have a final word with Kathy; second . . . Darktower. Yes, he would make his monumental effort—it was the least he could do.

If reconciliation was possible, *if* . . . then, yes, he would say farewell to Lilly. He could scarcely bear the thought of a parting but . . . the complexities were enormous, the stakes too high.

His fabled nest-egg, the million he was supposed to have made before ever meeting Katharine Darktower Ratoff, that money which was supposed to establish his credentials as a most honorable man. . . . "Good Lord, no, Erik had made his first million by the time he was twenty-five. . . ." Or twenty-one, why not twelve? During those days when he'd black-marketeered American cigarettes in what was left of the vaunted *Dritte Reich,* when all about him lay in ruins, all gone, and he wasted, tormented, living on like the rodents and maggots would after the final *nuclear* solution. Damnation. Goddamn it! Again, Erik forced himself into the present. No, his *treasure,* such as it was, had been knocked full of holes by declining markets, recession, fear, profit-taking, inflation, all those ills capitalism was supposed to be proof against. Plain and simply, it was a matter of money and unless Richard Darktower came forward cooperatively, magnanimously, generously, with enough for Erik to start afresh, then there was no way he could leave, with darling Lilly or without darling Lilly.

"*Verdamnt*! Goddamn." Erik Moss was in a box and the box was narrow and short, as tight as a punishment-cell, with no room for maneuver, much less a way of escape.

"And Daddy. . . ." Margaret could force his dark mood aside with a word. "And, Daddy, when we're in Wainscott, I'm going to have my puppy."

Erik could easily have shrieked. But he held himself in control, always aware of Conrad's eyes on the back of his head and watching his expression in the mirror. "Yes, of course."

"You had a puppy when you were a little boy, didn't you?"

Numbed, he shook his head. "No. Not in the war. They ate too much."

Margaret's eyes rounded with incredulity. A child in America, in America at peace, even though economically depressed, such a child could have no comprehension of what it had been like *then*.

He tried to explain. "You could perhaps have had a puppy in the war if you'd share your food with it."

"I would," she said solemnly.

He wanted to shout at her to get off it. But he smiled patiently. "Of course you would. You're a very kind little girl."

Erik stared grimly at the traffic which was beginning to thicken. Lucky they had left right after lunch. Glancing at the speedometer, he realized he had been driving too fast and slowed back to the fifty-five-mile limit. He looked at Conrad in the mirror.

"This car gets away from you."

"It runs very well," Conrad muttered.

In a few minutes, Margaret was curled in sleep. Conrad leaned forward, folding his arms on the back of her seat.

"You love her, don't you, Erik?"

"Of course!"

"That's good. It's good she's loved."

"Well, I said, *of course*!"

Conrad shrugged, his chin resting on his hands. "Sometimes I get the feeling Kate takes her for granted!"

"Don't be ridiculous. Of course she cares, very much." The prince—how dare he say such a thing?

Conrad shook his head. "I think she cares a lot but maybe doesn't show it—Kate."

"No! You are very wrong, Conny. Kathy is a good mother." He spoke softly.

"Just an opinion," Conrad said stubbornly.

"I know *you* care about her," Erik said, motioning at Margaret.

"And I'm a friend of yours, if you would accept it," he added.

Conrad smiled, nodding, acknowledging, possibly, that he had no reason, either, to think badly of Erik. He *had*, Erik told himself regretfully, but he didn't know it. Such was life.

"I heard Margo saying Richard Darktower has got a girlfriend," Conrad whispered.

Erik nodded. "Yes. May I say—what business is it of hers? She divorced him. Does she expect him to live like a monk, saying prayers to Mrs. Himmelmann every day?"

Conrad laughed appreciatively. "That's what *I* told her!" His light tone, however, quickly changed to dark. "You and my . . . Kate? You're breaking up, aren't you?"

Erik kept his face reserved. "I do not know. It has been very difficult, as you know."

"I don't understand why, that's all."

Erik emitted a tortured sigh. He wished this little trip of theirs would soon end. "Aren't you old enough to understand these things? You are a man of the world, Conny."

"I'm not doing so well myself," Conrad sighed.

Ah! Now, he would find out more about the true state of Conrad's relationship with Lilly. "I notice," Erik said cautiously. "You are a bit depressed?"

"I am. I feel like shit!"

"Please. . . ." At that precise moment, he truly wished— almost—that nothing had happened between himself and Lilly. The poor boy—how could he know his sister's husband had stolen his girlfriend? Worse, how could Erik ever explain *why* he had done so, if it came to an explanation?

"Well? What *about* you and Kate?"

Erik scowled. "It is true we are in crisis, I cannot say why. I did fear your sister had fallen in love with someone else. . . ."

"Oh." Conrad's face registered sudden interest. "Somebody else?"

"Yes, but that does not seem to be the case." He eyed Conrad crossly. "I will tell you, perhaps as a man you will understand what I am saying . . . Kate seems to have lost interest in me . . . physically." He paused to let the words make their mark. "She has told me . . . it is of no interest to her where I . . . however . . . so long as I am discreet about it."

"Christ!" Conrad's smooth face tightened. "Image *is* everything, isn't it? Isn't *that* what happened to Ratoff? The old man kicked him out of the country. Discreet! Shit!"

"Please. . . ." But there was no reason he should defend Richard Darktower who would treat Erik Moss as harshly as he had Stefan Ratoff when the time came. "Essentially, yes, that is what happened, Conrad."

"I could learn to hate the old man. . . ."

"Hate is a very debilitating emotion."

"My father is a bastard, and you know it," Conrad said bitterly. "How much money did *he* steal when he was in business?"

"None that I ever heard of," Erik said quietly. "If there had been anything illegal he would have been sent to jail, like Dolly Percy's husband was supposed to be. . . ."

"Before he killed himself, *very discreetly*."

Erik gripped the steering wheel, glaring at a car which dared to pass him on the right. "You should not dwell on these things," he said slowly.

"My father is really what they call a rotten capitalist."

Erik chuckled calmly. Here it came: the ideological diatribe Lilly had warned him about. Mildly, he observed, "Capitalism has been good to you, my friend, and to me—so far. It's the only economic system that seems to work. As bad as it is sometimes, as unjust, it's proven to be the only efficient way for people to handle their affairs. . . ."

"All based on greed!" Conrad grunted.

Erik allowed himself a good laugh. "Who told you that? Haven't you ever heard of original sin? I'm almost afraid to say this but, the fact is, man is by nature a greedy, even rapacious creature. He yearns to own things and he will fight anyone to the death who tries to take away *his* house, *his* land, *his* treasure."

"You're cynical, Erik."

"No. If anything, *religious*. Man is a sinner. He is born that way. Baptism is supposed to wash away that original sin of greediness. Unfortunately, we have yet to hear of the man who is permanently Christlike after his baptism."

"Other people say man is meant to be beautiful. Not that I care much either way," Conrad murmured.

"You should!"

"Why? We're not going to change human nature. . . ."

How was Erik to broach the subject of the two bad-smelling young men who had been following him that day?

"Maybe with a little force," Erik said blithely. "Just the other day two unreformed human creatures followed me in the street and I was forced to confront them. They were more frightened than I was . . . I have a certain training in my background. . . ." He smiled thinly. "One merely fainted. The other I treated to what our diplomats call appropriate retaliation, retaliation tailored to the provocation."

"What did they want?" Conrad asked timidly. "Did you hurt them?"

"Not seriously. But I hope they will leave me alone now."

"I hope so too."

After a stop for gas and coffee, the approach to Port London was leisurely, less hard on his nerves. First, they saw the sea, the glinting, metallic sheen of it, and then the sharp spire of Old Church which pinpointed the center of Port London.

"I'll drive you past the house I'm in charge of restoring," Erik said. "You'll see it now—*before*; and in a few years—*after*."

Yes, indeed, provided he was still around to complete the job, provided *he* hadn't been discreetly run out of the country. Along Henley Street, Erik turned left into a narrow, winding side street which had once been a main thoroughfare leading to the harbor in old Port London. The Smithers House was in mid-block.

"There." Erik pointed, slowed down, stopped. "It's in shocking deterioration."

What paint remained on the clapboard sides of the house was peeling in great long shreds, like dead skin, and the front stoop was cocked at a dangerous angle, its portico braced from the side by a long two-by-four.

"It's named for its original owner, the man who had it built. Captain Smithers. He was an old sea captain."

Cruelly, Conrad said, "Looks like you should just tear it down."

"Oh, no," Erik exclaimed. "And put *what* up? A take-home chicken place? No, you should see the inside. It is beautiful. The wood is lovely. I know what you've always said, that I'm more interested in old things than I am in the present. Yes, maybe, but you can depend on history. It's already happened."

Margaret stopped him in his tracks. "I'm hungry," she said.

Mrs. Rogers seemed to have been poised by the front door, waiting for them. When the car drew up, she darted outside and, before Erik had ever turned off the motor, had little Margaret out and halfway up the steps. "Dearie, how are you? You look beautiful today. You just come along with me, Margaret!"

Erik laughed wryly. "I guess that leaves us to unpack the car."

He heard Katharine's voice as he bent to open the trunk, then saw her in the open door.

"Hello, little brother."

"Hi." He put down the two suitcases Erik had given him to carry and hugged her. "Hello, sister Kate."

"Good afternoon, Kathy," Erik said.

Her smile deepened. "I just this moment got back from Dolly's . . . good afternoon, *Herr Moss.* . . ."

Erik frowned. She knew he disliked this. He straightened, one hand on the open trunk of the Mercedes. "*Jawohl!*" he barked. "*Zum befehl* . . . at your service. . . ."

Conrad tried to help by laughing but his sister turned on him angrily. "What's so funny? I suppose *you two* have been making jokes about me all the way from New York."

"No, we haven't, Kate, not at all."

"I'm going inside," she said icily. "I'll be in the library."

She marched past Conrad, her heels clicking on the marble floor of the entry.

Conrad was irritated. "I'll take the bags up . . . then I'm going to have a drink."

"Easy does it," Erik cautioned him, trying to conceal his anxiety.

"I don't know how you put up with the bitch," Conrad said, shaking his head. But Erik knew he couldn't be serious.

"Have no fear." Erik gathered a couple of coats over his arm. "If you're serious about a drink, wait till after I talk to Kathy, and I'll have one with you. . . ."

"You'll need it."

She had shut the library door. Opening it, Erik found her sitting in a slip-covered easy chair by the long side window.

"Well, darling. . . ."

"I'm fed up with this place," Katharine announced bitterly.

"Oh? Please, my darling. . . ." What did she expect him to say? Once, he had been in total control but this was no longer so. Katharine stared at him dispassionately, with the same indifference Conrad was so good at when he was in *that* mood, not as he had been, thankfully, in the car, as if nothing mattered in the worst of all possible worlds.

"Well," she said bitingly, "you're here. I can't think why . . . I thought we'd established our *modus operandi.* . . ."

"Which is?" he demanded sharply. "That we share a house and do not speak? That we live together and do not see each other? Is that some sort of life to lead?"

"It suits me," she said. "If you don't like it, divorce me."

He stared at her pleasantly. "On what *grounds*?"

"Anything you like . . . mental cruelty . . . adultery. . . ."

"Adultery?" He smiled faintly. "My dear, is such a thing possible?"

Kathy shrugged. "Does it matter? *Say* it happened—I won't deny it."

His legs were leaden, fastened to the floor. All his good intentions . . . and now this? "You tell me this to drive me insane with jealousy. I realize that. But I am not a jealous person. *You* are a crude person, on the other hand."

She loosed a scorching laugh, then lifted one hand to put her fingers delicately under her fine chin. "Whatever I learned about crudeness, I learned from you . . . how can you forget *that*?"

"Forget what?" he responded with puzzlement.

"My God! That day . . . with Helen? I cut your back— you've forgotten?

He shook his head. "No. I still have a red welt. I have not forgiven you that."

"Forgiven *me*? And should I forgive *you*?" Her face turned white with disbelief, her veneer of haughtiness gone.

"Of course, you should forgive me," he stated. "I behaved like a madman and I regret it. I have already apologized, have I not? You were at fault—you drove me that day to a fury of despair. I was not myself."

Katharine looked away, absently stroking her forearms under a cashmere sweater. "I haven't been myself either lately," she said hazily. "I've been thinking of making love to Marco Fortuna, Dolly's new friend. Out of your bed and straight into his . . . my word!"

Loudly, so loudly she glanced at him in alarm, he groaned. "Darling, I want our marriage to survive for the sake of the child!"

"Child!" Her eyes said this was the most outlandish thing she'd ever heard. "Margaret has nothing to do with this."

"Today," he said softly, "I was very close to her. And to your dear brother."

"Hah!" Katharine snorted contemptuously. "Don't fool yourself. Conrad hates your guts because you followed Stefan into my embrace." Lividly, she plunged in the knife. "Because your prick replaced Stefan's, inside his sister. Yes!"

Erik wavered before her withering sneer.

"A woman possessed," he stammered. "I expect the devil to come, smoldering, through the window."

"No," she said, waving him away, "you're here already. No shocking you, Mr. Devil Moss . . . I'm saying that Marco stuffs Dolly grandly and he wants to do the same with me. Should I?" she demanded. "Yes? No? Why not?"

"And you're going with *these* people to Europe?"

"Maybe," Katharine said airily. "But Dolly's afraid I'll steal Marco away from her. She's a fine one to talk, isn't she? After *fucking* you every time she got the chance?"

"Oh, darling." Again he groaned.

"Darling . . . nothing! It's all true and Dolly is ready to swear to it!"

"Insane," Erik sputtered. "I recommend you see a psychiatrist. Again you have departed reality for your dream world."

"Dream world? Are you crazy? Dolly is ready to *swear* on a stack of Bibles that you screwed her—what kind of a dream world is that? Maybe," Katharine suggested ironically, "you'd like to shove a handful of pills into me. . . ."

"I think you could use a sedative," Erik murmured angrily.

"Like hell!" she cried fiercely. "I know *all* about you, everything there is to know. Was it only Dolly? Or others too? Tell me!"

Violently, Erik shook his head. "With no one, darling! I deny it all!"

She fixed him with a sickly grin and he realized with some pleasure that her hands were trembling. She didn't have it all her own way.

"We know!"

"You know *what*?" he asked scornfully.

"We know about the girl too."

"What girl, for heaven's sakes?" There was no way, he thought, that they could know anything.

"What's her name—in that apartment," Katharine exclaimed, tearful in her anger. "Yes, I know—Lilly

Royce. Lilly Royce. She comes from Chicago. We know everything!"

Erik absorbed the shock wave of her knowledge. He was stunned—now, soon, he thought, she must deliver him the *coup de grace*.

"Brazen it out, *darling*," Katharine exclaimed. "Yes, do please deny it!"

"I will not since, obviously, your sainted father had me followed."

Her lips quivered. She was the spoiled child, defied in her fondest wishes. "You bastard . . . she's so young. I suppose she worships you."

"Yes," he declared, "she does. Because she is a normal girl . . . I invite you to remember that you advised me to seek *solace* wherever I could find it. This I have done."

Katharine nodded, almost philosophically. "I have no feeling about it."

He shrugged. "You have had no feeling for some time."

"Divorce me then!"

"Perhaps I will. We will divide our fortune and say good-bye."

She shook her head. "No, we divide nothing. The house here, the apartment in New York, they belong to me. Everything was bought with my money. My father is determined."

A clammy hand gripped his throat, fear. "He had me followed to entrap me, to rob me of what is rightfully mine, despite all my suffering in your behalf."

"Suffering? Don't make me laugh."

"Mental anguish," he insisted bitterly. "Worry . . . anxiety. Goddamn it, all this is worth something," he stormed, whacking his fist in his palm. "Not a large fortune perhaps, but certainly a small one."

"You'll get nothing," she said coldly. "My father has made up his mind."

"Really?" Desperately, he tried to bring her down with mockery. "Your father? He doesn't understand the lengths to which I am prepared to go."

"He understands very well. He's planned it through."

"You," he announced, "will not have custody of Margaret."

"I will! How could they grant custody to a known philanderer?"

Erik smiled contemptuously. "Better to a philanderer than a neurotic woman who drinks too much, takes drugs and maintains a sick relationship with a homosexual ex-husband. Disgusting!" His voice was taut, like a whip, and, clearly, she suffered under it. "The sordid demands you made on me . . . I will speak of everything, my darling," he snarled. "No insects will be left under the stones. It will be as you have decided—dirty . . . filthy. And why? Simply," he said coolly, "because you have decided we can no longer live together, that I am a bore."

Slowly, she nodded. "Yes, it's as they say . . . you *are* awful."

"As *who* says?"

She averted her face. "Everybody. It doesn't matter. You would do that, wouldn't you? You have no regard for your own reputation, not to speak of mine."

He hit her again with a laugh like a slap. "My reputation will be unsullied. It is yours, that of the neurotic, which will be soiled beyond redemption . . . Even Ratoff, the decayed voluptuary, will reel out of your presence."

She was self-possessed enough—so much so that he feared again for his case. "Oh, I don't think it'll be that bad."

Ah, he remembered the other. "And our friend, Mr. Francotti, will run away, to the end of the Earth. . ."

This warning did cause her to start, her lips to tremble. "He wouldn't believe any of it!"

"Oh, no? My darling, let me advise you—juries, judges, the man in the street, the newspapers, are still inclined to believe in the basic *evil* of Woman and the basic *weakness* of poor Man. Yes, *woman*, the Devil's own receptacle. . . ."

Katharine's stern eyes failed her. She blinked rapidly, put her face in her hands. "God, you are awful . . . I hate you now. I'd almost rather be dead than see you again . . . please leave the room."

"No! Look at me."

She shook her head, refusing. "If I did die, then you'd have no worries. You're provided for in the nuptial agreements. . . ."

"Yes, what of it?" he said loftily.

"Why don't you just kill me?" she demanded wildly. "It's all the same, if he hears the filth . . . he already despises me."

Victory clutched from the jaws of defeat. Kathy sees the light! Darktower would see the same glow of truth, reality, *fait-accompli*. Either . . . or.

Carelessly, he said, "There is no reason for me to kill you—you will accomplish that by yourself, my darling. Even Conrad thinks you are cold and loveless. . . ."

"Conrad?" She looked at him anxiously. "That's a lie! He doesn't think that."

"He does. He said so in the car. I tried to disabuse him of it—I did lie! I told him his sister is capable of love. Obviously," he said softly, "I *lied*.!"

"You *will* kill me," she gasped.

"Whatever," he drawled casually. "In any case, I will not bring a divorce action. We will stay married as the best of several terrible options. I will *wait you out*."

"It's too ugly!" Her eyes were bloodshot from tears cried and uncried. Words tumbled out. "We'll go on then as before . . . I'll hate you more than anything. I'll live without love . . . sooner or later one of us will sicken and die. . . ."

Erik grimaced with amusement. "Possibly . . . that will be our bond then, not a bad one really. Perhaps, eventually, it will bring us together, this one thing we have in common: mutually we wait for sweet death, this thing so many people yearn for. . . ."

Her voice shook. "I see evil when you talk like that."

"Evil?" he retorted. "What do *you* know about evil, my darling? How many corpses have you seen, stacked and burning, the stench, the rape, the death, even the violations of death through the years of the plague . . . ?"

He stared at her, seeing past her, feeling his face flush. His hands began to quiver so much he had to put them behind his back and clasp them tightly.

"Christ. . . ." Kathy crept toward the far corner of the room. She was weeping. "You're evil. . . ."

"No, no," he protested. "You read too much into it—perhaps," he admitted, "I have a certain affinity to evil. I understand evil at first hand, so I believe. But whether I myself am evil is open to debate," he continued, saying more than he should, blundering proudly along. Yes, they whom the gods would destroy are first issued the sin of pride; out of that led madness. "I do have a close association with past evil. My darling," he said soothingly, extending a hand toward her, beseechingly. "we're neither of us bargains. But we're not bad people either. . . ."

"No, no!" Kathy stood with her back to the window, at the advantage, the light streaming into *his* eyes. "I know better than that."

"We've merely lost our innocence," he argued.

"Innocence?" She laughed incredulously. Her eyes came around with the light, directly on his. "There's nothing more to say. You are really the devil, all smoking and stinking. . . ."

Erik stepped back, chuckling modestly. "I? The devil? Don't be silly, my darling—you give me too much credit."

Thirty-Two

Conveniently for Erik Moss, during the last week he had brought to the Himmelmann company several long-range financial planning prospects potentially worth several hundreds of thousands of dollars in commissions to himself and the H.H. organization.

Thus, with the arrival of Herman and Margo in Port London, more particularly Maples, Erik could with some justification play the accomplished and successful host, at one with Herman's bullish Wall Street spirit, while Katharine, anxious and silent, took her mother upstairs.

Herman closed the library door while Erik made them Scotches.

"Good job with the Bertrands, Erik." Herman praised him guardedly.

"Thank you. But it fell in my lap."

"Exactly. We like things just falling into our laps. Helpful to the soft-sell image," Himmelmann said.

His heavy cheeks creased with his usual smile; the latter never varied, whatever the stimulus. Himmelmann was not an especially pretty person. One saw in his eyes the glazed evidence of good living, of the good years, a hundred thousand luncheons and cocktails, all in the service of the American Way.

There was, however, something besides the Bertrands on his mind. "What's this about you and Katharine . . . ?"

Erik lifted an eyebrow. "What have *you* heard?" A better question—where had Herman been?

''Margo says you're splitting up,'' Himmelman grunted. ''I hope not.''

What he was thinking was obvious—anything which served to separate Erik Moss from Darktower social status, money status, was not good for H.H. Inc.

Erik smiled pensively. ''Not on my initiative, I can tell you, Herman. I couldn't afford it . . . unfortunately,'' he said, ''I can't answer for Kathy.''

''Christ,'' Himmelmann complained, ''these two women are something else. I can't make head nor tail of Margo or her daughter.'' Disgustedly, he tasted his Scotch, as if it were an unfamiliar drink.

Erik nodded. ''Headstrong, would you say?''

''Headstrong? Bah! More than that—flighty, unpredictable, fickle and sometimes even cruel. Just when you think she's settled down and fairly satisfied with life, she's off on some tangent.''

''A tangent, yes,'' Erik said, ''aptly put. . . .''

Himmelmann was encouraged to continue. ''I can remember how Dick Darktower got thrown for a loop. He was right—Margo is goddamn uncontrollable, Erik.'' He stared at his drink, shaking his head. ''I'm almost sure she's got a boyfriend.''

Erik wanted to laugh, to rave, to yell. God! Is *that* all? If only it were so simple with his wife. ''A boyfriend,'' he repeated.

''Yes! At her age! Margo is almost sixty, you know.''

''She doesn't look it,'' Erik muttered idiotically.

''That's the goddamn trouble,'' Himmelman exclaimed. ''It's not that I mind *very* much—but I don't like to waste time worrying about things that don't bear on the business . . . You understand.''

Erik nodded soberly. ''You startle and dismay me. . . .''

''Well, it shouldn't startle and dismay you,'' Himmelman snapped. ''Margo has always played around.'' He smiled somewhat guiltily. ''I guess maybe I don't have any right to complain—that's how I met her . . . playing around.'' He paused, shrugged mightily, laughing. ''Hell, maybe we should divorce the two of them, and you and me take off on a cruise somewhere . . . get drunk and screw native girls. . . ." His eyes twinkled weakly, then dimmed. No, screwing native girls wasn't in Herman Himmelmann's line.

Solemnly, Erik clicked his glass against Himmelmann's. "Here's to us, Herman . . . may we prevail."

"Don't worry about *that*. I certainly intend to prevail." He glanced curiously at Erik. "You say you couldn't afford to split up? I thought you were well-heeled in your own right."

"Yes," Erik said swiftly, "but the market hasn't been very kind to me recently. Also," he admitted ruefully, "living in the Darktower style is expensive, Herman."

Himmelmann nodded sympathetically. "That's right . . . you can't live off her, can you?"

"Exactly. That's the reason I came to *you*."

His step-father-in-law was very touched. "We'll do well for each other, Erik." Himmelmann nodded thoughtfully. "I hope everything is going to be okay but . . . remember one thing: A man doesn't necessarily have to be married to one of Dick Darktower's breed to make a go of it."

Erik agreed bemusedly, taking the invitation to throw out a few more cards. Chuckling softly, he said, "If it did happen you know Dick wouldn't make it easy for me." He paused. "Kathy has convinced him whatever's wrong is all my fault."

"*What's* your fault?"

"Well. . . ." He hesitated. He wasn't merely simulating—it did pain him to discuss the relationship with a man who had never been more than a comparative stranger. "Over the last couple of months, things have gotten very strained . . . estranged. I've been unhappy about that . . . *frustrated*."

"You mean you're not getting any?"

"Darktower has had me followed!" Erik blurted.

"The bastard! I wouldn't put it past him."

"Herman, I haven't been totally discreet. I may as well tell you," he confessed.

Himmelmann set down his Scotch and folded his hands in elderly pose behind his back. He paced away from Erik, then back, glowering. "I'm not surprised," he stated.

"I've often felt like busting loose myself . . . what *mischief* have you gotten up to?"

Erik shrugged, as if it were the most common thing in the world. "I've had a . . . friend for a while. Nothing serious. As you know," he purred, speaking one to one with this man-of-the-world, "it's not difficult to arrange. The trouble is, Darktower seems to have found me out. . . ."

Himmelmann scowled. "Of course! Isn't Dick a fine one to get so goddamn pious all of a sudden? From what Margo tells me, he's is all over town with a blonde . . . I don't understand where Margo gets off making so much noise about that either—Dick's not her property anymore." He shook his head, diverted from the subject of Richard Darktower by mention of Margo. "I can tell you, she is no piece of cake, Erik. And Kathy's not either. What the hell are you going to do?" he asked earnestly.

"If they come after me, they're going to have to make it worth my while. That's it!"

Himmelmann's eyes gleamed. "Well said! Don't give that blasted Dick an inch. I remember how he raked me over the coals when Margo left him. He behaved like a real son-of-a-bitch, Erik."

Erik tutted. "I'll be looking to you for moral support, Herman."

"And you can goddamn well count on it. If Margo doesn't like it, she can shove it," Himmelmann announced bravely.

Margo Himmelmann was in the process of telling Katharine that she did not understand herself at all. "Why did I come? I didn't want to and now it seems *he* might be here with that *woman*!"

"You don't have to see them—look the other way."

"I will *not* go to Dolly's party just to face that humiliation . . . I have much better things to do." A secret look crossed her face, instantly alerting Katharine, but Margo recollected herself. "I suppose I had to come to find out what the hell's going on with you and Erik. *Is* it all over?"

Katharine tried to smile but didn't do well. "It is, yes . . . and it isn't."

"You look terrible," her mother said critically. "I thought you'd promised yourself to snap out of these moods of yours."

"I thought so too," Katharine muttered. "Look, Mother, I don't feel like talking about it . . . The answer to your question is that the marriage is over but we're not getting a divorce. He's afraid to force the issue . . . and I'm almost too embarrassed to force it."

"You're crazy," Margo Himmelmann sniffed.

Katharine shrugged. "Probably. Why should I *bother* to end it?" she asked miserably. "I don't have anybody else. . . ."

"I thought there was a man, Kate."

"Who told you that?"

"Helen Ryan." Mrs. Himmelmann's eyes narrowed.

Katharine scowled. "Helen Ryan is a fool. She doesn't know anything . . . I said I do *not* have anybody else and Erik is not going to walk away from the marriage with nothing."

Margo Himmelmann drew a long breath and bared her teeth. "He'd have to have something."

"Why? I've got the evidence—he slept with Dolly. He's keeping a girl. . . ."

"Dolly?" It was more of an exclamation than a question.

Katharine laughed loudly. "Of course. Haven't Dolly and I always shared everything?"

"Very funny, my dear," Margo Himmelmann said sarcastically. Again, her eyes sharpened. "And Erik—what's he got on you? Are you lily-white?"

"No. . . ." Katharine said quietly.

"So I gather," her mother said haltingly. "I told you I talked to Helen . . . she told me some very nice things. Yes, indeed." Mrs. Himmelmann looked as though she might cry. "Yes, some very nice stories about your family life . . . I never expected to hear things like that about my own daughter. . . ."

"Oh, yes?" Katharine murmured. "It's not as if I don't have a few things *I* can remember too."

"What do you mean by that exactly?"

Sadly, Katharine said, "Every once in a while, I get a vague feeling I've heard all this before."

"I wouldn't dwell on it, dear," Mrs. Himmelmann muttered sourly. "We're talking about *you*, not me. I can see why you don't want a divorce action, not if Erik gets up and spouts all *he* knows. You'd lose—judges prefer to believe in the *fallen* woman, not the wronged woman."

Kathy nodded indifferently. "Erik said the same thing— and he doesn't know the half of it. But I said I don't care. If it went to court, I wouldn't come out looking any dirtier than him and people do forget these things pretty quickly."

"Oh, yes? Your daughter too? And me? It would be just swell for us all, wouldn't it?" Mrs. Himmelmann charged emotionally. "I knew a few things from experience, Katharine Margaret . . ."

Katharine was startled. She sat up straight. "Why do you call me that?"

"It's your name, isn't it?" Margo Himmelmann said harshly. "Listen, dear, pay him, I'm telling you, and get him out of your life. If you need grounds, try simple adultery. That's very acceptable these days . . . like tax evasion."

Katharine flushed. She didn't answer directly. "In *your* day, screwing in the back seats of convertibles wasn't acceptable?"

Mrs. Himmelmann turned beet-red, more embarrassed than Kate. "It's not possible . . . you couldn't remember that. You were much too young. You must have heard people talking about it—probably that father of yours."

"No. I remember your dress up over your head."

"You don't remember *anything*," Mrs. Himmelmann cried faintly.

"It was pink."

Mrs. Himmelmann's face changed from red blush to white shock. "Was it? How could you remember that, dear?"

"I don't know," Katharine said morosely, "but it doesn't matter."

Softly, weepily, Margo Himmelmann murmured, "Has this been bothering you all these years?"

"No, no, I *said* it doesn't matter."

Numbly, Mrs. Himmelmann nodded. "All right—so what *are* you going to do? It's all *too* much!"

"I'm going to Europe with Dolly and the two boys . . . I'd like Margaret to stay with you while I'm away . . . or she can go out to Wainscott. . . ."

"Of course—with me!" Margo Himmelmann was stunned to quick reply. "My God, you're *not* going to go to Europe with Stefan and this Marco Fortuna! I understand he's a horrible man."

"Maybe. I don't care. Stefan is dying . . . Conny accuses me of never caring. I'm going with them. . . ."

"Yes, yes," Mrs. Himmelmann said breathlessly.

"What's wrong?" Katharine demanded.

"I don't know—it's just such a mess."

"It's a mess only if you think of it as a mess," she said coldly. "In reality, it's very simple. I'm going to Europe for a few months—call it a trial separation if you want to. Erik is very busy and so Margaret will be staying with her grandmother, her doting, oh-so-proper grandmother."

Margo blushed. "Well, almost. . . ."

"What *is* going on with you? Tell me."

"Nothing," Margo drawled, more confidently. "I think . . . um . . . news of Richard's misalliance disturbed my glands, that's all. I say no more, dear," she added slyly.

"Is it love again?" Katharine asked sardonically.

Margo Himmelmann pursed her lips. "Don't be corny . . . I don't know that *love* in capital letters is an important requirement."

"Mother," Katharine sighed. "You're the original bad girl."

She wandered across the guest room to its high, leaded windows and looked down at the lawn, a semi-circular half-acre of green bordered by rose beds. The garage, big enough for eight or ten cars, with a second-story apartment for Mrs. Rogers, lay to the right of the house, and behind it, a stable of sorts. In the old days, as a matter of course, riding horses had been kept on Port London properties. But by now, most of the old stables had been converted to other uses—guest cottages, potting sheds, workshops; in the case of Maples, to a kennel and storage space for garden equipment. On the other side of the out-buildings lay the Sound, blue, moderate whitecaps marching. Everything seemed so neatly arranged, it was difficult to imagine the rest of life in such a shambles.

Margo Himmelmann was chattering about something entirely different. Katharine was about to turn back to her when she saw Conrad and Margaret come out of the stable, the two dogs bounding around them.

The children: Conrad, who'd always seemed like her son, tall, skinny, over six feet. He should have been more mature. But he was still a child, as childlike as Margaret in many ways. . . . And Margaret, both so thrillingly blonde.

She interrupted Margo Himmelmann. "I'd better call Dolly . . . your former husband must have gotten here by now."

"With his new love." Mrs. Himmelmann flopped down on the chaise longue and pouted.

Downstairs, the library door was still closed. In the kitchen, Mrs. Rogers was arranging a tea tray for Katharine's mother.

"I think what I need," Katharine muttered, "is a huge drink."

Mrs. Rogers' expression became melancholy. Enviously, Katharine thought of her as a completely uncomplicated woman. The Rogers clan had been breeding quietly in these-here parts for generations, centuries, with nary a slip. There was no madness in those genes. The Rogers lived comfortably and died comfortably, usually at night in their sleep, a reward for long lives, well-led.

"Is Mrs. Himmelmann not well?"

Katharine was stuffing a water glass with ice. "She's well. . . . She's just a little worried my father will show up this weekend with his girlfriend. Worried—no, she's frantic."

"In that case," Mrs. Rogers said, "I'd best get this tea upstairs. . . ."

As Mrs. Rogers exited the kitchen toward the stairs, Conrad and Margaret appeared at the screendoor. "Don't let the dogs in," Katharine warned. Was it her imagination or, when they saw her, did their lighthearted movement become awkward? Was she such a wet blanket? "Well," she challenged them, "is everything exactly the same?"

"Nothing ever changes in historical old Port London," Conrad muttered.

Margaret tittered. "Even the historical dogs are the same."

Conrad frowned. "This is one clever kid." Then he smiled. "What about a drink for me? Is that vodka? I'd like one, please."

Katharine shook her head. "Get a beer out of the frig." He swung open the door, took out a beer and yanked its tab. "Give Margaret something." Conrad found a Coke. "Now," Katharine said, "go on upstairs and see your grandmother. I want to talk to your old uncle."

"What about?" the little girl demanded.

"None of your business. Go on." Katharine waited until Margaret had slowly dragged herself through the door. "Let's go outside," she suggested to Conrad.

He shrugged moodily, already bored, she supposed. Katharine smiled at him, hopefully. He was even more handsome now than he had been beautiful as a child. In temperament, brother and sister were very similar—watchful, sensitive, more introverted than one would suspect.

Katharine stopped to put another ice cube in her glass before they left the house and strolled across the lawn in the direction of the stable. Finally, Conrad asked her what she wanted to talk about.

She shook her head wearily. "Us, I guess."

"Us? Who's us?"

"You . . . me . . . Erik . . . Margaret."

"Why me?" he asked. "I'm not *your* problem."

Conrad pulled back the creaky stable door for her and Katharine led the way inside. It was amazing that after so many years it could still smell of horses, straw and manure, surely one of the most permanent of scents. Like a specific perfume, it reminded Katharine of her youth, instantly of riding classes, jumping and the pony, that white, almost albino, pony with its crazy eyes, its pink eyes. She shivered and laughed aloud.

"What's the matter?"

She laughed again. "I just thought of something I've been trying to remember for months . . . years."

"What's that?"

Katharine shook her head. "It's too complicated to explain. A dream, wrapped in a hundred other dreams." She flexed her shoulders, as if some small burden, at least, had been lifted from her. And so it had. "Now . . . about *us*."

"Yes," he repeated archly, "*us* . . ."

"You do know what's going on, don't you?"

"You mean you and Erik? He calls it a crisis."

"Does he?" Katharine wondered what Erik had told him in the car. She continued quickly, "I'm thinking about going to Europe with Dolly. I will be spending time with Stefan and Marco . . . after all."

"Fine." Conrad put the beer can to his lips. He emptied it, then carelessly let it fall to the dusty floor.

"Don't do that. Pick it up."

He stooped and retrieved the can, dangling it between his fingers. "I'll go with you . . . can I?"

Katharine murmured, "If you like. One of the reasons I'm going is to be with Stefan. I . . . you accused me of not caring. I do care!"

"Then we'll go together, Kate." He laughed embarrassedly. "It's sort of funny, isn't it?"

"How so?"

"Just . . . well, where does that leave Erik?"

Irritably, she demanded, "Why are we suddenly so concerned about Erik? You were never great chums."

He put his elbows on the wooden partition that stood between them. Katharine faced him, her own forearms on the rough wood, the glass balanced on her knuckles.

"We're *not* great chums. I was thinking—they're so different. I don't know. . . ."

"Good Christ," Katharine grunted, "don't tell me at this late date you're finding Erik preferable to Stefan."

"Don't be stupid, Kate." He closed his eyes, dropped his forehead down on her wrist.

"Just, please, Conny, don't choose up sides. I guess," Katharine acknowledged, "I'll always have trouble with my men."

Carefully, he asked, "What about . . . the guy we visited?"

"Francotti? You saw, didn't you?" she responded bitterly.

"Saw *what*? I thought he was very . . . attracted to you," he said, as thoughtful of her feelings as he could be. "Is that right? Is he supposed to be?"

"Oh, yes," Katharine sighed. "Did you think he was . . . I. . . ." She chuckled embarrassedly. "You're going to think worse of me than ever."

"No, I'm not."

"Darling," she murmured, smiling up at him, "why can't *you* protect me from all this? I'd probably be just as miserable with him. . . ."

"You were *miserable* with Stefan Ratoff?"

"No, no. Actually, I wasn't. I wasn't outrageously happy either—but I definitely wasn't unhappy."

"So you're going back to him? For a trial reunion?" he asked suddenly.

"Why do you say that? Yes, all right, why not?"

Conrad nodded, wisely, she thought, judiciously, affectionately. "You'll have to divorce Erik, Kate."

She shook her head slightly. "Not necessarily. It would be messy . . . we have to think of Margaret."

"Her? That kid is so self-centered she wouldn't give a damn," he said.

"She loves Erik."

Tiredly, Conrad said, "I don't know what to think— why did you marry Erik in the first place?"

"I don't know," she confessed. "I was with Mother in Europe. I was . . . getting over Stefan. Erik seemed so strong, just what I needed, all that fortitude and strength. I didn't realize what else went with it."

"What else?" His face was strained.

Firmly, she shook her head. She could never describe it. "I can't tell you. It's too horrible."

Anxiety burst from him. "What the hell *am* I supposed to think? Why are you all so miserable? Why am *I* so miserable myself?"

"Don't be, you're not, Conny," Katharine pleaded. She put her hands over his, clutching his fingers. "Please try to be happy."

"Happy?" he echoed her mockingly. "What's happy? Not you, not Mother, that's for sure."

"You *can* be happy, goddamn it." She wanted to shout it. "Stop worrying so much. Live your own life. Don't worry about us—we're out of it."

He scoffed, "You've run your course, Kate? Don't make me laugh!"

Katharine put her mouth against his blonde hair. It smelled so clean, so pure. She kissed the hair and he turned his face toward her, so beautifully, and she kissed his lips. Conny's breath was fresh, almost sweet. She licked his soft lips and bit them teasingly. Suddenly he pressed her mouth with his own and his tongue flicked out to taste her lips too. Kate's body pressed toward him, against the partition which separated them. She could feel his slimness even through the wood. His eyes blinked open and he bathed her in their blueness, in their gentleness.

God, what she yearned for now was to take Conrad in her arms and to kiss him all over, the hardnesses and softnesses of him. With a tinny rattle, his beer can dropped and her glass fell to the stable floor; a splash of coldness from a melted ice cube hit her ankle. She placed her palms on either side of his smooth face and kissed his eyelids, the tip of his nose and, again, the smooth, soft lips.

"Oh, little brother, please don't be miserable. . . ."

He did what she'd wanted without thinking, stepping around the partition so she could gather him in her arms, press his body against hers. He wept into her shoulder, trembling. Why? He was only a baby and babies should be happy. She felt his nose, cold and wet against her breast.

His hands went to the front of her blouse.

"Conny. . . ." She had no strength to stop him.

"Please, Kate," he begged, "let me, let me."

He wanted her breast, and she could deny him nothing. Whatever he wanted, it was his to take. "Yes, yes, darling."

Reassuring him, yes, that it was all right, she shrugged out of her blouse and reached back to open her bra. He nursed at the sterility, or so it seemed to her, of her breast. Muttering, he sucked and pulled. It hurt her a little but she tried to help him on.

"Sit down," she suggested humbly.

Together, they slumped to the floor and he wet her breasts with his tears, bringing them to a tautness she had forgotten. Kate caressed his chest through his shirt, stroking him, her eyes closed, crooning, "My darling Conny. . . ."

Kate sloped toward blankness, unthinkingly dropping her hand to his thigh and feeling his manhood through his trousers.

Conrad's groan was hushed; deep in his throat he gasped, a yell it would have been from the other side of the mountain, through the trees.

Kate knew that she had gone crazy but she didn't care. She unfastened his belt, the top button and pulled down his zipper. Inside, underneath, were pure white boxer shorts. She thrust her hand in the opening and took his manhood in her hand.

He found his voice. "No . . . you can't. . . ."

"Yes, I can," she said, "you're *my boy.* I used to take care of you and make you clean when you were a baby."

He struggled but very weakly. "Please . . . Kate. . . ."

"It doesn't matter, my darling."

Kate shifted so she had a better sight of it sticking up at her and then, worshipfully, she bent to kiss and run her tongue through the cleft at the end of it.

"Your little pecker has grown so."

He panted, in fright, it seemed, torn between need and worry that this was wrong, *forbidden* by all convention. But yet, there were tribes in the world whose survival made it right, not wrong. . . . What about this endangered species called Kate?

Conrad cried out. She had forgotten how close young men were to the threshold. He loosed a torrent of vital juices on her tongue and she pushed down with her lips, taking it all in her mouth, gulping, draining him of it. At last, the quivering stopped. She opened her eyes.

His expression was so tragic. His voice trembled. "Why did you do that, Kate?"

She had a ready answer: she didn't care. But she said, "I've always wanted to. I was going to comfort you and then I went beyond comfort. I'm sorry if it's made you feel bad."

"Isn't it terrible?"

"People say so," she admitted defiantly, "but I don't feel terrible. Do you?"

He shook his head, and his eyes cleared. "No, I'm glad you did it, Kate."

Kate petted him and realized it was getting hard again. "God, you're so young, Conny . . . *I love you.*"

She knew they should stop now but he was eyeing her probingly. "*Shall* I? Would *that* be so terrible?"

"More terrible, yes, but not as terrible as a lot of other things."

No one would see. No one would ever know. They were hidden here and she let him continue. He kissed her breasts again urgently and staring at his blonde head she had to remind herself who he was. He groped at her thighs and obediently she lifted herself and pulled down her panties. Shrieking to herself, she felt his wetness and the hot point, as lethal for them as a stiletto, so sharp she was sure he was cutting her; in her desperation, she slipped, as if she'd lost her grip on the ledge or precipice, and down she went, his pecker pushed into her and not so little either.

She did not move much, feeling, somehow, that reciprocation would compound the transgression, make it more lurid than it was already, by definition. Kate lay quite still, gently stroking his buttocks. But then, even this resolution diminished, then vanished, before his pulsing energy and once more she forgot. At the long reach of him, on the tether of his life-force, she squirmed wantonly, making Conrad yelp in pain, anger, whatever, and jab wildly at her swaying hips. Alarmingly, Kate realized that she could not stop herself from climaxing . . . and she did so with fright like a scream stuck in her throat, her eyes clamped shut so she could not see him any longer, waiting to be struck down by a vengeful lightning bolt. Conrad whined as he divested himself the second time.

It was over. Kate lay panting, regretting it now when he wept. It had come to this, in a horse stall in an old stable.

Conrad stirred. In a single movement, he pulled himself away from her in a fury of embarrassment. Aching with a different want, Kate got on her knees, then her feet.

"Give me those."

Not speaking, he handed her the bra and panties.

"We have a deep, dark secret now, little brother," she whispered.

Conrad gulped noisily. "Everybody will know. . . ."

"There is no way," Kate said firmly, "that anybody can know, or even suspect. . . ."

"Every time I look at you, I'll turn red, Kate. I love you, Kate."

"You are my *lover*?"

"Don't say it," he exclaimed fearfully.

Kate put her hands on his shoulders. "You'll just kiss my cheek now with a little more conviction, darling, and when I wink at you, you'll know what I'm thinking."

She smiled broadly at him and winked.

"Kate!"

"Smile, damn it!"

He managed a tremulous grimace. "I'm sorry . . . I shouldn't have. . . ."

"Forget it," she said bluntly. "You're good, you know, quite the best I've ever had, Conny."

"Don't talk like that!"

"Better than Erik too," she murmured. Why tell him that?

"Erik? Shit, I feel guilty."

"Don't be silly. Erik will be fine, I can tell you," Kate said acidly. "He' s got Dolly—among others—and a girlfriend in New York that he's supporting. That's another reason I'm going away. You see," she said sardonically, "my dear husband has established a little love nest in a dingy apartment on the East Side and there he keeps a tiny girl in filthy jeans and unwashed hair. . . ."

"You've been spying on him!"

Kate laughed. "Not spying . . . well, yes, *spying*. I had to, didn't I, for my own protection?" She could not stop herself. She rushed on, determined to have everything said. "You've got to understand, darling," she murmured, tiptoeing slightly to kiss him another time on the corner of the mouth, "there's a ton of money involved."

"As Stefan Ratoff discovered. . . ."

Kate nodded. "Yes, true. It's supposed to be a responsibility, you know. It belongs to us all and we have to protect it."

"Money!" he mumbled. "I hate it . . . I feel sorry for Erik."

"Well, I don't," she barked. "I'm sure she's quite a nice girl, actually. One can't blame her, I suppose, for falling in with a fortune hunter."

"Is he . . . that?"

"We don't know for a fact but we have to play our cards with that in mind."

"You're all so cold-blooded about it," Conrad drooped wearily against the stall.

"Sometimes you don't approve of me at all, do you?"

His laugh was hopeless. "Approve of you, *dearest*?" he rasped. "How could you say a thing like that? Not approve of *you* when I love you? I do, you know."

Kate's tone was hard. "Don't be cruel . . . You don't have to approve of me. I'm not asking you to. You can stop insulting if you love me, Conny."

"All right," Conrad said. "But I can't help it—I feel sorry for all of you—you and Erik and the girl."

Kate laughed. "And *yourself* too? No need to feel sorry for the girl—she's having a good time of it. She's installed in a studio apartment and spends all day painting and Erik brings her food or takes her out to eat. I wouldn't feel sorry for her, oh no."

Conrad's face passed through a drastic alteration. "She's an *artist*?"

He began to turn away even as Kate was answering that, yes, the girl, a tiny redhead evidently, painted pictures. They didn't know where or how Erik had met her but apparently she'd come to New York from Chicago—and that, judging by the mailbox, her name was Royce.

Conrad choked off an exclamation.

"Where are you going?"

"I'm leaving," he cried, his voice muffled. "I can't *stand* it anymore."

Thirty-Three

Along with everything else, the weather changed that night, a spectacular sunset leading into blustery dusk. When Katharine drove into the parking lot by the docks, wind was gusting into the Sound from the open eastern ocean. She slipped into the heavy sweater she'd brought along and bucked the wind down the dock where a dinghy Stefan had sent in from the *Seaworthy* was waiting.

Gibber Higgens' two-master was anchored a couple of hundred yards offshore, rolling greasily in the swell which, beyond the breakwater, was heavy, performing vengefully as the tailend of spring. There wouldn't be much sailing on Sunday if it kept on like this.

Oh, sailor-boy, it was cold tonight, and storming. The young man pointed the bobbing dinghy toward the sea-steps at the stern of the *Seaworthy*. "Can you see Gene Francotti's boat out here?" she yelled at him.

He shook his head. "I wouldn't know it, Mrs. Moss . . . I just come out here the weekends to work."

Katharine peered into the wind. There were masts enough in the sheltered anchorage but no way she could discover which boat was his. She was soon scrambling up into the cockpit of the *Seaworthy*.

"Mrs. Moss, when do you think you'll want to go back to shore?"

"I don't know. It's so rough, I might get stuck out here."

"I'm up forward. Give a holler." He pushed open a hatch and Katharine presented herself to the warm glow of the main cabin of the *Seaworthy*, snug and secure in the unquiet sea.

Stefan leaned back from one side of a backgammon table. "We weren't sure you'd come."

Marco Fortuna grinned boyishly. "Join us, we who are banished from the social whirl."

"You'll meet everybody tomorrow." Katharine chuckled dryly. "I promise you won't regret the delay. True, Stefan?"

Stefan smiled aloofly, from the distance granted him by severe illness. "About meeting Richard Darktower, my dear, there can be no hurry," he agreed. "He is an ogre of very high caliber, Marco."

Marco shrugged. "I am so frightened. Come, Stef, we must finish this now, or never, and I continue as reigning champion of all backgammon boards . . . Katharine, sweetheart, make yourself something to drink. . . ."

Over the years, she had been aboard the *Seaworthy* now and then. It was a neat ship, not geared so much to luxury or comfort as to be an honest-to-God racing sloop. She wondered if Francotti's ship was likewise fitted for all kinds of weather. Chances are she would never know. But it didn't matter much now, did it? Nothing did—the dice had been thrown and both had tumbled off the table.

Katharine admired their concentration as they played the fatuous game. Marco swore terribly, the next moment chuckled inanely. Stefan, on the other hand, sat motionlessly, completely absorbed, his face peaked in profile, eyes half-closed. His hair had thinned dramatically too, she noted. It was brushed straight back from his waning widow's peak, scarcely disguising the scalp. Katharine didn't think she would have recognized him alongside that firm-fleshed athlete she had first come to know in Europe.

The bar was tiny, set precisely between a slanting map table and the interior hatch, which led to the bow of the ship. Each bottle had its own tight hole in a wooden wall-rack. Below, a refrigerator-icemaker with a wooden chopping-block top provided work space. Gleaming glasses had been arranged on a white towel. A fresh lemon, beaded with juice where it had been cut, rested on the wood. By Stefan's right hand was a glass of soda with a lemon slice in it.

"I'm making a vodka martini," Katharine announced. "Can I get you two something?"

Stefan glanced over his shoulder and shook his head sourly.

"Brandy, *cherie*," Marco muttered, flicking at his snifter with his thumb.

She made her own drink first, generous vodka on plenty of ice, and a curl of lemon peel. She tasted appreciatively, thankful for the bite of alcohol on her lips and tongue. Maybe she could deal with it now . . . what was going to become of her? Katharine leaned against the bar, her eyes closed. Of such insanity as this, she told herself grimly, were legends made.

The vodka sent a chill down her spine, but at least made her think more clearly. Clarity told her she should not give a damn about Conny—it had been nothing more than a quick physical contact, like a long kiss, not touching the spirit, once you had scuttled convention and superstition.

Katharine replenished Marco's brandy glass and placed it by his pudgy hand.

"*Merci*, darling," Marco mumbled.

Stefan looked up, smiling inquisitively. He would want to know what had driven her out here on such a night. The dark circles under his eyes were making graves of the sockets. His lips were colorless, almost white.

Katharine would not be able to tell him what had happened with Conrad even though Stefan was the only person who had a hope of understanding. Stefan had placed *himself* above convention years before. He had dared all! He had thumbed his nose at morality. Perhaps she *could* tell him. Later. Not now. Maybe when they were in Europe.

She sat down quietly with her drink and picked up a copy of the Port London weekly paper. She scanned the pages, with no clue what she was reading. Had Francotti gone to sea, or had he been put off by the weather? She lifted the vodka again. It didn't matter now about Francotti. That part of her life was finished too.

She and Conny . . . Katharine daydreamed, remembering

his unblemished skin and what *they* had done. They had pricked the bare nerve of civilization. She did love Conny more than she had any man. But what to do, what to do? To hell with everything else! She gulped the drink, tossed down the newspaper and jumped to her feet. "Shit! Are you two going to play all night?"

They glanced at her in surprise.

"Almost finished, sweetheart," Stefan said soothingly. "Just a little patience."

"Si," Marco whispered, touching his lips with his tongue. "A small patience."

"Sorry," she said.

Katharine wondered if Marco was really a Sicilian, whether he was even Italian. He was probably from Brooklyn. Perhaps he was a mongrel Maltese. The way he had begun to look at her, he evidently believed she was ready to fall on her back, panting to receive him. Not likely, not now.

Marco's next utterance was a scream of rage. *"Du schwein!"*

The game had ended and Marco was calling Stefan a pig because Stefan had won. Stefan laughed, then coughed rackingly, pulling his handkerchief out of the breast pocket of his blazer and holding it over his nose and mouth until the seizure subsided.

"Oh, son-of-a-bitch, Stefan," Marco complained. "It is against the agreement. You are *not* to beat the champion."

"You see, Kat," Stefan said, "if he does not win he becomes churlish and petulant."

Marco stared across the backgammon table at Stefan. Despite his studied effort to frown and scowl, a smile forced itself on his downturned lips. For a second, Katharine was touched to observe their relationship. She wondered if it was as simple as Stefan described it—family friend? But why not? Not everything had to be dark and dismal.

She had not forgotten that the two of them, in a manner of speaking, had made love to Dolly. But Marco must not get the wrong idea. She was not as wanton as Dolly. No . . . no, she wasn't, not really.

''Well,'' Stefan asked disinterestedly, ''what's new back at the ranch?''

She shrugged. ''Mr. and Mrs. Himmelmann arrived from New York on schedule. Erik came out with Margaret . . . and Conrad.'' Conrad, yes! ''I guess you'd already retreated to the boat by the time Daddy got here with his girlfriend.''

Stefan grinned gauntly. ''He actually did bring her? What a scandal. Good for the old boy!''

It was quite amazing, she thought, that Stefan did not bear Darktower any ill-will, not at all. Her father might have drawn a *moral* lesson from that! Even though Stefan had left first-class, the circumstances of his departure had been bitter. But, nonetheless, he remained generous, open, forgiving.

''Margo—my mother,'' she explained to Marco, ''is beside herself.''

''Shitting bricks,'' Marco bawled. ''Marco had better have a talk with Margo. Marco-Margo, yes, perhaps we will make music together.''

''Marco, she is too old for you,'' Stefan chuckled.

''Age! Poof!'' Marco laughed moistly. His laughter seemed to spring from his crotch. Sure enough, he swung his swivel chair away from the backgammon table and put his hand in his pocket, ostentatiously fingering his equipment. ''You put the bag over their head. One of your countrymen said that,'' he told Katharine.

''Yes,'' Stefan joked solemnly, ''a Tiffany bag.''

''*Punto!*'' Marco cried. He yanked his hand out of his pocket, slapped his knee and stood up. ''One more brandy for me. One more vodka for sweet-slit. One more soda water for Pa-Pa.''

All one could do with Marco was ignore him. Katharine glanced around the cabin and remarked, ''Very ambitious of Dolly to lease this, just for a weekend.''

''Ha, ha!'' Marco chortled. He was busy at the bar. ''Only to get horny Marco out of the way so she could pursue her designs on your father. . . . It is possible I will buy this barge. It is for sale.''

Marco smiled at her rapturously but, for him, unusually,

in that his eyes for once seemed open and intelligent, rather than foolish or leering, intimating she must be in a positive fever to get him between her legs. "Beautiful lady, I am all a ga-ga to meet your father. Any man who could deal so mercilessly with Stefan Ratoff . . . any man who has Dolly Percy frothing . . . this man must be quite a man."

"Sure," Katharine murmured. "He'll want to meet you too, darling."

Stefan chuckled. "Already King Richard is suspicious that Marco Fortuna is in Port London for the sole purpose of stealing all Dolly's money."

Highly insulted, Marco yelled, "Yes! *Dieu!* But the whole world knows Marco Fortuna does not need to steal any woman's money. More than that, *if* your father does not interfere," he demanded superciliously, "am I not nearly betrothed to Mrs. Percy?"

"Don't worry—we'll all give you character references," Katharine said laconically.

"My character is unimpeachable—whatever that means," Marco laughed. "I assure you, sweet-buns, that Marco is also completely solvent. It is the truth, is it not, Stef, *cher?*"

Stefan nodded. "True. Not only solvent—Marco is very rich. The oil pumps day in, day out."

"Yes," Marco pouted, "I cannot spend it fast enough. I cannot find enough women to squander it upon—and, as Stefan has no doubt told you, *j'adore* women with big breasts. I think we saw one, once, in Serbia." He giggled. "Not so, Stef?"

"Yes." Stefan agreed languidly. "Or in Bessarabia. . . ."

"Exactly!" Marco screamed. "Or England—there the women have the biggest breasts of all the world. But, darling, Dolly tells me this friend of your father's . . . well. . . ." Marco looked excitedly at Stefan. "Remember, *cher*, I am to stare at the breasts of this . . . what is her name?"

"Clara-something."

"Oh, Clara," Marco moaned, rolling his eyes up in his head.

Katharine said, "Please don't make a scene, that's all. My father will be in a bad enough mood as it is."

"Oh, hell," Marco grunted, "why does everyone always take such an offense? I am a mere innocent . . . and so lonely," he wailed. "How I wish Dolly had come with you."

"Marco," Stefan said gently, "you could do with a good night's sleep."

"Yes, quite so! My nerves are at screaming pitch. *Dio, cher,* we live so hard and fast." He glanced significantly at Katharine. "I am still quite undone from the afternoon."

"Me too," she said.

"And I," Stefan added sardonically. "But we will have to get you back to shore, Kat."

She shook her head. "No. Nobody's going to miss me. I'd just as soon wait 'til morning now."

Marco's body came to attention. "Yes, beautiful lady, do stay! We will make you so *very* comfortable."

Stefan was not so sure. "You should be home. Where is *Mossberg?*"

"Home, I guess. I don't know," she said carelessly.

Stefan looked at her curiously. "So, it *is* over?"

She nodded. "Oh, yes. That's how come I'll be with Dolly and you in Europe."

Marco beamed. "On *our* territory, beautiful lady! In *Geneve.*" He hopped to his feet and took her hand, kissed her fingers, then the inside of her wrist, his tongue darting like a serpent's. "Why put off the inevitable, beautiful lady?"

He glanced at Stefan apologetically and Stefan stared down at his hands. It was, he was silently saying, up to her.

"Sorry, Marco, that's not what I want."

"What! Surely, you jest!" he yelped comically. He hadn't *really* expected it, had he? He was clowning.

"Tonight, sir," she said roundly, "if with any man I bed, it will be with my beloved Stefan!"

"Ah-ha," Marco hissed, "*bene.* That is all right then. Marco will stand aside for Prince Stefan." Marco put out his hand to Stefan and dragged him to his feet. "Goodnight, sweet prince."

When Erik had extricated himself from another business discussion after dinner with Herman Himmelmann he found, to his dismay, that both cars were gone, the station wagon *and* the Mercedes. So was Kathy gone . . . and Conrad. Well, he would have to go on foot through the gathering storm if he intended to reach Dolly's that night for his talk with Richard Darktower.

Everyone was upstairs when Erik opened the front door and put his head into the wind. Hands jammed in raincoat pockets, he strode down the driveway to the main road, turning in the direction of Dolly Percy's house.

The weather had changed so decisively it would be a minor miracle if the weekend was fine and fair. Dolly's spectacular party would have to be moved inside. Even now, a burst of wind splattered raindrops on Erik's cheek. Blast! He would be soaked to the bone by the time he got to Doll House.

Erik was feeling so depressed, things were so hopelessly out of kilter that it didn't seem to matter much if he did get rained upon. Kathy hated him—he could not devise a way around that. How *were* they to coexist in this worst of all possible worlds? It was a pity Kathy did not love Francotti better—that would have precipitated an appropriate settlement of their relationship, for, he calculated, it was more Darktower's idea than hers to be hardhearted.

Erik kicked at the gravel along the side of the road. He disliked being put in a spot where he must plead with Darktower for something that should automatically be his: the right to existence. How was he to manipulate the situation? If it was impossible to exist in the bosom of the family, then he must leave; but he must have fair compensation for his years of service to the clan. He *had* forsaken all for love, or at least on the vague premise, not promise, that Richard Darktower would make him rich and wonderfully secure if he came to New York as Kathy's consort. The fact, Erik had recognized some time ago, was that Darktower had been as enamored of *stealing* Erik from

James Merriwether as he had in making his daughter happy. What stupidity—*clever* Erik Moss had already fallen between the two executive chairs, *ka-thump* on the boardroom floor, and it hurt very much.

Love? It was nauseating to think about love. Could he really have been in love with this neurotic, pampered lush? He, a cultured, well-educated European? A member of nature's own aristocracy? Erik mocked himself harshly, laughing into the spiteful wind. Implacable logic pinched his temples. Reality was upon him. There was no point, and indeed it was self-defeating to brood about what might have been. He would just have to wrest what he could out of the fire and take his leave.

He paid little attention to the sweep of bright headlights from behind him. He stepped well to the side and waited for the car to pass. It bore down on him, whistling in the wind, headlights picking him out of the darkness, practically blinding him. Erik heard the brakes being applied; the car slowed but not by much. He caught sight of the white face inside as it passed, lit eerily by the instrument panel. Conrad!

Erik shouted out: "Conrad! You're driving too fast. Slow down. Turn. Come back and give me a lift." But the car picked up speed again, tail lights shrinking in the blackness. Erik growled angrily—how dare the boy take his car without asking?

Down the road, the red tail lights beat steadily. Ah, Conrad had stopped and was turning to come back. In a moment, the bright front lights were dead-center in the road.

Erik stepped forward, raising his arm. He would have a few choice words for Conrad. The Mercedes came nearer, gliding silently. Again, Erik waved. It *had* been Conrad, hadn't it, Conrad's blond face and long blond hair? The face was blurred through the windshield.

Erik realized in this instant that the car was not preparing to stop, that whoever was driving it meant *not* to stop, meant to run him down! In this second of comprehension, Erik jumped clumsily to the side, like an aging matador pirouetting away from a young bull.

He had not been quick enough. The rough edge of fender caught the skirt of his raincoat, just that much, but it was enough to spin him forcibly, away from the road and headfirst into the ditch.

He knew he had been stunned for, by the time he could turn his head, the car had spurted away, its exhaust spewing smoky contempt. Erik slowly pushed himself into a sitting position and rubbed his leg. No, nothing was broken. He would ache and he would have bruises but he was not damaged. Erik got to his feet shakily and brushed off his coat.

He stared down the road. By now, there was not even a hint of disappearing car. *So.* It must have been Conrad driving. But that was impossible—why would Conrad do this?

Just after ten P.M., Margo Himmelmann led young Margaret down the hallway to her room overlooking the rear lawn of Maples. Margaret was half-asleep, tottering with exhaustion, then out like a light when her head hit the pillow. Mrs. Himmelmann kissed her on the forehead, smiling benevolently for a while, then quietly retracing her way along the corridor. She peered into the lighted room where they'd been watching television—Herman Himmelmann was slumped in his robe, fast asleep. Scowling for a second at his inert form, Margo continued down the hallway to the staircase.

In the library, at last, she closed the door and crossed quickly to the telephone. She had two calls to make, one to New York and one local.

In the metropolis, the phone rang only twice before a voice said guardedly, "*Ya*-lo."

"Sam," she gushed. "Me. Margo."

"Whatayasay, sugar?" The voice did not warm her much but it had about it a common lisping insouciance that encouraged her.

"You miss me, big boy?" She felt like a fool saying it, but that's the way Sam liked to talk. She'd have put up with even more of the vernacular if it assured her his lumpy-muscled body.

"Sugar. . . ." Sam paused for effect. "Does a dog have fleas?" His chuckle scratched at her ear. Next came the rasping noise of him striking a match. "Ya'know I do, sweetheart. I wish't you were here right now, with me."

"Whatayadoin' right now, Sam?"

"Sittin' here, sugar, drinkin' a brew and watchin' the tenaclock."

"Tenaclock what, big boy?"

"The tenaclock high, sugar. I wish't you were here 'cause I got a idea you'd like it a lot."

Margo breathed a sharp piece of air. The way he talked made her tingle. "What's that, lover-boy?"

Sam snickered. He had such a filthy laugh. "It hastado with dunkin' for donuts, sugar."

"You. . . ." She caught herself, fevered. "You're not high, are you, Sam?"

"Nah, don't be crazy, sugar. Just one little snort keeps the doctor away."

"It's not good for you, lover," she whispered anxiously.

"Huh? Look, sugar, blow it out your barracks bag. . . . When you getting back to town?"

Margo was conscious of breathlessness. She didn't know what it was about Sam—maybe his simple cruelty, verging on sadism, his very uncouthness, disregard for any of the niceties. On the surface, he looked and acted quite the gentleman; underneath, however, he was a savage. Margo Himmelmann had always adored savages.

"I'll be back Monday, lover."

He repeated his lowdown laugh, making her skin crawl. God, terrible! They all had their little aberrations, didn't they? Katharine . . . she . . . Richard. Not Herman, though, no, not Herman.

"Sugar, keep the little honey-pot warm for me, willya? Be seein' you, huh?"

"Oh, Sam. . . ." She stopped herself; he didn't like sentimentality. "I'll be seein' you, Sam."

"Hey, don't do anything I wouldn't do, okay? Keep your legs crossed there, sugar. . . ."

He hung up, just like that, without any ritual farewell, leaving her with the phone in her hand, shaking with

loathing and desire. Goddamn him. She'd have liked
somebody to beat him up; she was seized with a sudden
hateful desire to advise Richard Darktower that his detective
was a cocaine freak, along with being a horny-handed
lover.

Briefly, Margo closed her eyes, picturing in quick
succession Herman Himmelmann of the magnificent paunch,
and the quick, wolflike lout called Sam Merchant who
preferred slapping her to actually doing her, but then did
her willingly when she threatened to lock her purse.

There was an extra dimension of bitterness and vindic-
tiveness in her mood when Margo got Richard Darktower
to the phone at Dolly Percy's house.

"Yes, what is it, Margo?"

"I'm told you brought that . . . woman . . . with you."

"True, Mrs. Himmelmann."

"And do you intend she will be at Dolly's party Sunday
afternoon to embarrass me to the death, Mr. Darktower?"

"Yes." He didn't even have to think about it, the pig!
"As to you being embarrassed, that's your lookout, Mrs.
Himmelmann. I've never found *myself* embarrassed in front
of Mr. Himmelmann, as you may have noted."

"That's beside the point!" Margo's voice rose sharply.
No one was going to blame her for becoming hysterical,
either.

"What *is* the point?"

"You're not *supposed* to embarrass me. You know
that's not in good form, Mr. Darktower."

"Oh, *blither-balls*, Mrs. Himmelmann."

"You dog," Margo cried.

"Arf . . . arf, Mrs. Himmelmann," he barked, then
broke into mocking laughter. "Getting so excited, Mrs.
Himmelmann, you know what you're going to do—you're
going to scare all the moths off of your beaver."

Not believing his crudeness for an instant, she nonetheless
heard the raucous laughter. Margo gasped, but forced
herself to say maliciously, "I must say you are learning
some revolting things from your friend, Miss Berger. . . ."

"Who did you say?"

"Rotten snake that you are! Don't think the whole

world doesn't know the name of the *other woman*, Mr. Darktower. *Henrietta Berger*, from White Plains, or wherever," she sneered.

Richard Darktower whooped. "What! I don't believe it."

"I said her name is Henrietta Berger and everybody knows it, Mr. Darktower."

"Well, Mrs. Himmelmann, for your information, her name is not Henrietta Berger. I can promise you that."

Oh, oh! Margo put her foremost knuckle between her front teeth and bit down, hard. God, had she made a fool of herself? Had Sam Merchant misinformed her, the little rodent?

"You bastard!" Her teeth made marks on the words. "You unspeakable dog. I hope it gives you pleasure to make people miserable, Mr. Darktower, for you are an expert at it. You've made all of us miserable—me . . . Katharine . . . all her husbands."

His voice cut another swath through her self-esteem.

"That's enough, Mrs. Himmelmann. I've other things to do than listen to you prattling."

"What then?" she exclaimed. "Ask me what *I'm* doing, why my life is so interesting with this man you forced me to marry . . . Himmelmann . . . *El Gordo*, they call him in Spain. Fatty! Snoring. . . ."

Darktower chuckled softly. "You found him, not me, Mrs. Himmelmann . . . now, would you *please* excuse me. Dolly and . . . *they're* doing the Tarot cards in the other room and my number is up."

"Oh, shut up!" Margo said tearfully. "I hate you."

When Helen Ryan asked him who it was that had called, Sam Merchant told her it was his psychiatrist. She hadn't been listening very closely anyway—just before Margo Himmelmann's interruption, he had shown Helen how to snort a thin line of coke up into her large Irish nose. The "white lady" did the job. He could have told her he'd been on the phone to Cardinal O'Farrell and she'd have bought it; and by the time he got old Margo off the blower, Helen was into an even deeper spin, as well she might be if this was really and truly her first-ever dance in a white dress.

Sam had invited Helen over to his place for hamburgers and french fries, never tipping his hand to being the raging cocksman that he was, or letting her know he'd been banging Mrs. H., no—acting for all the world like Mr. Straight Arrow who wanted and hungered only for a bit of intellectual conversation and heaven forbid he'd ever do a thing like he'd just done, namely pull off her clothes and inveigling her into taking a few drags on his joss-stick, which Helen thereupon continued to do with a verve that surprised him. Maybe it had to do with oral satisfaction, if you listened to what the doctors said, and what the hell did they know?

Hands clasped under his head, Merchant lay back quite comfortably while Helen huffed and puffed on him. She enjoyed it so much he didn't try to stop her, even when her face turned red and she might have a seizure holding her breath so long.

Sam was hazily mapping future strategy when she got his attention with a squeeze of his balls. Glaring up at him across his hairy stomach and concave chest, her eyes were unhitched, her voice slurred. Thank God, for that would make it easier for him to deny later that he'd heard the awful thing she said.

Which, namely, was that since he had taken advantage of her in this filthy way, she expected him to marry her.

"Hey, baby, whoa!" Sam guffawed. "Lemme tell you something: Suck! You know what they say—*blow* is only an expression."

"Shut up!" Helen Ryan hiccoughed. She came up for air, wrapping her meaty arms around his midriff and turning him over on top of her. Wonder of wonders, she strung her muscled legs around him and unceremoniously found his roger and slammed it into her mousetrap. Closing her eyes, she was overtaken by a blissful look of contemplation that swept the worrylines off her face.

Riding atop her, like a cork in the water, Sam made a fist with his hand and put it under her chin. "Hey, sugar, did I say I was ready?"

"Shut up, Sam," she growled, "or I'll grind up your nuts. Get working."

"I thought you were a Catholic girl!"

"I am. The Catholics invented this, in case you didn't know. More's the pity they're trying to take it away from us now."

He struggled to impress her but all his vigor wasn't a match for her. Helen bore him down, pulled him in and inside out. Her heels punched at his kidneys until he came, almost in self-defense.

"Now you've done it—I'm pregnant."

"How do you know?" he yelled. "It's too soon. You can't get pregnant that fast. You bitch, Helen! You're taking advantage of me. I can't get sidetracked like this. I got too much to do." He might have panicked if he weren't always under such tight control. From a harmless little stick-up job it had come to this five months later? Marrying an Irish witch? No sireee, that wasn't how Sam Merchant read his tea leaves.

Her testimonial was enough to make him vomit. "I fell in love with you," Helen gushed, "like all of a sudden, you were the only person in Central Park."

"Don't be so fuckin' romantic, sugar."

"It *was* love at first sight," she insisted.

"In a pig's ass!"

But she paid absolutely no attention rocking him on her chest like a baby, not noticing either that his dingus had fallen out.

"I feel it's time for me to marry," she mused, "and why not? I should remove myself from that whole Moss mess, don't you think, sweetie?"

"Yeah, sure," he said peevishly. "Dump the imbroglio in my lap, sugar."

Rough knuckles caressed his spine. "When we marry you'll have to take Catholic instruction."

Bitterly, he corrected her. "When? You mean *if*, don't you? *If* is the operational word, sugar."

"On the phone . . . you called that other woman sugar." Sam recognized the wistful tone, the leading edge of jealousy.

"You know who *that* was," he said proudly. He thought the news might throw off her marriage plot. "None other than Mrs. Herman Himmelmann."

"You're not telling the truth."

"I am. It was."

"You wouldn't *dare* call her sugar."

"Yes, I would. She's very sweet on me, sugar. We're shacked up."

Sam realized at once that he should never have told. Even if she didn't believe it now, the idea would fester within her and, whether she believed it to be true or not, it was information she could drop anywhere if he made one false move. Shit, he was dumb!

Eyes wide, Helen searched his face. "You want me to believe, Mr. Sam Merchant, that you made love to old Mrs. Himmelmann?"

"She's not *that* old," he murmured. Having committed the unpardonable, maybe he could shock her into permanent disbelief. "She's built like a brick shithouse, tits just won't stop and a little birdcage snug as a seventeen-year-old's. Hey, sugar! Why you crying?"

He learned next that he had made a definite strategic mistake by leveling with her. He did not see her right hand coming—it caught him alongside the head and sent him sailing off the cot onto the very hard, uncarpeted floor.

Her condemnation followed. "That's a horrible thing for you to say. I don't ever want to hear you talk like that again."

"Hey, *momento*, sugar!" Sam sat up dizzily, trying to stiffarm his way out of this. "I don't go for getting banged around by dames. . . ."

"Oh, no?" Helen sat up on the edge of the bed and in the most casual way possible, before he could dodge away, she grabbed his nose between her thumb and forefinger and twisted it. As he came within range, her ankle jerked up between his legs and caught him smack in the balls. Sam cried out, in hideous pain, and, when she released her grip on his nose, collapsed on the floor holding himself with both hands. This was unbelievable. Sam Merchant had never been beaten up by a woman and no one must ever hear about it.

"I want you to leave my apartment," he glugged.

"I *am* going."

"I don't want to see you anymore."

"Oh, no?" She repeated the ominous words and Sam huddled protectively. Helen towered over him—his upward view was of stalwart legs, the hairy tigertrap, prominent stomach and the tits. Her bare toes nudged his belly.

"Christ! Please don't kick me!"

"I'm not going to kick you," she remarked complacently, "if you're a good boy. Just remember—I could. Now, get up and give me my clothes."

Sam pressed to his knees. First, he picked up her black panties and held them out to her.

"Over my feet, Sambo."

He opened the gauzy bottoms to her feet, pulling them over her hips.

"If I was wearing stockings, you could have the pleasure of putting them on me, Sambo. Wouldn't you like doing that? Or would you rather wear them yourself?"

"Now you're calling me some kind of a fag," he complained.

"Stand up and help me with my bra."

If it was the only way he could get rid of her, okay, he'd do it. He fit one tit and the other into the twin parachutes and managed to close the clasp on her back.

"Dress. . . ."

"Yeah, yeah. . . ."

Eventually she was suited up and ready to leave.

"Well, so long," Sam said heartily, trying to smile and wink, thinking his first order of business would be to get another place to live and a new phone number.

"Don't *so long* me," Helen told him curtly. "I know what you're planning. You think you can get away. I'm telling you right now, forget that. If you try, I'll track you down and I'll take care of you."

"What would you do?" Cautiously, he moved out of her space.

"I dunno—maybe kill you, throw you out the window and call it suicide."

"You wouldn't!" He knew, however, that she could be serious. She was a potential killer. "What do you want with me? I'm a nobody."

"You had your way with me, sweetie."

"Whatayamean?" he sputtered. "You pulled me on top of you."

She shook her head stubbornly. "You made me take that dope and then you made me do it. Now, if you don't make me an honest women, I'll have to commit suicide."

"Bullshit!" He chanced a sneer, hoping the worst of her sadistic seizure was past. "Catholics don't commit suicide—that's an absolute no-no for you guys. Hey, sugar," he pleaded feebly, "life's not so bad."

She looked at him witheringly. "How would *you* know? No, I'd risk damnation, just to get even."

"With *me*?" he cried softly.

"No. With Erik Moss—I hate him. I'd do it in his study. I'd get a gun and blow my brains out in his study, get blood all over everything."

"You're crazy. You popped all your buttons, sugar."

"I'd like to hurt him," she insisted. "I could even make it look like murder maybe . . . that'd really get him, wouldn't it?"

"Yeah. Really," he agreed discouragedly. "I don't understand what everybody's got against this poor son-of-a-bitch Moss."

Helen shrugged. Her answer was simplicity itself. "He's bad."

Sam shivered. This goddamn thing, he told himself worriedly, was going from imbroglio to maelstrom.

Thirty-Four

Erik was limping, not badly but noticeably, by the time he'd finished the walk to Dolly Percy's house. He was, not unreasonably he thought, in a furious state of mind. He was sure now that it was Conrad who had tried to run him down with the Mercedes. It was not the most soothing thing in the world to know that an in-law had tried to kill you. The outside world was unfriendly enough without that.

And it was definitely not a good omen to be greeted at Doll House as though he were carrying a case of the bubonic plague. In front of the women, Richard Darktower was not openly hostile but merely perfunctory. Erik understood he was going to be unyielding.

"Darling," Dolly exclaimed flippantly, "you're limping. What have you done to your leg?"

"Nothing important," he muttered. "It will pass."

As if Dolly gave a damn—she did not. She'd not have cared if he'd come in minus the leg.

The Darktower paramour was something else. Darktower was forced by sheer propriety to introduce him to Miss Clara Riding.

Miss Riding was civil enough, but only because she hadn't had the time yet to become a fierce enemy, he thought. "It is nice to meet you, Mr. Moss. I've heard so much about you."

"Yes, I'm sure," he said, smiling sardonically at Darktower.

350

Erik noticed the cards in front of Clara Riding. "What's your fortune?" he asked Dolly.

She chuckled, too brilliantly. "It appears I'm to be traveling to foreign parts . . . and soon."

"And," he said, trying to sound unconcerned, "you'll meet a tall, dark stranger."

"Yes! However *did* you know, darling? Maybe you should do Erik's fortune, Clara."

Clara Riding looked at him closely, then shook her head. "My intuition tells me Mr. Moss is not one to believe in such things."

"That's right," he said, "I'm a realist."

"Well," Dolly said impatiently, "if your leg hurts, sit down, Erik."

"Thank you. I'm all right," he said for the second time. "I'd hoped I might have a word with Richard."

Darktower looked away, as if embarrassed. "I see you didn't bring Kate. If we're to talk about things. . . ."

Things? Erik shook his head. "I couldn't find her. She's gone out somewhere."

Dolly looked up alertly, her eyes flashing. He saw she was inviting personal inspection that evening. Her long, red, at-home gown was unzipped far enough to show a tanned curve of breast and it was also made in such a way that a slit in the side of the skirt revealed a kaleidoscope of trim brown calf and taut thigh.

"I expect she's gone down to see the boys on the *Seaworthy*," said Dolly.

Blackly, Darktower growled, "What the hell is wrong with her? She's completely unpredictable. I don't like the idea of her being around that Ratoff again."

"Uncle Dick," Dolly reproved him, "don't worry! Katharine has a good time with Steve and she's taken a *great* liking to my fiancé, Marco Fortuna."

"Fiancé!" Darktower snorted disgustedly. "Fairy Sicilian!"

Erik stared at her. Dolly's head jerked in confirmation. "Yes, it's true. Little Dolly is about to make her move."

"*When* are you getting married?" he asked distantly.

"Sometime this summer. Not here," she said, "more

likely in *Geneve*." Self-consciously, Dolly applied the French pronunciation.

"Congratulations."

"Thank you, darling." He knew she was chortling inside over his discomfort.

"Well," Darktower said, "shall we walk down the hall? I won't be long, girls."

Darktower had put on weight, at least in rear-view; the girth was larger, the back of his neck stouter too. Less vigorously, but with his usual determination he stepped into the glassed sun room in the rear of the house. Outside, in the far distance, the water glinted as it caught bits of starlight from between fast-moving clouds.

"It's going to be stormy tomorrow," Darktower muttered. "It'll screw up Dolly's party plans."

"The sailing part for certain."

"Yes." Darktower faced Erik squarely, at eye level. "Well," he said, "have you decided? No point in denying it's over. When will you be leaving us?"

Erik drew a deliberate breath, knotting his tingling fingers behind his back. "Separation is not of my choosing," he said steadily, punctuating each word with a pause.

"Doesn't matter whose choosing it is. Kate hasn't been herself for the last four or five months—or years. We don't want to prolong that, do we?"

"I do not understand her condition," Erik said very carefully. "I have told you so before now."

"Understand it or not," Darktower snapped, "it doesn't matter, does it? Best to start divorce proceedings. It doesn't have to be difficult, not if we agree on everything ahead of time."

"Divorce is not my idea," Erik declared. "It is not good for the child."

"Of course it's not good for the child," Darktower said irately, "but once in a while drastic medicine is required . . . in this case, surgery. Kate can bring the action—we'll go with incompatibility. No problem."

"No problem?" Erik echoed. "What about the child?"

"What about her?"

"I will require custody," Erik said softly.

"Out of the question!"

"*Not* out of the question," Erik retorted as roughly as he could. "There is no possibility I would allow your daughter to have custody of that child."

Darktower's voice was dead. "You have no option."

"*You* are wrong, sir," Erik said severely. "It is clear to me, and would be to others, that Kate is too neurotic—too unpredictable, as you just said—to be a good mother. This very night she left without a word; what if the child had been *alone* in the house? Fortunately, Mrs. Himmelmann is there." He caught Darktower's wince of disgust. "By accident," Erik went on, aggrievedly, "I discover she has gone to visit her ex-husband, a *well-known* pervert, whose reputation is so bad women rush their daughters out of the room when he appears. Am I to stand by as my daughter, *quite possibly*, is introduced into the company of Stefan Ratoff and Marco Fortuna?"

Erik basted the two names in venom. But Darktower was not greatly impressed. Voice sharp as steel, he said, "It's not likely either that a judge is going to grant custody to a man who is a notorious adulterer, whose infidelities are the *cause* of the breakdown of the marriage."

Erik could have used the iron in his spine as a sword on the older man. "Wrong! It was Kathy who cast me aside. She told me I was free to take my pleasure elsewhere while she, yes, pursued her own sick and dismal proclivities. . . ."

Darktower was first to lose control. "That's a goddamn lie!"

Erik did not budge, merely smiled. "I am very sorry you say that. It does not help matters. You notice I do not reciprocate."

"Reciprocate if you want to, you son-of-a-bitch," Darktower glowered. "You wouldn't dare say a thing like that in court."

Erik shook his head. "If it is true, yes. If necessary, yes."

"It is *not* true!"

Sorrowfully, Erik murmured, "Were that it is not true. Sir, I agree it is a terrible thing when a child loses daily contact with her mother, but more than that I would not want my daughter's spirit to be poisoned.''

"Poisoned?" Darktower thundered. "Are you insane? None of this is true. I know Kate!"

Again, Erik moved his head in polite but determined disagreement. "You will find, I strongly believe, that Katharine is an emotional hysteric—sexually confused. . . ." He stuck in the lance and left it there to dangle.

"Emotional hysteric? You're a goddamn fool, Moss," Darktower spat contemptuously. "No, the fact is you're a proper son-of-a-bitch." Darktower squinted at Erik, his eyes full of bitter tears. "You *are* a son-of-a-bitch," he repeated, "and I'm going to fix your wagon. You're not going to win this, I don't care what you do. Don't you know, you Germanic bastard, that that woman in there. . . ." He pointed, panting.

"Dolly Percy, yes."

"Christ Almighty, she's admitted sleeping with you. She's ready to say so on the witness stand. You don't have a leg to stand on, goddamn it!"

Calmly, Erik rebutted, "And Helen Ryan, if sworn, will testify to disgusting events on Park Avenue. . . ."

Darktower glared. "I'm not buying that, Moss. I know exactly what you're up to—you want money, the kind of money I gave Ratoff to get him off our back. But I don't have to do it for you—I don't care what dirt comes out."

"Indeed!" Erik scoffed haughtily. "I must say, sir, I do not understand you—was Ratoff worse, did he shame you more, or make you more uncomfortable that you were so eager to settle two or three million on him?"

"Never mind! How much do *you* want? Give me a ballpark figure."

Erik joggled the lance a little. "I am not interested in the money, I assure you, sir. What concerns me is my daughter's well-being. If you insist there be a divorce, very well. I cannot fight that—but I *can* insist that my daughter's mental health be protected from a neurotic, unbalanced, sexual hysteric."

Darktower quivered. "If I had a gun, I'd blow out your goddamn brains, here and now."

Erik shrugged scornfully. "Why not have your detective do it, the *person* you have had following me?"

"That's right," Darktower exclaimed. "We've got the other one too, not only Dolly. Your love nest with that girl!"

Erik replied solemnly, "You exaggerate, sir. This girl you mention is merely a protege. I support her artistic endeavors—there is nothing *intimate* between us. If your detective suggests that, then he is lying."

Darktower cried, "Bullshit, Moss. Nobody would buy that either." He paused, something else occurring to him. "Maybe," he whispered confidentially, "maybe I will get him, or somebody, to kill you. For a couple of thousand I could have you snuffed out, like a germ."

Erik shrugged casually. "Now I am threatened with death? *Unless* I remove myself, cease to be an embarrassment to the wonderful House of Darktower I will be snuffed out? Is that it?" he demanded. "Think again, sir. It is not likely a death threat would impress me. I have been too close to death to be frightened of it."

Darktower sneered, his patrician nose pinched white. "Testify I threatened you, Moss! Nobody would believe you."

Erik chuckled. "I know how to protect myself. And, as you say in this godforsaken country, sir, *I am not kidding*."

Darktower was silent for several seconds. Finally, he hissed, "You're an evil man."

"Evil? What do you know of *evil*?"

"I can spot it, don't worry." Darktower retreated several steps. "Just tell me how much you want to go away."

"I have told you I *will* protect my own!"

He knew he had won. Darktower could not stand up to him. Perhaps . . . if he'd been younger, but not now. Darktower's voice was no more than a sigh. "One million . . . cash . . . on the table. . . ."

"I beg your pardon?"

"One million, I said," Darktower whispered.

Erik shook his head, as if astounded that Darktower could be so vulgar. "You know, for the sake of argument, sir, if Kathy were to *die*, I'd receive more than that.

Perhaps, since you brought up the subject of sudden death, that would be the most convenient thing for all of us—if Kathy's so *unhappy* life came to a merciful conclusion," he murmured.

The words were so raw that Darktower groaned. "Two million."

"I think I will leave now. Excuse me."

As he started to move past Darktower, he was stopped by a stab of pain in his damaged leg. He turned to Darktower and muttered, "My limp, sir. I thought it best not to say so inside but your son tried to run me down tonight with my own Mercedes. Perhaps your plot is already in motion."

Darktower shook his head. "I don't believe that either."

"Believe it or not," Erik said scornfully. "I am tired of convincing you of the truth."

"Whoever it was," Darktower said softly, "it's a pity they didn't do a better job."

"Yes, you would feel that way. I will discover the facts, however, and then, if I think it proper, I will possibly alert the Port London police. Conrad *could* be charged with attempted murder."

"He'd get off—people don't get convicted for killing sick dogs," Darktower said viciously.

Thirty-Five

Poor Stefan, he lay so still, so exhausted beside her, already deeply asleep, yet restless, muttering and murmuring words she did not understand. It was twelve, more than twelve, years since they had slept together like this, his head nestled against her shoulder. He was more craggy now—the imperial nose lorded it over his emaciated face. The full-lipped, sensual mouth had turned down, but his chin, always a shade too weak, now jutted powerfully out of his skeletal features.

Katharine felt the flannel of his pajamas against her bare leg—he was so cold at night. But this night she would keep him warm. Why had he come out on this godforsaken boat? It was so damp and it would rain soon. As she drifted on the edge of disturbed sleep, Katharine was aware of the gathering storm. Wind shrieked in the superstructure of the *Seaworthy*; the ship swung at anchor, buffeted by cross waves, rolling erratically.

Oh, Stefan, how stupidly it had all turned out, all to no purpose. *If it's purpose you need, then best go with a religious order. But they wouldn't have us—to enter you must bring something with you and we have nothing to offer, neither true belief, nor hope. No hope because we've given up, not that we have anything much except life, a few heartbeats, to give up.*

Katharine moaned and turned to the side, tucking her arm around his waist, pulling him to her and remembering Conrad. . . . Why had she let that happen? She recognized now that it'd had something to do with Stefan, even then. . . .

It could not have been much later when she heard the faint sound of voices from the main cabin, low and steady, then louder, quarrelsome. The noise was only a bulkhead away but the *Seaworthy* was built so tightly there was little acoustical leakage.

Stefan did not budge when she removed her arm and slid out of bed. She opened the cabin door and stuck her head into the gangway. Now she could hear.

It was Erik. Erik was telling Marco that he'd come to take his wife ashore. She was *his* wife and he, Erik Moss, demanded that Marco rouse her, wherever she was—he *knew* Kathy was on the *Seaworthy*.

Marco wheezed mockingly. No, he told Erik, his wife Katharine was not aboard and had not been here earlier either. Marco was a very good liar.

Erik objected curtly, "I am told Kah–ty came down to the boat to visit you and Stefan Ratoff."

"And I am telling you, Mr. Moss, she is not here."

"I will have a look in the cabins."

"No—you will not have a look in the cabins," Marco decreed petulantly. "Who are you, my dear man, that you will just blithely, *comme ca*, if you please, inspect my cabins?"

"This is *not* your vessel."

"It is mine tonight, Mr. Moss," Marco declared, "by the laws of the sea. . . ." He tittered. "Or is it Mossberg?"

Erik's voice was terse. "What do you mean by that?"

Marco said prissily, "I am told certain researches have been done."

This oblique remark was followed by dead silence. Katharine trembled, and not from the chill on her bare body. She could visualize Erik's face—God, he would be absolutely livid.

Erik's retort was hateful, threatening. "Fortuna," he rasped, "if ever a charlatan stepped foot in Port London, it is you. Fortuna—an invented name."

"Oh, yes?" Marco lisped again, just as maddeningly. "Let me tell you, Mossberg, that my Sicilian cousins would be very annoyed to hear you say so. Fortunately for you, I am a civilized man, Herr Erik *Ignoto*, Erik the Unknown. There is *no* Mossberg! What is your real name, Herr Von *Ignoto*?"

Erik's calm was deadly. "You accuse *me* of being an imposter, Fortuna? That is very funny."

Insidiously, Marco drawled, "What is known is that you were a waif of the war, Herr *Ignoto*. Your entire *curriculum vitae* is a fiction."

"Indeed?" She heard an intake of air, as he struggled to maintain his equilibrium. "And how, Fortuna, have you come to this conclusion?"

"It is a simple matter of detective work. One hires a tracker," Marco said, "and pursues the elusive quarry through the jungles and swamps of his cover-up."

"One hires a tracker?" Erik repeated curiously. "Would *you* have done that?"

"We were curious," Marco explained smoothly. "Stefan had heard various stories about this fabled Mossberg, right-hand to James Merriwether."

"And so you investigated me?"

"There was nothing to discover, however, except for one fact—that there *is* nothing to discover about you, . . . You are a man without a face, past. even a shadow, Mossberg," Marco declared.

Katharine was frozen. Marco—who was Marco? A hero to put Erik down, but, not being able to see him, she was quite unable to associate what he said, the way he said it, with the features, posture, expression of the Marco she had seen an hour or two before.

Erik evidently was bothered by the same question. "I am afraid I do not understand you, Fortuna. What is your game?"

"No game," Marco said carelessly. "Sit down. Have a drink with me. Will you take a whiskey?"

"Yes," Erik said slowly. "Why not? With a little soda, please."

She heard movement in the main cabin, the noise of bottle against glass, liquid.

"I drink to you, Mossberg," Marco said cheerfully.

"To you, Fortuna." Erik was still puzzled. "I do not understand why you would take the trouble to establish that I am a man who does not cast a shadow."

Marco's chair creaked as he sat down again. "And why not? I told you—Stef wanted to be amused. He was curious about you. And, as I say, we were intrigued by the Merriwether connection."

"Do you work for Merriwether?" Erik asked suddenly.

"Heaven forbid," Marco cried. "No, no. Why would you think so?"

"Merriwether has very long arms," Erik replied simply.

"But there was only the one thing," Marco pointed out, now sounding a little mystified himself. "The accident. . . ."

Erik didn't answer the question. Rather he said, "May I be assured that my wife is not on this vessel?"

Marco giggled, more like his usual self. "If she were, my dear sir, I can assure you I would not be sitting here talking with you. I would be doing my very best to seduce your wife and with luck would already have done so."

Erik's surprise was genuine. "You have a way with words, Fortuna."

"What I am saying is that you are in the wrong place if you are searching for an unfaithful wife."

"I did not say she was unfaithful. I said merely that I have come to get her ashore safely because I love her."

Oh, Katharine told herself, the goddamn liar. They were both liars, a match for each other. No, she would be ill-advised to go for a boat ride with Erik on a night like this.

"But I was told you are divorcing," Marco said.

"That is far from settled."

Katharine forced herself back into the cabin. Fear of him, frustration, anger, all combined like fingers clutching around her throat. She had to escape, otherwise she would charge into the main salon and confront him, scream and rage.

She put her slacks and sweater on and, carrying her shoes, stepped back into the narrow corridor. Katharine remembered a stairway or ladder up forward and in a moment she had climbed out on the rain-slick deck.

Free, yes, but now what would she do? Crouch here like a rat until he had left, or get away first? Careful to stay out of the light of the portholes, she edged along the skimpy walkway toward the stern of the *Seaworthy*. The dinghy was there, bobbing and scraping against the rowboat Erik had borrowed or appropriated.

The job was to get from the rolling deck of the *Seaworthy* into the unstable little dinghy. Once there, she could easily reach ashore and be home, locked in her room, long before him. She squatted on the stern apron of the sloop and pulled the small boat up close enough to get one foot down inside. Then, bravely, she heaved herself forward, intending at worst to fall into it. But the abrupt movement served only to spin the dinghy away and leave her suspended for a second in mid-air and then toss her into the cold water.

Frantically, Katharine grabbed for the side of the small boat. Choppy waves and wind were already dragging it away from the *Seaworthy*. Panting, she held tight; the water-soaked slacks made it impossible for her to heave herself up into the dinghy. She would not panic, but she was drifting. There were many yachts in the protected basin but not one was visible through the fog and mist. Even the bulky shape of the *Seaworthy* had quickly disappeared. Very faintly, shore lights glimmered and faded. How far out could she be? She would simply kick toward shore, using the dinghy as her life preserver. Holding the gunnel with one hand, Katharine pulled the slacks off and slung them up in the boat. Kicking was easier now, but it didn't appear she was making any headway. For all she knew, the little boat was dragging her around in circles in the wind. Then, frighteningly, the shore lights were gone.

Katharine knew what was going to happen. The tide would suck her into the narrow channel at the end of the breakwater and into open water. Surely the fishermen would spot her, still alive, but very weak, clinging to the dinghy and they'd haul her in making bold remarks about catching a bare-assed mermaid. But never mind—she'd be alive, that was the main thing. Katharine realized with a start, as a white-hot revelation, that she didn't want to die.

But how long must the ordeal go on? She was so cold,

gasping for air . . . getting tired. The best thing would be to tie the light rope off the front of the dinghy around her neck. That way, if she lost her grip or fell asleep or fainted, she wouldn't lose her life preserver. But what if she just went under? Well, then they'd find her easily, her body marked by the buoy of the dinghy and they'd take her dead body ashore to be mourned by hundreds, maybe thousands, and cremated. Why not? Dead by water and removed from the face of the earth by fire.

But Katharine was not ready to die, not yet, not so prematurely, having never known love. As if she weren't wet enough already, she began to cry, freely, bitterly, loudly, yelling her grief into the wind, as she fought to stay afloat. No one was around to hear her.

God, please, a few more years just to correct all the mistakes? Please, God, a little luck and the chance of some kind of redemption? If God took her right now, how would she atone? To make it good to Stefan . . . Conrad . . . Erik? She would even promise not to hate Erik if she could be saved.

Her voice made no impression on the wind. "Help . . . help . . . help!" Never in her life had she called for help and now, plainly, obviously, without shame, she was begging for help, as the waves splashed her face. How weird. . . . The dinghy twisted around again and the lights of Port London reappeared, but just as dim and faraway, maybe farther away. It was true—she was going to float out to sea and she was going to die. It was all over . . . and she was so tired.

Then, the miracle happened. Her heart leapt. A long shadow, the prow of a boat, cut between the shore and her weary eyes. Her dinghy bumped against it. She heard feet echo against the hull of the boat, a soft laugh.

Oh, God, she told herself in sudden fear, don't let it be Erik Moss!

A hand came down beside her in the water, then another. Grunting, the man—for it had to be a man—grabbed her under the arms and lifted her from the water into his boat. Not speaking, he threw a blanket over her bare legs, the soaking sweater. Katharine was shivering so hard she couldn't focus.

"Thank you," she mumbled, "Oh, thank you for saving my life. My name is Katharine Moss. *Who are you*?"

"Barnacle Bill the Sailor," he grunted.

She knew the voice.

Thirty-Six

They said that if the rain had not come down in such tropical torrents in the very early morning the wind would have spread the fire through the entire old town of Port London. It was bad enough as it was—the Joshua Smithers House where, evidently, the fire had started, was burned to the ground.

The destruction of the house would be a tragic loss to the Heritage Assembly but, fortunately, there hadn't yet been any heavy investment of funds and the ramshackle building had been stripped of furnishings in preparation for the beginning of restoration in the coming fall-winter slack season.

Erik heard about the fire at six A.M. It was Wadsworth on the phone, the curator of the assembly's modest museum, its house on Plymouth Avenue and the various properties under the assembly's jurisdiction.

It was not wonderful to be awakened from fitful sleep by the sound of a weeping man and Erik advised Wadsworth brusquely to control himself.

"Mr. Wadsworth, there is nothing you can do now. Such a thing is an act of God."

"No, no, Mr. Moss, not at all," Wadsworth wailed. "The fire department thinks it was deliberately set. There's a fire-bug loose in Port London."

"Oh . . . My God!" That was a different thing. Arson, the most terrible of crimes.

Bitterly, Wadsworth said, "Probably one of those goddamned derelicts passing through town on his way north for the summer. They should all be shot at the city limits!''

"No clues, Mr. Wadsworth?"

"No," Wadsworth cried. "Why would anybody want to burn down a beautiful old house?"

Erik answered the question with another question. "Mr. Wadsworth, why do whole armies destroy antiquities with such delight? The library in Alexandria, Mr. Wadsworth— priceless scrolls used indiscriminately as fuel to heat the water in barbarian baths. The Smithers House became the fire to warm the hands of some besotten wino!''

"Yes, yes, I hear what you're saying, Mr. Moss. Things never change. The price of liberty is eternal vigilance.''

"Yes," Erik said mildly, "at least that. Are you at the scene, Mr. Wadsworth? I'll join you in a few moments.''

Erik got out of bed and limped into the bathroom. His leg had stiffened during the night, in sleep and from the damp exposure in the middle of the night rowing around the harbor. Nowhere had there been a trace of Kathy—not on the *Seaworthy*, though he had not persisted in his demand for a search, not in town, not at Maples.

Quickly, Erik brushed his teeth and hair. He could put off shaving. He dressed in a white turtleneck sweater and tan corduroy slacks, pulled on his heavy-weather boots and found a fishing hat in the closet. His raincoat was downstairs.

In the murky morning light, Erik paced the quiet hallway to Kathy's room, opened the door a crack and looked inside. Empty! He stared morosely at her neat bed.

Halfway down the stairs he remembered he still didn't have a car; he'd spent half the night walking. No wonder his leg bothered him. Angrily, he took a yellow rain-slicker from the closet by the front door and stepped outside. The weather was still foul, the early morning gray; drabness hung in the soaked trees and still the rain made rustling noises in the gravel of the driveway.

But—the Mercedes was there. Erik circled it, stopping to inspect the left front fender. There wasn't a bump or scratch upon it, no smudge even of the paint job. He was puzzled, but not relieved. Whether Conrad or not, somebody had tried to run him down. Obviously, this was not the only Mercedes convertible in Port London. Why, yes, Dolly had a similar car parked alongside the other three sports-cars in her garage. Perhaps the driver had been the ghost of sports-car enthusiast Harrison Percy, come back to take his revenge too on Erik Moss, despoiler of his widow.

Was it wrong of him to think badly of Conrad? Could Conrad have turned on him so abruptly? Why, just hours before they'd been having such a friendly chat on the way from New York.

Windshield wipers stroked steadily as Erik drove into Port London. He whistled softly, actually not very disturbed at all this morning by the unsettled condition of his world. He had done rather well with Richard Darktower the night before. The cards were on the table now: Erik would fight, he would not easily give up his daughter whom he adored above all else. At the same time, he openly acknowledged that much damage could be done her by an open legal battle. Above all, he would proclaim, Margaret must be able to see that her parents respected each other, even after love was lost. Wasn't it obvious, therefore, that he was prepared to compromise? Margaret would come to visit him in Europe, of course, at the Moss chalet in Austria or the lush farm in Tuscany or, later possibly, once his finances were blooming again, somewhere chic along the Mediterranean.

Erik smiled, contemplating the future. Even his little discussion with Marco Fortuna had gone well despite his dark and terrible mood when he'd rowed out to the *Seaworthy*. He had been prepared to do murder, but Fortuna was really not such a filthy chap; Erik had actually rather enjoyed talking to the wanton Sicilian. Fortuna's mother had been an American, of course, but judging by Marco's personality, hers must have been a negligible force when sperm impacted ovum at the moment of the conception of her son.

How aptly Marco was named, Erik mused, and how unjust Fate had proved herself again to be. Why couldn't *his* mother have been an American instead of the besotted mate of one of Hitler's own? He would never have begrudged her pampered profligacy—better that than the knowledge he bore of his mother.

He thereupon cursed her and the memory of her in gutter German. From her, he had sprung and he might as well have been stillborn. In fact, Erik sometimes wished, as at such moments as these, that he had been born dead.

The strength of the hate, the genetic guilt, the regret, forced him to the side of the road. Suddenly, he hadn't the will to drive the Mercedes. He put his forehead on his hands on the steering wheel. God, *verdamnt*, over the years he had trained himself to put aside these feelings; or, when they pounced, to dodge and push them away. Now and then, however, despite his resolve, the despair flooded him. What had set it off this time? Fire! Yes! Fire devoured everything, bodies, buildings, history, tradition. There was not much left in the world now to be destroyed, if that could be any comfort. One or two more wars and nothing would remain except debris, the shells of buildings and the shells of people. Yes, in time, Master Satan would take care of everything.

Erik shook his head and rolled down the side window of the Mercedes. Cold air swept in and cleared his head. Slowly, he was able to pull himself back, to convince himself that he had better reason to be elated than to feel suicidal. After all, what had Fortuna confessed? That they had tracked Erik Moss through the years and found nothing—nothing beyond the fact he was a man without a history, a man without a past. What a beautiful and appropriate way to describe him.

What was it the Americans said? *Have a good day!*

Nonetheless, he could not prevent his heart from dipping sickeningly when he saw what was left of the Smithers House, namely the chimney, a stack of bricks teetering in the storm, and a smouldering mess of rubbish, a burning garbage dump. This time, pulling the car over, he could focus on a devastation different from his own.

The fire engine was parked in the middle of the road and raincoated men were cranking hoses back on their drums. Wadsworth was standing, stooped, at the edge of the devastation, his hands behind his back, bare-headed, talking to a tall man in a fireman's helmet.

Erik could see what had happened. In the heat, the old wood had simply disintegrated like brittle bones. It must have been all over in a matter of minutes. Fortunately, as people would say, it *had* been raining hard; fortunate too that the Smithers heirloom had been well separated from the frame houses on the other side of the street.

"Chief," Wadsworth said, "this is Erik Moss. He was going to be in charge of restoring the old place."

"It seems that job is beyond our reach now, gentlemen," Erik said.

"Yep," the chief agreed, "no doubting she's a goner, is there?"

"It was quick, wasn't it?"

"Very quick, merciful," the chief said. "There was never any hope, even though we got here fast. There's never any hope for these old places. They're dry inside and they've got a couple of hundred years worth of wax and old polish on 'em. Burn like gun powder."

Erik had never thought of it in just that way. "Patina is very combustible, gentlemen."

Wadsworth stared at him, blinking tearfully and nodding.

The chief interrupted the sadness. "Is there anything in particular we should be watching for when we start sifting through the mess?"

"Such as what?" Wadsworth asked.

"Metal objects, like pewter, old coins, tools, silverware, that kind of thing."

Wadsworth shook his head. "I think not. We stripped it of everything."

"Well, we'll go over the remains with a fine-tooth comb after it stops raining."

Erik nodded soberly. "It had to be arson, didn't it, unless it was struck by lightning—the gas was turned off. The electricity was disconnected."

"I just can't understand why anybody would want to burn the place down," Wadsworth mourned.

"Arsonists," chief muttered. "Hanging's too good for them."

They stood humbly for a few minutes more, gazing at the ashes, splintered glass, shards of clapboard half-burned. It was too depressing. Erik looked past the house, toward the water, which rolled on, undeterred.

"Mr. Wadsworth," he said, "I suggest we go down to the Claw and have some coffee. There's nothing more we can do here. Is there, chief?"

"Nope, nothing left now but the autopsy."

Thirty-Seven

Katharine awoke to the comforting rattle of rain, the briny smell of sea and aroma of coffee. She was wrapped in blankets on a bunk in the cabin of the Chris-Craft, the rough wool warming to her skin.

She turned her head, then sat up to see over the steps. He was sitting, hunched over, in the stern of the boat; beyond him she could see the tip of a fishing pole dipping and lifting with the movement of the waves. The voluminous, crackling folds of a yellow sou'wester covered him, the back of his head surmounted by a black knit sailor's cap. Francotti was sitting so still he might have been asleep. It was dawn.

"It's only me from over the sea, Barnacle Bill the Sailor." His singing voice was not marvelous.

She laughed. "I'm awake, Francotti."

"I know. Have some coffee. I found an old shirt, old pants, a sweater, all too big for you. But your stuff won't be dry in a month."

"Are they biting?"

"They will."

"How do you know?"

"Rain will usually bring them up," he muttered.

His back was broader than she remembered. He was bigger all over than she remembered.

"I forgot to ask you what you call this boat," Katharine asked, since he seemed determined not to talk.

"I call it *Windward*. Appropriate since it doesn't have any sails."

"It's big," she said.

"No, it's just an oversized speedboat. Goes like hell. I'll show you the engines later, if you want to see them."

"I'd love to," Katharine said.

Her tone was so quizzical, Francotti turned finally and stared at her. She was just in the act of pulling on a pair of patched white cotton pants.

"Sorry."

"That's perfectly all right," Katharine said. "A woman can't expect to be dragged out of the ocean with no clothes on and then blush. Francotti," she asked directly. "Did you sleep with me?"

"Can't you remember?" he asked calmly. "I slept *beside* you, yes, so you wouldn't fall overboard again, not *with* you."

"Shucks!"

"Shucks, hell. You think I take advantage of half-drowned women?"

Katharine lifted the sweater and dropped it over her head. "How do I look?"

"Not bad, Katharine Margaret."

Bare-footed, she climbed the short flight of stairs and stood under the protective jutting of cockpit. "How's the weather?"

"Raining. Stay inside."

"I'll have to borrow these clothes."

"Didn't I say you could borrow them?" he said sharply. "I said so last night."

"You said a lot of things last night," Katharine reminded him, "and not all of them so nice, Francotti, considering that I'm in love with you."

"Did I read you out?" He smiled. "Well, what the hell do you mean by trying to row yourself ashore on a night like that? It's just so typical of you—goddamn stubborn, foolish, spoiled. . . ."

"Don't start again," she said. "You were out of my life. And then you came back. You can't keep doing that to me. Otherwise, you shouldn't have rescued me. You should have just let me keep going."

"Yeah," he muttered, "that's right."

"Well?"

"Well, what? Are you going to get me some coffee, or not?"

The galley was forward of the windowed cabin. As ordered, Kathy put coffee in two cups. "Do you want cream and sugar, master?" she called.

"There's a bottle of rum there. Put a jigger of rum in. No sugar. No cream."

"Yes, master." She carried him the steaming cup, then moved a chair to be behind him, out of the rain.

"You better put a blanket around yourself, Katharine," Francotti said, concentrating on his fishing pole. "Some weather for the beginning of June, ain't it?"

"I love it," she said waywardly. "Is it all right if I sit here like this? It doesn't scare off the fish, does it?"

"Not if you talk sensibly. Fish are very rational. They hate inconsequential chatter."

"In that case," Katharine muttered, "I'll try to be consequential." She continued softly, returning to the subject of main concern. "You saved my life, Francotti. You're responsible for me now. What are you going to do with me?"

"I dunno," he said. "Should I set you up in business? Send you to college?" Idly, he flicked his pole, dragged line in, then let it out again. "Thought I had a bite there."

"God," she groaned disgustedly, "anything to avoid a direct question—I asked what you're going to do with me."

"Jesus, didn't I say I'd send you to college?" He grinned cagily. "What the hell more do you want?"

"Could you find it in yourself to be nice to me?"

He nodded thoughtfully. "I do like you, Katharine Margaret, I've got to admit it. But sometimes, all that bullshit. . . . I'm just afraid we don't operate in the same league."

"Goddamn it!" she exclaimed, pulling herself forward, "if you look at me now, like this, can you believe the only thing I'm interested in is lunch at *Le Cirque*, going to parties and the hairdresser? I'm not really like that at all," she told him angrily. "Why do you keep insulting me?

There *is* such a thing as a male chauvinist pig, isn't there? What do I have to do to prove I'd rather be here, *like this*, any day of the week?''

''Holy Christ,'' he mumbled, holding up his hand, soothing the air. ''Easy, easy, Katharine Margaret, don't get so excited.''

But she went on irately, ''I didn't blame you for getting mad when Erik showed up, especially when he caused that accident. But, good Lord, Francotti, I didn't send him! How long does it take you to cool off?''

''Too long,'' he said gruffly. ''You're right. I am an ass in lots of ways.''

''No, I'm the ass, not you. You're just a very hard case,'' Katharine said. ''But I'm telling you one thing— you can't keep jumping in and out of my life. You can't keep *saving* my life like this. How *did* you know I was there in the water?''

He laughed, slightly embarrassed. ''I saw you going out to the *Seaworthy* in the dinghy last night.''

She was shocked. ''You were watching for me? You didn't know I'd be going there.''

''I was watching the boat. I knew Mrs. Percy rented it for the weekend. I was layin' out here, just watchin'. I thought you might show up. I was going to come over, to say hello.''

''*Say hello?*''

''Yeah.'' He nodded carelessly. ''Then I thought better of it. Forgot about it,'' he declared. ''Next thing I hear: Help . . . Help . . . Help!'' He mimicked her screams.

''*You lie,*'' she said happily. ''You were waiting for me all the time.''

''Nope. I just wondered why you were going to see those two oddballs.''

''I thought you were sailing off on a big cruise.''

''In this weather? No way. I'm not as crazy as you are.''

Katharine nodded. ''That could be. One of the oddballs over there, you know,'' she said, ''is my first husband. You met him. Stefan Ratoff.''

''Yes, I know.'' He turned back to his fishing rod.

"Stefan is not a bad man," she said. "He's a better man than Erik."

"Well, at least he didn't come over here with a pocketful of money for me."

"Please," she said, "will you listen to me? You do want to know the truth, don't you? You want me to be honest with you, don't you?"

Francotti glanced at her, nodding. "The *whole* truth?"

"You want me to grow up, don't you? Isn't that one of your complaints?"

"Yeah, I guess," he agreed warily.

"Stefan is very sick," Katharine said quietly. "I don't think he's going to live very long. He's alone."

"No," Francotti said darkly, "he's got that fat little fag."

"Marco isn't a fag," she said patiently, "and people say I never cared, that it's all my fault, everything that happened to Stefan. I did care. I do. Now, I have to go to Europe with him. He's frightened. I have to be with him."

Francotti shrugged. "Well, that's easy. Go!"

Tears started up in her eyes. Couldn't he understand this? If he couldn't understand just this much, then was there any hope?

"He's dying, Francotti! He needs me. I don't love him anymore. You're the one I love. And, goddamn it! You won't listen. You won't even try to hear me."

He didn't look at her. His voice was enough. "No— you're wrong, Katharine Margaret. I understand exactly what you're saying. I think you *should* go with him. But don't go just because you want to make yourself feel good."

"No, no," she said hastily, "feeling good would be to stay here. It's something I *have* to do. I don't know why."

"If you don't, I do," he said positively. "So, go! Do it!"

"I'll be back," she exclaimed softly.

"You will be back! Yes."

"And?"

"And what?" he demanded. "I'm here. I live here, in New York and here."

"Are you going to Pearl Harbor again?"

He shrugged. "How do I know, Katharine? If duty calls. . . ."

"I'm saying. . . ."

"Sweetheart," he butted in sardonically, "you're saying—will you wait for me?"

She bobbed her head tearfully. "Yes . . . you bastard!" she murmured. "Can I ask you a very direct question?"

"Depends what it is," he said suspiciously.

"I told you I love you," Katharine said. "Now here's the question: Do you love me . . . at all?"

"Jesus, I knew you were going to ask me that! Yes."

"Yes?" She stared at him. "What does that mean?"

"What does *yes* mean?" he said sarcastically. "Don't you know what *yes* means? It's the opposite of *no*, for Christ's sake."

"Do you mean it?"

"*Or* am I just trying to shut you up? If I didn't mean it, you can be goddamn sure I wouldn't say it." He yanked at the fishing line.

Warmth spread through her. Katharine cradled her coffee cup in her hands, tasting the bite of the bean, relishing it, loving the misty early morning, adoring the gray and threatening skies.

"We're going to be happy, Francotti."

"If we're not, it won't be my fault."

She watched him, her eyes soaking him in. She wondered what he was thinking now, staring off the stern of the boat at the spot where fishing line met water.

"I'm not going to say anything else right now," she said gently. "I'm going to let you fish. Do you want some more coffee? Is there anything I can get for you?"

He looked at her, his mouth pursed skeptically. "Maybe a little coffee, a drop more rum. Thank you."

Katharine went back to the galley. God, she loved it; it was so neat, so efficiently designed. What a lovely little garbage can. She was bordering on hysteria, certainly fully submerged in euphoria.

She carried the cup to him, placing it reverently in his free hand.

"Now I'll just sit here," she whispered. "How long are you going to *fish*, Francotti?"

"Till I catch something."

"Then could we go to bed? I'd like to. . . ."

He held up his hand. "Hey! Quiet!" He pulled on the pole. "I got something."

Thirty-Eight

It was still only seven-thirty in the morning when Wadsworth took himself home to his wife and children, and Erik decided he'd might as well have breakfast. There was no particular reason for him to rush back to Maples—if Kathy had come home, he told himself, she'd have gone straight to bed. Not that he wanted to talk to her anyway. It was over, damnation, no doubt of that, and only a question now of how much Darktower would offer to get rid of him.

He ordered a huge breakfast. This weather did give one an appetite and nothing, absolutely nothing, ever disturbed Erik's appetite. After ordering, he waited quietly over fresh coffee and another cigarette, gazing through the oceanside window of the Claw at the misty harbor. Vaguely, he could make out the tall masts of the sailing boats anchored in the tidal waters.

The stench of the burned-out Smithers House was still in his nose. Erik wondered why *he* should be so affected by the destruction of an old tangle of boards and bricks known so affectionately as a colonial era treasure. Cherished things had been burned before. Most things dear to him had been obliterated—in fact, his training had been to view such inevitable loss with calm indifference.

Again, he remembered what Marco Fortuna, in a flash of intuition, had said. *Erik Moss was a man who did not cast a shadow!* When he died, his remains would instantly disintegrate and blow away in the wind.

He would leave no trace, no mark upon the world—save

for Margaret. Strange it was that he should have fathered a child at all. Erik stared at the surrealistic harbor scene. He shivered, feeling so alien to the Port London trappings— the boats, the houses, the cars, the people. He didn't belong here. But then, he didn't really belong anywhere.

Perhaps, he thought, it would be better for the child if he were to disappear into thin air, like dust. It would bother her for a while but she would get over it; and, in due course, Richard Darktower and his daughter would invent a story impressive and believable enough to satisfy all the curious.

Erik had no great regard, or love, for himself or anybody else. People existed a few years, arranged their lives in chapters: beginning, middle and end. The truth was that he did not give a *damn* about the Smithers House. He cared *nothing* about old wood or history. All the churches and museums and libraries in the world could be blown sky-high and Erik Moss would in fact welcome the explosion. And, if present at the time, he would dance happily through the vaporization of the human race. Let the whole world go—*good-bye*.

But first, he thought sardonically, he would read today's *New York Times*. Outside, in the sundries shop, he bought the *Times* and the local paper. The waitress was just bringing his food when Erik returned. He laid into the breakfast, wolfing the eggs, sausage, toast; quickly finished, he poured more coffee, lit a cigarette and looked at the harbor. There was no improvement in the weather. If anything, the fog seemed heavier than before, the rain squalls continued to beat the docks.

Dolly, Erik thought, would be going crazy. Her party, she would complain, was completely fucked. She'd have to replan it, maybe even cancel it. There was no way anybody was going to pitch a big catering tent on her back lawn in weather like this. Tennis, croquet and swimming were out of the question and no one but a raving maniac would dream of going sailing. The question was how he, a person most definitely *personna non grata* in two house-holds, his own and the Percy establishment, was going to spend such a rotten day.

Dolly, Dolly, he muttered to himself, how she had turned against him. And he had always admired her so much; of all the women, he loved Dolly best. But, in the end, she'd stayed true to her old alliance with the Darktowers. Could she be *serious* about Fortuna? Was Fortuna preferable to Erik in *any* way?

There must be a way of recapturing Dolly, for, soon, he would be free. He had shocked Darktower into surrender. He could be exclusively Dolly's. After all, it was what she had always wanted. Damn Darktower! He decided he would go to Dolly that morning, offer his organizational genius, reorganize her party. He could afford to promise her the moon now. Yes, yes, this strategy pleased him. It was the *intelligent* course. Lilly would have to be dismissed. She was too young and demanding. She was blatantly ambitious for her art, while Dolly's ambition lay in one direction only.

But when he thought of Lilly, he grew breathless. She was remarkably talented for one so young, so imaginative. Yes, he should have stayed in New York. No—Lilly had not minded his going away. It gave her a chance to work, she said; she couldn't *forever* be on her back in bed.

Erik's eyes narrowed. How did he know that as soon as he was clear of the city Lilly hadn't returned to her old crowd, wild and wicked youth, terrorist friends?

Face it—he was middle-aged. His future was with Dolly. He and Dolly, yes, they would take the money and run, head for Europe, to hedonize on the Riviera, along the Nile, in the south of Spain, in the Alps . . . yes! He became quite agitated merely thinking how sweet it would be.

Methodically, he stubbed out his cigarette. It was after nine now. He folded the newspapers and pushed his chair back. It was time to go to Dolly's.

Then he saw Kathy. She was climbing out of a skiff, laughing breathlessly, her fine blonde hair blowing in the wind. A large man tossed her the rope and she held it as he clambered up beside her.

It was Francotti.

Erik's jaw muscles were rigid and he felt a jagged pain

in his stomach. He knew from the look of her, the soft angles of her face and the sickening way the man gazed down at her that Francotti had made love to the simple-minded fool.

Francotti put a large hand on each of her shoulders. He was saying something endearing no doubt, for Kathy listened raptly, like the trusting village idiot. Then Francotti stopped talking and they merely looked at each other for what seemed to Erik an eternity. The look said it all—they had an arrangement. Kathy hooked her hand in the crook of Francotti's elbow and together they walked down the dock between the Claw and the water and turned at the end of the building into the parking lot.

Abruptly, Erik sat down. Hands shaking, he lit another cigarette. He remembered, trembling, that day when he had thrust the money at Francotti. Francotti had broken his arm and with his good arm he had punched Erik, knocking him down. That was the day he might have removed Francotti. But he hadn't taken him seriously enough.

Thirty-Nine

"Well, my little darlings," Dolly's voice preceded her into the breakfast room. "Even the best-laid plans. . . ." She stopped. "Where's Clara, Richard?"

Darktower looked up from the *Times*. One of the big pains-in-the-neck about having Richard for a weekend was that he had to have, absolutely, the *New York Times* every day or he went berserk.

"She'll be down in a few moments. She didn't sleep very well."

"What's the problem? Nothing she ate here, I hope," Dolly joked. "Maybe she's pregnant, Dickie."

"Hardly." He turned red.

"Come on, Dickie, don't be such a prude," Dolly jollied him. "Although you're really not a prude, are you?"

"Young woman, your patter is too fast for me," Darktower huffed.

"I know." Dolly paused a second. "I know you don't approve of me. But never mind—I don't care." She stopped again. It was difficult to plot out a line of conversation with him. "You know," she said slowly, "the fact I slept with Erik once or twice . . . in moments of *great* weakness, or a little drunk . . . anyway, what I'm saying is, wasn't that more convenient than if he'd been making way with a complete unknown? I mean I *am* easier to find."

"Oh, my God." He seemed to blush the more deeply. "I don't know what to say. Dolly, you are a very wayward child."

"That's the way to judge me, darling—not bad, just very wayward."

He sighed and put his newspaper aside, realizing that he was not going to get any more reading done just now. "Dolly, I won't make light of the fact you committed adultery with my daughter 's husband. He may be a rotter and everything, but you did do it." He spoke deliberately, in his eyes small sympathy. "I'm grateful you're ready to admit it, but otherwise, young lady, I don't think it's something you should be proud of."

Dolly shrugged irritably. "All right, so I'm not proud of it."

"Kate seemed to think that there was some possibility of your marrying him, once he's . . . uh . . . free."

Dolly shook her head cynically. "Oh, no, Richard, not if you don't approve—I know you've got your finger in all my trusts. What devilish retribution would Harrison take on me?"

Darktower smiled slyly. "If you step out of line, I think the principal goes to the Boy Scouts of America or something like that."

"So you see?" she cried. "It's almost a relief to know I can only be promiscuous, not marriageable. I'll just have to take my solace with my Sicilian count."

"Another goddamn fortune hunter," Darktower sputtered.

"You don't approve?" she demanded, delightedly. "I'm so pleased you don't. But there's nothing in the trusts saying I can't screw around with a Sicilian, is there?"

"You two women! Why is it these bastards always home in on you and Kate?"

"Maybe because we've got so much loot," she sang cheerily. "But it's not necessary to marry 'em, you know. Kate should learn that. We poor heiresses don't necessarily have to get the short end of the stick—so to speak—Richard, darling."

His face tightened with distaste. "You're incorrigible . . . I've decided," he added wearily, "to pay off Moss. The prospect of a dirty divorce action is more than I can stand."

She whistled, impressed by the news. "I thought you were going to fight him to the death, Richard."

"Well," he grumped, "I've changed my mind. I'm too old to fight. I've got other, more pleasant things to occupy myself with."

"Yes, Dickie, yes," Dolly smiled. "Aren't you and Clara going off to Europe?"

He shrugged. "We may delay it. Clara is getting a physical next week. Indigestion isn't something to take along on a gourmet's tour of France."

Absently, for she was thinking of something quite different, Dolly remarked, "Speaking of gourmets, you're getting as chubby as old Joe Six-Pack."

He patted his stomach smugly. "Are you ever going to sit down, Dolly? You're hopping around the room like a bird."

"I'm worried about the weather—obviously. The party is really in trouble, isn't it?" She was going from window to window, glaring up at the sky from every compass degree. One moment, rain blurred the windows; next, the sky grew lighter as if the sun were going to break through. As swiftly, another cloud replaced the last and cast gloom across the earth. Finally, pouting, Dolly pulled out a Windsor chair at the long oak table and sat down, arranging her robe modestly between her knees. Did Darktower's eyes flick? Ah, men. . . .

"Richard, please to pour me *un peu cafe, cher*."

The languid tone of her voice was enough to restore flush to his cheeks. He poured the coffee with a steady hand—but he *was* very aware of her.

"How much are you going to give Erik?" Dolly asked, as if the question had popped up as afterthought.

"I'm going to try to get away with two million," he muttered bitterly.

"Two? Didn't you give Stefan two? What about inflation?" she asked flippantly.

He frowned. "He'll just have to make do."

"Well. . . ." She let the matter go by, turning back to the weather. There was no reason she should let Darktower know she was more than idly interested. "Obviously,"

Dolly said, turning toward the window, "we are not going to put a tent up out *there*. We are *not* having croquet or tennis. If anybody is crazy enough to want to go for a sail, they can be my guest. I'm not going out of the house."

"The party is off?" He sounded hopeful.

Dolly smiled sweetly. "No, no, we'll put the tables up in the garden room, in here and in the foyer if we have to. We'll have the party inside, where it's *dry*. Richard, we'll have room enough for eighty to a hundred, won't we?"

"I don't see why not. But you *could* just cancel the whole deal."

"No, no, never! I've just got to call everybody to come dressed for the indoors and to arrive a little bit later. What if we have drinks at one-thirty and lunch at two-thirty? Is that too late?"

"It's a little late for lunch, isn't it?"

She tapped her thumbnail against her teeth. "Drinks at twelve-thirty and lunch at one. How's that?"

"That's perfect," he said. "That's when lunch should be anyway."

"You're wonderful." His eyes turned inward. "I mean, you've helped me. Will Clara help too—with the phone calls? Then, if anybody comes early, you can entertain them with your party stories."

"Now, Dolly. . . ."

"You can help, can't you?"

"I'll help but I'm not telling party jokes, Dolly."

"You can compliment the women. You're always good at that."

"Dolly!"

She plastered a soft smile on him, as if in a fit of preoccupation, and pulled the zipper at the top of her robe, toward her navel. But she didn't show him anything fundamental, just a flash of brown breast. Then, coyly, gasping, she yanked the zipper back up, closing the robe all the way to her neck, for she'd heard Clara outside saying good morning to Mrs. Donovan. It would be *their* secret that Richard had almost received the full treatment.

Clara trundled into the breakfast room. Dolly warned herself she shouldn't think in terms of *trundle*—Clara might have trundled once but she didn't now. Even in the day she and Richard had been in Port London Clara seemed to have transferred five pounds to Richard. Dolly made a mental note to ask her about her diet, whether she took pills, whatever.

"Good morning, Clara, darling!" Dolly cried.

"Good morning, all," Clara said. "Sorry I'm late coming down."

Darktower bobbed to his feet and pulled out the chair facing Dolly. "Dolly and I have been talking about how to save her party."

"I was hoping," Dolly mentioned, "that you'd help me make a few of the necessary phone calls, Clara."

"Gladly, gladly," Clara said. She was exaggerating her vitality. She didn't look well. There was a bloated pastiness in her face and her eyes were uneasy, a trifle glassy, as if she had gas on her stomach.

"Did you tell Mrs. Donovan what you want?"

Clara belched lightly. "Just tea and toast."

"The phoning is nothing major," Dolly said, smiling again at Richard. "We're moving the party inside and we'd like people to come at twelve-thirty instead of eleven."

"Dolly," Clara murmured, "give me the names and numbers and I'll get right to it. I had a feeling it'd rain all this weekend."

"A premonition?" Dolly cried. "I wish I'd consulted you earlier. Clara, you should get into party planning."

Darktower chuckled fondly. "You could do the weather predictions on TV, ducks."

Dolly glanced at him. Ducks? He'd called her that the night before too. Ducks? It was probably, Dolly decided, a reference to Clara's breasts. Geese would be more like it.

Clara's eyes rose sternly. "Richard, you know I get premonitions and I have the cards too and the stars. Don't mock me—you know, there are psychics who have foretold the exact moment of their death."

Her pronouncement came down on the morning like a shroud—just what they needed with weather like this, Dolly thought. Darktower flushed impatiently.

"Clara, what the hell are you talking about?"

Dolly got up. "Whatever it is, I don't want to hear it. I'm going to get my address book." She hurried upstairs. God, how she hated superstitious talk. If disaster were about to strike, she'd definitely prefer not to have warning.

Dolly took the address book and a legal pad and pen to write with and headed downstairs again. As she reached the bottom of the steps, the front doorbell rang. She opened the door and before her, abjectly, stood an unshaven Erik Moss. "For Christ's sake!" She was surprised to see him.

"I have bad, bad news, my darling."

She wouldn't believe him for a second. Jeering, she said, "I know! Somebody put sand in your vaseline!"

"Do not joke, my darling!" he cried, his face hurt. "The Smithers House—it burned to the ground during the night."

"Did it?" she asked slowly, smiling again, fleetingly. "I *thought* I smelled burnt history. For God's sake, is that all? You look like a Russian missile is on the way."

His face drooped, his eyes dropped. "May I come inside? I'd like to talk to you."

"Well," she hesitated, "come in, if you can face Darktower again." Dolly put a hand on his forearm. "He's been at me all morning," she whispered. "He thinks I should feel guilty about trying to steal you from Kate."

He clapped his hand on hers. His eyes blazed. "And so you should. I can say it now. It's love for you that ruined my marriage."

Brusquely, Dolly pulled her hand away. "Cut it out! You don't give a goddamn for anybody but yourself." She chuckled, trying to sound highly amused. "Why, they're even talking about you keeping a tootsie in New York. Look, darling, don't make me laugh—I don't mind admitting we had a good frolic or two but don't lay it on love and don't tell me I busted up your pathetic little marriage. Are you coming inside or not?"

"Yes. I am not embarrassed to see Richard Darktower."

Dolly wondered for an instant whether she should tell him he'd won. No, let him find out for himself. She led him boldly into the breakfast room. Clara and Darktower were sitting where she'd left them. Darktower looked very haggard, Clara had on her face the self-satisfied expression of someone who had passed on the plague.

"Here's Erik," Dolly introduced him, "come to report that one of our old colonial houses has burned up."

"Yes," Erik said glumly, "and it looks like arson."

Darktower *hr-rumphed* disgustedly. "*That* all you've got to worry about, Moss?"

Dolly didn't give Erik a chance to answer. "I've got the address book and guest list, Clara. I'll just scribble down the names and addresses of about twenty people. Clara, the thing to tell them is that due to the weather we're moving inside and to delay their arrival a little bit, preferably to twelve-thirty or so."

Darktower got up. "I'm going to read the newspaper." He left the room.

Erik stood stiffly, motionlessly, at one of the windows, facing the sea, hands clasped behind his back and waited while Dolly listed names and phone numbers on a piece of yellow paper.

"There you are, Clara. You can use the phone in your bedroom, where it's comfy for you. Just punch the second line. I'll do mine on the first."

"It's a real pleasure, Dolly," Clara said, smiling dewily. She pushed herself out of her chair and followed Darktower upstairs. Only then did Dolly turn to Erik Moss.

"Well, darling, what is it we're talking about?"

He turned slowly. His voice trembled as he pleaded, "My darling, won't *you* be kind to me? Why is everyone so hateful? I'm not the world's greatest villain, you know."

She didn't mention the money. If he'd known what Darktower had said, he'd not have had a kind word for her. He wanted the money; he didn't care anything about people. No, let him think Darktower was going to shaft him mercilessly.

"Richard Darktower thinks you're the greatest villain and then some," she said flatly.

"I repeat—I am not frightened of that man. The fact remains and it will be seen to be the truth, I destroyed my career when I married Kathy on the promise of a situation with the Darktower company and a secure income of my own. Instead," he went on spitefully, "I find myself leashed to a neurotic and now, without warning, the neurotic decides she no longer needs a *nurse*. So I am dismissed? Oh, no," he exclaimed arrogantly, "Darktower should be prepared for more than surrender. I told him last night I am not prepared to deliver my daughter to the custody of a mad woman."

"She's not mad," Dolly said calmly. "Far from it. You can have some coffee—after you finish your speech, of course."

"Goddamn it," he cried, "you are mocking *me*."

"I wouldn't dare," she drawled. "You're too fierce."

"What of *us* then?" he demanded angrily. "Just a matter of here today, gone tomorrow? Ta-ta! Good-bye, Charley."

Dolly giggled. "I'll pour you some coffee. How funny you are, darling, when you're incensed. I'll always remember you lovingly. After all, you were one of my best *lovers*."

"A thing of the past," he growled.

Dolly pushed the cup toward him. "Who knows?" she asked blithely. "Nobody ever knows what's going to happen."

Hope softened the lines in his face. The deepset eyes warmed. "At least, we should give ourselves a chance. Believe it or not, I yearn for you."

"But, remember," she warned, "I'll testify against you."

Erik snapped his fingers. "I don't care. I know why you're doing it—just to be cute, perhaps get yourself a little publicity. Even with that, I love you madly."

"Oh, yes?" she said acidly. "I'm a publicity hound? Well, let's see if we can't drag in your little redhead then."

He shrugged. "I am only sponsoring her as an investment. She is a gifted artist."

"That's an old one," Dolly cried. "Little protege. . . ."

He smiled faintly, not bothering to expand his denial. "I went out to the *Seaworthy* last night. Kathy was not there."

"Where was she then?"

"I don't know."

Dolly permitted herself a little concern. Katharine, after all, was, by definition, her friend. "I've always expected Kitty to do something stupid sooner or later."

He nodded tragically. "She has not taken it so lightly as you might think, this business of me falling in love with you, my darling."

"Please, let me tell you one more time. She might not like our little *contretemps* but *that* did not wreck her marriage. That's something else, nothing to do with me."

"With what then?"

Dolly shook her head. "How do I know? How do I know what you do to her?" She eyed him inquisitively. "She hinted there was something she didn't dare talk about."

He scowled. "As usual, she is hallucinating."

"Not screwing in snowbanks, I hope," she chided him good-naturedly.

"Your idea, not mine."

She shrugged. "It seemed like the thing to do. It occurred to me at the time, that given your love of death. . . ."

Erik was genuinely shocked. "If there is anything I do not love it is death, or dead bodies."

Dolly nodded smugly, knowing she could shock him again. "I know. I heard later it was actually *Marco* who's the junior necrophiliac. It seems he loved his mother too much—and too long, over in jolly old Sicily."

Erik gasped. "And this is the man you talk of. . . ."

She said flippantly, "Well, darling, so long as I'm alive, he's quite . . . interesting. After I'm dead, should I care?"

Erik made a choking sound. "My darling, you are torturing me unmercifully."

Dolly laughed lightly at his pain. She was, in fact, doing her best to hurt him, but there was more. She watched his face. In his eyes there was a fevered glare. He put his large square hand on her wrist and she felt the beat of his blood through his thumb. He pushed the hands at her breast, caressing the lower lift of it with his knuckles.

She felt faint. She wanted him so much, yes, even now, especially now. Could she resist? *Should* she resist?

He slid forward, moving the chair so that his knee touched her leg. Even his kneecap was warm, insistent. His face approached her cheek and Dolly shifted her head so she could look into those eyes. He smelled of cigarettes and smoke and his beard was heavy, prickly. Dolly breathed deeply, trying to control herself. She should not succumb so easily.

"Darling," she muttered, "I don't know what to do about you. You're such a liar. Marco I *understand*—he's silly but he's manageable and I know he doesn't need money."

Erik's lips brushed her ear and he chuckled huskily. "Then Marco is completely unreliable, my darling," he whispered. "I *do* need your money. Therefore, I am supremely reliable."

"You never gave a goddamn for Kitty, did you?" she asked. "It's always been the money, hasn't it? And you don't love me either—that's what you're saying."

He wasn't put off by the indictment, only held her more closely than before, not caring, she realized, whether Mrs. Donovan burst into the room, as she had a habit of doing. Rather the reverse—perhaps he hoped she would come into the room and discover them. He was rolling the dice, throwing all his cards down.

"Love is a big emotion, my darling," he whispered. "I love *everyone*, all God's creatures, big and small."

"Beautiful or ugly. . . ."

"Does any of it matter so much?" he insisted. "Why can't I love you *and* money? I love you—ergo, I am *forbidden* to love money? I am not totally without means, you know. I am not as rich as Marco Fortuna with his oilwells but I am not penniless either."

Dolly protested weakly, wanting him, hating him. Perversely, knowing she was beaten, she muttered, "Tell me you've got enough for cab fares and I'm yours, darling."

"I do."

"You could love me a *little*, at least?"

"I will love you to distraction," he said solemnly, "in

such a way that even if it were not love at all, you would
bloom as though it were the greatest love since Romeo's
showered on Juliet. The love of the ship for its port, the
ring for its finger, the key for lock.''

"It'd be so embarrassing, darling. What will they all
say?'' she asked delightedly.

"What does it matter what anyone says?'' His voice
was more persuasive than before. "If it becomes too nasty,
we will simply leave. We need no one.''

"Only money.''

Erik nodded, frankly enough. "Money buys freedom.''
Urgently, he gazed into her eyes. "Now, you needn't go
to Europe.''

Dolly nodded pensively. "But I promised Kitty. I think I
should. The arrangements are being made.''

"Marco. . . .''

She winked at him. "Darling, it'll give us time for *both*
of us to straighten out our affairs, won't it?''

He shrugged. "All right. If you feel you must, what can
I say? Don't offend Kathy, by all means.''

"Don't be a baby, darling,'' Dolly said. "Whatever we
have will wait.''

He was so bitter. "Of course. Perhaps one day Kathy
will go out in her rowboat and not come back. Who cares?
You asked me where she was last night—she spent the
night with Francotti.''

"Good God! Did she now?'' Dolly smiled broadly. That
seemed to clinch it then. She pushed her breasts at his
hands so that he would caress her through her robe.
"Darling,'' she mumbled thickly, "I want to go somewhere
with you . . . right now. Is your car outside?''

"Yes. I. . . .''

"We better put your car in the garage.'' She grinned at
him warmly. "We don't want it getting . . . dry . . . do
we? Come on.''

"We could go for a little drive, my darling,'' he
murmured, not getting the point at all.

"No!'' Her voice was charged. Dolly did not believe
she could still feel so physically passionate about him. She
hated herself for it, knowing very well that Erik was every

bit as bad, untrustworthy, cruel, despicable, and even more of all that, as people said he was. "Never mind about love," Dolly muttered edgily. "Can't you see I'm dying for it?"

She made him stand up, then pulled him along after her, down the hall to the front door. She ran outside and jumped in the Mercedes, slamming the door after her.

More measured, Erik climbed in beside her and keyed the motor. "My darling, we'll drive around the block for propriety's sake and then I'll circle back and into the garage."

"I don't give a goddamn what you do," she cried. "Just get going."

She could not help herself. Even as he was in the driveway, she freed his business from his corduroy pants and ducked her head.

Richard Darktower was standing woefully at the window upstairs, bending his mind toward hate for the man he'd just seen downstairs, and contempt for himself that he was going to give this same man money, lots of money. He saw Dolly run down the steps and hurl herself into Moss's car, then somewhat surprised, realized Moss was taking her somewhere. Why must she, he demanded of himself angrily, persist with Moss who was his primary enemy?

Primary enemy? Perhaps not. A more threatening adversary than Moss had appeared—although this new adversary would surely become Darktower's friend if he, or she, would merely contract to treat Moss to the final kiss, the kiss of death.

What a nerve Clara had saying she'd had a premonition of her own death. Plain stupid, he told himself grumpily. He did not believe in these things; yet, she had frightened the bejesus out of him.

He tried not to listen as she made the inane and, in the circumstances, irrelevant phone calls telling Dolly's friends to come, please, at twelve-thirty instead of eleven on Sunday because, barring a minor miracle, the storm was going to continue through the weekend.

Never mind. According to Clara's extrasensory advisory,

she was to die quietly in her sleep not so long from now, never to wake again this side of eternity. Richard Darktower was not to grieve.

Oh, yes, he told himself angrily—and bullshit too! He didn't accept it for a moment. He refused to consider it, being too much a man of reality for such nonsense. Horoscopes and palmistry and the cards, that was all for secretaries, not for Wall Street bankers who lived and died by prime rate.

"Clara," he said loudly, "I want to get the hell out of here!"

But she didn't hear, so busy was she chattering, not like a woman who was going to be dead before the end of the year. He did not appreciate all these goings-on, or, come to think of it, staying in a house belonging to a woman who, for all he knew, was singlehandedly responsible for almost all of his daughter's unhappiness.

Now, to his renewed surprise, he saw the Mercedes coming back toward the house. But Moss didn't pull up to the front door. Rather, he throttled down the motor, and glided into the garage on the far side of the house. Ah, Darktower understood—it was a maneuver. Moss was going to have Dolly now in the back seat of one of her antique Rolls Royces.

Royce . . . Royce? Yes, he remembered—the girl from Chicago. Moss's city mistress. He closed his eyes for a second and leaned his head on the window frame. Dolly was two-faced, such a hypocrite. Darktower refocused his eyes on Clara. She had just put the phone down to consult Dolly's list for her next call.

"I said I want to leave here," Darktower barked. "Let's get packed. I want to get back to the farm."

She was stricken. "Dickie, not because of what I told you?"

"No, no, not that. I just want to go. This place depresses me. I don't want to hang around for her party."

"Well. . . ." Clara pointed at the list.

"If you're worried about that, Clara, forget it. Sweet little Dolly hasn't even started making her calls yet."

"She hasn't? How do you know that, Dickie?"

"I just know," he said grimly.

Clara looked hurt. "I understand," she said piteously, "you're ashamed of me. You're afraid that the former Mrs. Darktower will come to the party and laugh at me and you'll be embarrassed." She planted her elbows on the desk, put her head in her hands and began to weep.

"No, goddamn it!" Darktower stormed. "That's not it at all. I am *not* ashamed of you."

"I know you are, whatever you say," she sobbed.

"And I know I'm not," he said angrily. "Do I have to stay here just to prove it?"

Clara's dimpled cheeks came out of hiding. She smiled. "Thank you, Dickie. If you knew how much I wanted this, you'd be very proud of yourself. I'd never ask you for anything I didn't really want."

"Okay," he said wearily, "I understand, ducks."

He understood all right. He understood he'd just lost one of life's minor battles with the opposite sex; and that Clara wanted the seal of approval, the first step toward becoming essential to his household.

Forty

"Conny, it's me." God, she was so scared of him, she could scarcely talk.

"I hear you."

"Conrad, we didn't know what happened to you. When did you get back to New York? I called Saturday . . . Sunday. . . ."

"I left early Saturday morning," he said, his voice pitched dead. "I walked downtown and caught a bus and got out of there."

Katharine tried to think of what to say to him, *how* to say it. "You know we're leaving for Europe in a week? Will you come with me? Will you meet me today?"

"Will you come here?"

"No, no! Better we meet somewhere public. . . ."

She heard him catch his breath. Miserably, he murmured, "You feel bad about it, don't you? I knew you would. You tried to pass it off as nothing . . . meaningless! But you were wrong, weren't you?"

"Conny," she said fraily, "Stop it! It happened. I'm sorry."

"You're afraid it'll happen again, aren't you?" he exclaimed.

"Yes," she admitted. "But it won't. It taught me a lesson."

"Lesson?" he mocked, "what lesson? It didn't teach me anything I didn't know—women are stupid."

"Don't say that!"

"Well?" he demanded defiantly. "Tell me it's not true
. . . *I'm sorry*," he whispered. "Oh, shit."

"*Are* you going to come to Europe with me?"

"No, I can't. How could I? No, it wouldn't work . . .
not with you."

"Come and have lunch today and we'll talk about it,"
she said hopefully. "We'll go to *Le Cirque*."

"Don't you ever go anywhere else?" he asked dully.

"It'll be fun." She tried to sound gay, *toujours gai*.
"We'll look at the people. Your grandfather might even be
there with Miss Riding. You haven't met her yet."

"Who wants to see him?" Conrad demanded sullenly.
"The Robber Baron and his moll."

"Conny dear, I must see you before I leave."

His voice shifted again. Now it was very curt, distant.
"You won't see me again. Never again. Not unless you
come here. I. . . ."

He didn't finish the thought. She knew what he would
have said—that he needed her, needed comforting. No, it
could not happen again. Katharine thought desperately of
Francotti—would Francotti understand a thing like this?
But she could never tell him. It would be impossible to
explain how it had happened—as all else in her life,
everything out of desperation and defeat. Nothing mattered.
No, goddamn it, Katharine told herself angrily, *everything*
mattered.

"I won't come there," she said forcefully. "I can't. I
promised."

"Promised? *Who did you promise*?"

There—and now he was jealous. In his confusion, he
would hate any of her men even more.

"I promised myself," she said humbly.

He grunted disbelievingly. "Have you taken up with
that guy again? The guy with the engines?"

"No," she said.

"If I thought so, I'd go over there and tell him about
us."

"You'd embarrass me like that?"

"Yes," he shouted into the phone, "I would. You're
not to fool around anymore. I won't stand for it."

Her soul seemed to shrink inside her. She was perspiring. Her armpits were wet and her hand clammy on the phone.

"No," she pleaded, "please. How could I be taking up with him again if I'm going to Europe?"

A good argument, God, yes. It would hold him, hopefully, until he'd had time to recover his senses. He could not object to her going to Stefan, or could he?

"That's right. I forgot."

"Well, *remember* then! Will you come?"

"With the two of *you*? No!"

"Don't hate me so."

"Should I love you?" he said scornfully.

"You'll forget. You're young."

"Bullshit. I'm not young. I was *never* young!"

"Conny," she groaned.

"Oh . . . *Kate*." He chuckled intensely. "If you come here, I'll see you today. Otherwise . . . no way."

She began to cry. "You're so nasty to me."

He was calm again. "Yes, I am. I'll tell you what—I'll go to Europe if you and I can travel alone. We'll book suites in the hotels. No one will ever know."

"It's impossible," she groaned. "You'll drive me crazy if you go on like this!"

"Then go crazy," he cried jubilantly. "Like me."

She could not talk to him any longer. "I'll call you. I don't know you anymore."

All very well, Conrad told himself as he hung up the phone, to be cruel to *her*. But it did not solve his problem, problems. God, there were so many. What had happened in the barn, simple incest, was not his main concern.

In fact, Conrad was almost concussed with the terror he felt in himself, about himself—he had tried to kill Erik Moss. God, a few feet of difference in the trajectory of the car and he would have succeeded. Only by his own quick reactions, had Erik escaped death. Conrad recognized in himself the lunacy. If he had succeeded in hitting Erik squarely, he would have driven the Mercedes back and forth over him, crushing him into an unrecognizable pulp.

Conrad slumped on the couch, hands over his face. He'd been like this, practically comatose since getting back from Port London and discovered Lilly was gone. Kate said she'd called; he couldn't recall having heard the phone ring either. What the hell was he going to do? He wanted to kill everybody. It was just as well Kate wasn't coming down here—he could visualize murder-suicide.

Lilly? Moss had stolen his girlfriend, callously, in a seignorial gesture—what's mine is mine; what's yours is also mine. He had enticed Lilly away, to a studio where she could be fed and fucked. Lilly, the whore; she *was* a whore to allow herself to be bought like that. He, Conrad, could have given her everything; instead, she'd gone with Moss. And Conrad didn't know where she was. He should kill her too. No, he wouldn't. It shouldn't be that important. Lilly wasn't malicious. She didn't consciously do him harm. Moss had merely been the more fascinating.

The truth was, Conrad told himself despairingly, he did not have the necessary resolution or the depth of hate to kill. To hell with it. God, now he wished Kate had come down to the Village. He could have told her about it. She would understand and she would comfort him.

Conrad threw himself back on the couch. He lay there motionlessly until the phone rang again. Lilly . . . *or* Kate saying she would come after all?

"Hallo—it is Captain Roberto speaking."

Oh, shit! He could have howled the word. "What do *you* want?"

Roberto's fluty voice was guarded. "We require to use your apartment for temporary storage of some things."

"Require? Fuck you! What is it?"

"Only a box. It will be no trouble for you. I know, little man, that you are not one of us. This is for friendship, that's all."

Conrad shrugged to himself. "Okay . . . I don't care."

"We will be there tonight, after dark," Roberto said. "I and my lieutenants." He hesitated. "It's just as well that the redhead isn't there anymore."

"Is it really?"

"Yes," Roberto said slowly. "You do know where she's gone, don't you?"

"I don't know where she is. And I really don't give a shit." Nevertheless, Conrad's body snapped to attention.

"Good that you don't give a shit," Roberto drawled scornfully, "since she has moved into an apartment provided by that pig, Moss."

"I know that."

"Well? Your girlfriend stolen by your own brother-in-law? This doesn't make you mad? You don't require *revenge*?"

Conrad laughed lightly. "Revenge is for babies . . . since when are you a captain?"

Roberto said severely, "I was elected captain by my lieutenants. Evidently, comrade, you don't know where the apartment is."

"No, I don't. And I told you I don't give a shit."

Roberto laughed mockingly. "Perhaps one day we will tell you."

"Oh, yes? Well, you can tell me right now—or you can go hide your stuff somewhere else. I do have in mind a *certain* revenge."

"On that pig Moss?" Roberto demanded coldly. "He believes he is very tough. He is not tough enough to stop a dum-dum bullet. Carl and Dork have already had a certain revenge. They burned down his fucking *Smithers* House. Did you know?"

"*They* did that?"

"Yes," Roberto said proudly. "You gave us the information." He chortled maliciously. "We did the rest."

"I don't think that's so wonderful, burning down an old house," Conrad said slowly.

"Asshole! What does history matter? I thought we agreed on that much."

"Where is she?"

Roberto snarled at him. "Lilly is where she belongs, fucking that Moss, keeping him on the string. Knowing where she is, we can get at Moss whenever we decide the time is right. How much do you think *she'd* be worth to Moss?"

"Don't be stupid," Conrad snapped. "Moss doesn't have any money. My father's got all the money."

"True," Roberto muttered. "I wonder how much Daddy Darktower would come up with to save *your* life, little man."

Coldly, Conrad said, "Talk like that, *captain*, and don't bother to come over here. I'm not kidding."

Roberto thought it through, weighing what he wanted—against his secret. "When I come I will tell you where she is."

Lilly, of course, sweet Lilly, Erik learned with some relief, was way ahead of everybody. Ah, youth! So enterprising and energetic . . . so insensitive and ruthless.

When he arrived, she was sitting in the canvas director's chair several yards from her easel, swinging one sandaled foot and nonchalantly smoking a very long filtered cigarette, tipping ash on the littered floor. Erik had the feeling there was nothing he could tell her that would surprise her. She knew it all.

He explained that they had been the target of an investigation by a private detective hired by his father-in-law, Richard Darktower and it was possible, if everything went *wrong*, that her name would come up in a rather distasteful divorce action brought by his wife, Kathy, nee Darktower, and formerly Ratoff.

"Lovey," Lilly said breezily, "I could not care less."

In the soft light of early evening in which the studio basked, Lilly's freckles seemed to run together across her cheekbones and pert nose. Already, or was it his imagination, the orange-red of her hair was running toward a deeper titian shade. Yes, he told himself regretfully, Lilly was maturing fast. Pity he wouldn't be around to watch her in the full bloom of womanhood.

"It's very convenient you don't care," he said acidly. "But perhaps you don't realize how much publicity this case is likely to get. Your parents, even in Chicago, will be in for a bad shock, darling Lilly."

She shrugged. "Tough beans. It'll all help sell pictures, lovey." She stared at him smugly. "I'm going to have a show. I arranged it over the weekend."

"Oh, I thought arranging shows was supposed to be my department?"

She named a gallery on Fifty-Seventh Street, one of the most prestigious in the city. "It took a bit of doing, lovey," she confessed archly. "I had to lay for Hank Homeric."

Stupid, epic jealousy knotted his belly muscles.

"You know," she added, not sparing him, "the movie actor. He's a good friend of Snidford Fontainbleu, the man who owns the gallery. I guess, you'd probably say, he's a silent partner."

She might have been describing a symptom of madness. "I don't understand what you're saying, Lilly. You inveigled. . . ."

"Not inveigled," she disagreed impatiently. "I laid Homeric, knowing he was close to Fontainbleu."

"Lilly. . . ." Erik studied her as calmly as he could over his arced fingertips. "I was led to believe that you and I had a somewhat exclusive relationship."

"Yes. . . ." She shook her head doubtfully and her foot more rapidly. "I thought so too, lovey, but you know I'm not really so sure I want to go live in Europe. Everything I want is beginning to happen right here, in the Big Apple."

"I hate that expression, *Big Apple*, Lilly."

"See, you would, wouldn't you?" she demanded, too eagerly. "You're too proper for me, too much the classicist."

"Possibly," he agreed, "but isn't that beside the point? An agreement is an agreement, it seems to me."

He shouldn't talk her out of it, he reminded himself. She was presenting him a perfect extrication from the Lilly situation.

Lilly stretched her arm to find a place to put out her cigarette in the overflowing ashtray. Then, nimbly, she crossed to him and perched on his knee. "Lovey, are you really annoyed with me? We didn't sign anything, remember? I asked if you'd marry me and you hemm'ed and haw'ed. What's a girl to think? I wouldn't have done it with Hank if I'd figured we were engaged."

"See—you don't *think* you would have."

Defensively, as if she could be justified in blaming him for the whole episode, Lilly said, "You know how I get when I'm left alone. I think it's the red hair. Anyway, I was pretty circumspect, I think that's the word. I just laid. I didn't blow him or anything even though that's what he really wanted."

Erik put his hand to his forehead. "Oh, Lilly. . . ."

"I suppose you'll kick me out of here now?" she said resignedly. "I was hoping we could just continue on. I'd be just as good to you."

Erik laughed gently. "You'd be *good* to me. How wonderful." He ran the palm of his hand down the flatness of her back. The vertebrae stuck out distinctly, like beads.

She squirmed pleasurably. "I do love it here but I can see where you might want it back. I'm trying to be honest with you. I just can't go to Europe. I'm so attached to the Apple."

He nodded. "I know you are, Lilly. I admire you for knowing what you want. In a way, I'm sorry you didn't stick to Conrad. You'd have put some direction in his life."

"I know," she said philosophically, "but you see, I don't have time for Conrad. I'm in a big hurry."

"Yes," he sighed, smiling. "What makes Lilly run? One word of caution, my darling. Don't run too fast, or in the wrong direction. Now, for instance, with this actor."

"You don't think he's going to come across, *do you*?"

Erik moved his shoulders. "Perhaps he will. I can make sure—I'll call him and say I'm your 'legal advisor' and when is the show to be scheduled? That would serve to activate the promise."

Lilly's eyes sparkled. "You're a genius. Not a threat, or anything, just a reminder."

"Naturally."

Lilly twined her small-boned forearms around his neck and kissed him lingeringly on the mouth. "Should we have a little wine?"

"Let's, Lilly."

Very deliberately, she washed out two glasses in the kitchen alcove and poured the cheap red she bought as a matter of principle. "Here's to you. You're really a nice guy."

He grinned, wonderfully sardonic. "And to you, Lilly darling, the *artiste*—everything for the sake of art, body, mind and soul."

Tentatively, trying to decide if he was serious, she pushed back wisps of red hair. "Well, I *do* believe that, you know, lovey. For me, that's all that matters."

"That's what I've just been saying."

Erik put his hand on the round of her hip and pulled her closer, caressing her through the dirty blue jeans, running his hand to her knee, then up her thigh to the tightly fit crotch, skintight over the babyish mound of her femaleness. Lilly licked her lips appreciatively and sighed when he undid the top button of the jeans and worked the zipper down. Underneath, she was naked.

"You still like me then, lovey?" she whispered.

"Of a certainty."

He tugged the jeans down, no easy task, placing her on his knee again to get them off her feet. Erik stroked the tender and transparent flesh of her rump, the flat belly and the sweet meat of her inner thighs.

Eyes glittery with lust, Lilly mouthed the wine, rolled it on her tongue, salivated on her chin. She drew out his weapon. "The best," she muttered, fondling it to hardness and then applying her wine-stained lips to it.

"Shouldn't I, perhaps, undress?" Erik asked.

"Yes."

There was nothing of him she hadn't seen and experienced. As she watched, one hand like a patch over her pubic zone, he hung up his suit, shirt, tie and arranged his shoes and socks. It amused Lilly that he would take such care with something so unimportant as clothes.

"Now then, darling Lilly." Leering at him in a way she obviously thought would transform him into a fiend, she thrust, no threw, her body at him, stroking him with her skin, draping herself on him, as if daring him to do his worst, or best. Erik sat down again in her chair and beckoned for her to sit in his lap so he could hold her like a child. He kissed her neck and then the breasts, so frisky, again counted off her vertebrae to swelling rump and behind, with one finger pressed her anus.

Her body jerked. She moaned and tried to pull away but he was not going to let her go now. He had decided it was time Lilly had a big surprise. Although she struggled and protested, there was nothing she could do to prevent him working the weapon, stiff and unrelenting, into the forbidden zone. Her contortions, her resistance, helped the way.

"Christ!" she exclaimed. "Oh. . . ." From behind, he couldn't see her face but assumed she was crying. She should be.

"It is not entirely unpleasant, is it, my little darling?"

"Why are you doing this?" she whimpered.

Oh, no, she was not quite so full of herself now.

"It is a form of punishment," Erik grated.

But it was more than that. It was also a way of branding her his property. He hadn't time to relish the victory for with an angry thrust, he crested, spent himself and just as abruptly withdrew.

Lilly fell forward, her arms around her knees. "You did that to hurt, not to love."

"Correct."

"I feel busted in half," she moaned.

"The first time this was done to you?"

"Yes."

"How virginal," he murmured acridly.

"I don't think being sodomized is much fun," she said bitterly.

"So! You know the word."

"I'm not as simpleminded as you think. Our generation knows a lot," she said stoutly.

"Indeed? You know so much?"

She nodded, almost fearfully. It was the tone of his voice and his temper. He felt the blood rushing through him, his muscles tremble, as though she had triggered a nervous phenomenon.

"You little fool," he snarled, "you know so much, *do you*? You have seen it all, have you? Darling little Lilly, American Lilly, born and raised in the cocoon of Chicago in the state of Illinois. Damnation!"

"Well?" she demanded defiantly.

He felt like striking her. "Well? What shall I tell you,
little Miss Lilly? About life? I think I was eight years old
when I was first sodomized by one of the *Fuehrer's* own.
Yes, buggered, sweet Lilly. At the age of . . . ten, was it?
I saw men violating dead bodies."

"Jesus!" She pulled away from him. "I don't believe
that."

"Believe it!" he exclaimed. "Germany in nineteen hundred
and forty-five . . . I was in boarding school then, you
realize, my *alma mater*, so fine where we were taught to
rip off the head of our favorite puppy. My *alma mater*,
yes, perhaps I should send them money for a crematorium
. . . The Erik Moss Memorial Abattoir."

Lilly gasped. Her eyes stood out, revolted. "I knew, I
knew."

"Knew what?"

"I knew you had secrets, things that would come out."

"Jesus Christ!" he swore. "You are hilarious, my
darling."

Her nose twitched. "Awful things. Horrible things! I'm
sorry for that little boy."

"*Scheisse, nein*, you are not to feel sorry for that little
boy. That little boy is now none other than *me*. And I am
quite well, thank you."

Sorrowfully, she remembered. "You wanted me to go
back to that . . . place . . . *Europe* . . . with you?"

"And why not?" he demanded furiously. "Is there a
law that says I cannot adore youth and innocence just
because my own youth and innocence was violated? Then
. . . listen!" he thundered. "I come here and you have for
me a sordid little tale of *laying* for some ruined actor to
buy your way into an art show! *Jesu Christu*, little Lilly, is
there no one in the world who is not tainted?"

Her face turned white. She twisted her fragile arms,
covering her breasts, her crotch, wrapping them around
each other and her belly. She understood now why he had
done to her what he had.

"I'm sorry." Her voice could not have been sorted out
of whispers.

"Don't be sorry," Erik rasped. "You merely reinforce my basic faith—that everybody in the world is rotten. When children theoretically reach the age of reason at age seven, it is not reason they reach at all. It is not. It is then that they begin to *rot*, dearest little Lilly."

"That's so awful."

"A different view of the world, eh, little Lilly?"

She turned toward the wall, covering her face, exposing her once cheeky and undefeated little behind. "I can't stand to look at you anymore."

"Good," he cried. "Look at your pictures. The baby Rothko! Shit! Your favorite word, shit. You have no idea of what haunted Rothko, or me, for that matter."

"Thanks," she muttered. "I understand better now— dead bodies, cruelty, war."

"Yes . . . and fire, ashes." Stolidly, unmercifully, he reeled off his litany, the stuff of nightmares, driving her to the wall. She held her face against it, anguishing, in her hands.

"Why are you telling me these things?" she wailed.

"It is very simple. I've never told anyone else. No one, Lilly. Perhaps it is right that I pass it along, my remembrance of history. It is not good that such documentation be lost to the world. Torture should be recorded too."

"So that's what you're telling me? The history of torture?"

"Or torture in recent history," he said ironically. "Understand, I do not care. I am a dead man, Lilly."

"You look alive to me, lovey," she said faintly, bravely trying to swing away from the horror.

He took her up on it. "Your innocence has always provoked me, sweet little Lilly," he said wearily.

"Innocence is a provocation?" She did her best to sound playful, in her very innocence not realizing they were at the heart of the matter.

"Of course." His head was light. "In a manner of speaking, innocence itself is ugly. I discover, to my relief, that you are not an innocent after all."

Wickedly, Lilly nodded. "Yes, thanks to what you just did to me."

Erik smiled coolly. "Sarcasm doesn't suit you, darling. No, let me recapitulate. You think you have, perhaps, plumbed the lower depths, a la Gogol, but you do not comprehend that lower depths are a hundred times deeper . . . or that the *bottom* of the depths is a place called *Hell*."

"Oh, Christ." Now she turned, facing him, her back glued to the wall, her nakedness forgotten. Her hands fell to her side. "You're getting to me. You're scaring me!"

He seized her arm and placed her again on his knee. "I could scare you even more. If I were to strangle you now, just at the moment of death, or a few seconds before you lost consciousness, staring deeply into my eyes you would understand the lower depths."

Lilly shivered. "But you wouldn't do that?"

"Of course not. I'm not that anxious to prove my point."

She giggled in relief. "I was worried. Jesus, I don't want to end up as an experiment."

"Goddamn it," Erik complained, "how can you be so flippant just at the moment of truth?"

Lilly shrugged. "Well, I'm happy you're not going to strangle me."

"Damnation." He put his fingers on her bare throat, stroking to the tiny crimson nipples of her breasts, then back to her throat, the tips of his fingers registering the pulsing of her veins, the artery pulling heart's blood to her brain, where it all began. "I could do it," he said.

"Do it a little," she whispered. "Not hard, lovey. Just a little."

"You'd like me to snuff you out, wouldn't you?" he asked disbelievingly. "Just as I said; you yearn for the sensation."

"It's sexy," she agreed, nodding.

Erik closed his fingers on her windpipe. He could have snapped it with a twist of his wrist, dispatching her, transforming her in an instant into a limp, redheaded rag doll.

Dolly's eyes dilated. Huskily, she muttered, "If it

happened when you were making love . . . an incredible sensation.''

He jerked his hand away from her throat. ''Also a very terminal one. Why are you making me do these things?''

Lilly rubbed her throat, the red marks of his thumb and fingers distinct where he had gripped her. ''We do have to experience all sorts of things, don't we?'' In the end, Erik realized, she was totally unimpressed. She laid her hand on his flaccid weapon. ''I think I'll suck you off now.''

''Women!'' he cried. ''I am constantly amazed.''

Her laugh was spirited. ''I think our secret is that we're much more optimistic about life than men. You know, as much as you go on, I'm not really very shook-up. I think we're not as frightened of death as men are—after all, we're in at the birth and we know we're always going to be alive in a certain way, through the children we have.''

''Good God,'' Erik exclaimed. He was stunned by her reasoning. ''You *are* naive. . . .''

''No,'' He wanted to put his hands back on her throat. Complacently, she told him, ''I'm innocent . . . innocent little me.''

Forty-One

Nobody was going to argue that Dolly Percy wouldn't be very pleased and relieved when Katharine and Stefan Ratoff took off for the Riviera in one of Marco Fortuna's cars. The four of them had been together day and night now for nearly three weeks and, as soporific as the June weather was along the shore of Lake Geneva, the companionship was beginning to wear thin.

Dolly of course hated illness—it depressed her unspeakably. The sight of Stefan, every day more feeble, creeping around Marco's colossal home, annoyed her. Stefan could not get warm, even in the stifling humidity; he complained constantly, asking for sweaters, blankets, heat, heat, heat. Even worse, if that were possible, was Katharine's cloying, insipid behavior as she played nurse, medicant, female Doctor Schweitzer.

Everything was hanging fire and by itself that was enough to make her jittery. She hadn't the nerve to call Erik and she hadn't heard anything from him. All she did know for sure was that Darktower had apparently changed his mind—there would be no money. . . . Erik could roast or fry or freeze first.

Marco's jovial but coarse attempts to keep their little group up to a lighthearted pitch had a reverse effect. And, having failed to make Stefan smile or Dolly to flirt with him or Katharine just to relax a little, Marco himself would withdraw into silence.

Dolly could not arouse herself to even a shadow of passion—was it possible she could pine for Erik Moss so much? She knew all about him; yet she wanted him here, the two of them to be alone. Why had she come to Europe anyway? Hopefully, the answer was, so that Erik could get things settled with Darktower without further scandal. Marco was a bore. Dolly kept to her own room even though it was abundantly clear Katharine was sleeping in the same room as Stefan, close by in case he needed her.

Finally, on the evening before Katharine and Stefan were due to leave, Marco flew into a rage.

"Blast all of you! Why should I bear this misery? Tomorrow, I'm leaving too—I'm going to Marbella and have some fun."

Dolly said quickly, "I'll go with you."

He turned on her furiously. "Why should you? *You* are no fun, Dolly. You sit and sulk and Marco cannot lay a finger on you—even when it is my one ambition to love you morning, noon and night."

She made a face. "It must be the weather, Marco. I'm sorry," she murmured contritely. At least, Marbella might make a difference.

"Bah!" he yelled crudely. "It cannot be the salt that had shut your sweet slit. Lake Geneva is fresh water." Despite his effort to be nasty, he collapsed in laughter.

Dolly was newly miffed; Erik never talked in such a way. "Goddman it, must you always behave like a slut, Marco? You're not funny!"

He scowled again. "You see? You are no fun, Dolly." He wagged a finger at her. "I am telling you right now, if you come with me you will have to open the silken portals to *Marco Il Magnifico* or you will be out on your ass, high and dry, and Marco will take his comfort with a Flamenco dancer, no less."

Somewhat stimulated just by the thought of getting away from somnolent Geneva, Dolly screamed, "You hear? The man is shameless. How can you talk to me like that, Marco? Aren't I your betrothed?"

Marco tossed his hands wildly. "It is not betrothal I am interested in—it is crawling between your luxurious thighs, Dolly."

"Good God."

"But true, oh God," he exclaimed devoutly.

Stefan chuckled breathlessly. "We'll be gone tomorrow."

"Yes," Marco shouted, "in the Lamborghini. Go with God—*but go*! You two creatures are depressing us fun-loving kids."

"What he's trying to say, darling," Dolly said to Katharine wryly, "is it's just as well we're splitting up for a while. We're getting on each other's nerves."

Katharine nodded agreeably enough. "He's right. We're all on edge sitting around here."

Marco was astonished. "You do not like my beautiful *casa*?"

"We love it." Katharine smiled. "It's just that we're all going nuts listening to the cuckoo clocks go *coo-coo*."

Marco nodded sadly. "You will take good care of my best friend in the world?"

Give him credit, Dolly thought—he was a kinder person than she was.

Katharine and Stefan were ready to leave early in the morning. When the luggage was packed in the bright blue Lamborghini, they went to say good-bye to Marco. He was sitting disconsolately on the glassed terrace overlooking pool and shining lake. A moody smile played on his pudgy face.

"Marco," Stefan said, "we go, my dear."

Marco jumped to his feet, whatever he'd been thinking about forgotten. "You go," he muttered, "I see that. Be careful. When will you come back?"

"That we don't know," Stefan said quietly. "Kat is directing this expedition."

She said the same thing. "We don't even know where we're going, Marco, let alone when we'll be back. Maybe never."

"Never? Do not say such a thing. *Never* is a final word and I hate final things."

Anxiously, Marco gazed at Stefan and Stefan's face became more drawn. "Thank you for making us happy here, Marco. You know that *I* have always been happy here."

Marco tried not to cry. A sob burst from his throat. "Tell me, Stef—we will see each other again, won't we?"

Stefan moved his shoulders, not indifferently. He didn't know, that was all. Katharine felt a pang of the same anxiety that moved Marco.

"Say good-bye to Dolly for us, please," she said quickly.

Marco stiffened, glad to be distracted. "That miserable tease," he yelped. "She has been leading me a frantic race. *Kathrina*," he continued archly, "tell me, was she ever so? In your country she was eager and insatiable. But arriving here she slammed the door in my face, telling me she is worried about Swiss law coming down hard on *in flagrante*, though knowing we are in my private place and consenting adults. And she does not consent." Wildly, he appealed to their sense of justice. "Only last night, *Stef*, upon allowing me in her room, she submitted to my most loving advances, relishing the feel of my lips on her smooth thighs and against her fun house, but more she would not do."

"Marco. . . ." Stefan tried to slow him.

"No, no, let me finish! And then, upon my becoming so hot and bothered, Dolly tells me cruelly to go into the bathroom and whack off! Is that any way for a woman to talk? No! I shall not marry her. She is too hard to please. When she is good, she is a very good person; but when she is bad, she is hell on wheels, my dears."

"So, Marco?" Stefan asked.

"So?" Marco shrugged. "So I am going to take her to Marbella until Bastille Day and find if that improves her generosity."

Stefan's red-rimmed eyes glistened. Not speaking again, he held out his arms in farewell and Marco came to him. They embraced. Stefan turned and they went out to the car.

Katharine drove away rapidly, glad for the feel of the powerful automobile and the sensation of making space. She drove silently for a half-hour; beside her, Stefan collapsed in fatigue, with his eyes closed. Perhaps, given his condition, this was not the best thing for Stefan; but it was what he wanted, to move on.

He spoke. "Poor Marco. What will he do without me?"

Katharine shrugged. "He's got Dolly—do you think he treats her too badly?"

"Probably. But no worse than Dolly treats him. It is not a match made in heaven, sweetheart. You drive so well, Kat. I cannot take my eyes off your hands."

She smiled at him and, as she did so, she thought, as she usually did, of Francotti. "I always drove us, don't you remember?"

He slouched in the seat. His body had shrunk. He seemed no larger than a child. "I remember everything," he said, his voice little more than a whisper. "We did not turn out so well, did we?"

She frowned at the heavy oncoming traffic. They would cross the border at the well-traveled spot near Annecy, then drive south through France. "I have no complaints."

"Ah, yes, love," Stefan sighed. "The great leveler. The great deceiver." He chuckled grimly. "That's me— the gay deceiver."

"Oh hush! Goddamn it, why didn't you just tell Richard Darktower to go to hell? I'd have stuck up for you."

He shook his head, as if he didn't care. "No, you wouldn't have, sweetheart. I know better." She was afraid to look at him. "That's why you're with me now, isn't it? You feel guilt." He didn't really want her to answer. He gripped his shoulders, shivering. "Goddamn chills. They never stop, even with the windows shut, sun beating in."

"It's very hot in here," she said worriedly. Katharine hoped he was not going to say anything else. But he did.

"Sweetheart, it's pointless for you to waste time with me. Healthwise. . . ." He laughed briefly. "Healthwise, I'm nowhere's-ville." He was staring at the side of her face. "I know you've got somebody else."

Katharine gripped the wheel more intently, focusing more sharply ahead of her, not even glancing at him. "How do you know that?"

"Dolly told me."

It angered her. By what right? "That bitch! I wish she'd stop sticking her nose in."

"Well?"

"Well, nothing," she said fiercely. "I'm here because I want to be." She paused. "I am sorry we didn't do better . . . that I didn't do better."

"But no guilt, right? No pity."

She nodded emphatically. "Right!"

"We'll have a few laughs," he cried, for a second sounding like he'd used to. And then, sweetheart, you promised—bury me not on the lone prairie."

"Jesus, Stefan!"

"I mean it. Promise!"

Her skin crawling with self-hate, she said, "I don't see any lone prairies around here, do you?"

"I don't want to be cremated, sweetheart."

"Shit, stop it!" Tears blurred her vision. "I won't be able to drive."

"I'm telling you once—quickly. I want to be buried in Rome. Anywhere in Rome. I was born a Catholic. Bury me next to an English poet—English poets are always having themselves buried in Rome."

He said nothing else and Katharine still dared not look at him. When she did, finally, she saw he'd dropped off to sleep. His breath came hoarsely and there was a look of hurt in his expression; under his eyes the dark circles were darker but the illness, whatever it was—and God forbid he would ever tell anyone what it was—had softened his face. From this angle, in this light, he looked like a worn-out angel.

Forty-Two

Conrad, for all practical purposes, had moved out of his apartment. Perhaps, better said, he'd been forced out by "Captain" Roberto and his two minions, Dork and Carl. He had the worrying feeling that, even then, taking advantage of his hospitality, they were debating among themselves whether it actually would make sense to ransom him off to Richard Darktower.

Conrad found the three of them disgusting; Lilly had certainly been right about that. Their talk bored him and they were filthy. The worrying fact, however, was that the innocent box Roberto had said they were bringing to store with him didn't contain papers at all; soon enough, he'd discovered it contained gunpowder, caps, wire, all the ingredients for bombs. This was why they couldn't carry the stuff around in the heat of the day. Conrad *was* surprised. He'd always figured it was talk, just bullshit and boasting. Conrad could always claim they were squatters, and if worse came to worst, that is, if they went sky-high, he'd known nothing about any explosives.

Roberto did, after a few days, condescend to give Conrad the address of Lilly's studio.

By mid-June, he was uptown at the Himmelmann place on Fifth Avenue, telling his mother he wouldn't be staying long; he'd be on the move, off to Europe, off somewhere. The truth was Conrad didn't know what to do, or where to go. On the other hand, maybe it would be a good idea to go with the Himmelmanns and Margaret to their house in

Maine in July. He simply did not know. He was preoccupied and worried by so many things.

During the day, Conrad had his work cut out for him. He had to be up early and across town to the address Roberto had given him. He was most concerned to establish when Erik Moss came to visit Lilly and how long he stayed. Erik did not go to Lilly's much in the morning; usually, Conrad discovered, as he became increasingly familiar with the Moss routine, Erik went straight downtown to Himmelmann et Cie. Conrad even learned which elevator Erik habitually used. In the middle of the afternoon, sometimes a bit later, Erik went to the studio, and almost every day. The duration of his stay varied and often enough, Conrad had to assume, when he'd given up his vigil at midnight or so, Erik had slept the night with Lilly.

Naturally, Conrad didn't know what to do. His emotions were confused, especially since he'd fallen so violently in love with Kate. He couldn't very well continue to love Lilly if *this* were so. About Lilly, he assured himself, he cared nothing. Why then did he spy on her and Erik?

It was of little consequence now that Moss had stolen his girlfriend, for, hadn't Conrad stolen Moss's wife? The situation was ironic, funny in a way. A pity he could not tell the story as a joke.

Lilly might have appreciated it but Conrad couldn't summon the courage to confront her until finally one morning, it suddenly seemed the obvious thing to do; having seen Erik all the way down to Wall Street, Conrad cabbed back to the Sixties and calmly climbed the steps to her studio. That morning, he was wearing a good suit, lightweight beige, a cotton shirt and light blue tie.

Whistling to himself, he knocked staccato on her door.

Her voice. "Yes, who is it?"

"May I come in?"

"Conrad!" She giggled, somehow joyfully, and pulled open the door. It was as if they had never parted. Her jeans were the same, messy, paint-streaked, the sweatshirt identical, even in the doldrums of summer; her hands, thin and nervous, were grimy with ash and dried paint.

"Hi, Lilly."

"You found me." She seemed surprised, but pleased, that he had.

"It wasn't so hard—I just followed Erik."

He realized she was not going to be at all embarrassed. "Come in, lovey. You look so prosperous—are you working on Wall Street too?" she asked brightly.

"No," Conrad said sarcastically, "only one per family."

"Now look. . . ." Lilly's face tightened and she backed away. "I don't want any lectures. I moved out to get away from your goddamn friends."

"My friends? You brought them to me. Roberto. . . ."

"And those other two cretins . . . so what?"

"Now they've moved in with a box of dynamite," he said grimly.

Her eyes were stony cold. "If so, call the police. Right away. They'll blow you up. I told you they were crazy. Two of those bastards followed Erik—he made them sorry."

"I know," he said.

"Sit down," Lilly urged. "I'll get us some wine."

"No, no, too early," he said. He sat down in one of her straight chairs, and Lilly lit a cigarette. "You look good."

Lilly nodded. "You don't approve. You hate me. I did you wrong."

"No, I don't hate you." Curiously, he asked, "Are you in love with him?" She didn't answer, merely moving her head stubbornly, telling him it was none of his business. "I don't care if you do or don't, Lilly."

"You don't care? Good. Well," she said impatiently, "the only thing I love is my work."

"Oh . . . wonderful for you."

"It's true. That's all I do love." She puffed on her cigarette furiously. "You could have some coffee." He said yes and she went into the kitchenette and turned gas on under a kettle. Smoking, she leaned against the sink. "We can be friends, can't we? I know you always liked me, never mind about love. That doesn't matter, does it, like or love? It's easier being liked than loved. Fewer complications. The problem is I think Erik loves me."

He chuckled acridly. "I doubt that, Lilly."

She tossed her red hair. "He's a case, Erik is. Christ, he can be so morbid."

"You know, they had a detective following him, and discovered you. That's how I found out about it."

"I know, I know," Lilly said. "Erik told me. Fucking spies."

Calmly, very quietly, Conrad said, "The night I heard, I came close to killing him, Lilly. I tried to run him down with the Mercedes. He jumped out of the way just in time."

"*That* he didn't tell me. *Are* you crazy or something?"

"I don't think so. I'm glad now I didn't kill him."

"So am I, for your sake," Lilly said disgustedly. "Can you imagine what they'd do to you? The rest of your life in some jail. Crazy little son-of-a-bitch!" Her voice rose excitedly. "I suppose you're the one who burned down his beloved house too?"

"No, that wasn't me. I didn't hear about it till I got back here." He didn't tell her who had done it—it was better she didn't know. He didn't want Erik knowing either. He continued seriously, "You know, I'm all alone now. My sister has gone off to Europe, with Stefan. Isn't that a strange twist?"

Lilly remembered something he'd forgotten. "You accused her of never caring, doing nothing for him. Now she is. He's sick, isn't he? You told me that."

"Yes, yes!" he cried. "But you see, she's got another man here too."

"Who's that?" Lilly asked curiously.

Cleverly, feeling sly, Conrad said, "He's an engineer named Francotti."

"If that's so, he must be an understanding man," Lilly said.

Ah, damn it, he hadn't thought of that. Francotti was an *understanding* man. He had let her go off to Europe, hadn't he, the kindly man?

"Well, why all of a sudden so silent?" Lilly demanded. She'd turned her back again, to stir hot water into instant coffee.

"I'm thinking," Conrad said. Should he tell her about

Kate? That would catch her attention, wouldn't it? Toss out the magic word: *Incest!*

Lilly carried him a mug of coffee. She'd taken wine for herself. "Here you are, sourpuss," she said. "Wine for me; I'm nervous."

"So am I," Conrad mused.

"Because of me?" As he agreed evasively, knowing the truth was somewhere else, Lilly said, "You know, Erik wanted me to go away with him, I guess after everything is settled with your sister. But, hell, I can't go. I'm too attached to the Big Apple." She shrugged grandly. "Besides, I'm getting my show—in a good place on Fifty-seventh."

"Lilly Royce—hot property," he sighed.

"You bet—and I've decided something else too."

"You've decided a lot of things."

"I'm beholden to no man. Erik is too possessive—he believes in woman-subservient."

"Well, I never believed that, did I?"

"Nope," Lilly said decidedly. "If anything, you were subservient to me. But Erik likes to sit around and be petted and stroked and told how wonderful he is."

Conrad chuckled. Acidly. "I feel sorry for the poor bastard . . . almost."

"Don't feel sorry for him. He'll be all right."

He nodded. "You *know* he will. Old Daddy Darktower will take care of him. Listen, after he's gone, think about me. Okay?"

"I don't have to wait until after he's gone. As far as I'm concerned, he's gone right now."

Self-consciously, Lilly came to stand in front of him. She rested one hand on the top of his head. "I'm sorry for everything, I didn't mean to hurt you. I don't know what got into me. I wasn't normal. Is it all right, now?"

He nodded, looking up at her. "Yeah. Pretty much. It'll get better."

"Erik says when all this hits the newspapers, it'll be like you-know-what hitting the fan."

"Heavens! Not good for the image."

She laughed gleefully, bending to kiss his mouth, the tip

of her rubbery little tongue making contact. "That doesn't worry *me*, lovey." She laughed, gasping throatily.

Now, he thought—if he were going to kill her, now would be the time to do it.

"Listen," Conrad said grimly. "Two to one, none of this gets to the papers. Daddy Darktower will see to that—unless somebody does something crazy."

Forty-Three

"It is not fair!" Richard Darktower declared at the top of his voice. "We were going to France for Bastille Day."

"Sssh, Dickie," Clara said, holding a finger to her lips. "You can still go. Join your daughter there."

"No, I want to be with you."

"Now don't be a baby about this," she chided. "You must accept it like a grown man."

"No," he raged, "I'm not accepting anything like a grown man. I don't believe your goddamn doctors and I'm *not* accepting it. We'll get some more opinions."

"Dickie," Clara murmured coyly, "I've known for a while that I'm a partial diabetic."

"Partial?" he cried. "What you really are is a *full* idiot—giving yourself diet injections only aggravates whatever else is wrong with you. It's a goddamn insult to the body, Clara. All the time you're cooking and getting me fatter and you're taking appetite depressants—that's not fair either, goddamn it!"

"Try to be calm," she pleaded. "I was only trying to make myself nice for you."

"Oh, bullshit!" he stuttered. "I don't care if you're a little bit fat—that's one of the things that I liked about you in the first place."

She had to interrupt him with more nonsense. "I look at all your friends. They're so slim and svelte, like your first wife."

Was she trying to kill him on the spot? "That goddamn tramp," he yelled. "Don't talk to me about her. She's thin because she made a pact with the devil, sold herself for a couple of pounds.''

Clara pitched on the queen-sized bed in the Darktower suite at the Carlyle, throwing one arm across his body and facing him up close. "Dick, it'll be all right. It's not the end of the world. I've expected all these things to happen. You'll see!''

Darktower thrust his face into her cleavage. He puffed air to produce a sound like a man farting. Clara laughed boisterously.

"What's your quack say about hormones?''

"The more, the better, Dickie.''

"I've got some perking in the back burner. My gonads were working overtime last night, ducks.''

Clara squealed merrily. "Gonads? Don't you mean your lovely little nutties, Dickie, all tucked in there like marbles in a little leathery bag? Um, let's see. . . .'' She thrust her plump hand between his legs. The squeeze was a form of inquiry.

"Whew! That's it, all right, ducks,'' Darktower breathed.

"Would you care for a little face, Dickie?''

"Frankly,'' he said, for they'd come to talk to each other that way, "I think I'd rather just shove it right in, if you're acquiescent, before I lose my head of steam.''

"I'm always prepared for you, Dickie.''

He felt her just to be sure, running his hand across her stately, befurred mansion, placing one finger at the front door. Something grabbed at his finger, trying to pull him inside.

"Dickie,'' she whispered, "please to assume the position of superiority.''

With an agility that said he'd live to two hundred, Darktower hoisted himself above her and felt himself manipulated into the GO posture. Damn! There was plenty of life in him yet. Clara groaned lavishly, swathing him in flattery. He the swordsman, as quick and deft as Errol Flynn or Fairbanks Senior, thrust, counterthrust, *clang!*, *swack!*

Clara, he realized, was in a condition of high passion. Usually, she took him slowly, hedonistically savoring the long moments. This time, she did not wait for his normally precipitous ejaculation. No, her cheeks puffed; air whistled from her bronchial platform upon which, the two snowy-white breasts were rolling stupendously. *"Oooo."* The sound was as neat as a dove's call, rounded at both ends. Her lips pursed prissily to form lusty words of fulfillment. *"Oooo,* Dickie, your remarkable dingus has transported me."

"They don't call me McGee for nothing, ducks," he grunted.

Clara held him cozily by the buttocks, bumping and grinding this way and that against his tool, repeating her *"Oooo"* until, in extremis, she exuded a rapturous cry and the *"Oooo"* became *"Awwwh. . . ."*

As always, Darktower was impressed with Clara's performance. This time he outlasted her, but not for long. With a final great heave she extracted from him another dollop of life force.

"Oh, Dickie, what a miraculous gift you have given me," she sighed beautifully.

Christ, she was so *real* about it. Simulation was beyond Clara. He'd asked her several times—was it really as good as all that, ducks? Oh, yes, better than good, superb, superlatively superb. And she always did come? Oh, yes, it was a physical thing with her, she told him, for her clitoris was forward-canted. My, just the act of walking along the street on a hot day was often enough to give her the vapors. Of course, over the years she had learned to control herself . . . usually.

Darktower was quite swamped by her rollicking affection. "Clara, you must take care of yourself—I think I love you."

"Dickie—you dear!" Her chest shook disturbingly. He had made her cry. Sobs wracked her, threatening to toss him aside. "You touch me to the bottom of my heart, to my very soul. . . ."

"Don't get carried away," he said. "All I'm telling you is to take care of yourself. I don't want anything to happen to you."

She purred in his ear. "How do I make you happy with me, Dickie?"

He knew what he was supposed to say—Clara was incurably cute. "I'm happy with all of you, ducks, but especially the romance and mystery of your love canal."

"Oh, and you, Dickie, my little gondolier."

He stopped himself from wincing. If anyone else in the world had talked to him like this, he would have vomited. But from her, it was all acceptable. Now, as if released from a pledge of silence by his declaration of love, such as it'd been, Clara proceeded to surprise the life out of him.

"Dickie, I will now tell you the biggest secret of all. Forget partial diabetes. Dickie Darktower. . . ." Her eyes bugged at him in thyroid mesmerization. "You are going to be a *da-da* again."

He stared at her dumbly, numbly, so astonished he stopped breathing. "That's impossible, Clara. I'm too old!"

Weepily, she told him that was not so. She basked in his consternation. "That was the real secret. I wasn't sure I should tell you at all."

"Clara, for Christ's sake, I'm sixty-five years old!"

"So?" she sang. "You are going to be a new daddy-ums."

"You can't be sure. You *can't* be a hundred percent sure."

"Yes, Dickie," Clara said complacently. "It's sure. The tests were done. Daddy-ums has glued his little seed to duck's little seed and a new life has begun in my little tummy."

Darktower rolled off her tummy to lay clammy and frightened at her side. He closed his eyes tightly and pinched the bridge of his nose to stop himself from crying. A life begins . . . a life ends. Ah, yes, he had *that* on his mind: a life that deserved to be ended. He had been thinking about Erik Moss.

"Holy Jumping Jesus," he sighed.

"And Mary and Joseph," Clara added piously. "Dickie, I pray this will make you happy. As for me, I am unspeakably happy."

The next thing that occurred to him was that Mrs. Himmelmann would probably have a stroke when she heard about it. Then he realized he was going to have to redo his will.

Later, after breakfast, as it came time for him to keep his appointment with Sam Merchant, which meant he would have to leave Clara alone for a few hours. Darktower became much calmer. By the time he reached Grand Central Station he was very calm, indeed, exceedingly calm.

Briefly, only briefly, he had considered having Merchant come to the Oak Bar at the Plaza. No, too likely he'd see somebody he knew. Thus, the rendezvous was set for the Grand Central Station, the west entrance off Forty-Second Street. Merchant was to follow him through the station and up Lexington Avenue until Darktower picked out a bar sufficiently off the beaten track.

Though the late morning of a July day like this was warm and muggy, Merchant was wrapped in a trenchcoat that seemed too long for him and he wore a hat whose snap-brim kept his eyes private.

Seeing Darktower, Merchant hurled the butt of the cigarette he'd been smoking to the sidewalk and ground it viciously with his heel. Not looking at Sam directly, Darktower entered the station and headed eastwards across the marble floor, now and then slowing his pace to make sure he hadn't lost the slippery dick.

Back on the street, Darktower walked uptown several blocks until he came upon a bar called Murphy's. An Irish bar, good—the Irish were so self-centered they'd never remember two strangers. He waited inside the door for Merchant.

"Hello, Sam, my lad."

"Hi, ya, Chief," Merchant said, pulling at the nib of his upper lip as if to squeeze off his lisp. "Howyadoin'?"

"First-class. Let's take a booth in the back."

"Yeah, so's we can see the door."

As his eyes adjusted to the midmorning gloom of the bar, Darktower appreciated the fact the place was almost empty, except for the bartender and one customer. They were discussing baseball—what else?

"Sam, drinks, okay? I'll take a Scotch and soda. Here's money. . . ."

"Hey, Chief!" Merchant lifted his hand. "It's covered. On me."

Darktower smiled as Merchant swaggered up to the bar and ordered Scotch and soda and, for himself, a draft beer. He drummed on the bar with his fingers.

"Four and a half," the bartender said.

Merchant nodded. "Here's a fin. The rest is for you, buddy."

The bartender paused. "Jeese, thanks, big spender."

"Don't get wise," Merchant growled.

"You don't like it? Piss off, buddy."

"Hey! Listen. . . ."

Darktower interrupted. Merchant was defeating the whole purpose of the exercise: to be anonymous. "Sam!"

Merchant whirled around. "Oh, yeah, okay, Chief."

"Christ Almighty," Darktower hissed at Merchant. "Do you go out looking for trouble? Don't we have enough of it?"

"Sorry, Chief," Merchant said, unperturbed. "I just can't stand wise guys. I'd like to take that monkey apart."

"He looks big enough to rip your head off," Darktower grunted. "Save yourself for more important things, that's my advice."

He stared flatly at Merchant and, rather uncomfortably, Merchant grimaced back, showing his chipmunk teeth. Darktower had been pitching things all his life, mainly stocks and bonds, so this was nothing new to him. Specifically, his idea was to lead Merchant along in such a way that when the desired destination was reached, Merchant would think he'd found it by himself.

His eyes concerned, Merchant lifted the beer glass to his lips, asking, "Trouble, Chief?"

"Yes." Darktower nodded, then put him off. "Aren't you going to take off that coat?"

"Uh, uh, Chief." Merchant showed his teeth. "See, I'm not wearing a shirt underneath. Too hot out."

Darktower smiled, not believing it. "If you weren't wearing a heavy coat, you could wear a shirt."

Merchant shook his head. "Naw, gotta wear the coat,

Chief. I gotta lot of stuff to carry. Chief, the *trouble*, what is it?''

"I don't know how serious. . . ."

"Gimme it straight, Chief," Merchant said bravely.

Again Darktower stalled him. "You can smoke if you want to."

"I thought you didn't like it."

"I don't—but go ahead."

Merchant nodded and fumbled in the right-hand pocket of the trenchcoat. He got out his pack of unfiltered Camels, clicked one free with his thumbnail, lit it and inhaled mightily. Then he looked at Darktower and scowled. "Okay, let's have it, *huh*, Chief?"

"It's Moss."

"What about him? I kow he's a tough cookie—has he been threatening you?"

"No, no, Sam. The trouble is he knows about *you*."

"About me?" Merchant plucked the cigarette out of the corner of his mouth. "That's bad shit, Chief."

Darktower shrugged, as if to say what did Sam think he was getting paid for. "I had to tell him I knew about the redhead, Sam. He got the picture right away—that I'd been having him tailed." Darktower congratulated himself on how easily he had picked up the jargon. His children could be proud, too, yes, *all* his children, that he was protecting them from the predators.

"Jesus," Merchant whined, "you didn't give him my card, didja?"

"No, no, of course not. The *trouble* is, even with the goods we got on him, he's going to fight. You'll probably have to testify in court, Sam."

"Bad, Chief, bad," Merchant muttered. "That means I'd gotta come out of deep cover. Everybody's going to say, that guy there, that's Sam Merchant, private eye. My career could be ruined. Shit, I thought we were goin' to France."

"We're not going," Darktower said testily. "Trip's off."

"Aw, shit."

"Come on, cut it out. I never promised you. So what if

you did have to testify? You'd still be on my retainer. Private eyes testify all the time. What bothers me is what he might do before that. You can't trust him, you know."

Merchant nodded vigorously. "Guys like him you *cannot* trust."

Darktower nodded, wishing Merchant would not interrupt. "What he wants is custody of my granddaughter. He's going to make my daughter out to be neurotic, unstable, unfit to take care of a child."

"The son-of-a-bitch," Sam glowered, "and him shacked up with that redhead. Where does he get off?"

"More than that, Sam, more than that. If we go to trial, he's going to accuse my daughter of all kinds of weird stuff. He's got another woman—he'll call her for a witness to Kate's . . . uh . . . I don't know what."

Merchant's face was disfigured by an expression of disgust. "What? Some kind of pervertations? Won't work, Chief, take it from me."

"I know that, for Christ's sake, and you know that, but who's to say a judge might not fall for it? No, no, I can't have that. I can't let it go to court, Sam. I'm going to have to pay him off."

"Chief, what about warning him that if he goes ahead, his ass is in one big sling?"

Darktower shook his head from side to side. "No, no—my only choice is to pay him off, Sam, to protect my family. You did a good job, Sam, but we didn't get enough on him. We'd need something that'd really burn him if it came out. You need fire to fight fire."

"Jesus, Chief," Merchant grieved, "I done the best I could. How much you gonna have to pay off the turkey?"

Darktower shrugged. "Probably on the order of two million."

"Dollars?" Merchant's face twitched and he giggled nervously. "Christ," he whispered, "you could get him *hit* for an awful lot less than that."

Darktower knew he must look very puzzled. "*Hit, Sam*?"

Merchant grinned wildly; his chipmunk teeth seemed to chatter. He pushed himself back in the booth and looked preoccupied. "Well, just suppose, Chief . . . we're supposing, right?"

"Hypothetically."

"Yeah . . . well, suppose I could talk this turkey out of it . . . somehow?"

Stolidly, Darktower shrugged. "He'll never go for it, Sam."

"Well, if that don't work. . . ." Merchant grinned fearfully. "What if Moss was persuaded to go on a long trip?" His lips drew away from his teeth. "Maybe a one-way trip, get it, Chief?" He chortled, then stopped, having frightened himself.

Darktower smiled fondly. "If he went away on a long trip, it certainly would save everybody a lot of trouble, Sam."

"You know what . . . uh . . . I'm saying? You're cool, Chief."

"Not cool . . . hypothetical, Sam, very, very hypothetical."

"Yeah, okay." Merchant didn't understand, did he? "What about this broad that he'd call for a witness?"

Wryly, Darktower said, "Helen Ryan, the maid. I thought you interviewed her."

He hadn't expected he'd surprise Merchant as much as he had apparently done. Merchant's face parted incredulously. "You're shittin' me, Chief. She's a witness to this . . . whatever it is?"

"Yes, Helen Ryan, she's probably invented the whole thing, Sam."

"Shit! I never would've believed it."

"Well," Darktower pursued him, "didn't we agree that Moss has made up the *whole* goddamn story? We can't believe either one of them."

Merchant nodded dumbly. *"We do not believe it, no sir!"*

"Do you carry a gun?"

Merchant's body whip-sawed. "You know I do . . . it's in my pocket, for Christ's sake," he whispered frantically. "That's why I'm wearing the coat."

Darktower stared at him significantly. "Do you trust Moss? I don't."

Merchant looked ill as he shakily lit another Camel. "Fist things first, Chief. I'll talk to this Ryan. If she's not going to make a stink, it changes the lay-of-the-land, right? Right! We go on from there."

"Sure," Darktower agreed smoothly. "What about a couple more drinks, Sam?"

"Yeah, why not?" Merchant did not move right away. He stared at Darktower respectfully, schemingly. "I just want to say one thing, Chief—however I handle this thing, it's going to cost you a lot less than two million big ones." He licked his lips greedily and tried to smile.

Darktower nodded. "Don't worry, Sam. I'm going to be very, very grateful."

Forty-Four

Stefan could abide only two nights in St. Tropez—it was too hot, it was too cold, too crowded with the international jet-set, the beautiful people, all out of his past, and he was sick to death of them all.

"Yes, it is true," he told Kate at dinner in the most out-of-the-way bistro they could find. "I despise them all now—finally, but too late. *Honestly*."

"Never mind honestly. Don't dwell on it."

"No. In the end," he muttered, picking distastefully at a bland fish dish, "when one is playing one's last hand, honesty is all one has."

Kate looked up at him angrily. "I won't believe you're as far gone as you keep saying."

"Believe it or not." He stared at her tolerantly, in a way that was beginning to annoy her very much, as if *he* knew all too well and *she* knew nothing. "Now, believe *this*—I want you to be . . . *happy*." His eyes were warm, so warm she stopped being annoyed. "I do remember this man, you know. He was next to Moss and I said *that* must be your new husband. Remember? I took him for your husband—his name is Francotti."

Katharine nodded. "Yes—that was at Frank Berliner's party for Dolly."

"I hope you love him."

"Since we're being honest," she said, "I'll tell you that I do love him . . . yes, quietly."

"The best way," Stefan murmured.

431

"And I love you too," she added softly. "You may have noticed. Deeply, far inside me. . . ."

He smiled gratefully. "Ah, thank you . . . that is very nice."

"You're welcome," she said. "I didn't tell you something else—Francotti saved my life."

"No! When?"

"The night of the storm, remember, when Erik came out to the boat and I left."

"You left to get away from that swine," he said bitterly. "You did not wake me."

"No, I didn't. Never mind. When I tried to get in the dinghy, I fell in the ocean. I was drifting out to sea. Francotti dragged me in. That's when we. . . ."

He smiled appreciatively. "Fate . . . the best way," he said again. "That is a very good story, sweetheart."

"It's true!"

"I know it is," he assured her. Pushing his plate away, he said, "*No more.* I said I was happy for you, didn't I?" Chin on his folded hands, he gazed at her speculatively. "You know, you are much the same—Miss Innocence Incorporated, as if twelve years have not flown away. You are, I admit, more mature here. . . ." He tapped his head. "But your body, the physical being, is much the same. I think you and I should have had children." He laughed regretfully. "It was not *un*enjoyable making love. But. . . ." He reared back in his chair. "Too late for that now. Too late for me, that is. For you—never! You are a natural child-bearer, even more so now. Your body has changed only for the better. It is fuller at hip and breast."

"Please," she muttered, "don't."

But he went on, again very frankly. "I recommend to you this Francotti, sweetheart. It would give me the greatest pleasure." His eyes watered easily. "You know, you are being very kind to me." Being so ill had brought his emotional circuits closer to the surface. "You do not have to be so kind; it is uncalled for. Our contract . . . expired." His voice fell sorrowfully.

"Goddamn it," she whispered, "will you stop!"

With an effort, Stefan pushed his chair back. "Come. Get the check. We leave here tomorrow."

They went early the next morning, Katharine guiding the Lamborghini east through the dense summer traffic and into Italy. They skirted Genoa and made for Rapallo. Stefan was willing to give Rapallo only one night of their precious time and so they turned inland. Stefan decided it was not good to be too near the sea. Katharine aimed the car for Florence.

Florence was not what it had used to be. They walked the few blocks from the hotel along drought-emptied River Arno to the Ponte Vecchio, the old bridge arched with curio shops, and no, it wasn't what it had used to be either. Florence was too muggy, too dirty, too noisy—the speeding Fiats kept Stefan awake all night.

No, no, they couldn't stay in Florence. Moving—had to keep moving. Katharine tried to lose whoever it was, in Stefan's mind, that was following them in the maze of Tuscan hills. On the old road to Rome, they reached Volttera, hilltop city, one of the ancient capitals of Etruria whose natives, since time's beginning, had specialized in two things: big, handmade green umbrellas against the rain which swept in from the Mediterranean several times a day flooding the gray-stoned streets and squares and running down into the lush plains; and in the artifacts of death: the tombs, the graveside statuary, the chiseled catafaults of a pre-Roman civilization which, for some reason lost to history, had worshipped Death and the Princes of Death above all else.

The constant travel was beginning to show on Stefan now. He sat wearily beneath the awning of a cafe on the main, stone-paved, stone-walled square, looking around apprehensively. Perhaps whoever was pursuing, had now trapped them here where they had been meant to be all along.

"This is a fierce place, isn't it?" he asked, surveying the square, stone, all stone, all gray. "It is severe, medieval. The whole city is paved, there is no blade of grass. It wears its stone like a suit of armor. I love it! We will order an aperitif. Yes! An aperitif. I am so bored with this abstinence.''

"Can you?" she asked cautiously. God, if only he could, what a drink might do for him.

"Why not?" he cried. "I'll order a small vermouth, one of this region.''

When the drinks came, Stefan sat for ten minutes staring at the dark, rich liquid. If it had been possible, he could have finished it off with his eyes, never touching glass with his lips. Finally, he did lift the small, fluted glass, holding it under his nose, sniffing, beaming his anticipation. He put the glass to his mouth, sipped quickly . . . put the glass down . . . sat back . . . twirled the vermouth on his tongue. His throat moved agonizingly as he swallowed. Solemnly, he looked at Katharine, his long fingers jerking spasmatically in his lap, waiting for the reaction.

She did not dare touch her own glass. She watched him, wondering if she could catch him before he hit the cobblestones. But no, nothing so drastic was going to happen. Carefully, Stefan smiled, tentatively. It was still too soon for a final triumphant grin.

At length, he picked up the glass again, sipped a second time. "It is so *good*," he sighed. "Not whisky . . . not vodka . . . not brandy, heaven forbid . . . but very, very *good*." His expression brightened. "You look wonderful, sweetheart. This dampness makes your skin blossom. Ah, it is so beautiful to be alive.''

"What shall we eat?" She realized that being so unused to alcohol now, Stefan's body might not tolerate it well.

"Pasta!" he cried softly, "some spaghetti, with a little butter, a little cheese. Wonderful!''

He finished all the light meal and the vermouth. For a while, he felt quite recovered. It was the air, he said, fresh and cool above the plains. "Shall we stop here a few days?''

Katharine rented the biggest room available in the Hotel Nacional around the corner from the square and then came back to the restaurant to get him. Stefan was sitting as she'd left him, but he was dozing, his chin on his chest. The proprietor watched worriedly, even more concerned when Katharine made Stefan stand up. He was suddenly irritable. He shook her hand away, telling her he could get there by himself.

When she'd seen to the car and went up to the room, Stefan was stretched out on the bed, his face was white and drawn. "Tired?"

"Very," he muttered, "But at rest." He opened his eyes and watched her warily as she opened the doors at the end of the room and walked out on the terrace.

"You can see down into the whole valley from here. But it's getting hazy," she said quietly.

"And cold," Stefan said.

"It's going to rain."

He struggled to raise himself in the bed. "Close the door, please. I'm cold. I need the blanket."

Katharine came inside and relatched the balcony doors. She pulled away the bed covers and helped him underneath. He was shivering. His lips seemed to have been stained from the vermouth, but she realized they were merely bluish from the chill.

"How long are you going to stay with me? he demanded faintly. "You can't go on like this. How long?"

How long? An impossible question. "I am staying with you," she said firmly.

She lay down beside him in the bed, putting her arms around him.

He shook away. "Don't do that. It makes me nervous. I'm not cold now. I'm warmer." His eyes were distant. "You can't stay with me much longer. You've got to get back. Your life. . . . ."

"Shut up," Katharine said.

Stefan wouldn't go downstairs with her for dinner that night. He ordered her to go by herself, his mood nasty again, impatient, wounding.

"Go, go, for God's sake, leave me alone. I don't want to talk anymore. I'm sick and tired of arguing with you."

She promised she'd bring something back and he said bitterly that all he really wanted was brandy and this he could not drink. "Go!"

"All right. But don't treat me so—don't be so angry just because I'm worried."

"I'm angry with you *because* you're worried. I forbid you to worry about me."

She put on her raincoat and went, downstairs and out to the cobblestoned street. But she wasn't hungry either. She walked, careless of the light rain that was falling. Finally, the warm and companionable drizzle improved her spirits and she went back to the hotel. She ordered an espresso, descending into deeper reverie.

How long could she stay with him? She was committed now. She would remain with him . . . until the end. The end, that was the next step. The end.

The woman who'd made her the espresso asked if she'd like another. Katharine nodded, yes: and why not? And, yes, again, she'd like a brandy to go with it. At least *she* could drink brandy. She'd drink it for him.

Then she saw the telephone on the wall next to the espresso machine. She asked the woman if she could place a call for her. It would be about four P.M. in New York. She jotted Francotti's number down on a slip of paper.

It was easy, it happened every day. The woman muttered *Momento* into the phone and handed it to Katharine.

"Hello?"

There was only a tick of a pause. "It's Katharine Margaret," Francotti said.

"Yes, me. I wanted to hear your voice. How are you?"

"Fine," he said evenly. "How are *you*?"

"Bearing up," she said slowly.

She must not have sounded very good, for he said, "*Are* you all right? How is it . . . going?"

"I. . . ." She didn't know how to put it, what to say. "I'm afraid . . . I. . . ."

"That's okay," he said cheerfully, his cheeriness forced, she reckoned. "Your brother is here. How about that for a coincidence? We went out to lunch. . . . Say hello!"

Breathlessly, she listened. "Hello . . . Kate" Conny's voice was low.

God, she was frightened. "Are you okay, Conny?"

"Yes, *fine*," he said. "How is Stefan?"

"Not good—not at all," she confessed. She couldn't bring herself to tell him what she knew—that Stefan would be dead soon. "We're on our way to Rome. How did you . . . why?"

"I thought I'd like to talk to somebody, that's all," Conrad said. "Don't worry, Kate." He spoke so loudly she knew it was for Francotti's benefit. "I'll mind my manners. I wouldn't want to shock Mr. Francotti out of your orbit."

"Oh . . ." She was limp. "Darling. I love you. I'll call you from Rome. You could come, if I needed you?"

She heard his intake of breath. "Yes."

Francotti came back on. "Look, everything's fine. "You're *not* to worry," he said. "Do your thing. So long."

Katharine was sniffling as she hung up. She gulped the brandy and motioned for another. Sympathetically, the Italian woman stared at her, on the verge of tears herself.

In a few moments, Katharine felt better, much better. Suppose Conrad *had* told everything to Francotti as he had threatened? What was the man's depth of compassion? Was it better to find out now, rather than later?

Finally, Katharine climbed slowly to their room. She would place herself beside him, circle him with her arms and hold him warmly, and sleep, and in the morning he would be fine.

Stefan was not in the room. The balcony doors were open and he was sitting outside in his shirtsleeves, with nothing on his head, in the rain.

"My God! What are you doing?"

He stared at her calmly. "I'm merely watching the distant lightning."

"Come inside, for God's sake!"

Obediently, Stefan stood up, wobbling. When he came into the light, Katharine realized he was trembling violently.

"You're sopping wet," she sobbed. She clapped her hand to his forehead. "And you've got an awful fever."

Calmly, smiling mistily, Stefan said, "I'm sorry, sweetheart. I simply had to go outside. The air is so sweet."

"And wet . . . and cold! You stupid ass!" she raged. She tore off his shirt, ran for a towel, dried him off, wrapping him in blankets.

He smiled again contritely. "I'm sorry to worry you."

"Get in bed."

Despite her sleepless efforts to keep him warm, he shivered and shook all night, his temperature blazing. In the morning, the fever dropped and he became stubborn and angry again. No, he would not see a doctor. No, he would stay here no longer. "Quick! Pack the bags! We must go to Rome. Yes, Rome."

She drove badly and he slept all the way, fitfully. In Rome, Katharine drove straight to the Hassler, demanded a suite and got it. She knew this would be their last stop.

Forty-Five

When Sam Merchant told Helen Ryan what the trouble was and how worried Mr. Darktower was, he might have been threatening to sit her down and tear out her fingernails. Helen dropped to her knees beside the couch in the Park Avenue living room and lofted her hands in supplication, whether to Sam Merchant or the Almighty was open to question.

"It's a terrible lie, I swear it's a lie! Why would the dirty and awful Devil say such a thing like that about me? It's not true and you can tell Mr. Darktower I would never testify to lies. Oh, what am I going to do with a Devil making up dirty and terrible stories so he can get money out of the Darktower fortune. What should I do about a Devil who always wants to have his way with me even when I resist, to push me down and have me, the dirty rotten bastard! I should kill him, or me, or both, rather than be dragged into a public place with that written all over me. No, no . . . if I had a gun, I'd wait for him to come and when he did I'd confront him with what he'd said about me and then I'd not even give him a chance to explain but I'd blow his brains out and say it was self-defense, no more a lie than the other, that I thought he was a burglar. He'd be dead as doornail and my honor would be swept clean of all blemishes before God and Man alike. Heavens above, who would believe a thing like this? Not you, Sam, I know you don't, for I can tell by your shocked eyes that you don't want it to be true, do you? And you better say no or I'll smash in your jaw just like

439

I'm going to smash him, the Devil, the next time I see him.''

Quite suddenly, she halted her soliloquy, hobbling toward him on her knees and seizing Merchant about the hips, burying her red, wet face in his crotch.

''Baby,'' Merchant murmured, as if his heart was broken, which it was not. ''Moss is going to say terrible, terrible things about you whether they're true or not. And if you back down now, not say what he tells you to say, he'll hurt you, you know. He'll come in here with a whip and he'll whip you black and blue . . . and silly.''

''Oh,'' she howled, ''the son-of-a-bitch, he wouldn't. Why would a woman like me who enjoys the love of a man such as you engage in dirty things with him? Moss, he's the Devil and he projects the evil right into you, as with osmosis, and brings you down to his level, in the dirty old sewer pipe. Oh, give me your hand. Put your hands on my head, Sam, my dear, and just let me see. I'm opening your pants here. Oh, God, the Devil he is. . . .''

''Baby, this is no time for playing around,'' Merchant said sternly. ''This is a serious moment. This confluence of forces has brought us to a miasmic imbroglio.''

''A what? *Do as I say*, Sam, darling, come down here on the Persian carpet while I just move my skirt out of the way. Come down, you little pipsqueak, as I say!''

Son-of-a-bitch, he muttered to himself, she wasn't impressed really, not at all. She didn't give a goddamn what Moss said about her.

''There, now, my little dear, just push it in a little and *we'll see* what Helen Ryan likes best. Oh, could a person who likes such as this so much tell lies about it? I don't think so. And if I have to testify, by God, to my honor, then you're going to testify too that I'm a pure lover of male organ.''

''Slide trombone,'' Merchant hissed, ''more like it, slide trombone. Get it, baby?''

In reply, she pinched his right buttock so hard he knew he would get cancer from it, then felt what he had in his back pocket, a revolver, a snub-nosed .38, and she squealed in fright.

"And it's loaded," Merchant growled. "I've got it, just in case. See, Moss is not a man who can be trusted, sugar. You know he'd do murder to anyone standing in his way."

"Murder most foul," she exclaimed ominously. "Oh, yes, I don't doubt it, for he is the Devil. Sam, push harder into me," she cried piteously, "for who knows it may but be the last time you and I will ever do this loving act."

She practically yanked a load of liquid dynamite out of his goatlike loins, even as he was telling her again that Moss was lethal, homicidal, and in fact plain insane. "He's a man who's not to be trusted," Sam warned her hotly, "and I'm going to let you keep the gun here, just in case, for I don't want anything happening to your sweet ass."

"Oh, I do hate the Devil," she panted. "Imagine him saying a thing like that about me who's been so faithful all these years to the Darktower family?"

Perspiring, he muttered, "It's the priests I'm worried about, sugar, and us not being able to show our faces in Brooklyn for twenty years. Brooklyn, my homeland."

"Oh, yes, oh, yes," she squalled, her eyes going blank while, with an excruciating heave and follow-up rabbit punch she performed her version of climax. "Oh, dearest, you do love me, don't you?" Her breathing descended to the expiration point.

He stared down at her, deep into her eyes, as she nailed him into her, once again, thrice, again, four times and yowled. Trying to fathom what lay behind her wild eyes, he fancied he could see into the curlicues of her brain. It was a long shot, he warned himself, but he believed that with the proper provocation, Helen would surprise them all.

"Sam!" She sliced him in the kidney.

"What, for Christ's sake?"

"I asked, didn't I, if you love me?"

"All the way, sugar. You betcha."

Forty-Six

With Dolly away in Europe and his affairs in general no more than hanging fire, Erik Moss devoted himself conscientiously to Himmelmann et Cie all through the month of June. His reward came from a not-unexpected quarter, namely Casper Rockbottham, of a law firm which handled legal and other problems of the Darktower family and estate.

Erik had met Rockbottham on numerous occasions and they had been on a first-name basis for several years at least, if not longer.

But not on this day. Severely formal, Casper Rockbottham informed him over the telephone that, acting on the instructions of Richard Darktower, on the occasion of the cancellation of the marriage contract between Erik Moss to Katharine Darktower, formerly Ratoff, Moss, on the date of said cancellation, the Erik Moss share of the business would be set and agreed at the sum of three million dollars, and for which settlement Mr. Moss would enter into a supplemental agreement not to sue or otherwise legally molest the Darktower estate *ad infinitum* et cetera, et cetera.

"My *charge*, Mr. Moss is . . . is to ask you whether this is agreeable to you?"

He could play the game too. Frigidly, Erik replied, "Since there is no hope of reconciliation, and since we are now at this sad state of affairs, lawyer to principal, then, I say yes, to spare myself further pain and mental anguish."

442

"Yes. . . ." Rockbottham's drawl was positively insulting. "No doubt. No doubt at all, Mr. Moss."

"Send me the necessary papers, Mr. Rockbottham, made out to *Erik Moss* and I will sign them. I will expect the money in the form of a cashier's check."

"At which address?" Rockbottham asked, his voice like a cutting edge.

Erik paused. "Not at the apartment for I will be moving immediately. I should say I will be moving after the July Fourth holiday weekend. Messenger me the papers Tuesday at the Regency Hotel."

"Very well," Rockbottham said. Erik could visualize his lip curling— oh yes, a smell of money.

After he'd hung up, Erik drew a long breath, exhaled, and breathed deliberately again to quiet his nerves. Three million was not unsatisfactory, not at all. It was more than he had figured Darktower would offer.

What to do? Very gently, Erik opened his desk drawer. Was there anything in here that he desperately needed? Financial statements, corporate prospectuses, bond offerings, a telephone index, pencils, pens, discarded cigarette lighters. He closed the drawer, stood up and walked out of the office, down the carpeted hall. He nodded to the receptionist-telephonist in the outer office, and left. Downstairs, he caught a cab and directed the driver to the Park Avenue address. He did not bother to go upstairs, merely asked the doorman to have the Mercedes brought around.

In ten minutes, he left for his last visit to Port London. As he drove, Erik went over the figures in his head. Three million, moved, along with himself, quickly out of the country to a safe and tax-free haven . . . carefully invested, at even a modest return of 8 percent would net him nearly three hundred thousand a year, certainly enough to support life in a small Austrian village; yes, he smiled faintly to himself, his eyes warming his skull, yes indeed, far from the maddening crowd. *Herr Mossberg, jawohl*, Erik Moss . . . who he? *Who he, Mr. Tax-Man*?

For the first time in an hour or so, he frowned; altogether, it had been a trying time. Painful, yes, anguished, so hated and despised and why? Because: He had tried always to do the *right* thing, for he was a righteous man, an honest man, a kindly man, an honorable man, a man of his word. His word is his bond. *Of course*, Erik would sign the paper and he would keep the bargain. *Naturally*, he would be able to see Margaret from time to time—they could not sensibly forbid him that. If they did, despite the agreement, he would bring an action. It would never be too late for an action.

Things, as they said in this outrageous country, were going great! He needed no one now—except, perhaps, Lilly. For what had looked like a long-term relationship with Dolly Percy, he had begun to withdraw from Lilly's life; slowly, a few moments fewer with her every day and in a month she'd have forgotten what he looked like. Dolly, he reminded himself, was behaving strangely, keeping herself so incommunicado in Switzerland. Perhaps he should let her know she should remain there, that he would arrive soon to join her. Should he tell her this . . . *should* he resume with Lilly? Should he search out entirely fresh territory? Perhaps the latter was better, more intelligent, for he would not especially want anyone tracing his whereabouts, would he, not for a time in any case?

Erik lit a cigarette and puffed luxuriously as he dawdled along in the Mercedes, keeping to the speed limit, enjoying the weather from the air-conditioned atmosphere of the car. Thank God everything was settled, that there would be no long dragged-out legal process. He had begun feeling very nervous about the volatility of the situation. He could never have left America with all that hanging over him, not if he wanted his rightful, yes, damnation, *rightful* share of the estate—rightful in the sense that this was precisely what he'd have gotten if Kathy had died.

He would close down Lilly's studio as of, say, the end of September. Be generous with the little thing, yes, why not? It would simply happen; she'd be advised by the landlord. Erik Moss would be gone.

Mrs. Rogers was already retired to her apartment over the garage when he arrived at Maples. Hearing him, she came down but Erik, in such grand and kindly fashion he was even impressed with himself, told her, no, never to mind. He'd fend for himself. Moving slowly, he drove on down to the Claw for a sandwich and several beers, keeping to himself, but alert to the local crowd. Thankful not to be required to carry on light conversation about business or the weather, he went back home, had a Scotch and so to bed.

In the morning, Erik made a call to Wadsworth, the Hermitage Assembly curator. No, Wadsworth wouldn't have heard anything yet. Wadsworth took it for granted Erik wanted to hear the verdict on the Smithers House. The fire department investigation had turned up nothing in the way of clues though sifting through the ashes with a fine-toothed comb. By now even the unstable chimney had been pulled down. The assembly could salvage only a few bricks to be used on restoration work elsewhere. Very, very sad it was, yes indeed.

"I'm sorry, Erik," Wadsworth intoned in funeral style. "It would have been a grand project and a great monument to everybody concerned, a wonderful addition to our roster of colonial treasures."

"Yes," Erik said flatly, "it was one of the few things to which one could look forward in these painful times."

"Yes . . . everything well with the family?" Wadsworth asked, the usual next point of business in Port London.

Erik could have thundered laughter. The House of Moss was in about the same condition as that of Smithers, except the strong central pillar, Moss himself, was still very much intact.

Wadsworth finished the civilities by inviting Erik to coffee and cakes at the assembly's headquarters Sunday afternoon at five—a little meeting of the fireplaces committee. Erik declined. He was driving back to the city after lunch.

Not staying for the weekend of the Fourth? No, no, too crowded.

At midmorning, Erik drove over to Dolly's house, telling Mrs. Donovan that Mrs. Percy had asked him to check if everything was all right. No problems? No, and Mrs. Donovan had only had the one phone call from Geneva, Switzerland, at least three weeks ago.

"Oh, yes," he said, "I've left that number in New York. Do you have it handy, Mrs. Donovan? Why don't I just give her a call right now? It'd be about teatime in Europe, wouldn't it?"

Naturally, Mrs. Donovan had no idea of any time save Port London time, since the entire world revolved around Port London. But she had the number. "Say hello for me, Mr. Moss," Mrs. Donovan said, trying to smile, achieving a frosty grimace.

Erik went into the library and closed the door. The call went through soon enough but static on the line and a lag in tempo told him it was a satellite hook-up.

He recognized the voice which answered to be that of the Sicilian lush, Marco Fortuna.

"Mr. Fortuna," he cried cordially, "it is Erik Moss. You remember . . ."

"*Quoi*?" Marco's voice overlapped. "Sorry . . . Erik Moss . . . *Si!* Hello."

"Yes . . . excuse me. Mrs. Percy. . . ."

" 'Allo." Marco bubbled with laughter. "You say . . . oh, yes, Dolly . . . *Senora Fortuna*!"

Dismay stampeded in Erik's head. What had he said? Senora Fortuna? Mrs. Fortuna? Jesus Christ, had they married?

Her voice echoed.

"You married him?" Erik shouted.

Dolly laughed, the atmospherics distorting her words. "He likes to think so. Darling, I can't marry, you know it. Or do you? The trusts . . . Richard Darktower would break my neck. I can only marry a man with a ton of money, like you."

She was joking lightheartedly, little knowing . . . little knowing.

"Yes, like me."

Her next words obscured what he'd said. "We had a marriage ceremony off the coast of Spain, outside the coastal limits. The captain did it. Marco thinks it's legal but I know better."

"*Legalo, legalo*." Marco boomed boisterously from somewhere near her.

She was saying something else. "Bad news about Stefan— Kitty's had to put him in a hospital in Rome."

"I'm sorry," he murmured. In a way, he did pity Ratoff; he could afford to now.

She didn't hear what he'd said. "Darling! You sound like Mickey Mouse . . . Marco says it's not serious, that Stefan nips brandy in secret and has to be put away every so often."

"Dolly," he yelled, to stop her. "It's over now."

"Oh, that? Sure, I know. Don't worry—I'll always have a soft spot for you, whatever happens between us. Marco says good-bye, darling. He's pouring champagne and we're having caviar. Oh, God!" She began to giggle hysterically. "Can you believe it—he's just ladled some on my belly. God, he's licking it. Marco . . . Oh, Christ, Marco! You'd better get it all, you fat little wop."

She'd dropped the phone, forgotten all about him, Erik Moss! Was it possible? He heard the crusty sound of rustling fabrics, grunts and labial slavering. Mother of God!

Forty-Seven

It was upon one of the hottest, muggiest nights of the year over the Fourth of July weekend that "Captain" Roberto chose to make his grandest gesture.

Somehow, Conrad was not surprised to see Roberto at the door of Lilly's studio, his aides, scruffy Carl and Dork, behind him.

Roberto pushed inside. "Sit down," he commanded Conrad. "And you too—you're not dressed," he scolded Lilly.

"I'm dressed enough for a night like this." She was barechested with panties on below. "We weren't expecting company. Company, Jesus! Who asked you here? Take those two scumbags and beat it, Charley."

"Shut up, I said," he cried furiously. "Sit down, the both of you. You're hostages, so keep your goddamn mouths shut."

"I said, *leave!*" Lilly yelled. "Or I'll call the police!"

"And I said, sit down," Roberto grunted. He drew his arm back and slapped her across the face. Lilly slumped into her canvas chair. Conrad stepped forward angrily. Roberto shoved him back. "Sit down, you bastard! Can't you see what Dork's carrying?"

Dork, grinning stupidly, held up a black plastic bag.

Roberto's second assistant, Carl, declared viciously, "That bag drops, all our asses go up."

"You. . . ." Roberto pointed at Conrad. "Get on the phone to your fucking father and tell him we're holding you for money."

"They're crazy," Lilly screamed. "Didn't I tell you?"

Roberto hurled himself forward and slammed his hand over her mouth. Leaning down, he said softly, "If you don't shut up your goddamn screaming, I'll get Carl to shove something in your mouth."

"Big cock," Carl goggled.

"We'll gag your fucking mouth," Roberto raved. "I don't give a shit what happens to you, Lilly, remember that. We were friends before but that's all done now. We're serious—we're making our move, our gesture."

"Up the ass of society," Carl grunted.

There might be some doubt about the other two, Conrad realized, but not about Carl. Carl was insane and frightening. Roberto whirled and told Carl to shut up, then directed himself at Conrad the second time.

"Tell him we want five hundred thousand dollars in hundred dollar bills."

Lilly started to laugh. Nervousness made her voice shrill But she was cool, given the circumstances. "Anytime you're ready to leave, Charley."

"Roberto," he corrected her, "say it—Roberto!"

"Roberto, my ass," she snarled.

"All right," Roberto said. He nodded at Carl.

Carl seemed to have been told what he was expected to do. He grabbed Lilly roughly and pulled her to her feet. Holding her by the throat with one hand, he inserted his grimy fingers in the elastic top of her white panties and ripped them down the front.

Her face reddened in anger but she made no move to cover herself from Carl's loose-lipped drool or Dork's jumping eyes. "You son-of-a-bitch."

"Now, do you understand?" Roberto asked grimly. "*Maximum terror*, little Lilly. I'll scare you so goddamn much, you'll do anything I say. You!" He glared at Conrad. "Call Darktower. Get on the phone, asshole!"

Conrad was frightened. He didn't doubt that he was and he was not ashamed of it, either. "I don't know where he is."

"What do you mean you don't know where he is?"

"I don't know if he's out at his farm or here in New York . . . or where."

"Then we'll just have to call until we find him, won't we?" Roberto sneered. "Call the goddamn farm."

Lilly suddenly yelled, "Fuck him! Don't call. He's just playing terrorist."

"Yeah?" Roberto said, his eyes slitting. "You'll see. After we get Pig Darktower organized for the money, then we call the police and we tell them what we're doing. We want coverage. We want the fucking TV and the cameras. Along with the money, we want a plane. We're goin' to Cuba."

Lilly pushed Carl's hand away from her. "You're full of shit," she yelled.

Again, Roberto nodded at Carl. "Okay. She wants trouble. I figured you might be a tough nut, Lilly. Not him." He gestured contemptuously at Conrad. "Go on, comrade."

It was obvious enough what Carl was going to do. He backed her against the bed in the corner of the studio and pushed her down. "Get ready, cunt!" he snarled.

Lilly still didn't lose control. "I see—you're going to rape me."

"No, no, I'm just giving you a little screw like that pig Moss and pretty boy. Then Dork can get his rocks off too."

"Go ahead, you fucking animal!"

"Cut out that goddamn yelling!" Roberto ordered.

Carl ripped at the pillow and shoved it on her face.

"Wait a minute," Conrad exclaimed. "I'm going to call him. You don't have to do this."

Lilly was kicking her legs, trying to get Carl in a vulnerable place, as he fumbled with his pants.

"No!" Conrad yelled. "Stop it!"

"Shut up!" Roberto hissed.

Dork swung the black bag threateningly. "We're not kidding—we got a beauty in here, prick!"

The pillow fell off Lilly's face and she screamed again.

"You're getting it, cunt!" Carl said furiously. He put

his hand over her face and pressed. Then he yelled angrily when she bit his finger.

Roberto, cursing wildly, rushed to the window to close it. "You noisy bastards. We're going to kill you all."

Dork complacently twirled the handles of the black bag in his fingers, making no move to intervene. Carl dropped his dirty trousers and knelt between Lilly's bare legs. She scowled at him, gasping, choking, lifted her knee and caught him in the crotch. He howled and went on his knees.

"You rotten son-of-a-bitch," she shouted, "how do you like that?"

Roberto forgot about the window and lunged toward her. His hand had gone to his pocket and out came a knife, a switchblade which he popped open.

The moment had come. Conrad felt himself possessed by fury. Leaping forward he pushed Dork out of the way, grabbed Lilly's heavy ashtray off the table by the easel and cracked it into Roberto's black curls. Then, with all his might, he kicked the scrambling, moaning Carl in the side and reached for Lilly. He yanked her off the bed. Roberto, on his knees, swaying, grappled for her. Lilly chopped him across the bridge of the nose with the heel of her hand. He cried out and went face down on the floor.

"Conrad, keep away from that other cocksucker," Lilly yammered. "Keep away from him."

But Conrad was gone, his bloodlust running high. Not caring if they went up in flames, he launched himself at Dork.

"I'll drop it! I'll drop it! You crazy fucker!"

Conrad punched at Dork's face, hitting his mouth, seeing blood spurt, hitting his eyes, his nose. Dork was against the wall, moaning.

And the black bag dropped.

It hit the floor. Nothing happened.

"See!" Conrad panted. He slammed Dork against the wall. "Come on, Lilly, come on!"

He took her hand, forgetting about her clothes and pushed her ahead of him through the door.

Then suddenly, deafeningly, somebody, something, hit him from behind, tackled him at the knees, the hips, the shoulders, and propelled him forward into the hallway. He tottered, holding his ears, hearing the sound of exploding rockets, bells, thunder, lightning, and then he was falling . . . mercifully falling free.

Forty-Eight

Erik, on top of the world, in command of his destiny again, parked the Mercedes on Second Avenue that afternoon and turned toward the brownstone where people would say he had "kept" Lilly Royce.

He realized, without too much concern, that a police cordon had been erected in the middle of the block—probably something of a nasty domestic nature going on. In another second, he realized the trouble was localized in Lilly's house.

His eyes drifted upward and Erik saw the hole where the windows of the studio had looked down on the street. It was precisely that—a gaping hole, a blackened hole. Below, on the sidewalk, chunks of brick and mortar had landed on car roofs, denting them, breaking windshields. Across the street, windows had been shattered. Broken glass was everywhere. All too evidently, it had been an explosion, and obviously from inside the studio.

It was hot enough already in the early evening. Now clammy wet fear soaked his suit. Numbly, Erik watched two ambulances careen onto the scene from the opposite end of the street, lights swirling. White-coated men jumped out and rushed up the brownstone steps, through the front door, into the blasted place.

A TV crew arrived and then another, and another. The crowd grew from small to medium to large, cameras *whirred*. No one said much, as far as he could tell, although he was not sure his hearing was working. Erik stared at the socket where a wall had been, and at the front door of the brownstone.

What little noise there had been dropped as the ambulance attendants reappeared, bearing stretchers. One stretcher, two, then two more, a body on each, each body covered . . . dead.

Lilly was dead. He understood. But what the hell had happened?

But Lilly was not dead. Another figure appeared in the doorway, a stalwart policeman, and in his arms he was carrying a slight figure, white-faced, all the more white-faced because of the blazing red hair.

Erik started forward, then stopped. No, no, he would not go to her. Best he stayed away. No, things were going too well for him; he must not get involved in anything that might throw his plans awry. The thing for Erik Moss to do was to go back to his Mercedes and to drive north to the Park Avenue place, make himself a drink, and rest.

"Poor devils," Erik murmured to a man who happened to be standing next to him.

He left, walking steadily, remembering that, damnation, the studio had been rented in his name. But, of course, for Lilly Royce, a friend, a friend of a friend, a protegé. It was not so difficult. He got to the car, unlocked it and climbed in. A cigarette steadied him more. He'd be home in time to answer the first police inquiry.

The weekend doorman was outside to take the car. "Nice trip, Mr. Moss?"

"Yes, Peter, uneventful," Erik said, as if bored out of his wits.

Upstairs, he let himself in, appreciating the deep silence of the duplex, and made straight for the library. The first taste of the Scotch was welcome, soothing. He got rid of his sweaty jacket, loosened his collar and tie, then added ice to the Scotch and squirted in soda. Flopping down in front of the TV set, he debated whether to turn it on. By now, they should be getting eye-witness reports from the disaster area.

No! First, he must put his head against the back of the chair and close his eyes. Ah, the ways of the world were forever mysterious. Lilly . . . concussed; but who had been killed? Why? Who had she had up in the studio? He thought of Dolly . . . her awful Sicilian. Kathy . . . yes, of Erik Moss, sitting alone with a Scotch and soda waiting for the first startling call from the police. What! My studio apartment blown into a million pieces? Unbelievable!

The imponderables. Erik smiled to himself. When he opened his eyes, he found himself looking straight at Helen Ryan. Good God! So engrossed had he been in his consideration of infinity that he had not heard her approach. But how would he? She was in her bare feet, ready for bed, in a loose-fitting robe, belt knotted at the waist.

"Helen, dear," he said gently, "you gave me a start."

"I heard the noise," she said calmly, "and I didn't know who it'd be."

"I just got in from Port London. It didn't occur to me you'd be here tonight."

"I have nowhere else to go," she said.

"Well, now that we've discovered each other, would you care for a drink?" He stood up. "I'm about to have another Scotch. What will you have, Helen?"

She shifted her weight clumsily from one bare foot to the other. "Should I drink with you? You treat me so badly."

"Badly? Helen, I treat you royally and you know it."

She stared at him, as if sorting out his face. "I remember you doing terrible things to me, Mr. Moss."

"Not I, Helen," he said gaily. "Only wonderful things."

"Sticking me from behind like I was some animal."

"Oh, bother," he snapped. "*What* do you want?"

"I'll have a drop of the brandy, if you insist."

"Done!" Erik poured Courvoisier into a brandy snifter. "Here, Helen." She was still standing, so shyly, in the doorway. "To your very good health, Helen." He held up his glass.

Naturally, she had to take offense. "You're so patronizing of a good girl like me." Her tone was wounded. "All I want to do is be of assistance, to do my duty and not to be molested, as you're so fond of doing.''

"Helen," Erik smiled, "you mustn't take on so. I don't mean you any harm, and don't say you haven't enjoyed it. Surely, Helen, you didn't mean to remain virtuous all your life.''

Contemplatively, she tasted the brandy, gazed at him frailly. "We're alone now. Is there something else you haven't done to me that you've wanted to do?''

Erik chuckled, pleased. "What did you have in mind, Helen?''

"I don't know," she shrugged. "You're the expert on those degenerate things. I'm a lost soul, so what does it matter to me?''

"Poor thing," he muttered.

"I'll go upstairs with you now.''

"Suit yourself, Helen, but don't feel so rotten about it. We could use up a few hours in a nice way, yes? God-given, isn't it?''

"Yes.''

"I'll bring the brandy bottle.''

"That would help me," she agreed listlessly. "I could pour some on me and set me on fire . . . a flambé.''

"Yes. Helen Flambé." He chuckled lightly. "What a good idea.''

Moodily, she preceded him up to Katharine's room. Facing him defiantly she untied the cord on her robe, let the latter fall loose, then shrugged herself out of it. Docilely, she stood, her arms at her sides.

"Can you remember me?''

Erik smiled encouragingly. It was always wise to encourage the servants. "Of course I remember. How could I forget? You surprised the life out of me with your knowledge, your own expertise of things degenerate," he observed sardonically. "If you agree, I'll take a shower first, so I'll be nice and spry for you, dear Helen.''

"Yes. But hurry," she said, her voice hushed and jittery.

She watched him unblinkingly while he undressed and

put his clothes over the back of a chair. Her face turned a little red in agitation; perspiration formed on her upper lip.

"Just wait for me right there," he said.

He took his time in the shower, enjoying cold water on his skin. He did his best to wash away everything, all the worry, the disappointment, telling himself he'd soon be free of all of it. Out of the shower, Erik rubbed himself down with a clean white towel. Slowly, his manhood engorged as he thought of her in the next room. He weighed his testicles, soon to be lighter. He was ready.

White towel wrapped around his waist, he opened the door and went back into the bedroom. Helen was flat on her back on Kathy's bed, arms and legs akimbo, her stomach rising and falling with quick breathing. She couldn't wait, could she? She was all a-twitter. Her body seemed to reach toward him.

"Well, Helen," he said clinically, "we're about ready, aren't we?"

"Yes." Her eyelashes slashed at her cheekbones.

He dropped the towel to the floor, presenting himself before her fascinated eyes. A gasp of joy, adulation, desire, escaped her. Slowly, he escorted it toward her, aim unerring. When he was close, she put one hand behind his knee and drew him toward her. "Will you be slow about it and help me?"

"Of course, Helen."

"Then come into me," she sighed deeply.

Carefully, Erik situated himself between her legs and waited while she shifted herself to her satisfaction. He lowered himself so she could feel the weight against her thighs and then, groaning, she positioned it. Erik let himself down, extending himself fully upon her, within her, thrusting quietly, making her breath come shorter. Her hands roamed his body restlessly, up and down his back, across his shoulders. She extended them behind her head, throwing herself at him and then he felt something else, something hard and metallic near his ear.

Then, very unexpectedly, as he considered it, because

there had been no hint of it, he sensed a movement under him, a huge noise, the sound of breaking and cracking. An earthquake here in New York? Strange. Very strange. The ceiling came down on his head. Strange—but he would go forward, acquitting himself with Helen as she always desired, honorably. Above all, Helen must be made happy. Whatever else happened, he warned himself, life did go on.

Forty-Nine

Hot, red, sticky blood gushed out of the wound next to his ear, down on Helen's face, across her chest, the sheets, choking her even when his eyes went dead and nauseous after death began to run from his open mouth, burning her skin until she could have screamed.

So it was done. Her hand, still holding Sam Merchant's gun, slipped limply off the bed. But Erik Moss did not stop. He was dead, she knew it, but his hips continued to pump, his thing, hard as a rock, harder now, kept banging into her, hurting. Why wouldn't he stop? He was dead. She had shot him, sent a bullet crashing into his head. A bullet at this range was supposed to kill instantly. Still . . . he did not stop.

Helen began to babble, hearing herself, and this was even more frightening, hearing herself saying terrible untrue things about herself, as he kept on fornicating her. Helen wanted to scream but she could not interrupt her senseless protesting. He continued, his hips jogging and Helen could not help it when her own hips began to respond, to writhe under him because, even though he was dead, she was coming. He was making her come, Oh God, with his battering ram. Christ, Oh, Christ, he was so hard she could not believe he was dead. Sam had been fooling. There hadn't been a real bullet in the gun. It was a joke, a loathsome joke, all of them part of it against her.

She knew better, yes, she did know better because of the blood. It was his motor mechanism running on, undeterred. He was like the chicken racing around the barnyard even after its head had been cut off . . . or the hanged man, for they said a man being hung got the most terrible erection. No, he *was* dead.

She clutched his hips with her hands. Here he was warm although his face was ashen and cold and his blood dripping away. Yet, the long, hard thing ploughed her, ripped her and again pushed her to the brink and she suffered another orgasm, for it was suffering now when it happened.

Nerves screamed within her. She could not stop him, could not control him. His hips bucked against her hands. She had to get him off her, to throw him to the side and escape or she would die under him, as his final spasms continued. It was God's doing, her punishment. Hell had already begun without even a judgment against her. She was guilty and now she was being fornicated to death as punishment.

Helen breathed hoarsely. Her lungs were fiery from panting and weeping and praying and she realized she had begun bleeding too, from the vagina, all over the sheets. God. And he kept on!

She had nearly dropped the gun in her feebleness. Now the metal was solid in her hand. Of course. Another shot. Of course, she decided, there was only one. Helen raised the hand, and the gun, and rubbed her temple with the cold steel.

Fifty

"Well, darling," Dolly announced herself breezil[y]
I am and all of a sudden it's October." She sat d[own at]
Katharine's right. "Isn't this . . . somehow . . . whe[re we]
came in?"

Katharine watched her doubtfully. There was so m[uch]
to doubt these days. "If you mean we're back at *Le Cirq[ue]*
. . . you look beautiful, Dolly."

Dolly winked. "I never change. *Well*?"

"Well, indeed."

"Well, how *are* you, Kit?"

"I'm fine." Katharine did her best to sound sure of
herself. "A little tired. We've been on the road over a
month."

"Exciting, darling!" Dolly did look envious. and at
once curious. "How is everything? You know—*Gizmo*?"

As if Katharine wouldn't understand what Dolly was
thinking about. "Oh? Francotti?" She drew a breath and
smiled. "He's fine . . . just fine. We traveled practically
all the way around the world, you know. It was good
medicine. I didn't think it would work—but it did."

"Of course it did!" Dolly shrieked lightly. "The man
worships you. It had to work."

"I suppose," Katharine murmured. "Here's hoping."
She held up a glass of white wine, then motioned for the
waiter.

"I. . . ." Dolly stopped. "I want to know—are you all
right now, about Conny?"

Katharine breathed silently, then nodded. "I've gotten

461

...at it happened. It'll never be all

used to t... ...ered, staring down at her brightly
right ...," Dolly ... She moved her hand a few inches
...nicured fingewrist. "Conrad saved that girl's life."
to grasp Katha... ...e agreed, almost drolly. "The life of
"True," ... is, Erik Moss's mistress. Can you
his girlfri... ...d up it all was?" She couldn't avoid the
believe ...en ...orrow. "If Conrad hadn't loved her; he
famili... ...en there to save her life. He wouldn't be
wou... severely. "You have to give Fate the
... ...or the blame."

...," Katharine grunted, purposefully clearing
... of anxiety. Francotti had told her often
...e was nothing, absolutely nothing, she could
...ow, or could have done then, if the truth be
...cotti was her man, a man of towering logic,
...e'd forced her out of the brooding. What was
...ast. It was true, Katharine knew: Francotti was
...onal as the next man, and more so, but he wouldn't
... her, not if she insisted on living in the past. She
couldn't blame him; she'd done her best. She was trying.
Christ, she was trying!

Katharine pulled her hand away from Dolly. "Enough
about me! You're here to cheer me up, remember? What's
with Marco? Tell me about Marco, goddamn it!"

But thinking about Marco made her remember Stefan
and that was enough to make her quiver too. Couldn't she
ever escape it? But Dolly was happy enough to talk about
Marco, to deal him out and away.

"In the final instance," she said sourly, "Marco was a
revolting pig, darling. After a while his childishness was
only that. We had some good times, but life does go on."
She drank absently of the white wine the waiter had brought
her. "I suppose," Dolly said morosely, "there was nobody
around who was going to save Erik, was there?"

"Fate, sweetheart," Katharine said sardonically.

"Shit—what a way to go. Disgusting."

"Yes," Katharine said quietly, "but the trouble is he

didn't go. I'm seeing the doctor again this afternoon. We have to decide what to do. What do you think?''

Dolly shook her head evasively. "That's not my decision, darling. Not my responsibility, *darling*. It's all yours.''

Katharine glanced at her amusedly. "Not yours too? You loved him a little, didn't you, sweetheart? You went to bed with him enough.''

Dolly's face whitened. "Darling . . . please! You shouldn't say that. It's not kind.''

"Bullshit, sweetheart,'' Katharine growled, thinking she must sound like Francotti, hoping she did. "This isn't the time for the niceties. You would have run off with him, Dolly, and you know it.'' Katharine winked at her derisively. "Therefore, you get a vote. Do we keep him going on that machine or do we pull the plug?''

Dolly looked very faint. Definitely, perhaps for the first time ever, Katharine felt as though she had the drop on Dolly.

"Darling, *legally* it's nothing to do with me. I don't want you talking to me like this. You're very cruel.'' Dolly seemed ready to cry.

But Katharine persisted. "There's no hope, you see. One-half of the brain is totally dead. The rest of him runs out of habit.''

"Jesus Christ,'' Dolly whispered, "I'm not surprised. He's built like a bull.'' Her eyes glittered fearfully. "My God, shot in the head like that and he keeps right on humping that maniac of a maid.'' She tittered nervously. "Too much of a good thing *can* be too much. Hours later . . . Good God!''

"Yes. Amazing. You *could* come with me to the hospital.''

"Are you kiddihg? *No way* . . . do you think Helen actually knew what she was doing?''

"No, I think by then she was completely crazy. Erik drove her crazy. Let's face it.''

A faraway look came into Dolly's face. "Somebody was going to do it,'' she proclaimed softly. "Better her than either of us. Yes.'' She nodded, then abruptly added,

"It's cruel to keep him going, darling. He wouldn't have liked that. What does Francotti say?"

"That it makes no sense—and helps nothing or nobody."

Dolly nodded sagely. "You can't marry Francotti unless you get some kind of annulment or divorce . . . or if Erik dies."

"That doesn't matter either," Katharine said impatiently. "What use is marriage? It didn't do us much good, did it?"

"No," Dolly said laconically, "contrary to what our sweet families taught us, it was something we could have done without very nicely. But," she said, sounding for once sincere, "out of it you do have Margaret."

Tears came to Katharine's eyes. "If it hadn't been for Francotti. . . ." She paused, choking a cry. Her words rushed out. "We're going away again. He's got to get back to Hawaii. Six months. We'll take Margaret."

"You should," Dolly said. "You must, of course."

"I'm going to."

Dolly nodded. "Well, I know you are, darling." She smiled ingratiatingly. "I didn't tell you that I have a new lover, did I?"

"Do you? How wonderful. Who?"

"Darling! Would I tell you?"

"So," Richard Darktower said, "what *is* she going to do about him?"

Dolly perched on a blue-velvet cushioned chair and smiled prissily. From a tea tray, she passed Richard a cup with just a little milk, the way he liked it.

"What she'll do, Richard, I don't know. But what I told her she *should* do was turn off that awful machine and let the poor man die."

Darktower nodded briskly, in his most businesslike way. "Absolutely—it's just costing a hell of a lot of money for nothing. I never thought enough about Moss when he was one hundred percent alive that I should spend a couple of thousand dollars a week to keep him going—that stupid Helen should have aimed better."

"Richard!"

Darktower grinned craftily. No matter what, he was not going to tell Dolly any more about it, was he? It had, by George, come off beautifully. Had he managed his Wall Street affairs as cleverly as he had this matter of family he'd be the richest man in the world right now. A dark tragedy, it had been, no matter how you sliced it. Oh, yes, Christ, just tragic, he chortled. But fortuitous to the Darktower estate—for just at the moment of Erik Moss's untimely departure from consciousness the Darktower attorneys had been drawing up the final settlement.

Primly, Dolly said, "Richard, I think that as a father-to-be, you should be more charitable to your fallen enemies. How's Clara?"

Darktower smiled, not so much for Clara as for the personality she was carrying around inside her. "Fine, so long as she doesn't move a muscle," he said. "And she doesn't dare move, I can tell you. The tests are all okay—it's a boy, and very normal." He paused, suddenly gloomy. "For which I'm thankful."

"I understand," she said. "It is a gift. . . ."

He nodded, not telling Dolly either about another worry. Darwin had said it first—the dying species reproduces itself. Ergo, Richard Darktower was the dying species for in his final act he had reproduced a man-child. He wondered when it would come, how soon, or how long from now; he prayed he would be around long enough to see the boy . . . what? Walk, talk? . . . take a seat in the business? Damnation! To hell with that, he told himself. He didn't give a damn what line of work his only son chose for himself.

Dolly leaned forward to take his cup for a refill and he had a reviving look down her cleavage. Dolly had a fine and reassuring set of breasts, not big, not small, not floppy, not used up from all her dalliances.

He took the cup back. "Thank you. What'd Kate have to say about her Italian?"

Dolly shrugged. "She's mad for him."

"What the hell does that guy do?" Darktower growled. "Why does he always seem like such a goddamn secret."

"We know he designs motors. He must be very good at it."

"Sure," he snapped. "And I can't find out anything else about him. Jesus, why can't she ever fall for a plain American?"

"Now, Richard, he's an Italian-American, you know that," she muttered. "He's not an enemy alien, for heaven's sake."

"He's not super-rich," Darktower continued, overdoing it, he knew, "but he's solvent as all hell. He doesn't own anything except four bank accounts. He's a director of a couple of companies and he's got a handful of honorary degrees. He goes down to Washington a lot—who he sees I don't know, but I'm mighty suspicious. He's got a wife he's in the process of divorcing—she's a marine biologist or some weird goddamn thing."

"Nothing much, in other words, eh, Richard?"

"No," he said gloomily. "I can't believe he's so clean." But he wouldn't mope about it, would he? "You know, Dolly, when that child is born, he's Margaret's uncle—yes, my own granddaughter's uncle. Does that make any sense?"

Dolly nodded mischievously. He liked her best when she was being tricky. "You *are* an old dog, Richard. More tea?"

"He shook his head. "Uh, uh. I've had enough tea."

"Anything else then?"

"Yes." He chuckled hoarsely. "Some crumpet."

"Richard," she reproved him gently. "Why is it I always thought *you* didn't approve of me?"

"I *don't* approve of you, Miss Dolly. Come along now, Miss Dolly. . . ."

"Now, Richard, you can just wait until I've finished my tea and then we'll do some very proper things."

"I don't want to do proper things," he growled.

Margo Himmelmann didn't know how she was ever going to survive Richard Darktower's pregnancy with a surviving shred of self-respect. Good Heavens! A new Darktower heir! Why was it Mr. Darktower always seemed to have the last laugh? Blast, if she could have conceived, she'd be pregnant right now and racing Miss Clara Riding for the finish gate.

As it was, Margo was simply shamed. Shamed to death. She had begun to think the best out for her was a long stay in Europe. She might go and lend her charms to the decadent Sicilian whom Dolly Percy had dumped. Such a pity Erik Moss was out of circulation—to coin an expression. In a terrible snit over the Darktower business, she had told Herman Himmelmann that, indeed, she might just be leaving him and heading off with a young and untiring Lothario, in a word, a *stud*. And Herman? Be my guest, he'd replied.

"I suppose," she muttered huskily, "that you too think I'm nothing but an old has-been, Samuel?"

Her lips were sweaty, her bare body too, straining against him, holding him in her legs, feeling the weight of his slim chest caressing her breasts. It was so nice, so comforting.

"Not so, Margo," Sam said cockily. "What I've always said to anybody wants to listen is that while, or whereas, there might be winter in your bones, there's definitely spring in your ass."

Margo laughed brokenly, almost hysterical. "You are a *terrible* person."

"Yeah," he agreed, "ain't I ever, sugar?"

She moaned and whispered to him for a few minutes, urging him on, trying to keep him erect until she had climbed to her pinnacle. Sam had a tendency to wilt after a few moments.

"I'm not so bad looking, am I, lover?"

"Margo, didn't I just finish telling you? You're a knock-out, sugar. I had an uncle told me once—'Boy,' he said, 'Don't worry about takin' on an older woman 'cause they're always going to do their best, thinkin' every time might be the last.' "

Margo Himmelmann began to cry. Hot tears ran down her cheeks. What was she going to do with this awful man? She needed him now, very badly, to get through the Darktower weeks. He had to be kept, somehow. She'd bought him furniture and she gave him an allowance for his drinks and cigarettes. She ordered him clothes and he was the Lothario she might possibly be taking to Europe—if he was a good boy.

She wrapped him in her arms, held him tightly to her, angling her pelvis to take all of him into her, humping up to have it all, aware of every bit of it scrabbling around inside her. God, would the craving never end?

When he began to whimper in her ear, it was the signal that he was preparing his pathetic ejaculation. As a child he must have had a vitamin deficiency. It showed in his production of bodily fluids.

Margo tried to get to her climax at the same time but it was useless. She was a long way off. She was too preoccupied. There was so much to worry about. Kate . . . Margaret . . . Kate's Italian, their constant traveling. They were going to take Margaret to Hawaii with them—maybe just as well, get her out of the city, away from the place where the awful thing had happened. And Conrad—thought of him wrecked her ardor. A son . . . dead, the worst thing.

Merchant gurgled into her throat. That was it. *Finito*. . . . No, best if she went to Europe to pick up a local product, test-drive it, then maybe import it.

Groaning, he rolled off her and reached for one of his Camels. After he was puffing himself into renewed conviction that he really was a stud's stud, he drawled, "I really dig you, Margo. When we goin' to France and all that?"

"I don't know. We'll have to see," she said forlornly.

"Whatsamatter, sugar?" He propped his head on his fist and grinned at her. "I know—you've got the post-whatever blues."

"Yeah, probably, sugar," she said, hating him, hating him very much. "Do you ever think about Helen . . . about that awful thing that Helen did?"

"Yeah, I sure as hell do," he nodded. His eyes, however, didn't flicker in sadness. "That poor baby."

"I still can't understand what happened."

"Me neither, sugar, but it sure put Moss on ice, didn't it?"

"Yes." Margo nodded thoughtfully. "*Conveniently*, too.

It would've cost Mr. Darktower a lot of money to get rid of him.''

Sam nodded his head solemnly. "It was, indeed, sugar, a most convenient escape from that imbroglio. I just hate to talk about it. I think . . . maybe," he said humbly, "if I'd done my job better the Moss problem would have been solved before all that bloodshed eventuated."

"Probably," Margo agreed. She didn't really give a damn, did she?

Neither did Sam. His head engaged one of her fragile breasts, his lips taking the nipple, tongue darting at it. She shuddered, feeling the sensation to the very tips of her toes. Oh, what was the point? There was no hope. Might as well be the wild and abandoned creature everyone hinted she was. She pushed his head away and moved, ducking to his limp sword, about the only thing she knew to do in order to arouse him again. She wanted it badly, as much as she hated him.

He sucked in air, squirmed and yelled at the top of his voice, in a transport of ecstasy, "*Hey, wow, Margo!*"

A split second later, the apartment door burst open and, with simultaneity of such horrible events, flashbulbs began exploding, blinding Margo even as she turned her head, his poor tool in her mouth, to see what in the world was happening. She jerked back but curiously she could not get away for Sam's hand was wound in her hair and he kept her right there, where she was, in this publicly sordid position.

She understood instantly what was happening. Oh, the sneaky little bastard! Who was it paying him? Herman or that horrible Richard Darktower? The sneak! The traitor! After all she had done for him.

Very well! Margo bit vengefully on Sam's flaccid stub. A scream ruptured his throat. She bit and bit, deep, deep, and little Sam kept on screaming. Yes, she was going to amputate and she wasn't even a surgeon.

Hands pulled at her and then only did she let him go, spitting a mouthful of his own blood in his face.

*   *   *

Kathy sat in a straight-backed chair by the side of the hospital bed, not too close to him. Erik Moss was bound to the bed so he would not lapse continually into a fetal position and his hands were restrained too to prevent him from plucking hideously at his skin. His face was cadaverous, features transformed. She remembered Stefan had said Erik looked like a bird of prey; the bird was better defined now: eyes red-rimmed and staring, predatory nose and chin both jutting.

Tubing connected him with suspended vials and instruments. His breathing sounded as mechanical as a man pumping a bicycle tire.

Well, *my darling*, well, well, she murmured to herself.

There was really nothing to feel or fear about him now. But, as outrageous as it seemed, Katharine never failed to experience a terrible dread when she came to visit. Visit? A ridiculous way to describe it: sit down, watch, leave. . . .

The door opened. Katharine looked up, expecting the doctor or a nurse. Instead, a small, red-haired girl faced her, no more than a child, so frail and slight. She was wearing a cotton shirt and skirt, hair tied away from her thin, elfish face. A livid red scar ran almost the whole way across her forehead.

The truth came to her. "You're Lilly," Katharine whispered.

The girl nodded and came further into the room, to the end of the bed. She took her eyes away from Katharine's face for a second to stare at Erik. Then she rounded the bed to stand next to Katharine. She reached and took her hand.

"You're my brother's friend. . . ."

Lilly Royce, for that was her name, again inclined her head, gazing sorrowfully into Katharine's face. Finally, she spoke. "I'm sorry," she said softly. "Conrad saved me."

"You're all right?"

"I'm all right," the girl said.

"Come to see me." Katharine opened her purse and took out a pen and piece of notepaper. She wrote down

Francotti's phone number and handed the paper to Lilly Royce.

And then Lilly left, not saying another word, merely glancing once more at Erik's supine form.

At four-thirty, the doctor entered the room, and stood for a while staring at Erik Moss. He pursed his lips disparagingly, and then, for something to do, put his fingers to Erik's pulse.

Katharine stood up, suddenly weary of the whole thing, as weary of it as she sensed Erik must be. Dolly was right—the cruel, the vindictive thing would be to keep him alive, to make of his body a spectacle of slow decay.

Katharine looked at the doctor across Erik's deep chest. "I'm going to sign the paper," she said.

And it was done. Katharine sat afterward for a few minutes by herself in the doctor's office, somehow for this brief time as disassociated from her own body as Erik was from his, her mind numb but crawling with vague apprehension.

Well, it was over, wasn't it, the whole thing? He would die now, as he must, as he should, for there was no hope of recovery. Dolly had said just an hour or so before that Erik was as strong as a bull. But he was not stronger than this.

Katharine pushed herself upward, standing erectly by the chair, then opening the door, walking through the outer office, saying good-bye to the secretary. She went to the elevators and, downstairs, walked a long corridor until she found a public telephone.

"Hello. That's you!"

Katharine's eyes moistened for she realized he had been waiting. "You knew," she sighed. "Of course you knew. . . ." She stopped suddenly, ahead of her tears. "Francotti. . . ."

"Don't talk—please," he said firmly. "Don't say anything more. I want you to go to the front entrance and wait there. I'm going down to get the car."

Again she tried to speak. "Francotti. . . ." He stopped her once more.

"We'll talk later. We've got plenty of time. I have to go out to the Island to see a man . . . about a boat. You're invited to come along."

"But . . . Francotti, let me. . . ."

"Hey! I'll be there in twenty minutes . . . maybe ten."

She nodded mindlessly at the wall. "Yes . . . yes. All right, Francotti."

A Selection of Arrow Bestsellers

☐ Voices on the Wind	Evelyn Anthony	£2.50
☐ Someone Else's Money	Michael M. Thomas	£2.50
☐ The Executioner's Song	Norman Mailer	£3.50
☐ The Alexander Principle	Wilfred Barlow	£2.95
☐ Everything is Negotiable	Gavin Kennedy	£2.95
☐ The New Girlfriend & other stories	Ruth Rendell	£1.95
☐ An Unkindness of Ravens	Ruth Rendell	£1.95
☐ Dead in the Morning	Margaret Yorke	£1.75
☐ The Domesday Heritage	Ed. Elizabeth Hallam	£3.95
☐ Elvis and Me	Priscilla Presley	£2.95
☐ The World of Placido Domingo	Daniel Snowman	£4.95
☐ Maria Callas	Arianna Stassinopoulos	£2.50
☐ The Brendan Voyage	Tim Severin	£3.50
☐ A Shine of Rainbows	Lillian Beckwith	£1.95
☐ Rates of Exchange	Malcolm Bradbury	£2.95
☐ Thy Tears Might Cease	Michael Farrell	£2.95
☐ Pudding and Pie (Nancy Mitford Omnibus)	Nancy Mitford	£3.95

NAME ....

ADDRESS ....

....

....

U.K. CUSTOMERS: Please allow 22p per book to a maximum of £3.00.

B.F.P.O. & EIRE: Please allow 22p per book to a maximum of £3.00.

OVERSEAS CUSTOMERS: Please allow 22p per book.

Whilst every effort is made to keep prices low it is sometimes necessary to increase cover prices at short notice. Arrow Books reserve the right to show new retail prices on covers which may differ from those previously advertised in the text or elsewhere.

Bestselling Fiction

☐	Dancing Bear	Chaim Bermant	£2.95
☐	Hiroshima Joe	Martin Booth	£2.95
☐	1985	Anthony Burgess	£1.95
☐	The Other Woman	Colette	£1.95
☐	The Manchurian Candidate	Richard Condon	£2.25
☐	Letter to a Child Never Born	Oriana Fallaci	£1.25
☐	Duncton Wood	William Horwood	£3.50
☐	Aztec	Gary Jennings	£3.95
☐	The Journeyer	Gary Jennings	£3.50
☐	The Executioner's Song	Norman Mailer	£3.50
☐	Strumpet City	James Plunkett	£3.50
☐	Admiral	Dudley Pope	£1.95
☐	The Second Lady	Irving Wallace	£2.50
☐	An Unkindness of Ravens	Ruth Rendell	£1.95
☐	The History Man	Malcolm Bradbury	£2.95

NAME ....

ADDRESS ....

....

....

U.K. CUSTOMERS: Please allow 22p per book to a maximum of £3.00.

B.F.P.O. & EIRE: Please allow 22p per book to a maximum of £3.00.

OVERSEAS CUSTOMERS: Please allow 22p per book.

Whilst every effort is made to keep prices low it is sometimes necessary to increase cover prices at short notice. Arrow Books reserve the right to show new retail prices on covers which may differ from those previously advertised in the text or elsewhere.